The Ethics of Capital Punishment

The Ethics of Capital Punishment

A Philosophical Investigation of Evil and Its Consequences

Matthew H. Kramer

OXFORD
UNIVERSITY PRESS

OXFORD

UNIVERSITY PRESS

Great Clarendon Street, Oxford OX2 6DP

Oxford University Press is a department of the University of Oxford.
It furthers the University's objective of excellence in research, scholarship,
and education by publishing worldwide in

Oxford New York

Auckland Cape Town Dar es Salaam Hong Kong Karachi
Kuala Lumpur Madrid Melbourne Mexico City Nairobi
New Delhi Shanghai Taipei Toronto

With offices in

Argentina Austria Brazil Chile Czech Republic France Greece
Guatemala Hungary Italy Japan Poland Portugal Singapore
South Korea Switzerland Thailand Turkey Ukraine Vietnam

Oxford is a registered trade mark of Oxford University Press
in the UK and in certain other countries

Published in the United States
by Oxford University Press Inc., New York

British Library Cataloguing in Publication Data

Data available

Library of Congress Cataloging in Publication Data

Library of Congress Control Number: 2011943633

Typeset by Newgen Imaging Systems (P) Ltd, Chennai, India
Pinted and bound by
CPI Group (UK) Ltd
Croydon CR0 4YY

ISBN 978-0-19-964218-2

10 9 8 7 6 5 4 3 2 1

Preface

When I was eight years old, I learned about the Holocaust and the subsequent trials at Nuremberg. During the months that followed my discovery of those events, my ruminations led me to develop inchoately one of the ideas at the core of the pivotal sixth chapter in this book. I remember thinking that it would have been morally grotesque if the trials of some of the major Nazi leaders had ended with sentences that would involve the devotion of resources to sustaining the lives of those leaders. That line of thought—reinforced by my recognition that, in slightly different circumstances, Hitler and Goebbels and Mengele and Heydrich would have been among those who were placed on trial—ultimately evolved into the purgative rationale for capital punishment.

I am a philosopher, and this book is a work of philosophy. However, because I want the book to be accessible to readers who are unfamiliar with philosophical technicalities, I have usually sought to elucidate any specialized philosophical phrases when they first appear. My explanations are mostly in the form of terse footnotes, but at a few junctures I have provided longer expositions.

This is not a book on American constitutional law or on the law of punishment in any other jurisdiction. Though I occasionally refer to some features of American law and to some aspects of the role of capital punishment in American life, the philosophical orientation of this volume leads me generally to prescind from the specificities of any particular jurisdiction. Whereas some of my conclusions about capital punishment are in accordance with the current law in the United States, many of them are not, and I only intermittently touch upon the points of convergence and divergence. As this book presents a philosophical investigation of the death penalty, it does not undertake any sustained efforts to track the correspondence (or lack of correspondence) between the results of that investigation and the details of any existent legal doctrines. My aim is primarily prescriptive; this volume seeks to recount, at a very high level of abstraction, what the law concerning capital punishment in any liberal-democratic jurisdiction should be.

I owe thanks to many people—nearly all of whom are opposed to capital punishment—for their generous help in my writing of this book. Alex Flach at the Oxford University Press has been an excellent editor, in keeping with his adept handling of some of my previous books. The anonymous readers whom he recruited were likewise superb, with perceptive comments that have salutarily prompted many modifications. I am very grateful to them. I am grateful as well to Natasha Flemming, Matthew Humphrys, and the rest of the production team at the OUP.

Norman Geras several years ago asked me to write a short account of my views on capital punishment for his blog. Though I now regard that account as extremely rough and facile, it murkily prefigured the structure of this book. I wish to express warm thanks to Norm for his invitation, which he extended despite his own opposition to the death penalty.

Eve Garrard and Steve de Wijze provided some invaluable feedback on Chapter 6, and Eve in particular has engaged in some remarkably helpful correspondence concerning the nature of evil. I am extremely grateful to both of them for prodding me to sharpen my thinking about evil. Especially fruitful was my encounter with Eve and Steve at a conference in Manchester (England) in November 2009. Also present at that conference were some other people to whom I am very grateful for their thought-provoking comments: Ian Carter, Norm Geras (again), Eric Mack, Jonathan Quong, Hillel Steiner, Zofia Stemplowska, and Peter Vallentyne.

Of great value as well have been conversations with several of the philosophers who have visited Cambridge during the past few years: Thom Brooks, Alan Brudner, Robert Gibbs, Claire Grant, and Russ Shafer-Landau. (I am also grateful to Thom for supplying me with an offprint of his important article on capital punishment.) I have likewise benefited considerably from conversations with several Cantabrigians: Mark Hanin, Jules Holroyd, Antje du-Bois Pedain, Andrew Simester, and Andrew von Hirsch. Some email exchanges with my twin brother Mark Kramer have also been helpful.

Finally, I should make special mention of Dan Markel, whom I have never met. In the late autumn of 2010, he undertook the entirely supererogatory labour of reading every chapter and making extensive comments thereon. I have profited hugely from his suggestions and queries, and have responded to most of them (though of course I have not embraced his opposition to capital punishment). With his investment of so much time and intellectual effort in a project that runs partly contrary to his own sophisticated position on the death penalty, he has been a model of scholarly generosity and integrity.

Matthew H. Kramer

Cambridge, England

January 2011

Contents

1

Introduction

1.1. The limits of the enquiry

Although much of this book will be devoted to impugning all the standard rationales for capital punishment, the chief purpose of the volume is to advance an alternative justification for such punishment in a limited range of cases. By pursuing both a project of critical debunking and a project of partial vindication, this book adopts an approach quite different from that which has sometimes been attributed to proponents of the death penalty. Some theorists have asserted that 'citizens invariably signify their agreement with *all* the conventional rationales that point in the direction of their preferred position on the death penalty' (Kahan 1999, 445, emphasis in original). Whatever may be the veracity of such a bold assertion when it is applied solely to non-philosophers or non-academics, it is very wide of the mark in application to philosophical discussions of the death penalty and particularly in application to this book. On the one hand, my accounts of the standard rationales for capital punishment will seek to highlight the features of those rationales that have made them attractive to philosophers and ordinary citizens alike. On the other hand, however, the ultimate aim of each such account is to reveal that none of the standard rationales can genuinely justify the imposition of the death penalty. By showing that each of the currently prominent justifications is otiose even when elaborated sympathetically, my discussions of those justifications will indicate that the moral soundness of capital punishment must rest on some alternative basis—if such punishment is indeed ever morally sound.

Unlike the commonly proposed rationales for the death penalty, the purgative justification that will be championed in this book is not an offshoot or aspect of a general theory of punishment. Each of the commonly proposed rationales is associated with a wide-ranging theory that addresses all types of crimes rather than only the most rebarbative atrocities. Each such rationale for the death penalty thus consists in the application of a comprehensive account of punishment to the worst atrocities; the death sentences for such heinous misdeeds are perceived as lying at the extreme end of a spectrum of sanctions which in their sundry degrees of severity are respectively attached to various crimes in pursuit of the same underlying objective (deterrence or retribution or incapacitation or denunciation). By contrast, the rationale for capital

punishment that will be expounded herein is *sui generis*. It does not emerge as a ramification of a broader theory of punishment.

In two respects, then, this book's purgative rationale uniquely requires the imposition of the death penalty (in appropriate cases). In the first place, as the subsequent
chapters will argue—and as has been remarked above—the purgative rationale is
uniquely effective as a justification for capital punishment, since the competing justifications all fail. In the second place, the only type of punishment for which the
purgative rationale ever calls is the death penalty. It does not prescribe any lesser punishments, and does not address any crimes less grave than those that are extravagantly
heinous.

In that second respect, my approach to the death penalty runs counter to the
following declaration by William Edmundson: 'Anyone who reflects on the practice of capital punishment has to work through two issues. The first is that of the
justification of punishment in general, the second is that of the place of death within his
or her overall theory of punishment' (Edmundson 2002, 40). Though Edmundson's
comment accurately summarizes the ways in which the standard rationales for capital punishment have been propounded, it fails to capture the *sui generis* character of
the purgative rationale. Within this volume, I do not endeavour to present an overarching theory of punishment from which certain conclusions about the death penalty follow as special implications. Instead, the aim is to arrive at certain conclusions
about the death penalty through a free-standing justification. (To the extent that this
book's purgative justification of capital punishment is embedded in a broader theory,
the theory in question is an account of evil rather than of legal sanctions.)

Consequently, this book's contestation of the prevailing rationales for the death
penalty will address them predominantly as just such rationales rather than as doctrines that prescribe punitive measures across the board. To be sure, a few of my
objections to the commonly marshalled arguments for capital punishment will question whether the factors invoked by those arguments can ever truly justify any punishments. Furthermore, this book's expositions of those putative bases for the death
penalty will of course take account of their locations in comprehensive theories of
punishment. For the most part, however, my expositions and queries will concentrate on the distinctive difficulties surrounding the proposition that some criminals
are properly punishable with death. We shall be pondering the diverse efforts by
numerous philosophers to defend that proposition, and we shall only incidentally
consider whether the shortcomings in any of those efforts extend beyond the context
of executions. For example, when we contemplate the merits and weaknesses of the
incapacitative rationale for the death penalty, we can largely leave aside the question
whether a broad incapacitative approach to punishment would succeed in vindicating some lesser sanctions.

Because the justification of capital punishment advanced in this book is not a facet
or ramification of a general theory of punishment, it presupposes that any satisfactory
overall account of punishment will be pluralistic. That is, given that my purgative

rationale for the death penalty does not lend itself to being generalized to other sanctions, there is no single principle that serves as the justificatory foundation for all the punishments that might suitably be imposed by a morally worthy government. There is no single objective toward which all those punishments should be oriented. On this point, the present book is in agreement with some theorists who never mention the purgative rationale: 'Ultimately, all accounts of punishment are partial accounts. No one theory explains the whole enterprise.'[1]

1.2. A matter of justification

As is evident from what has been said already, the fundamental tenor of this book is justificatory. Both within the chapters that seek to discredit the most frequently proffered arguments in favour of capital punishment and within the chapter that expounds a purgative alternative to those arguments, the aim is to come up with solid grounds for the employment of the death penalty in response to especially horrific crimes. Now, if this justificatory project is to yield any practical consequences, the direction of the burden of proof has to be specified. For the operativeness of such consequences, it is not enough that the imposition of the death penalty in response to atrocious crimes is justified. In addition, we need to be warranted in believing that it is justified. When are we so warranted? Where does the burden of proof lie?

In line with most other philosophers and jurists who write about capital punishment, this book readily accepts that the burden of proof rests on the proponents of such punishment.[2] Thus, for example, if some people support the death penalty on the ground that it more effectively deters vile murders than does any other available type of punishment, their views should not carry any practical weight unless they adduce solid evidence of the deterrent effect to which they advert. They cannot rely simply on the absence of any clear-cut evidence that would disprove the occurrence of such an effect. Much the same is true, *mutatis mutandis*, of other rationales for capital punishment.

---

[1] Kennedy 2000, 850. For a similar view, see Hampton 1992, 1659 n 2, 1700–1. See also Shafer-Landau 1996, 296–7. In my insistence on the distinctiveness of the considerations that justify the imposition of the death penalty, this book's approach to punishment is more strongly pluralistic than the sophisticated blending of retributivism and consequentialism advocated in Cahill 2010. The purgative rationale for capital punishment is neither retributivistic nor consequentialist.

[2] See, for example, Finkelstein 2002, 12, 16, 20; Goldberg 1974, 74 n 5; Hurka 1982, 659 n 14; Symposium 2003, 152 (remarks by William Erlbaum). A few theorists proceed differently. For instance, Hugo Adam Bedau writes that he will 'ignore here the question of which side has the burden of argument and will proceed as if the abolitionist did' (Bedau 1999, 49). Likewise, Ernest van den Haag—Bedau's fiercest opponent—sometimes contended that 'the irrevocability of the death[s] of homicide victims justifies capital punishment until deterrence is positively disproved' (Book Review 1983, 1213). For a more sophisticated version of van den Haag's view, see Davis 1996, 42–3, 50–1. For non-committal stances on the matter of the burden of proof, see Jones and Potter 1981, 158–9; Schwarzschild 2002, 10–11. For a somewhat equivocal stance, see Sorell 2002, 28, 33. See also Edmundson 2002, 41: 'It will not do for either side to claim that his or her position is presumptively correct, and to cast upon the other side the burden of persuasion.'

Of course, not every such rationale joins the deterrence-focused theories in appealing centrally to empirical considerations. In particular, this book's purgative rationale for the death penalty depends on moral argumentation rather than on empirical investigations. (Naturally, any deterrence-focused theory also depends on moral argumentation; but the content of its moral argumentation commits it also to some major empirical claims that have to be substantiated.) Unless this book's lines of reasoning are strong enough to be plausible, its purgative rationale for capital punishment should not carry any practical weight. The sheer absence of any conclusive refutation of that rationale is hardly sufficient to discharge the burden of proof that confronts anyone who advocates the imposition of the death penalty.

Why does the relevant burden of proof lie on the supporters of capital punishment rather than on the opponents thereof? Under basic principles of liberal democracy, any significant use of governmental power and resources is illegitimate unless it has been credibly justified by reference to some worthy public purpose(s). Legal-governmental officials are not morally entitled—nor legally entitled, in any liberal democracy—to wield the mechanisms of government whimsically or selfishly. If their activation of those mechanisms is not undertaken on the basis of objectives that can properly be sought by a system of governance, then it violates the moral obligations that are incumbent upon them in their roles as public officials. Those obligations both constitute and express the morally subordinate status of any system of governance vis-à-vis the citizenry over whom it exercises authority.

Hence, the direction of the burden of proof in debates over capital punishment is a matter of fundamental liberal-democratic principles concerning the moral priority of individuals vis-à-vis governments. After all, the application of such punishment to anyone is a lethal exertion of governmental power. If executions were to go ahead without any credible argument that they are necessary for the achievement of an important public purpose, the respect due to citizens from those who govern them would be egregiously compromised. Liberal-democratic principles raise a presumption against virtually any use of governmental power. When a use of power involves the deliberate infliction of death, the presumption is strong indeed. Though the presumption is still rebuttable, the requisite rebuttal does not occur by default; it has to occur through moral argumentation, and the argumentation has to establish that capital punishment serves a major public end which cannot be satisfactorily served by any less severe penalty.[3]

---

[3] I am here subscribing to a moral principle that Bedau has styled as the 'Minimal Invasion Principle' (a fundamental precept as well in American constitutional law). According to that principle, any significant exertion of legal-governmental power must satisfy two conditions: it must be in furtherance of an important public purpose, and it must employ the least invasive or restrictive means that is sufficient to achieve that purpose. See Bedau 1999, 47; 2002, 4. Van den Haag was disconcertingly glib when he sought in effect to reconcile the death penalty and the Minimal Invasion Principle by discounting the invasiveness or restrictiveness of that penalty. He wrote that 'the [implementation of a] death sentence does not deprive one of a life one would otherwise keep. We all die even without a legally imposed sentence.... Whatever can be said against the death penalty, it cannot be said that it causes an otherwise

As will become clear in Chapter 6, the only tenable justification for capital punishment leads to the conclusion that such punishment is never legitimate except when imposed (in appropriate circumstances) by liberal-democratic governments. Hence, the liberal-democratic principles that determine the direction of the burden of proof in debates over capital punishment are dispositive. No applications of the death penalty are morally legitimate unless a satisfactory vindication of that penalty has emerged as the basis for those applications.

1.2.1. A first caveat

This section should close by averting two possible misunderstandings. First, although there is always initially a (rebuttable) presumption against the mobilizing of a government's coercive mechanisms, we should hardly infer that the absence of punitive measures on the part of a government is never itself in need of justification. On the contrary, a government's refusal or failure to intervene forcibly is sometimes morally indefensible. Joel Feinberg supplied an example of this phenomenon, when he reported that the penal code in the state of Texas had formerly permitted the slaying of a paramour by a cuckolded husband if the paramour and the adulterous wife were caught by the husband *in flagrante delicto*. As Feinberg wrote, 'a great injustice is done when such killings are left unpunished.... [I]n effect the law expresses the judgment of the "people of Texas," in whose name it speaks, that the vindictive satisfaction in the mind of a cuckolded husband is a thing of greater value than the very life of his wife's lover' (Feinberg 1970, 103). David Lyons has recently recollected an even more odious example. In the South of the United States during the closing decades of the nineteenth century and the first few decades of the twentieth century, prosecutors were extremely reluctant to pursue charges against the perpetrators of racist lynchings, and juries and judges were strongly disinclined to return guilty verdicts against the few who were prosecuted. As Lyons remarks: 'Lacking fear of prosecution, participants posed [for cameras] with impunity. Prosecutions were in fact rare and, thanks to jury nullification, convictions were rarer still' (Lyons 2008, 32).

As these examples and many other potential examples can attest, the withholding of punitive measures is quite often morally problematic. What is most important for our present purposes is that, whenever the absence of sanctions is objectionable, it is so because a general practice of levying sanctions is morally legitimate and vital. In other words, the moral dubiousness of the omission of punishments is always supervenient on a context in which the burden of proof for the legitimacy of punishments

---

avoidable death' (Van den Haag and Conrad 1983, 15, 16). If these quoted statements are to be evaluated as true, they have to be understood *de dicto*. That is, they have to be understood as focusing on an event-type—the event-type of death—with an indefinite temporal index. When so construed, the statements could just as well be uttered about murder, *mutatis mutandis*. Van den Haag himself eventually allowed that no conclusions about the moral status of the death penalty follow from the remarks just quoted: '[T]he death penalty is intended to hasten death. We as yet have to consider whether this can be justified as a punishment for any crime' (Van den Haag and Conrad 1983, 16).

has been met. That moral dubiousness 'presupposes the regular [and legitimate] use of the criminal sanction as a background condition, as the "baseline" against which deviations are measured' (Fletcher 1999, 62). Thus, far from there being any inconsistency between a presumption against a government's exercise of its coercive powers and a presumption against a government's failure or refusal to exercise its coercive powers, the satisfaction of the burden of proof imposed by the former presumption is a necessary condition for the existence of the latter presumption.

1.2.2. A second caveat

Although this book endeavours to vindicate the employment of the death penalty, it is certainly not seeking to justify every execution that has actually taken place in any country. For one thing, as has already been briefly noted, the use of the death penalty is morally legitimate only in countries that are governed by liberal-democratic regimes. Most executions in the present day (to say nothing of past centuries) have taken place in countries that are governed by regimes which lack the moral authority to put any prisoners to death. Furthermore, even in the liberal-democratic nations in which the death penalty is still employed—by far the most prominent of which is the United States, of course—the application of that penalty has been both overinclusive and underinclusive. Many convicts who should not be put to death are in fact executed, and some convicts who should be put to death are instead kept in prison for life (either because they are sentenced to lifelong imprisonment or because their death sentences are never given effect).

Two broad sets of considerations can separately or together militate against the appropriateness of any particular execution: procedural or administrative factors, and substantive factors. Shortcomings in the administration of capital punishment, which Chapter 7 will explore at length, can undermine the moral legitimacy of executions of criminals whose misdeeds are sufficiently heinous to be covered by this book's purgative rationale. Indeed, if the procedural shortcomings are serious and frequent, they can vitiate the whole practice of capital punishment within the criminal-justice system involved. After all, an execution is not legitimate unless it is performed for the right reasons. When death sentences are imposed and carried out largely because of administrative aberrations, they are morally illegitimate even if the executed criminals are defilingly evil. In such cases, substance does not trump procedure; the moral permissibility of the outcomes is undone by the unscrupulous or haphazard ways in which they have been reached. Just as liberal-democratic principles determine the direction of the burden of proof in debates over the moral status of capital punishment, those principles—particularly relating to due process and equality of opportunity—constrain the manner in which any applications of such punishment can legitimately unfold.[4] When the administration

---

[4] For an exposition of the formal and procedural principles of liberal democracy, see Kramer 2007, 143–86.

of the death penalty is in compliance with those constraints, it is informed by the same moral values on which the substantive correctness of any infliction of that penalty depends.

At least as important as the procedural legitimacy of executions, of course, is their substantive appropriateness. As has already been indicated—and as will become clear in Chapter 6—the purgative rationale for capital punishment, which articulates the conditions for the substantive appropriateness of executions, is fairly restrictive. It would not serve to justify quite a few of the death sentences that are handed down in the United States.

Hence, although the orientation of this book is justificatory, I am not striving to vindicate the current practice of capital punishment in the United States or anywhere else. Quite the contrary. If the arguments in this book are sound, then the systems of capital punishment in various American states are in need of considerable modifications. Some notable features of those systems are salutary, to be sure, but numerous people sentenced to death therein are not defilingly evil and are thus not properly subject to execution under the purgative rationale that will be expounded in this book. Accordingly, my championing of that rationale is more a manifesto for change than a vindication of existing practices. It does not constitute an apology for the status quo.

Indeed, although support for the death penalty is more often found on the right than on the left of the political spectrum in the contemporary United States, the regnant political associations of that support are contingent and somewhat superficial. Even Dan Kahan, who dwells on those associations, acknowledges that '[t]here is no necessary *philosophical* link between the death penalty and these [right-of-center] positions [on issues such as abortion and civil liberties and gun control].'[5] He avouches that, if support for the death penalty does stem principally from the right of the American political spectrum, 'that's only because the death penalty bears [contingent] connotations that make it fit better with certain evaluative stances than others' (Kahan 1999, 441).

These concessions by Kahan are wise, since the connections between conservatism and the advocacy of capital punishment are tenuous. For one thing, conservatives' distrust of governmental power lends itself quite readily to some forceful arguments against the adoption or retention of the death penalty (Rowan 2004). Although Chapter 7 will ultimately reject those arguments, they are not to be dismissed lightly. Moreover, as will become apparent in Chapter 6, this book's purgative rationale for capital punishment appeals to considerations that are more frequently invoked on the left of the American political spectrum than on the right. Those considerations, pertaining to the ties of solidarity and mutual responsibility among human beings, cannot easily be ignored or disclaimed by people who regularly resort to them for

---

[5] Kahan 1999, 440, emphasis in original. Let it be noted that I myself favour left-of-centre positions on abortion, civil liberties, and gun control.

other purposes. Such people should be chary of trying to squeeze this book into any ideological pigeonholes.

1.3. A pithy conspectus

Each of the next four chapters will critically scrutinize one of the standard rationales for capital punishment. Chapter 2 deals with the deterrence-oriented justification; Chapter 3 examines two main types of retributivism, the vindicatory variety and the desert-focused variety; Chapter 4 ponders the incapacitative rationale; and Chapter 5 probes the denunciatory theory. After those four chapters have rebutted the commonly invoked justifications for the death penalty, Chapter 6 presents a rationale—the purgative rationale—that stands as an alternative to those justifications. Chapter 7 then concludes the volume by considering whether the sundry problems that afflict the administration of capital punishment are inevitably so bad as to undo the moral legitimacy of every endeavour to institute such punishment.

Three of the standard justifications for capital punishment—the deterrence-oriented, incapacitative, and denunciatory rationales—are consequentialist. They favour the death penalty because of its presumed tendency to produce socially beneficial consequences (especially through the reduction of serious criminal activity). By contrast, retributivism in its primary form is deontological.[6] Retributivistic arguments in support of capital punishment contend that death is sometimes an appropriate sanction not because the imposition of it will tend to cause a diminution of criminal activity—though such a consequence may indeed ensue—but because the imposition of death is deserved or because it reasserts the moral dignity of those who have been harmed by serious crimes. My purgative rationale for capital punishment is likewise deontological rather than consequentialist, as I maintain that such punishment is appropriate when the application of it brings to an end the defilingly evil existence of someone who has committed particularly flagitious crimes.

1.3.1. Chapter 2: Deterrence-oriented theories

All the consequentialist justifications for capital punishment, especially the deterrence-oriented and denunciatory rationales, depend on far-reaching and controversial empirical claims. Thus, as will be discussed in my next chapter,

---

[6] Of course, as will intermittently become apparent in subsequent chapters, retributivism can be combined with consequentialist theories in a number of ways. Moreover, as is argued in Berman 2010, some contemporary versions of retributivism are consequentialist. According to those latter versions of the doctrine, the realization of any retributivistically valuable states of affairs is an especially weighty goal that should be pursued along with other goals in a consequentialist fashion. For reasons that will become evident from my comments on consequentialism in Chapter 2 (and from a few of my comments on retributivism in Chapter 3), the elaboration of retributivism along consequentialist lines is highly problematic; it weakens rather than enhances the insights of retributivists. Thus, because I want to come to grips with retributivism in its strongest form, I will generally treat it as a deontological justification of punishment.

much of the disputation surrounding the deterrence-oriented rationale has centered on numerous empirical studies that have been subjected again and again to complicated statistical analyses. Still, as was remarked earlier, the empirical claims of deterrence-oriented theories are coupled with moral principles that ascribe ethical significance to those claims. Though the moral theses of the deterrence-oriented rationale for the death penalty are perhaps not as frequently assailed as are its empirical theses, they have been far from uncontentious. Chapter 2 will concentrate chiefly on those moral tenets. It will endeavour to show that, even if the empirical propositions advanced by deterrence-oriented theories were all true, those theories would not succeed in establishing that capital punishment is morally legitimate in principle.

In a nutshell, the deterrence-oriented justification of capital punishment holds that executions of murderers are significantly more effective than any other acceptable penalties in lowering the incidence of premeditated homicides by frightening people away from committing them. (Deterrence-oriented arguments in favour of the death penalty can also advert to crimes other than murder, of course. However, very few proponents of such arguments in the present day have called for the use of capital punishment in response to crimes that do not involve murders.) As one of the most renowned exponents of the deterrence-oriented justification proclaimed: '[B]y a dozen or score of punishments, thousands of crimes are prevented. With the sufferings of the guilty few, the security of the many is purchased. By the lopping of a peccant member, the body is saved from decay' (Austin 1995, 43). When theorists commend capital punishment on such grounds, they usually hail any reduction in the incidence of premeditated homicides not as an ultimate end but instead as a means to the ultimate end of maximizing a society's aggregate or average level of utility. In the eyes of deterrence-oriented theorists, then, executions are instrumentally valuable for the fear-inducing ways in which they contribute to the realization of the value that is of ultimate importance.

Chapter 2 will address the debates over the multitudinous relevant empirical studies only to a very limited degree,[7] because the controversies over the findings and statistical significance of those studies are largely matters for social scientists rather than for philosophers. Still, even someone outside the social sciences can recognize that there is a dearth of evidence in support of the deterrence-oriented position. At best, the data and the statistical analyses of the data are inconclusive. Given the quantity of ink and intellectual energy bestowed on the question of the deterrent efficacy of capital punishment, the conclusion that can most plausibly be drawn is that there are no statistically significant deterrent effects waiting to be discovered.

Still, as has been stated, most of Chapter 2 proceeds (strictly *arguendo*) as if the empirical claims of the deterrence-oriented theorists have been at least partly substantiated. Should those claims, if correct, impel us to conclude that the institution

---

[7] I will, however, discuss some general reasons for doubting that capital punishment deters serious crimes more effectively than do alternative sanctions such as lifelong imprisonment-without-parole.

of capital punishment is morally legitimate and obligatory? For several reasons, the answer to this question is negative. As will be argued, the deterrent efficacy of capital punishment is not sufficient to justify the infliction of such punishment, nor can it become sufficient by being supplemented with any of the considerations on which the other standard rationales for the death penalty have concentrated. This book's second chapter will explore the moral inadequacies of the deterrence-oriented rationale partly by reference to a recent exchange between Cass Sunstein and Adrian Vermeule on the one hand and Carol Steiker on the other (Sunstein and Vermeule 2005a; Steiker 2005; Sunstein and Vermeule 2005b). Though their exchange does not address all the queries that will be raised in my critique of deterrence-oriented theories, it is a stimulating point of departure for a number of those queries.

1.3.2. Chapter 3: Retributivism

Chapter 3 moves away from the consequentialism of the deterrence-oriented rationale, as it shifts the focus to the deontological conceptions of punishment and the death penalty propounded by retributivists. Retributivism has emerged in multifarious varieties, which are often blended in the writings of particular theorists. Every variety lays emphasis on human equality and on the moral responsibility of individual human agents. In some versions of retributivism, the centre of attention is the malefactor who has unjustly indulged himself at the expense of others and who therefore deserves to be brought low by being subjected to the detriments of punitive measures. In other versions, the centre of attention is the victim whose rights and dignity have been transgressed; the object of retributive punishment is to reaffirm the rightful standing of the victim, who can be understood solely as some discrete individual(s) or also as the public at large. In either the desert-focused form or the vindicatory form—each of which is frequently conjoined with the other—retributivism aims to reassert the equality of all human agents by ensuring that nobody can unfairly set himself above his fellows with impunity.

Whereas the deterrence-oriented supporters of capital punishment commend it from a viewpoint that is thoroughly prospective and instrumentalist, the retributivistic supporters of capital punishment commend it from a retrospective viewpoint that characterizes such punishment as intrinsically fitting. For these latter proponents, executions are valuable not because of the consequences to which they lead, but because of their commensurateness with the heinous crimes in response to which they are carried out. Executions in appropriate cases are deserved and are to be performed for that reason, irrespective of whether they yield any salutary results such as deterrence.

As has been suggested in this chapter's opening section, my critique of the tenets of retributivism will not seek to impugn those tenets as a general theory of punishment. Rather, the precise issue to be addressed is whether retributivists can succeed in justifying the use of the death penalty. Can they show that the use of that sanction is morally obligatory and legitimate in principle? Chapter 3 delivers a negative answer to this question, as it argues that the considerations underlying retributivism cannot determinately call for executions in preference to certain other severe sanctions. In so arguing, the third chapter will align itself not only with many opponents of retributivism but also with quite a few retributivists (who oppose the institution of capital punishment). Though the chapter will not endorse all the objections raised by those retributivists against the use of the death penalty, it will join with them in maintaining that such a penalty is never morally required on the basis of retributivistic principles. The ends prescribed by those principles can be attained through lesser sanctions. Because retributivism cannot provide any grounds for the proposition that capital punishment is ever morally required, it cannot provide any grounds for the proposition that such punishment is ever morally permitted; after all, it cannot provide any grounds for the proposition that executions are the least severe means for the realization of a major public purpose.[8]

1.3.3. Chapter 4: The incapacitative rationale

According to the incapacitative rationale for the death penalty, the object of capital punishment is to eliminate extremely dangerous people in order to prevent them from wreaking havoc in the future. A justification along these lines is obviously consequentialist, as it upholds capital punishment for the sake of producing the socially beneficial consequence of enhanced public safety. It contends that the only way of protecting members of the public (including members of the public in prison) from the depredations of certain people is to terminate the existence of those people. Even if the executions of those thugs will not deter anyone else from indulging in criminal activity, the executed thugs themselves will no longer be around to prey on their fellow human beings. *Pro tanto*, the world will be a safer place; the numerous innocent lives spared will more than offset the relatively few lives extinguished.

Chapter 4 poses a host of objections to the incapacitative rationale for putting people to death. For one thing, the rationale on its own terms is unconcerned with moral responsibility. It deals with dangerously violent people as if those people were rabid animals rather than agents responsible for their misdeeds. Furthermore, the incapacitative justification for capital punishment does not even condition its applicability on the occurrence of misdeeds. If there is a solid basis for the claim that someone is strongly disposed to engage in murder and mayhem, then under the incapacitative rationale there is a solid basis for executing him regardless of whether he has yet committed any crimes.

Even more damaging is that the incapacitative justification cannot determinately call for executions in preference to alternative sanctions (such as lifelong imprisonment in solitary confinement) that would effectively deprive savage criminals of opportunities to harm others. Thus, notwithstanding that the incapacitative goal of safeguarding members of the public against the occurrence of lethal crimes is a

---

[8] Note that this argument does not rely at all on the principle that everything morally obligatory is morally permissible. I have repeatedly assailed that principle, most recently in Kramer 2009b.

worthy and important objective, the use of the death penalty for the realization of that goal is doubly illegitimate. It is illegitimate because it runs afoul of the problems broached in the preceding paragraph and also because it is not the least severe means for effectively promoting the desideratum that is being pursued.

1.3.4. Chapter 5: The denunciatory conception

Although the denunciatory conception of punishment is often mistaken for other conceptions, it comprises a distinctive array of consequentialist theses. Foremost among them is the idea that punishments give expression to a community's detestation of the misdeeds for which the punishments are levied. Denunciatory theorists hold that the expressive role of punishment is instrumentally valuable for two principal reasons. First, the manifestation of the community's attitude of revulsion toward serious crimes will help to solidify people's sentiments against the commission of those crimes. Like the deterrence-oriented rationale, then, the denunciatory theory maintains that a key function of punishment lies in the reduction of criminal activity. However, whereas the advocates of the deterrence-oriented approach contend that the reduction will occur through the evocation of fear in people, the advocates of the denunciatory rationale contend that the crime-diminishing effect of punishment will derive instead from the reinforcement and purification of people's moral sentiments.

A second valuable consequence of the expressive role of punishment consists in the defusing of people's vindictive impulses. By giving vent to people's feelings of hatred and resentment, punitive measures satisfy their instincts for revenge and thereby greatly lower the likelihood of their resorting to private acts of retaliation. When private vengeance and vendettas are thus obviated, the increase in public order and individual security is beneficial for everybody. As one of the most famous exponents of the denunciatory theory remarked with characteristic trenchancy:

[C]riminal law is in the nature of a persecution of the grosser forms of vice, and an emphatic assertion of the principle that the feeling of hatred and the desire of vengeance . . . are important elements of human nature which ought in such cases to be satisfied in a regular public and legal manner . . . [C]riminal law operates . . . indirectly, but very powerfully, by giving distinct shape to the feeling of anger, and a distinct satisfaction to the desire of vengeance which crime excites in a healthy mind. [Stephen 1993, 98, 100]

Although retributivism is often associated by its critics with a lust for revenge,[9] the denunciatory conception of punishment is in fact the rationale that accords a central place to vindictive feelings. Of course, in so doing, the denunciatory conception is not crassly pandering to people's baser impulses. It portrays punishment as the opti-

---

[9] Such an association has also been posited by some proponents of retributivism. See, for example, Oldenquist 2004, 339–40.

mal means of channelling and allaying people's vengeful sentiments, rather than as a means of untrammelling those sentiments to roam freely.

Applied to the matter of capital punishment, the denunciatory rationale submits that the only apposite way of expressing a community's repugnance toward the most heinous crimes is to execute the perpetrators of those crimes. Only thus can the functions of criminal law be satisfactorily performed in reaction to such ghastly wrongdoing. Unless the vilest criminals are put to death for their iniquities, the extreme wickedness of their actions will have been glossed over and will consequently not have been made sufficiently apparent to the community at large. Likewise, the instincts for revenge felt by many individuals against those criminals will not have been sated and thereby defused. Accordingly, if the most repellent crimes in a community are not punished with death, the community's moral cohesion and its level of public security will suffer considerably.

Chapter 5's critique of the denunciatory rationale for capital punishment will take exception to that rationale partly because of its consequentialism. Like the deterrence-oriented approach, the denunciatory theory does not in itself provide any basis for confining the death penalty to malefactors who have actually committed crimes. If someone is very widely and firmly thought to be responsible for an atrocious murder, and if there is no significant prospect of the emergence of any exculpatory evidence that will persuade people to the contrary, then the denunciatory rationale countenances the execution of the suspect regardless of whether he has actually carried out any misdeed. Furthermore, even if the denunciatory theorists supplement their rationale with retributivism's emphasis on desert in order to overcome this first problem—that is, even if they treat retributivism as a side-constraint that limits the applicability of their own theory to people who are actually guilty—a number of other difficulties remain, as Chapter 5 will make clear.

For the proponents of the denunciatory rationale, the most vexing of those additional difficulties is that that rationale cannot provide any solid grounds for favouring executions over severe alternative sanctions such as lifelong imprisonment-without-parole. The empirical studies adduced by supporters and detractors of the deterrence-oriented justification are focused solely on increases and decreases in rates of crime; those studies do not attempt to distinguish between decreases attributable to the dread of execution and decreases attributable to the reinforcement of morally upright sentiments. Consequently, the utter inconclusiveness of those studies (at best) is as damaging to the denunciatory rationale for capital punishment as to the deterrence-oriented rationale. No more than the empirical claims of the latter rationale are the empirical claims of the former rationale borne out by the available data. (Chapter 5 will present some general reasons for doubting that those empirical claims will ever be borne out.)

Moreover, even if the empirical evidence were largely in keeping with what the denunciatory theorists assert, their attempted justification of capital punishment would fail to establish that such punishment is morally legitimate in principle. Again the problem faced by the denunciatory rationale is parallel to a problem faced by the deterrence-oriented rationale. For each theory, the problem arises from the fact that punishments much more severe than the ordinary death penalty—such as the infliction of savage torture followed by death through dismemberment—are highly likely to be even more efficacious as deterrents or as reinforcers of morally upright sentiments. In many possible worlds,[10] those much more severe sanctions will be utility-maximizing (not least because their formidableness will mean that they seldom have to be used). Nonetheless, they are morally illegitimate. Given as much, the efficacy of sanctions as deterrents or as reinforcers of morally worthy sentiments is not a sufficient condition for their legitimacy. Ergo, to know whether any sanction such as the death penalty is morally legitimate in principle or not, we have to draw upon some independent touchstone of moral legitimacy. That touchstone must come from somewhere beyond the denunciatory theory, yet—for reasons explored in Chapters 2–4—it cannot come from any of the other standard rationales for capital punishment.

1.3.5. Chapter 6: The purgative rationale

Having impeached the standard justifications for the death penalty, this book proceeds in Chapter 6 to expound an alternative justification. Although the purgative rationale goes almost entirely unmentioned in the contemporary philosophical literature on the death penalty, it is one of the most prominent of the several justifications for capital punishment that are propounded in the Bible. In the Book of Deuteronomy, the following pronouncement occurs at many of the junctures at which the Israelites are enjoined to put certain miscreants to death: 'So you shall purge the evil from the midst of you' (Deuteronomy 13:5, 17:7, 19:19, 22:21, 22:24, 24:7). Several other closely similar pronouncements likewise appear in Deuteronomy.

Now, one reason for the nearly complete disregard of the purgative rationale in modern philosophical discussions of capital punishment is undoubtedly the association of that rationale with the Bible. One of the most salutary contrasts between modern philosophy and much of medieval philosophy is that the Bible cannot any longer be cited respectably as a source of authoritative insight that supposedly resolves thorny philosophical disputes. Quite rightly, no capable philosopher in the contemporary world would accept that the Bible's endorsement of the purgative rationale for the death penalty is somehow determinative of that penalty's moral status. Far from being invariably correct, the moral beliefs expressed in the Scriptures are often primitive and repellent. Hence, the sheer presence of the purgative rationale in Deuteronomy is hardly sufficient to guarantee its moral correctness. On the contrary,

---

[10] When philosophers speak of possible worlds, they are referring to the countless alternative ways in which the whole array of entities and events can unfold; the actual world is possible, of course, but so are innumerable counterfactual worlds. Any one of those latter worlds is classifiable as nearby or proximate insofar as its similarities to the actual world are close.

the salience of that rationale in the Bible is enough to discredit it altogether in the eyes of many philosophers.

Indeed, as we shall see in Chapter 6, a famous passage from Immanuel Kant that fleetingly gestures toward the purgative justification for the death penalty has frequently been derided on the ground that it peddles some outlandish ideas from the Bible. Still, despite the ridicule heaped upon that passage, the purgative rationale to which it somewhat confusedly adverts is sound and is quite detachable from any religious origins. Removing the purgative rationale from its religious provenance is in fact the central task to be carried out by Chapter 6, for this book firmly aligns itself with most modern philosophers in eschewing any appeals to the Scriptures as authoritative oracles.[11] Moral justifications have to be grounded on unremittingly secular moral argumentation rather than on Scriptural incantations. My elaboration of the purgative rationale for capital punishment will indeed be unremittingly secular in both its orientation and its motivation.

What, then, is the purgative rationale? It maintains that some misdeeds are so monstrously evil as to render morally noxious the lives of the people who have committed them. The continued existence of the perpetrator of any such misdeed(s) will have defiled the moral character of the community in whose control he or she abides. Though the community may well not have been complicit in the occurrence of the misdeed(s)—since the misdeed(s) in question may have been thoroughly at odds with the prevailing mores rather than in furtherance thereof—it becomes and remains complicit in the continued existence of the person who is responsible, insofar as that culprit has been brought or should have been brought under the control of the community. By failing or refusing to execute such a person after fair legal proceedings, a community becomes and remains defiled. (As will be seen in Chapter 6, the defilement pertains to the relationship between a community and the rest of humankind. It arises because certain offences are so horrific that they count as crimes against humanity.)

Unlike the commonly invoked rationales for capital punishment, the purgative justification calls uniquely for the death penalty—not only in the sense that it deals exclusively with the most heinous offences, but also in the sense that the sole remedy which it ever prescribes is the termination of a defilingly evil person's life. As Chapter 6 will argue, for example, banishment is never a suitable alternative to death under the purgative rationale. Nonetheless, the superiority of the purgative rationale in the respect just mentioned will obviously be unavailing unless the key elements of that rationale are sustainable. Most of Chapter 6 is devoted to providing support for those elements.

In particular, the chapter—drawing to some degree on recent philosophical discussions of the topic—expounds a thoroughly secular account of evil. In a closely related vein, it elaborates a thoroughly secular account of defilement. (Whereas the

---

[11] Although I study the Bible closely for 60–90 minutes every day, and although I believe that fruitful ideas can be gleaned from it, I have been robustly atheistic since the age of eight.

property of evil has received considerable scrutiny from philosophers in recent years, the intimately connected phenomenon of defilement has received very little attention from them.) On the basis of my explications of those notions, Chapter 6 affirms that the application of the death penalty in appropriate cases is the least severe means— indeed, the only means—for the effectuation of a major public purpose. The application of that penalty in such cases partly constitutes the moral probity of a community as a locus of liberal-democratic values.

As has already been indicated, the reach of the purgative justification is too cabined to comprehend many of the executions that have taken place in the United States in recent decades. Similarly, as has likewise been indicated, the emphasis of the purgative justification on the ideal of moral probity will mean that the justification does not support any executions carried out by a regime that is itself morally illegitimate (such as the Communist government in contemporary China). No such regime can correctly claim to be acting in furtherance of the moral purity of the community over which it governs, since most of the regime's own operations are so starkly at variance with genuine moral values.

Still, despite the restrictive scope of the purgative rationale for capital punishment, it does indeed establish that some executions in the United States (and other liberal democracies) are both morally obligatory and morally legitimate in principle. Any of the vilest murderers, such as Charles Manson and Richard Ramirez and Theodore Bundy and Richard Speck and Dennis Rader and Timothy McVeigh and Ian Brady and Khalid Sheikh Mohammed, would fall within the sway of the purgative rationale. The continued existence of any such person defiles the community in whose control he abides. Furthermore, as Chapter 6 will maintain, some actual or imaginable crimes other than murder can be sufficiently depraved and brutal to fall within the ambit of the purgative rationale. Hence, although this book's arguments are focused chiefly on matters of abstract moral principle, they yield a number of concrete practical implications.

1.3.6. Chapter 7: Problems of administration

Having debunked the standard justifications for capital punishment, and having then offered an alternative justification that surmounts the difficulties afflicting the previous rationales, this book concludes by investigating some problems that have figured prominently in the disputation over the death penalty in the United States for decades. Notwithstanding that the death penalty for some monstrous criminals is morally obligatory, any application of that penalty will be morally impermissible if shortcomings in the administration of capital cases are so grievous and widespread as to undermine the moral legitimacy of the institutions responsible for handling such cases. Critics of the death penalty in the United States have long dwelt on real or putative problems such as the following: the never fully eliminable possibility of mistaken convictions and executions of innocent people; racial biases in the administration of capital punishment, especially with regard to the racial affiliations of the victims of the crimes for which the death sentences are imposed; the arbitrariness of the selection between capital defendants who are to undergo executions and capital defendants who are instead imprisoned for life; the costliness of the death penalty; the shoddiness of the legal representation provided to indigent defendants; the protractedness of the delays in the carrying out of death sentences; and the notoriety gained by executed defendants whose victims, by contrast, tend to be largely overlooked.

My closing chapter will explore most of these problems. Two chief points should be noted straightaway. First, even if these administrative shortcomings are independently or cumulatively sufficient to delegitimize the death penalty as it is currently practised in the United States, they are not destructive of the moral legitimacy of that penalty in principle unless they are somehow inevitable. Surmountable faults in the administration of capital punishment, however flagrant, do not affect the moral status of such punishment as a general type of sanction. In a society whose institutions of criminal justice are not tarnished by those faults to any significant degree, the moral obligatoriness of executions under the purgative rationale will be accompanied by the executions' moral permissibility. In a society whose institutions of criminal justice are so tarnished, the best course of action is to improve those institutions and thereby to bring about a state of affairs in which the implementation of appropriate death sentences is morally legitimate. (Among the reasons for deeming such a course of action to be best is that, if administrative defects are grave, the factors consequently militating in favour of a moratorium on capital punishment would typically also militate in favour of a moratorium on any severe punishments.)

Secondly, most questions concerning the extent of the various imperfections in the administration of capital punishment in the United States are for social scientists rather than for philosophers. To ascertain whether and how much the problems listed above are occurrent in the criminal-justice system of any particular country, scholars have to engage in empirical enquiries. Though Chapter 7 will make reference to some empirical studies, I do not pretend to have conducted any such studies myself. Thus, instead of marshalling any newly obtained empirical data, the chapter will ponder some general points that arise from the data that are already available. In so doing, the chapter will suggest that some allegations of administrative irregularities are exaggerated or tendentious, and that some other such allegations are based at least partly on dubious arguments. In those respects, Chapter 7 will join with some opponents of the death penalty who chafe at finding that the debates over the morality of capital punishment have become preoccupied with administrative deficiencies (Dolinko 1986; Note 2001; Steiker and Steiker 2005). Still, while raising a number of queries, the chapter will of course not deny that the systems of capital punishment in various American states are procedurally imperfect. Every punitive system is procedurally imperfect. Whether the failings are so grave as to be sufficient in themselves to delegitimize the whole practice of capital punishment within any American jurisdiction is a more complicated matter. Answering that question for each jurisdiction is an endeavour that lies beyond the scope of this book, but there is no evident basis for presuming that the answer will be either uniformly positive or uniformly negative.

2

Deterrence through Capital Punishment

In everyday political debates over the death penalty in the United States and in other countries, deterrence-oriented arguments in favour of that penalty are extremely common (Abernethy 1996, 386–8; Sorell 1987, 32–8, 41–2). In scholarly disputation as well, such arguments figure saliently—though they are more frequently and sophisticatedly controverted in such disputation than in quotidian political debates. For many ordinary people and some philosophers, the deterrence-oriented lines of reasoning in support of capital punishment possess a compellingly common-sensical appeal. Nevertheless, despite the prevalence of the endeavours to justify the death penalty with reference to its deterrent efficacy, those endeavours are unavailing for a number of reasons. People who wish to vindicate the use of capital punishment will have to look elsewhere for a satisfactory rationale.

This chapter will first delineate the deterrence-oriented rationale for capital punishment, and will defend it against some unwise objections. A worthwhile engagement with that rationale has to highlight its apparent strengths, in order to reveal why people have so often invoked it; there is little point to contesting a theory in anything other than its most persuasive forms. Thereafter, however, the chapter will proceed to assail the deterrence-oriented justification.

My critical remarks will begin with some general reasons for doubting that the death penalty is indeed more effective in deterring people from committing serious crimes than are other severe sanctions such as lifelong imprisonment-without-parole. In other words, my critical discussion will begin by impeaching the empirical propositions on which the deterrence-oriented supporters of capital punishment have to rely (if they wish to maintain that the imposition of such punishment is warranted in the actual world). This chapter will also devote some attention to the myriad of empirical studies that have enquired into the deterrent efficacy of the death penalty. My brief treatment of those studies will be largely confined to accentuating the inconclusiveness of the data that are available. This chapter does not attempt to amplify those data or to carry out any new statistical analyses of them, for the empirical shakiness of deterrence-oriented theories is not the prime target of my critique.

Instead, my critique will concentrate principally on the moral dubiousness of the proposition that deterrence can serve as the basis for the moral legitimacy and moral obligatoriness of capital punishment. Though some of the dubiousness can be overcome through the supplementation of the deterrence-oriented rationale with elements of retributivism, the most damaging difficulties cannot be dodged in that fashion. Neither the ghastliness of the deterrence-oriented justification nor its indeterminacy can be surmounted through recourse to any of the other standard justifications for the death penalty.

2.1. The deterrence-oriented rationale expounded

As has been stated in Chapter 1, the key thesis of the deterrence-oriented rationale for capital punishment is that executions are more effective than are any gentler sanctions in lowering the incidence of murders by inducing people to fear the consequences of perpetrating such crimes. Several aspects of this thesis are in need of amplification. First, although deterrence-oriented theories have sometimes been associated with a model of human beings as rational calculators who tend to reflect carefully and knowledgeably on the consequences of their actions in sundry contexts (Murphy 1973, 232), that exaggerative model is dispensable. As has long been granted by both critics and supporters of the deterrence-oriented justification (Abernethy 1996, 383–5; Sunstein and Vermeule 2005a, 714; Van den Haag 1968, 285–6), the deterrent effect that is supposed to follow from the occurrence of executions does not have to ensue from any detailed and careful calculations on the part of prospective murderers. A general fear-suffused awareness of the dire consequences of committing murders can be enough to incline potential malefactors away from engaging in such misdeeds. As Ernest van den Haag wrote, the requisite outlook can consist simply in a 'general response to a severe but not necessarily specifically and explicitly apprehended or calculated threat' (van den Haag 1968, 285–6). Of course, the actuality of any deterrent effect presupposes that some or all miscreants possess at least modest abilities to assess risks and to adjust their conduct accordingly. As Richard Lempert rightly remarks: 'The threat of death can only deter potential criminals who [at least] loosely calculate the costs and rewards of their behavior' (Lempert 1981, 1193). Still, although neither capital punishment nor any other type of punishment can deter someone who is wholly incapable of balancing the risks and potential rewards of different courses of conduct, a meagre level of proficiency in balancing is sufficient to make deterrence—albeit perhaps a modest degree of deterrence—possible. Since some would-be murderers in any society are endowed with at least meagre levels of such proficiency, deterrent effects are possible.

A second point to be clarified here is that the debates over the deterrent efficacy of capital punishment are focused on its marginal deterrence rather than on its absolute deterrence (Abernethy 1996, 382; Bedau 1985, 901 n 89; Bedau 1993, 181; Conway 1974, 433; Donnelly 1978, 1144; Jones and Potter 1981, 161 n 7; Lempert 1981, 1192,

1211; Markel 2005, 470; Reiman 1985, 144–5). That is, they are focused not on the difference between the incidence of murders in the presence of capital punishment and the incidence of murders in the absence of any punishments whatsoever, but instead on the difference between the incidence of murders in the presence of capital punishment and the incidence of murders in the presence of only non-capital sanctions such as lifelong imprisonment-without-parole. Nobody could reasonably doubt that the death penalty for murder is a far more effective deterrent than is the wholesale absence of any sanctions for such a crime. That glaringly obvious point is not what is at issue in the disputes between opponents and advocates of deterrence-oriented theories. Rather, a key point at issue pertains to the disparity—if any—between the deterrent efficacy of the death penalty and the deterrent efficacy of punishments that are slightly less severe. If the latter punishments are sufficient to deter everyone who can be deterred at all from committing murders, then the death penalty does not produce any marginal deterrent effect; it adds nothing to the deterrent effect of the less severe sanctions. Consequently, given such a state of affairs, the death penalty would fail to satisfy the Minimal Invasion Principle that was broached in Chapter 1. It would not be the least severe means for realizing the worthy public purpose of minimizing the occurrence of murders. When deterrence-oriented theorists impute deterrent efficacy to capital punishment, they are claiming that the introduction or retention of such punishment does not in fact constitute a transgression of the Minimal Invasion Principle. They are claiming that the death penalty produces a *marginal* deterrent effect.

Thirdly, any deterrent effect of an execution is plainly general rather than specific. General deterrence consists in the fear-inducing impact of some punishment on members of the public at large, whereas specific deterrence consists in the fear-inducing impact of some punishment on the person who has undergone that punishment. Although the notion of specific deterrence in application to somebody who has undergone a term of imprisonment is perfectly sensible (even if the person has not in fact been deterred), that notion makes no sense in application to somebody who has been executed. Manifestly, a person who has undergone the death penalty is no longer in a position to experience fear or any other emotion.

Fourthly, as was noted in Chapter 1, the psychological reaction on which the deterrence-oriented approach to punishment trades is that of fear. Insofar as capital punishment or any other type of punishment is a deterrent, it tends to reduce the incidence of criminal activity by leading people to be frightened about the detriments that will be inflicted upon them if they engage in such activity. In this respect among others, the deterrence-oriented conception of capital punishment diverges notably from the denunciatory conception (though the two are compatible and are indeed combined in the writings of some of their chief exponents). Whereas the denunciatory theorists submit that capital punishment brings about a reduction in the rate of murder by strengthening people's feelings of moral revulsion toward such a heinous crime, the deterrence-oriented theorists claim that the reduction occurs because most would-be murderers are so daunted by the prospect of being put to death that they refrain from acting on their inclinations. This contrast between the two theories was famously captured by the foremost advocate of the denunciatory conception of punishment:

Some men, probably, abstain from murder because they fear that, if they committed murder, they would be hung. Hundreds of thousands abstain from it because they regard it with horror. One great reason why they regard it with horror is, that murderers are hung with the hearty approbation of all reasonable men. [Stephen 1863, 99]

This difference between the deterrence-oriented approach and the denunciatory approach to lowering the rate of criminal activity is not always kept in mind by scholars who write on these issues. For instance, when expressing some doubts about specific deterrence as an aim of punishment, Mary Ellen Gale writes as follows: 'Rather than foster an eager desire to conform to law, punishment may produce anger, resentment, and a determination to reject the values of a society whose authorities have inflicted pain on the offender' (Gale 1985, 992). Given that Gale is discussing deterrence—albeit specific deterrence—her worry about someone's lacking an eager desire to conform to legal requirements is misplaced. Though the denunciatory account and the retributivistic account of punishment do concern themselves (in quite different ways) with instilling into malefactors a ready desire for compliance with the law,[1] the deterrence-oriented approach in detachment from those accounts does not pursue such a concern. Instead, it attributes the salutary crime-reducing effect of punishment to the fear that is bred thereby. As John Austin put the matter, sanctions are attached to any legal mandate so that each person 'is restrained by his fear of the evil from doing the act which is forbidden'.[2] Gale herself slightly later recognizes clear-sightedly this point about the nature of deterrence, when she goes on to say that 'it also remains both intuitively and empirically probable that many rational criminals are deterred from committing future offenses by the fear of further punishment' (Gale 1985, 992).

A fifth aspect of the deterrence-oriented rationale to be noted here is the communicative role which that rationale ascribes to capital punishment. Although the communicative force of executions is perhaps more heavily emphasized in the retributivistic and denunciatory justifications of the death penalty, the deterrence-oriented

---

[1] Also concerned with the eliciting of such a desire, of course, is a rehabilitative account of punishment (or a theory that posits rehabilitation as an alternative to punishment). Although Chapter 3's exposition of retributivism will include an ancillary rehabilitative component, this book does not present a separate rehabilitative rationale for capital punishment—mainly because the idea of rehabilitating someone by executing him is obviously a non-starter (save when that idea is assigned the very limited role reserved for it in Chapter 3).

[2] Austin 1885, 444, italics removed. Austin later went on to suggest that habitual fear of the punishments attached to various crimes can eventually lead a person to develop genuine moral scruples about committing those crimes. See Austin 1885, 448–50. Austin's remarks along these lines are perceptive and are undoubtedly accurate in some cases, but they are not integral to the deterrence-oriented conception of punishment. Under such a conception, any punishment can play its role purely by eliciting persistent fear.

justification likewise accords a central place to communication. If executions were somehow kept concealed from all members of the public, they would not produce any deterrent effects. People are not frightened by occurrences of which they are unaware. Only by being publicized do any executions convey a deterrence-oriented message to people along the following lines: 'If you commit a similarly vile crime, you will suffer a similar fate.' Hence, inasmuch as a system of capital punishment is designed to further the objectives of a deterrence-oriented justification, it will aim to ensure that executions receive ample publicity. (As has been noted by some commentators—especially by Abernethy 1996—this feature of the deterrence-oriented rationale is not easily squared with the systems of capital punishment in various American states at the present day. Though the occurrence of executions is of course not concealed in any of those states, such events now each take place in front of very few people. Whereas executions in the early United States were public spectacles, they are now performed away from the public gaze behind prison walls. They are not televised or broadcast by other means. In sum, although deterrent effects are still possible in the American systems of capital punishment, the shift from public spectacles to sequestered events has significantly lowered the likelihood of such effects, *ceteris paribus*. If deterrence were the prime objective of those systems of capital punishment, then the secludedness of executions in the United States would be baffling. We at best would have to infer that some strong countervailing concerns have greatly attenuated the commitment of those systems to that supposedly prime objective.)

A sixth and final aspect of the deterrence-oriented rationale for capital punishment which should be mentioned here is that such a rationale is usually embedded in a general utilitarian theory. As Chapter 1 has remarked, nearly all deterrence-oriented theorists take diminutions in the rate of murders to be instrumentally valuable rather than intrinsically valuable. Most of them perceive such diminutions as effective means for realizing the intrinsically valuable end of maximizing a community's level of aggregate or average welfare (or some closely related property). As will become evident later in this chapter, the location of the deterrence-oriented rationale in a broader utilitarian framework enables that rationale to circumvent or finesse some objections that might be raised against it. However, the utilitarian bearings of the rationale will leave many other such objections undeflected, and will give rise to some additional difficulties. In light of the battery of criticisms directed against utilitarianism for many years, we should hardly expect the aforementioned bearings to be an unproblematic shield for the deterrence-oriented theorists.

2.2. Simplistic strictures

As a continuation of my exposition of the deterrence-oriented justification for capital punishment, this section of the chapter will parry a few misconceived strictures that have been levelled against that justification. Although the principal aim of this chapter is to expose the untenability of the deterrence-oriented rationale, the success of the endeavour requires an accurate understanding of that rationale. We thus have to fathom the strengths of the deterrence-oriented approach as well as its weaknesses. We have to see where it does not go astray, as well as where it does.

2.2.1. A misjudged recourse to Rawls

In an interesting article that draws on the philosophical methodology of John Rawls and Ronald Dworkin in order to deny the moral legitimacy of the death penalty, Samuel Donnelly argues in effect against the deterrence-oriented rationale for that penalty (Donnelly 1978, 1145–52). He accepts purely *arguendo* the claims by some deterrence-oriented theorists that each additional execution in the United States will spare several lives of innocent people, and he assumes *arguendo* that the parties in the Rawlsian Original Position will know that those claims are true. He asks whether such knowledge will lead the parties to favour the institution of the death penalty for their society. He notes that, because the parties do not know who will end up where in the society, they will take into consideration both the viewpoint of an executed murderer and the viewpoint of the victim of an undeterred murderer. 'The hypothetical contracting parties are required to imagine themselves in each of the positions: namely, that of the person threatened with execution and that of the person in danger of death from private violence' (Donnelly 1978, 1146). Donnelly offers three arguments for the proposition that the parties will reject the institution of capital punishment.

2.2.1.1. Donnelly's first line of reasoning: the matter of slavery

First, Donnelly recalls that Rawls himself maintained that the parties in the Original Position would forswear the institution of slavery even if the adoption of that institution could raise the level of aggregate or average welfare in their society (Rawls 1971, 168, 248). Donnelly submits that the maximin reasoning of the parties will likewise impel them to forswear the death penalty.[3] Such an analogy, however, is markedly inapposite. When the parties in the Original Position decide to disallow slavery, they are indeed complying with the maximin rule. The cost of forgoing the institution of slavery is a diminished level of utility for the people who would benefit overall from the presence of such an institution. Although those people will *pro tanto* be worse off as a result of the disallowance of slavery, it is overwhelmingly unlikely that they will thereby be brought below the level that would be occupied by subjugated people if slavery were to be countenanced. Hence, the decision of the parties in the Original Position to prohibit slavery is in conformity to the maximin rule. By contrast, given (*ex hypothesi*) that those

---

[3] Donnelly 1978, 1150. When people reason in a maximin fashion, they seek to fix upon social arrangements in which the lowest positions are higher than the lowest positions in any alternative social arrangements that could have been chosen. The Rawlsian Original Position is a situation in which principles of distributive justice are to be selected by parties under a Veil of Ignorance which prevents the parties from knowing anything about the individuating features that differentiate them one from another.

parties know the correctness of the deterrence-oriented theorists' claims about the power of capital punishment to spare innocent lives, their maximin reasoning will not impel them to disallow such punishment. The cost of forgoing the imposition of death sentences on murderers is the loss of many innocent lives. If the parties compare (1) the lot of the murderers who will be humanely executed in a world that includes the death penalty and (2) the lot of the far more numerous innocents who will be brutally slain in a world that excludes the death penalty, their maximin reasoning should lead them to embrace the institution of capital punishment for their society. Unlike the establishment of slavery, the establishment of the death penalty—in a world in which the deterrence-oriented theorists' bold empirical claims are true—is in accordance with the maximin rule's instruction 'to adopt the alternative the worst outcome of which is superior to the [worst] outcomes of the others' (Rawls 1971, 153).

2.2.1.2. Donnelly's second line of reasoning: an untenable asymmetry

A second line of reasoning by Donnelly is equally problematic. He writes as follows:

> In the presence of other means for restricting private violence, the contracting parties would not agree to take the risk of the uniquely devastating capital punishment, which they have examined from the point of view of those subject to it, for the sake of fulfilling their obligation, from another point of view, to take reasonable measures to reduce the risk of death by private violence. A death by capital punishment, then, cannot be simply balanced against a death by the haphazard violence of murder. [Donnelly 1978, 1150]

Given that the commendations of capital punishment by deterrence-oriented theorists are always focused on the *marginal* deterrence generated by such punishment, the initial clause of this passage's opening statement is puzzling. When deterrence-oriented theorists affirm that several lives can be saved by each additional execution, they are indicating the extent to which the deterrent impact of each execution salutarily exceeds the impact produced by any 'other means for restricting private violence'. At any rate, even more troubling is the other chief misstep in this passage.

Though the wording of the passage is not very lucid, Donnelly appears to construe as a certainty the prospect of being executed (for anyone who has been subjected to such a sanction) while construing as a mere possibility the prospect of being murdered. This asymmetry is especially salient in the closing portion of the passage, where the adjective 'haphazard' differentiates 'a death by the . . . violence of murder' from '[a] death by capital punishment.' That is, Donnelly seems to be comparing the perspective of everyone who is actually executed with the perspective of everyone who faces the possibility of being slain by an undeterred murderer.[4] Within the model of the Original Position as Donnelly draws upon it, however, such an asymmetry is untenable. There should be uncertainties on both sides of the relevant comparison—uncertainties which reflect the epistemic situation of every party in the Original Position. In other words, Donnelly should be comparing the possibility

---

[4] Claire Finkelstein appears to commit this same error in Finkelstein 2002, 18.

of turning out to be an executed criminal with the possibility of turning out to be the victim of an undeterred murderer. When those possibilities are compared, we can see that Donnelly's characterization of capital punishment as 'uniquely devastating' is unsustainable. Being murdered is at least as devastating. Hence, given *ex hypothesi* that the parties in the Original Position know that the empirical claims advanced by the deterrence-oriented proponents of capital punishment are correct, and given that those parties will engage in the comparison just outlined—rather than in Donnelly's tendentious comparison—they will favour the adoption of capital punishment for their society. (Of course, Rawls famously excluded all knowledge of specific probabilities from the ken of the parties in the Original Position. Nothing in Donnelly's discussion or in my riposte to his discussion is at odds with that Rawlsian exclusion. Even if the parties know that each additional execution will save several lives, no party under the Veil of Ignorance will know anything about the probability of his or her turning out to be either an executed murderer in the presence of capital punishment or the victim of an undeterred murderer in the absence of capital punishment.)

2.2.1.3. Donnelly's third line of reasoning: public order

Donnelly proceeds to contend that '[i]n the case of capital punishment, . . . there must be both a demonstrable deterrent effect and a showing that it is necessary to the preservation of a reasonably orderly society'. He insists that 'the contracting parties would not agree to capital punishment simply on the ground that it would deter some potential murderers but only if it were necessary to preserve reasonable order in society' (Donnelly 1978, 1158, 1161). It is quite unclear whence this new restriction comes. Few if any deterrence-oriented theorists have ever gone so far as to maintain that the institution of capital punishment is necessary for the preservation of a reasonably orderly society. Accordingly, the new test applied here by Donnelly to capital punishment is not based on anything internal to the claims of the deterrence-oriented writers. Yet that test likewise has no grounding in Rawls's methodology. When the parties in the Original Position are deliberating whether to embrace some institution for their community, they do not insist that that institution must be necessary for the preservation of a reasonably orderly society. Any such standard would be far too stringent, and would disallow many of the detailed institutions and principles that are endorsed by the parties in the Original Position as envisaged by Rawls. Instead, the parties ask whether any specified institution will improve the position of the worst-off group in the society for which they are choosing. If they ask that question about the practice of capital punishment while knowing that the empirical claims of the deterrence-oriented proponents of the death penalty are correct, they will endorse that practice for their society.

Donnelly seeks to vindicate his preservation-of-a-reasonably-orderly-society restriction by pointing out that 'Rawls's contracting parties, on occasion, would reject societal advantage in order to secure protection of the individual's basic interests'

(Donnelly 1978, 1161). Such an appeal to Rawls is unavailing, for essentially the same reasons that have been noted in my rejoinder to Donnelly's analogy between capital punishment and slavery. When the parties in the Original Position contemplate the benefits of the death penalty, they are not asking whether that penalty will increase 'societal advantage' (that is, the overall good of their society). Rather, they are asking whether it will 'secure protection of the individual's basic interests' and thereby enhance the position of their society's worst-off group. As has already been indicated, the parties—who are presumed to know that the empirical contentions of the deterrence-oriented theorists are correct—will supply an affirmative answer to that question.

2.2.1.4. Some further reflections

In sum, our brief exploration of Donnelly's arguments has made clear that Rawls's methodology in itself does not furnish any basis for repudiating the moral theses of the deterrence-oriented rationale for capital punishment. If the empirical theses associated with that rationale are correct and if they are known to the parties in the Original Position (as Donnelly assumes for the sake of argument in the portions of his article on which my discussion has concentrated), then the parties will choose the death penalty for their society. Moreover, even if the Veil of Ignorance precludes the parties' knowledge of those empirical theses—on the ground that, because the theses' truth-values are variable across societies, their contents are not sufficiently general to qualify as some of the 'general information' that gets past the Veil (Rawls 1971, 137–8)—the parties can reach a provisional judgement on the matter of capital punishment. Under the Veil, they will agree that such punishment is to be adopted by their society if and only if it has been shown to be strongly efficacious in deterring people from committing murders.

Of course, this formulation of the parties' decision tends to highlight a problem that confronts any version of the deterrence-oriented rationale or denunciatory rationale for capital punishment. If the introduction of such punishment on the basis of either such rationale is to be morally legitimate, it must proceed by reference to data that reveal the efficacy of the death penalty in reducing crime. Yet the collection of such data cannot occur unless the death penalty has already been practised. Hence, a necessary condition for the moral legitimacy of any deterrence-oriented or denunciatory institution of capital punishment is that such punishment has previously been imposed for quite some time illegitimately.

Although the problem just recounted is a genuine difficulty for deterrence-oriented theories, it is not wholly insurmountable. For one thing, the proponents of such theories are not morally obligated to ignore data from other jurisdictions. If the other jurisdictions are similar in relevant demographic and socioeconomic respects (as is true of many American states vis-à-vis one another), then the data can be a suitable basis from which those proponents can warrantedly extrapolate conclusions about their own jurisdictions. Furthermore, even within a single jurisdiction the deterrence-oriented advocates of capital punishment are not morally obligated to disregard all data concerning the effects of past executions. Although those data have been collected through observations of a practice that was not morally legitimate at the time when the observations were undertaken, the deterrence-oriented theorists are not morally obligated to imitate ostriches by refusing to recognize that the observations have indeed been undertaken. If the data reveal that past executions have significantly reduced the incidence of murders, then—in the eyes of the deterrence-oriented theorists—a necessary condition for the future legitimacy of the institution of capital punishment will have been established.

Two quick caveats should be entered, before we move on. First, my defence of the deterrence-oriented rationale in the preceding paragraph has not been suggesting that executions carried out on the basis of that rationale are morally legitimate if they are supported with empirical studies which show that past executions have tended to reduce the incidence of murders significantly. After all, much of the rest of this chapter will be arguing that the deterrence-oriented rationale is never sufficient to establish the moral legitimacy of capital punishment. Instead of implying that executions conducted on the basis of that rationale are morally legitimate, I have simply sought to indicate that the challenge sketched in the penultimate paragraph above is not fatal for deterrence-oriented theories. The point raised in that challenge does not preclude the proponents of those theories from showing that a condition which they perceive as prerequisite to the moral legitimacy of any applications of the death penalty can be satisfied.

Secondly, there is no need for us here to consider the following moral questions, interesting though they are. Let us suppose for a moment that the deterrence-oriented rationale for capital punishment is correct. If the death penalty were to be introduced for a certain period with the express aim of generating the deterrence-confirming data that could subsequently place that penalty on a solid moral footing, would the initial trial with the specified aim itself be morally legitimate? Will the initial trial be morally legitimate even if the data when gathered are inconclusive at best? (We can assume that the trial will be discontinued when the inconclusiveness of the data becomes apparent.) Although these are vital questions to be addressed by deterrence-oriented theorists, this chapter can put them aside. Such questions are of importance only if the deterrence-oriented rationale for capital punishment—or the denunciatory rationale—is correct. Since this chapter will be impugning that rationale at length, the questions just broached can be left by the wayside. If some sound justifications of other institutions rely heavily on empirical claims, then cognate questions about those institutions may well be pertinent in other contexts. However, in the context of this book (where my own arguments in favour of the death penalty do not rely on any controversial empirical propositions), such questions can properly go unaddressed.

2.2.2. Using people as means

Another misdirected objection to the deterrence-oriented rationale for the death penalty is the allegation that any executions based on that rationale would use capital defendants for the furtherance of public ends and would thus contravene the second formulation of Immanuel Kant's Categorical Imperative: 'Act in such a way that you always treat humanity, whether in your own person or in the person of any other, never simply as a means, but always at the same time as an end' (Kant 1964, 96, italics removed). Given that the deterrence-oriented rationale is typically a component of a broader utilitarian moral theory, the occurrence of complaints about violations of the Kantian injunction is scarcely surprising. Such complaints are a staple of the anti-utilitarian literature. Specifically in application to the deterrence-oriented justification of capital punishment, the concern is that executions are carried out purely for instru-mental reasons. Executions are deemed to be justified if and only if they bring about significant decreases in serious criminal activity. That is, they are deemed to be justified if and only if they further the public weal by enhancing public security. Consequently, a capital defendant's life is sacrificed for the sake of the public weal. There can hardly be a starker example of the use of somebody as a means for others' ends.

This line of complaint has been voiced by some sophisticated retributivists: robustly by Jeffrie Murphy and more cautiously by Tom Sorell (Murphy 1973, 219; Sorell 1987, 124). As we shall see later in this chapter, some genuine weaknesses in the deterrence-oriented approach are quite closely related to this point about using people as means. Nonetheless, the objection focused on that point does not withstand scrutiny. As has been separately observed by Jeffrey Reiman and Dan Markel—who are themselves sophisticated retributivists—capital defendants are not being used *only* as means when they are executed for the purpose of deterring others from committing murders.[5]

If executions possess deterrent efficacy, they do so as elements of an ongoing prac-tice. Set within such a practice, executions are indicators of the fate that awaits other people who commit nefarious crimes. Only because they signal what is likely to befall murderous miscreants in the future, do the executions currently have any marginal deterrent force. To be sure, a strictly isolated instance of capital punish-ment can serve as a marginal deterrent for a limited period if it is wrongly believed to betoken the way in which other murderers will be treated. After quite a short time, however, the isolatedness of such a punitive measure will become apparent and will deprive that measure of its efficacy as a marginal deterrent. (Note that the sheer fact that a lone execution has not been followed by any other such punish-ments does not necessarily mean that the execution is isolated in the relevant sense. If its power as a deterrent is so great that no additional murders occur at any future juncture, and if there are consequently no occasions for any further instances of

[5] Markel 2005, 469 n 259; Reiman 1985, 118–19. See also Pearl 1982, 277–80.

capital punishment, the deterrent power of that one execution might persist for an extended period. However, in any realistic setting that involves a sizeable community, no lone instance of capital punishment will yield such a sweepingly formidable deterrent effect. Some additional murders will occur. If nobody responsible for any of those subsequent murders is ever executed, then the marginal deterrent impact of a lone instance of capital punishment will dissipate. People will recognize that that instance was isolated in the sense that it was not an element of an ongoing practice that will continue to put murderers to death.)

Hence, inasmuch as applications of capital punishment in any society are conducted in accordance with the deterrence-oriented rationale, they are situated in an ongoing institution that endows them with their marginal deterrent efficacy. Yet, precisely because those applications are so situated, no executed defendant will have been used only as a means. After all, the system of capital punishment in which the defendants lose their lives is an institution that enhances public security (if the empirical theses of the deterrence-oriented rationale are correct). As such, that system has benefited the executed defendants as well as everybody else. It has protected them against violent interference with their pursuit of their respective ends, and has thus not used any of them only as means for the ends of others. As Reiman writes: 'If…what deters potential criminals is the existence of a functioning punishment system, then everyone is benefited by that system, including those who end up being punished by it, since they too have received the benefit of enhanced security due to the deterring of some potential criminals. Even criminals benefit from what deters other criminals from preying on them.' Reiman concludes that 'no one is used or sacrificed *merely* for the benefit of others' (Reiman 1985, 119, emphasis in original).

Even if an execution is the first such occurrence in a deterrence-oriented institution of capital punishment, the institution—at its inception as well as thereafter—is not only for the benefit of everybody else but also for the benefit of the executed defendant. Given the correctness of the deterrence-oriented theorists' empirical claims, the emergence of the aforementioned institution will have discouraged any violent interference by others with the executed defendant's pursuit of his ends, just as it will have discouraged violent interference by others with everyone else's pursuit of various ends. Ergo, although the defendant has indeed been used as a means, he has also been treated as an end. His execution does not run athwart any Kantian injunction.

2.3. Empirical doubts

Notwithstanding that some criticisms of the deterrence-oriented rationale for capital punishment are misguided, numerous other criticisms of that rationale are well founded. A focus on deterrence is not a tenable justificatory basis for the introduction and retention of capital punishment. In this fairly brief section, my exploration of the shortcomings of the deterrence-oriented justification will begin with some reflections on the dubiousness of the empirical propositions that are presupposed by actual applications of that justification. On the one hand, as has already been stated plainly, this book is not a work of social science. It does not present any new empirical findings or any new statistical analyses of the data that have been gathered by social scientists for decades. On the other hand, any satisfactory critique of the deterrence-oriented rationale has to deal at least in passing with the myriad of empirical studies that have enquired into the deterrent efficacy of the death penalty. After some laconic remarks on those studies, this section will turn to some general doubts about the proposition that the death penalty is likely to reduce the incidence of serious crime significantly. Though the empirical bearings of the deterrence-oriented rationale are not the main concern of this chapter, those bearings are shaky indeed.

2.3.1. The meagreness of the evidence

Anyone familiar with the empirical literature on the effects of capital punishment can hardly fail to be aware of the intensity and protractedness of the wrangling among social scientists over the nature and extent of those effects. Until the mid-1970s, nearly all the relevant data and statistical analyses in the social-scientific literature had militated against the hypothesis that the death penalty is an effective marginal deterrent. They had not strictly disconfirmed that hypothesis, but they had furnished no support for it (Abernethy 1996, 380 n 4; Bedau 1993, 181; Conway 1974, 442–3; Donohue and Wolfers 2005, 792, 796–7, 842; Hart 1968, 83–5; Lempert 1981, 1196–206; Primorac 1982, 135–6; Sorell 1987, 35; Van den Haag 1968, 285–6). In 1975, Isaac Ehrlich published a famous paper in which he employed some arcane techniques of statistical analysis to argue that executions do substantially lower the rate of murders (Ehrlich 1975a). Although Ehrlich's findings caused a great stir, and although Ehrlich replied forcefully to the barrage of strictures that were directed against his methods and conclusions (Ehrlich 1975b; 1977a; 1977b), his work on the issue has been discredited for quite some time. As has been remarked by two scholars who are far from dismissive of the notion that capital punishment is a significant deterrent: 'It would be fair to say that the deterrence hypothesis could not be confirmed by the studies that have been completed in the twenty years after Ehrlich first wrote.'[6]

More recently, some further empirical studies have sought to overcome the flaws in Ehrlich's methodology while endorsing the gist of his conclusions (Sunstein and Vermeule 2005a, 711–15). The authors of these more recent studies have sometimes made bold pronouncements about the definitiveness of their findings,[7] but their protocols and

---

[6] Sunstein and Vermeule 2005a, 711. For some extended criticism of Ehrlich, with abundant citations to other critiques, see Lempert 1981, 1206–15, 1218–21. For some further general remarks on Ehrlich's work, see Van den Haag and Conrad 1983, 139–40.

[7] See, for example, the quotations in Donohue and Wolfers 2005, 793 n 11. See also Marquis 2005, 505, where we are told that the conclusions of the recent studies are 'undeniable'.

conclusions have now been oppugned as tellingly as have Ehrlich's (Cohen-Cole *et al* 2009; Donohue and Wolfers 2005; Donohue and Wolfers 2006). Though the critiques of those studies have not strictly disproved the occurrence of deterrent effects associated with executions, they have undermined the idea that the ostensible discoveries of such effects are more than conjectural. John Donohue and Justin Wolfers have nicely summarized the upshot of their ripostes to Ehrlich's successors:

Our estimates suggest not just 'reasonable doubt' about whether there is any deterrent effect of the death penalty, but profound uncertainty. We are confident that the effects are not large, but we remain unsure even of whether they are positive or negative. The difficulty is not just one of statistical significance: whether one measures positive or negative effects of the death penalty is extremely sensitive to very small changes in econometric specifications. Moreover, we are pessimistic that existing data can resolve this uncertainty. [Donohue and Wolfers 2005, 794]

At best inconclusive, then, is the empirical evidence adduced for the purpose of showing that capital punishment deters the commission of murders. Even if the moral tenets of the deterrence-oriented rationale for capital punishment were impeccable, the shakiness of its empirical theses would block it from constituting a satisfactory basis for putting anyone to death. As Chapter 1 has emphasized, the onus of proof lies on the proponents of the death penalty to establish that their reasons for favouring the application of such a penalty are sound. Deterrence-oriented supporters of the death penalty have not met that burden of proof.

Chapter 1 at its outset referred to Dan Kahan's view that the advocates of capital punishment, like the opponents thereof, generally subscribe to all the arguments and hypotheses that chime with their firmly held position on the issue. Recently, Cass Sunstein and Adrian Vermeule have made a similar claim about people's assessments of the empirical literature on the efficacy of the death penalty as a deterrent:

[A]s new entrants into the death penalty debate, we are struck by the intensity of people's beliefs on the empirical issues, and the extent to which their empirical judgments seem to be driven by their moral commitments. Those who oppose the death penalty on moral grounds often seem entirely unwilling to consider apparent evidence of deterrence and are happy to dismiss such evidence whenever even modest questions are raised about it. Those who accept the death penalty on moral grounds often seem to accept the claim of deterrence whether or not good evidence has been provided on its behalf. [Sunstein and Vermeule 2005b, 848 n 10]

In application to some participants in the debates over the morality of the death penalty, these remarks by Sunstein and Vermeule are apt enough. For example, having written in 1968 that 'I doubt that the presence or absence of a deterrent effect of the death penalty is likely to be demonstrable by statistical means', Ernest van den Haag in 1990 declared that some studies from the early 1980s—which are now discredited—had managed to 'confirm the results obtained by Isaac Ehrlich' (van den Haag 1968, 286; van den Haag 1990, 508). Such a trimming of sails to the intellectual winds is deserving of Sunstein's and Vermeule's wariness. All the same, their remarks are doubly misdirected in application to my own assessment of the empirical literature on capital punishment and deterrence. (Admittedly, their remarks profess to state what is often the case rather than what is always the case.)

In the first place, my jaundiced appraisal of the evidence for the deterrent efficacy of capital punishment is based neither on opposition to such punishment nor on unwillingness to ponder the empirical evidence seriously. After all, my purpose in this book is to argue in favour of the death penalty. My negative assessment of the studies carried out by Ehrlich's successors—my assessment of those studies as utterly inconclusive—is focused on their methodological confines and on the heavy model-dependence of their results. Precisely those failings are what the critics of Ehrlich's successors have highlighted.

Moreover, if the findings of the aforementioned studies were persuasive, there would be no reason for me to refrain from acknowledging as much. As this chapter will presently argue, the deterrence-oriented rationale for capital punishment would founder even if its empirical presuppositions were correct. Its *moral* failings are the prime concern of this chapter. Hence, my strong doubts about those empirical presuppositions—and specifically about the evidence offered in support of them—do not stem from any *parti pris*.

2.3.2. General misgivings

Quite apart from the methodological shortcomings of the studies and statistical analyses that have purported to demonstrate the efficacy of capital punishment in deterring the commission of murders, there are some general reasons for querying whether the death penalty will be more effective as a deterrent than will lifelong imprisonment-without-parole (perhaps in solitary confinement or in other austere conditions). These general considerations are themselves empirical, of course, in that they cannot be rigorously substantiated except through empirical investigation. Nonetheless, they are not to be understood as rejoinders to the empirical studies that have just been discussed. They are pitched at a higher level of abstraction. My presentation of them here serves two interrelated purposes.

First, the factors adduced in this subsection can help to counter the notion—a notion enshrined in common sense—that the prospect of death must be a more effective deterrent than the prospect of lifelong imprisonment because death is feared by the large majority of people more than is lifelong imprisonment. Although the premise about death's greater fearsomeness is undoubtedly true, the conclusion about death's greater deterrent efficacy does not perforce follow. Secondly, the points to be enumerated here can help to explain why social scientists have encountered such difficulty when they try to show that executions play a statistically significant role in reducing the incidence of serious crimes. While the fearsomeness of the death penalty generally militates in favour of the proposition that that penalty is likely to be an effective marginal deterrent, other considerations militate against such a proposition.

Taken together, the various factors that influence the actions and decisions of potential evildoers are complicatedly cross-cutting and are therefore apt to confound most
empirical enquiries (Reiff 2005, 185).

2.3.2.1. Prospects versus certainties

Although the certainty of death is more frightening for most people than the certainty
of lifelong imprisonment, the disparity between a quite remote prospect of death and
a quite remote prospect of lifelong imprisonment is generally of considerably less significance. The latter disparity may well be proportionately the same as the former, but
its absolute magnitude is typically much smaller. As HLA Hart and many other commentators have recognized, there is only a tenuous 'parallel between the situation of a
convicted murderer offered the alternative of life imprisonment in the shadow of the
gallows, and the situation of the murderer contemplating his crime'.[8] This point about
uncertainty is especially weighty because most potential murderers—particularly those
inclined to commit slayings that are vile enough to attract the death penalty—tend to
overestimate their chances of eluding detection and apprehension. Such people will of
course overestimate the likelihood of their escaping lifelong imprisonment just as they
will overestimate the likelihood of their escaping the death penalty, but what is of key
importance is that the deterrent force of each sanction diminishes as the perceived probability of the imposition of each sanction diminishes. Hence, the absolute magnitude of
the disparity between the deterrent force of the one sanction and the deterrent force of
the other will almost always be far smaller than a glib comparison between death and
lifelong imprisonment would lead us to expect.

  Of course, the present point about the contrast between certainties and quite slim
possibilities does not in itself entirely undermine the plausibility of the empirical
claims that are associated with the deterrence-oriented rationale. This point is about
the *attenuation* of the marginal deterrent efficacy of capital punishment, rather than
about the *elimination* of that efficacy. Still, in combination with the other factors to
be recounted here, this weakening of the death penalty's deterrent power can go a
long way toward accounting for the inconclusiveness of the social scientists' empirical
studies.

2.3.2.2. Beyond deliberation

As was stated earlier in this chapter, the deterrence-oriented justification of capital
punishment does not presuppose that people inclined toward murder will carefully
and knowledgeably calculate the consequences of their actions. Nevertheless, as was
also stated earlier, neither capital punishment nor any other punishment can be efficacious as a deterrent unless the people subject to it do pay some attention to the
disagreeable consequences that may follow for them from their conduct. Yet, as Hart

---

[8] Hart 1968, 86. For some other writings that have made similar points, see Abernethy 1996, 393–4 n 71;
Conway 1974, 433–4; Lempert 1981, 1192–4; Markel 2005, 470; Marshall 2004, 582; Reiman 1985, 145.

observed, 'murder is committed to a very large extent either by persons who, though sane, do not in fact count the cost, or [by persons who] are so mentally deranged that they cannot count it' (Hart 1968, 87). Again Hart's observation is especially weighty in connection with the people who are inclined to commit the most repugnant murders. Of course, people severely unhinged to the point of being legally classifiable as insane are not currently subject to the death penalty in any event; but even many of the potential murderers whose derangement falls short of legal insanity will take no account or virtually no account of the remote prospect of being executed.

Admittedly, nothing just said is inconsistent with the thesis that the use of the death penalty can deter any potential murderers whose psyches are not as woefully unattuned to reality. Such people can be expected to act with a general sense of the danger that attends their homicidal misdeeds. However, the effectiveness of the death penalty as a deterrent even in respect of such people is weakened by at least four considerations.

First, as this chapter has made clear in § 2.1, the relevant deterrent effect is marginal rather than wholesale. Any non-suicidal person with some grip on reality will obviously be deterred more by the prospect of death than by the absence of any punishment at all, but the pertinent question is whether such a person will be deterred significantly more by the prospect of death than by the prospect of lifelong imprisonment (perhaps with long periods in solitary confinement or in other grimly austere conditions). As Lempert and many other critics of the deterrence-oriented rationale have remarked, the answer to such a question is by no means plainly affirmative: 'It is difficult to select from the array of activities which a death threat might induce us to drop any which we would engage in if the threat were instead that we would *only* be imprisoned for life.'[9]

Secondly, far more felons are killed each year in the United States by police officers in the line of duty than by executions.[10] Further felons are killed each year by ordinary citizens who act in defence of themselves or others. Such killings by police officers and citizens occur, of course, in jurisdictions without capital punishment as well as in jurisdictions that do apply such punishment. Thus, as Reiman has aptly commented, 'anyone contemplating committing a crime *already* faces a substantial risk of ending up dead as a result. It's hard to see why anyone *who is not already deterred by this* would be deterred by the addition of the more distant risk of death after apprehension, conviction, and appeal' (Reiman 1985, 145, emphases in original, footnote omitted).

---

[9] Lempert 1981, 1192, emphasis in original. The point made in this paragraph is overlooked by William Edmundson when he writes as follows: 'If the abolitionist takes the position that death is *worse* than life without parole, she supplies ammunition to the advocate's deterrence argument: How can what is admittedly worse not have a greater deterrent power, whether or not social science can measure it?' (Edmundson 2002, 41, emphasis in original.)

[10] For an interesting discussion of killings of felons by police officers in the United States, see MacInnis 2002.

Thirdly, in addition to the risk of one's being killed during one's perpetration of a serious crime—and during the aftermath of that perpetration—is the risk of one's being murdered while one is incarcerated. In the United States each year, the number of convicts murdered in prison by fellow inmates has until recently been much higher than the number of convicts executed.[11] When we compare a death sentence with a term of lifelong imprisonment, we should not make the mistake of thinking that only the former type of punishment involves a substantial likelihood of a premature demise.

Fourthly, even people with largely normal mentalities are prone to discount quite a few risks that could be averted or minimized through alterations in their behaviour. For example, in the absence of mandatory seatbelt laws—and often in the presence of such laws—most people do not wear seatbelts while driving or riding in cars (Lempert 1981, 1193; Reiman 1985, 145). Because they underestimate or disregard the risks to which they are exposed when engaging in such activities, people significantly increase those risks for the sake of avoiding some minor inconvenience. '[H]owever much people fear death, they commonly prefer immediate gratification to a statistically [lower] chance of an unduly early demise' (Lempert 1981, 1193).

2.3.2.3. Brutalization

Quite a common theme in the literature on capital punishment and deterrence is the concern that the use of such punishment in a criminal-justice system will tend to coarsen people's ethical sentiments (Abernethy 1996, 380 n 4; Allen and Shavell 2005, 627, 631–2, 634; Bedau 2002, 5; Berns 1979, 24–8; Bowers and Pierce 1980; Hart 1968, 88; Lempert 1981, 1190, 1196, 1216–17, 1223 n 153; McCord 1998, 13, 15; Nathanson 1985, 162; Reiman 1985, 134–42, 145–6; Shepherd 2005; Sorell 1987, 48–50, 85; Steiker 2005, 773–4, 786–9; Sunstein and Vermeule 2005a, 713 n 37; Van den Haag 1986, 1665 n 15, 1667; Van den Haag 1990, 508; Van den Haag and Conrad 1983, 9–10, 140; Waldron 1992, 39). Complaints along these lines need not involve any endorsement of the notion that executions of murderers are somehow ethically on a par with the acts of murder in response to which the executions are carried out. Instead of relying on that outlandish notion, someone who complains about the likely occurrence of brutalization can simply be presuming that many people who are exposed to repeated instances of lethal violence will become inured to them. Such people's moral sensibilities tend to harden, and the whole ethos of their society becomes rougher as a result. For example, when savage executions and tortures were public spectacles organized by governments in bygone centuries, the prevailing attitudes toward human dignity were cheapened. Such events impaired the level

---

[11] Allen & Shavell 2005, 631. Of course, the total number of convicts in prison is much higher than the total number of such convicts who have committed capital crimes. However, most of the people who are murdered in prisons have committed very serious crimes; they are incarcerated alongside the other offenders whose homicidal dispositions are most pronounced.

of respect for human life and well-being in medieval and early modern societies, and thereby contributed to the violence that was pervasive in those societies. Quite a few opponents (and some supporters) of capital punishment in the present day have worried that, although executions are now considerably less savage, they still devalue the preciousness of human life. As exercises in the authoritative and deliberate killing of human beings by governments outside the special contexts of emergencies and military conflicts, applications of the death penalty degrade the overall ethos of any society in which they occur.

Like the other matters recounted here as general reasons for querying whether the death penalty will yield any deterrent upshot, this matter of brutalization is an empirical phenomenon that can be verified or disconfirmed only through wide-ranging empirical investigations. Any full substantiation or disconfirmation would have to examine not only the rates of murders and executions but also the ethical outlooks of people. Such a herculean task will very likely not be undertaken by anybody for quite some time, if ever. Even the somewhat more modest task of exploring the rates of murders and executions through appropriate statistical analyses is problematic, as my short discussion of the recent empirical studies of deterrence has underscored. Empirical evidence for the brutalizing effects of executions is at present no more solid than the empirical evidence for their deterrent effects. Nonetheless, as was stated earlier, my general reasons for doubts about the deterrent efficacy of capital punishment are not put forward here as rejoinders to any empirical studies that have actually been undertaken. Rather, the point is to broach some plausible general considerations that tell against the likelihood of one's finding any significant deterrent effects associated with executions. Even if any brutalizing tendencies of capital punishment themselves elude empirical substantiation, their presence can partly explain why the endeavours to detect the aforementioned deterrent effects have proved to be so frustrating. Those latter effects are perhaps offset by the coarsening of citizens' ethical sentiments that may ensue when a government sets its imprimatur on the practice of deliberately putting people to death (outside the contexts of emergencies and military campaigns).

Of course, two techniques for minimizing any incidence of brutalization are the relocation of executions away from the public gaze and the employment of the most humane methods of execution available. Just such techniques have been implemented in the United States. However, as was indicated earlier in this chapter, those techniques are in clear tension with the deterrence-oriented rationale for capital punishment (Abernethy 1996). The communicative reach of deterrence-oriented executions is markedly curtailed when they take place in secluded settings, and the dauntingness of those executions is likewise attenuated when they are performed in the gentlest possible ways. Hence, the implementation of these techniques in the United States is a factor that partly accounts for the inconclusiveness of the efforts to show that capital punishment significantly lowers the rate of murders. By minimizing the brutalizing effects that might follow from executions whose locations and methods would be more in keeping with the deterrence-oriented rationale, the secludedness and humaneness of instances of capital punishment in the United States minimize any consequent increases in the frequency of murders; in so doing, however, those civilizing features countervail the efficacy of capital punishment as a means of lowering the incidence of murders through deterrence.

Let us close this discussion by noting briefly (and proleptically) that my purgative rationale for the death penalty does not confront any dilemma of the sort that afflicts the deterrence-oriented rationale. Unlike most of the justifications for capital punishment that have been propounded by other theorists—including the deterrence-oriented justification, of course—the purgative rationale does not involve any substantial communicative dimension. Nor does it countenance cruelty in the administration of the death penalty. Cruelty does not help to realize the purgative objective of removing a source of defilement from a community, and the pursuit of that objective is not aimed at producing any extrinsic effects that require vivid communication. Hence, although executions conducted on the basis of the purgative justification will of course be a matter of public record in a liberal democracy (the only type of society in which the executions can ever be morally legitimate), they can quite properly be performed in seclusion through humane methods. Some central trends in the administration of capital punishment in the United States are thus fully consistent with the purgative rationale for such punishment, whereas they are largely incompatible with the deterrence-oriented rationale.

2.4. The moral untenability of the deterrence-oriented rationale

Legion are the shortcomings in the empirical presuppositions of the deterrence-oriented justification of capital punishment, but they are only a secondary concern in this chapter. Of considerably greater importance are the shortcomings in the moral tenets of the deterrence-oriented justification. Even if the empirical claims advanced by deterrence-oriented theorists were true, the moral arguments marshalled by those theorists in support of the death penalty would be unsound. Moreover, the failings in their arguments cannot be remedied through recourse to any of the other standard rationales for the death penalty. In the rest of this chapter, we shall ponder a number of those failings.

In a recent exchange with Sunstein and Vermeule, Carol Steiker has levelled an array of telling objections against the deterrence-oriented rationale for capital punishment. Although my own critique of that rationale differs from hers in several important respects, the two overlap nearly as much as they diverge. Accordingly, the discussions in the rest of this chapter will intermittently make reference to her illuminating exchange with Sunstein and Vermeule.

2.4.1. The manner of use

As has been argued in § 2.2.2, the deterrence-oriented justification of capital punishment is not damaged by the sheer fact that it envisages the use of executed convicts as means for the furtherance of societal ends. Because the convicts are not treated *only* as means, the killing of them for the purpose of deterring others from engaging in serious criminal activity does not violate the Kantian Categorical Imperative. Still, although an invocation of the second formulation of the Categorical Imperative is inapposite in this context, the manner in which the executed convicts are used as means is indeed morally problematic. To see as much, we should probe a variant of a scenario that depicts a practice which is paradigmatically wrong.

The original scenario, propounded by Philippa Foot and many other moral philosophers for a somewhat different purpose (Foot 1978, 24–5, 27–8), pertains to a healthy and innocent man who is murdered by doctors so that his vital organs can be harvested to save the lives of several other people. Now, this scenario is usually taken to portray an isolated incident rather than an occurrence in an ongoing practice. When so construed, the scenario recounts a clear-cut transgression of the Categorical Imperative; by slaying the healthy man in order to obtain his organs, the doctors use him solely as a means for the promotion of the well-being of others. However, the narrative can be modified to assimilate the depicted situation (in morally relevant respects) to the workings of a deterrence-oriented system of capital punishment.

Suppose that the killing of the healthy man for the harvesting of his organs is not an isolated incident. Instead, it is an element of an ongoing practice in some country Ghoulishia, where each year a small number of healthy people are selected—by an aleatory device such as a lottery—for sacrifice and harvesting. Everyone in Ghoulishia stands to benefit from the practice, since anyone can fall ill and come to be in need of new vital organs; like an insurance policy, the greater availability of such organs is beneficial even for people who never actually have to undergo any transplants. Consequently, the people who are selected each year for the harvesting of their vital organs are not being used solely as means. They too have benefited from the existence of the institution in which they are now sacrificed. Their ends, like those of everyone else in their community, have been served by the enhanced medical security that such an institution provides.

Suppose further that, in any given year, some or all of the people in Ghoulishia who have been singled out for disembowelment are unwilling to cooperate. Declining to acquiesce in their fate, they actively resist when the doctors and governmental officials arrive to take them away. Eventually they are overpowered, and their vital organs are duly harvested.

Let us assume that the institution just described is utility-maximizing. Any distress suffered by the sacrificed people and any apprehension which the institution elicits among the general population of Ghoulishia are more than offset by the gratification that ensues from the invaluable augmentation of the supply of vital organs. No alternative arrangement would bring about a larger excess of utility over disutility. All the same, the institution just described is morally illegitimate. The fact that it would be approved by an unremittingly utilitarian doctrine is something that counts against utilitarianism.

2.4.1.1. Blocking the analogy?

Now, if this conclusion about the Ghoulishian practice of killing people for their vital organs is to be transferable to a deterrence-oriented system of capital punishment, then that practice and that system have to be analogous in morally relevant respects. Yet the proponents of the deterrence-oriented approach will surely insist that there is a major disanalogy between the two. Whereas the convicts executed in a deterrence-oriented system of capital punishment have committed very serious crimes, the healthy people sacrificed by the Ghoulishian doctors have not committed any crimes. The convicts are guilty, whereas the involuntary donors of organs are innocent. Accordingly, so the deterrence-oriented theorists will assert, my conclusion about the moral illegitimacy of the Ghoulishian harvesting of organs is not a basis for any similar conclusion about a deterrence-oriented system of capital punishment.

For the moment, we should leave aside a point that will be taken up later: namely, the fact that the deterrence-oriented rationale can call for executions of people who have not committed any crimes. Even if that point is temporarily pretermitted, the response of the deterrence-oriented theorists that has just been outlined is unsuccessful. Let us remember that the deterrence-oriented justification of capital punishment is embedded in a broader utilitarian theory. Hence, when deterrence-oriented theorists appeal to notions of guilt and innocence, they have to cash out those notions along utilitarian lines. (Of course, the Ghoulishians themselves probably do not understand guilt and innocence along those lines. Many utilitarians believe that people such as the Ghoulishians are more likely to arrive at utility-maximizing practices and arrangements if the people in question do not knowingly seek to maximize utility.)

If the deterrence-oriented theorists are rule-utilitarians, then they will regard behaviour as guilty if it contravenes any laws or other norms that promote utility by channelling people's conduct into generally beneficial paths. If the deterrence-oriented theorists are instead act-utilitarians, then they will regard any instance of behaviour as guilty if it falls short of utility-maximization by foreseeably engendering—or threatening to engender—more disutility than utility. Everyone who commits a murder is guilty in the eyes of rule-utilitarians, and nearly everyone who commits a murder is guilty in the eyes of act-utilitarians (though they would not ascribe guilt to a murderer whose capacity for sadistic pleasure is sufficiently expansive). Also guilty in the eyes of utilitarians of either type, however, are any people selected for sacrifice in Ghoulishia who resist the efforts of the Ghoulishian doctors to kill them. A proponent of rule-utilitarianism will deem such people to be guilty because their behaviour contravenes some legal and social norms that promote utility. Their refractoriness impairs, or threatens to impair, the workings of a utility-maximizing practice. A proponent of act-utilitarianism will deem all or nearly all of the Ghoulishian resisters to be guilty, because compliance with the practice of organ-harvesting would always or nearly always be the utility-maximizing course of action. Given that the several lives saved through the provision of vital organs from any selected Ghoulishian person will outweigh the one life ended, a refusal to comply will have fallen markedly short of utility-maximization and will therefore be guilt-incurring. By the lights of act-utilitarians as well as by the lights of rule-utilitarians, such conduct is egregiously illegitimate.

Thus, in the eyes of the deterrence-oriented theorists with their allegiance to utilitarianism, anyone selected in the Ghoulishian lottery who resists being sacrificed for his vital organs is far from innocent. In that respect (though not in most other respects), such a person is akin to a convict who is executed for the purpose of discouraging other people from engaging in serious criminal activity. Of course, the recalcitrant Ghoulishian person is killed not because of his resistance, but because of his having been selected in the lottery. He is not killed for having acted wrongly. Still, the deterrence-oriented theorists cannot capitalize on that point. After all, as has been mentioned in Chapter 1—and as should also be clear from the present chapter—the deterrence-oriented conception of capital punishment, like utilitarianism generally, is strictly prospective in its orientation.

Under the deterrence-oriented rationale for the death penalty, the dispositive reason for the justifiability of an execution is that the authoritative killing of a serious criminal (or of someone widely believed to be a serious criminal) will improve a community's future by inducing other people to abstain from major misdeeds. The emphasis is entirely on the benignity of the future states of affairs that will be brought about by a current execution. Viewed from a utilitarian perspective, the past is gone and cannot now be undone. From such a perspective, executions and other punishments have to be oriented toward the future. More specifically, executions and other punishments have to be oriented toward the objective of maximizing a community's aggregate or average utility in the future. By discouraging the perpetration of murders henceforth, executions now contribute to the fulfilment of that objective and are thereby justified.

The rationale for sacrificing the Ghoulishians selected in the lottery is fundamentally the same. Each sacrifice goes ahead because it contributes to valuable future states of affairs. Each sacrifice promotes the maximization of utility by making several vital organs directly available and by helping to sustain a practice that makes such organs available on a broader scale. Indeed, the sacrifice of any selected Ghoulishian will partake of this rigidly prospective orientation regardless of whether he has acquiesced in his fate or actively resisted it. Whether or not a selected Ghoulishian has ever acted wrongly (by utilitarian standards), the killing of him for his organs will help to realize the objective of utility-maximization. By utilitarian standards, then, each such killing is both morally legitimate and morally obligatory.

Thus, given that the deterrence-oriented rationale for capital punishment is located in a utilitarian framework, the proponents of that rationale cannot relevantly distinguish between an executed murderer and a sacrificed Ghoulishian. Utilitarianism lacks the resources that would enable the deterrence-oriented theorists to fall back upon a distinction between the guilt of a murderer and the innocence of a Ghoulishian (the innocence of an acquiescent Ghoulishian, at any rate). Executions of murderers in a deterrence-oriented system of punishment are countenanced by utilitarianism because they give rise to valuable states of affairs in the future, and the harvesting of organs from the people selected by the lottery in Ghoulishia is countenanced by utilitarians because it gives rise to valuable states of affairs in the future. In each case, the justificatory foundation for putting people to death lies in the utility-maximizing consequences of doing so. With that foundation in place, a failure to sacrifice a selected Ghoulishian is fundamentally on a par with a failure to execute a convicted murderer, in being morally illegitimate. In each case, utilitarian theorists will perceive such a failure as morally illegitimate because of its impact on future states of affairs and not because of the guilt or innocence of anyone in an ordinary (non-utilitarian) sense.

Yet, patently, the Ghoulishian practice of killing people in order to harvest their vital organs is morally illegitimate—whatever a diehard utilitarian might think. Even though such a practice is utility-maximizing (*ex hypothesi*), and even though it does not use the sacrificed people solely as means, it uses them wrongly. Hence, given that there is no relevant basis for distinguishing between the killings in the Ghoulishian practice and the executions in a deterrence-oriented system of capital punishment, any such system and the executions within it are likewise morally illegitimate. We should agree with utilitarians that those killings and those executions are fundamentally on a par, but we should draw the anti-utilitarian conclusion that the killings and the executions alike are morally impermissible.

2.4.1.2. Help from an unexpected quarter?

Some proponents of retributivism might wonder whether the foregoing objection to the deterrence-oriented rationale for capital punishment has moved too quickly. Such theorists might contend that, notwithstanding the inability of doctrinaire utilitarians to distinguish germanely between the execution of a convicted murderer (in a deterrence-oriented institution of capital punishment) and the sacrifice of a selected Ghoulishian, the exponents of retributivism can draw such a distinction perfectly well. That is, although utilitarians cannot fall back upon the difference between the guilt of a convicted murderer and the innocence of a selected Ghoulishian—because the justificatory foundation for executions in a deterrence-oriented system of capital punishment, like the justificatory foundation for sacrifices in the Ghoulishian organ-harvesting arrangement, is purely prospective—retributivists can certainly avail themselves of that difference. A cornerstone of retributivism is that a necessary condition for the legitimacy of the subjection of a person to punishment in a criminal-justice system is the fact that the person has committed a crime. A necessary condition for the legitimacy of the subjection of a person to capital punishment, accordingly, is the fact that the person has committed a capital crime. A condition of that sort is not satisfied by the Ghoulishian arrangement, whereas it is satisfied by any well-functioning system of capital punishment in a liberal democracy. Consequently, the executions in such a system and the sacrifices in Ghoulishia are not morally on a par. Only the former are morally legitimate; or, at any rate, only the former can be morally legitimate. In other words, once the deterrence-oriented rationale for capital punishment is supplemented by the retributivistic rationale, the analogy between deterrence-oriented executions and Ghoulishian sacrifices can be blocked—or so a retributivistic defender of the deterrence-oriented rationale might contend.

We shall later explore in more detail the strategy of supplementing the deterrence-oriented rationale with retributivistic side-constraints. For now, we can simply note that the posited defence of that rationale against my current line of critique is misconceived in two respects. First, the Ghoulishian practice of killing people for their vital organs is not punitive in character. It does not address, and does not purport to address, the misdeeds committed by Ghoulishians against one another. Killings undertaken by doctors within that practice are not responses to wrongdoing, but are instead anticipatory public-health measures. Consequently, the retributivistic conception of punishment is beside the point in the present context. That conception applies to punitive institutions and punitive measures; it does not apply to institutions that have nothing to do with punishment. Thus, neither here nor there is the fact that the Ghoulishian practice does not satisfy one of the necessary conditions laid down by retributivism for the moral legitimacy of any punishment. The moral legitimacy or illegitimacy of a non-punitive institution is not to be gauged by standards that determine the moral legitimacy or illegitimacy of punitive institutions. Retributivism as a side-constraint on the operations of systems of punishment—a side-constraint insisting that the punishment of innocent people is never morally permissible—will not have any purchase on the Ghoulishian system of compulsory organ extractions. Accordingly, the deterrence-oriented theorists with their allegiances to utilitarianism cannot avail themselves of such a side-constraint in order to differentiate between the moral status of that Ghoulishian system and the moral status of a deterrence-oriented regime of capital punishment.

Secondly, and of equal importance, the Ghoulishian system of compulsory organ extractions would be morally illegitimate even if it were partly punitive in its nature and even if it were in compliance with retributivism's insistence that guilt is a necessary condition for the moral legitimacy of punishments. Suppose that not every healthy person in Ghoulishia is liable to be selected by the lottery. Instead, the only people liable to be so selected are those who have committed certain crimes; the punishment for any such crime includes the removal of one's exemption from being randomly selected for the harvesting of one's vital organs. Though the chief purpose of this modified version of the Ghoulishian scheme is still the promotion of public health, an important ancillary purpose is punitive. Hence, the revised scheme—which, we can assume, is still utility-maximizing—falls within the compass of a retributivistic side-constraint. Let us suppose that the side-constraint is fully satisfied by the scheme. That is, no Ghoulishian ever becomes susceptible to being selected by the lottery unless he or she has committed one of the aforementioned crimes. Therefore, this new arrangement is in keeping both with the retributivistic side-constraint and with the paramount objective of utilitarianism. Even so, the Ghoulishian practice of compulsory organ extractions is morally illegitimate. It is, indeed, ghoulish.

One of the many repellent aspects of the practice of capital punishment in China at present is the non-consensual extraction of organs from executed prisoners. That aspect alone is sufficient to render the contemporary administration of the death penalty in China morally illegitimate, even if all the executed prisoners there have genuinely committed vile murders. If that feature of the Chinese approach to capital punishment is nonetheless utility-maximizing, then the deterrence-oriented theorists lack the resources to differentiate morally between the Chinese approach and their own preferred regime of capital punishment (without compulsory organ extractions). Neither their own utilitarian tenets nor the retributivistic side-constraint discussed above will enable them to put any moral distance between themselves and the Chinese. Still worse, as has been argued, neither those tenets nor that side-constraint will enable the deterrence-oriented theorists to put any moral distance between themselves and the Ghoulishians. Since the Ghoulishian arrangement for the harvesting of organs is morally illegitimate—in either of its two main forms that we have plumbed here—we should conclude that a deterrence-oriented system of capital punishment is likewise devoid of moral legitimacy.

2.4.2. No limits

John Finnis, after mounting a forceful critique of the coherence and intelligibility of utilitarianism and other closely related doctrines (Finnis 1980, 112–19), goes on to declare that a champion of utilitarianism 'holds himself ready to do *anything*' (Finnis 1980, 121, emphasis in original). Here Finnis articulates a widespread and longstanding sense of consternation over the implications of the maximizing imperative in any standard version of utilitarianism. Most critics and some advocates of utilitarian ideas have expressed unease along similar lines. That is, they are concerned about the absence of any intrinsic limits to what utilitarianism prescribes (Abernethy 1996; Bedau 2002, 7; Gardner 1978, 1187, 1211–14; Hart 1968, 75–82; Hudson 1983, 229–30; Hurka 1982, 651, 658; Lempert 1981, 1188; Moore 1984, 238–40; Mortenson 2003, 1149; Nozick 1974, 28–9, 39–42; Pugsley 1981, 1510; Reiman 1985, 147; Schwarzschild 2002, 10, 11; Steiker 2005, 774–82; Steiker and Steiker 2005, 601–2).

Deterrence-oriented theories of capital punishment, with their utilitarian bearings, are manifestly vulnerable to worries of this sort. We shall here consider two main sets of problems that afflict those theories: problems pertaining to the class of individuals who can fall within the sway of deterrence-oriented systems of capital punishment, and problems pertaining to the types of punishments that can be required under the operative terms of those systems. These sets of difficulties over-lap—in particular, one major difficulty (explored in § 2.4.2.1.2) straddles the two categories—but we shall ponder them separately.

2.4.2.1. The massacre of the innocents

For many years, one of the most common complaints about deterrence-oriented the-ories of punishment has been that such theories condone the punishment of innocent people in certain cases. More specifically, if some person is very widely believed to be responsible for an outrageous crime, and if there is very little likelihood of the emer-gence of any exonerative evidence that will alter others' opinions, then the execution of the person is warranted under the deterrence-oriented rationale irrespective of his underlying guilt or innocence. Even if he is actually innocent, the execution of him will yield the same deterrent effect that it would have yielded in the event of his having been guilty. What is important for the achievement of deterrence through an execution is the perceived guilt, rather than the actual guilt, of the person who has been put to death. Whenever the widely perceived guilt and the actual guilt diverge, a deterrence-oriented system of capital punishment ascribes dispositive importance to the former. Such a system demands the execution of innocent people so long as they are very widely and firmly thought to be guilty.

Defenders of the deterrence-oriented rationale for capital punishment, and of utilitarianism more broadly, have sought in several ways to allay concerns about that rationale's potential countenancing of executions of innocent people. For example, some of those defenders affirm that such executions would ultimately impede the realization of utilitarian goals. Others contend that such executions can be ruled out through the incorporation of retributivistic side-constraints into a deterrence-oriented system of criminal justice. Most recently, Sunstein and Vermeule have suggested that executions of innocent people are indeed morally justified in extraordinary circumstances. Let us examine each of these replies in turn.

2.4.2.1.1. Ineffective dissimulation?

Deterrence-oriented theorists can seek to avail themselves of the general utilitarian framework in which their conception of capital punishment is embedded, by main-taining that executions of innocent people would hardly ever be utility-maximizing in just about any credibly possible world. This response is in fact surprisingly com-mon. John Rawls, for instance, famously adopted this tack in his discussion of the utilitarian conception of punishment (Rawls 1955, 9–13). Rawls emphasized the insti-tutional regularity of any system of punishment, and he contended that anxieties over the possibility of utilitarian grounds for executions of innocent people are unfounded unless 'it can be shown that there are utilitarian arguments which justify an institu-tion whose publicly ascertainable offices and powers are such as to permit officials to exercise that kind of discretion in particular cases'. He asserted that 'the requirement of having to build the arbitrary features of the particular decision into the institutional practice makes the [utilitarian] justification much less likely to go through' (Rawls 1955, 13). In support of his assertion, Rawls maintained that citizens would become aware of the policy of punishing the innocent and would become distressed and confused in their attitudes toward their legal-governmental system. He further maintained that the discretion bestowed upon officials would very likely be abused. For these reasons, a 'utilitarian justification for this institution is most unlikely' (Rawls 1955, 12).

Many supporters and some opponents of the deterrence-oriented rationale for capital punishment have endorsed Rawls's reflections on this issue (Binder 2002, 322–7, 348–9; Binder and Smith 2000, 132–6; Gale 1985, 1005–6; Goodin 1995, ch 4; Lyons 1974; Markel 2005, 435 n 124; Sunstein and Vermeule 2005a, 735–6; Sunstein and Vermeule 2005b, 856). Nevertheless, his lines of reasoning are dubious in several respects. First, although Rawls is to be commended for trying to inject greater sophistication into the discussions of utilitarian punishment through his emphasis on the institutionality of criminal-justice systems, his remarks on that institutionality are somewhat simplistic. Not all the legal powers possessed by legal-governmental officials are conferred upon them by explicit authorizations and policies.[12] Those officials also possess interstitial legal powers that accrue to them independently of such authorizations and policies. For example, the adjudicators and administrators in any system of governance are legally empowered to alter certain implications of existing laws by reaching mistaken judgments that will stand with legal force unless they are reversed by some superior official(s). Though utility-maximizing executions of innocent people are not classifiable as mistakes within a deterrence-oriented system of criminal justice, they too can proceed from officials' exercises of interstitial powers. Such a system will be run in accordance with general norms along rule-utilitarian lines, but, on the very rare occasions when executions of innocents will foreseeably be utility-maximizing, the officials can be legally empowered by the underlying principles of their system—rather than by any explicit policies or authorizations—to order and administer those executions.

Because the legal powers exercised in ordering and administering the executions of innocents can be interstitial, the concealment of the guiltlessness of the executed people can be relatively easy. Rawls, presumably because he took for granted that those powers will be based on explicit policies or authorizations, also took for granted that all or most citizens will come to know that the officials who run their legal-governmental system sometimes knowingly execute innocent people. Subsequent

---

[12] I am invoking the notion of a legal power here in a standard Hohfeldian sense. That is, I am referring to any ability to effect changes in legal relations through some volitional course of conduct. See Kramer 1998, 20–1. For some discussions of the interstitial legal powers of adjudicators and administrators to alter implications of existing laws by reaching mistaken judgments, see Kramer 2004, 115–40; Kramer 2007, 9–12, 78–9, 196–201. My current paragraph is a riposte not only to Rawls but also to Pearl 1982, 280–6.

theorists who endorse Rawls's position have not simply taken that point for granted; they have argued that legal-governmental officials will encounter great difficulty in concealing any policy of deliberately executing innocent people. The confidence of these theorists on this point would probably be well-founded if the legal powers exercised by officials in ordering and administering the executions of innocents had to derive from explicit authorizations. However, given that those powers can be interstitial, and given that they are operative only in the rare contexts where innocents are very widely believed to be guilty and where no significant exculpatory evidence is accessible, the confidence of Rawls and his successors is misplaced. Naturally, there are never any firm guarantees that the guiltlessness of an executed prisoner will remain permanently undiscerned by members of the public, but the balance of probabilities can sometimes be the opposite of what Rawls proclaimed. Across many credibly possible worlds, the utilitarian deterrence-oriented rationale for capital punishment will call for executions of innocents in the rare contexts just mentioned.

Of course, if legal-governmental officials do order and administer executions of innocent people in those uncommon contexts, they might then become inclined to carry out similar measures in much less apposite circumstances (that is, circumstances that are much less apposite from a utilitarian perspective). In some societies in some credibly possible worlds, official overreaching of that sort will indeed occur. *Pro tanto*, the predictions of Rawls and his successors are not baseless. Nonetheless, this very observation leads into my second main criticism of Rawls's remarks on the utilitarian conception of punishment. In his rejoinder to the allegation that the utilitarian conception countenances the execution of innocent people, Rawls concentrated entirely on empirical contingencies. His empirical surmises are correct in application to some possible worlds and unfounded in application to other possible worlds, but the key point here is that those surmises altogether miss the principal force of the allegation to which they are a response. As was recognized by Hart—who was himself a proponent of the deterrence-oriented conception of punishment—empirical suppositions like those advanced by Rawls do not engage with 'the real moral objection that most thinking people have to the application of the pains of punishment to the innocent'. Hart continued:

This moral objection normally would be couched as the insistence that it is *unjust*, or *unfair*, to take someone who has not broken the law ... and use him as a mere instrument to protect society and increase its welfare. Such an objection in the name of *fairness* or *justice* to individuals would still remain even if we were certain that in the case of the 'punishment' of one who had not broken the law the fact of his innocence would not get out or would not cause great alarm if it did. [Hart 1968, 77–8, emphases in original]

In other words, the defenders of the deterrence-oriented conception of capital punishment are mistaken insofar as they think that the strictures directed against that conception's condonation of executions of innocent people are focused on empirical contingencies.[13] On the one hand—as has already been argued, and as will be further argued presently—those defenders underestimate the likelihood that in the actual world there will arise some rare circumstances in which executions of innocent people are foreseeably utility-maximizing. On the other hand, even if they were correct about the actual world, and thus even if the aforementioned circumstances were present only in credibly possible worlds that are not actual, the deterrence-oriented conception would deliver odious verdicts concerning those circumstances. That conception should be rejected because of its repellent counterfactual implications, whether or not it carries any equally rebarbative implications for the actual world. Those repellent counterfactual implications are enough to reveal the nefariousness of the doctrine that generates them. What Ronald Dworkin says about the creed of wealth-maximization in legal theory can be said, *mutatis mutandis*, about the deterrence-oriented account of punishment: '[T]he argument [against the moral force of wealth-maximization] is meant to show, not that the duty [to maximize wealth] would produce horrifying results in practice, but that what it recommends [in certain rare contexts], if this were feasible, is deeply wrong in principle' (Dworkin 1986, 287). Because in a multitude of credibly possible contexts the utilitarian principles of the deterrence-oriented rationale for capital punishment prescribe results that are morally outlandish, those principles lack all justificatory force in the contexts in which they call for sensible results. Whatever may account for the sensibleness of the latter results, it is not the sheer fact that the deterrence-oriented rationale prescribes them. That fact is never sufficient for moral legitimacy.

Let us now briefly contemplate a third objection to the arguments of Rawls and his successors. Rawls was responding to scenarios in which innocent people are very widely perceived as guilty by members of the public but not by the legal-governmental officials who have to administer any punishments. He therefore took as given that the officials in relevant settings will be aware of the innocence of the people whom they put to death. However, the tellingness of the scenarios does not depend on any such restriction. Let us assume instead that the officials themselves are as firmly persuaded of some innocent person's guilt as are his or her fellow citizens. If the person is executed as a vile murderer on the basis of the deterrence-oriented rationale for capital punishment, and if no exonerative evidence subsequently comes to light, then the terms of that rationale have been fulfilled perfectly (at least if its empirical presuppositions are accurate). Under those terms, no wrong whatsoever has been committed through the execution of the innocent person. On the contrary, the execution—according to those terms—has been both morally legitimate and morally obligatory. The deterrence-oriented rationale's countenancing of the imposition of death sentences on innocents is scarcely confined to circumstances in which the officials who pronounce and administer the sentences are resorting to chicanery.

---

[13] For a largely similar point in a different context, see Dworkin 1986, 285–6.

Hence, we have yet another reason to query the suggestions by Rawls and his successors that the innocence of a guiltless person who is put to death will almost inevitably become a matter of public knowledge. After all, if the legal-governmental officials who execute an innocent person are as firmly convinced of his guilt as is virtually everyone else, then there are no machinations that have to be kept hidden. Consequently, any deterrent effect of the execution will remain unweakened (and will contribute to the maximization of utility) unless some compelling exculpatory evidence surfaces at some point in the future—an eventuality that is highly contingent rather than virtually inevitable.

Note that, even if no machinations and deception are perpetrated by the officials, a serious wrong is committed against the guiltless person who is put to death. Indeed, even if no carelessness or any other faultiness has been involved, the execution of an innocent person has grievously wronged him or her. As I have argued at length elsewhere (Kramer 2004, 249–94; Kramer 2005), some outcomes can be wrong even when brought about by people whose precautions against errors and mishaps have been impeccable. Such precautions always at least extenuate the gravity of the outcomes by preventing them from being blameworthy, but do not always prevent them from being wrong.

What is of central importance in this whole discussion is that a utilitarian deterrence-oriented account of capital punishment cannot acknowledge that anything wrong has occurred when an innocent person is executed in circumstances in which the infliction of the lethal punishment is utility-maximizing. Whether the officials involved have been deceitful or careless or faultless, they have done nothing wrong in such circumstances (in the eyes of steadfast deterrence-oriented theorists). The officials' deceitfulness or carelessness or faultlessness is relevant only insofar as it bears on the probability that the innocence of the executed person will eventually become known—and on the probability that the officials will be tempted to act inappropriately in other contexts. So long as those probabilities are very low, a deterrence-oriented theory approves of the sanction undertaken against the executed person. In sum, such a theory asks misdirected questions and occasionally supplies unconscionable answers.

2.4.2.1.2. A retributivistic side-constraint?

Perhaps the most straightforward way for a deterrence-oriented theorist to address the problem of the massacre of the innocents is to incorporate a retributivistic side-constraint into his or her theory. Such a tactic was broached by Rawls himself before he went on to elaborate the lines of reasoning which we have examined. He fleetingly adverted to the possibility of 'adding to [the maximizing imperative of utilitarianism] a principle which distributes certain rights to individuals. Then the amended criterion is not the greatest benefit of society *simpliciter*, but the greatest benefit of society subject to the constraint that no one's rights may be violated' (Rawls 1955, 9). Such a tactic furthermore is precisely what Hart famously pursued, as he sought to present 'a utilitarian justification of punishment qualified by recognition of the innocent individual's claim not to be sacrificed to society' (Hart 1968, 81). A largely similar approach is also touched upon—though not clearly adopted—by Sunstein and Vermeule in their debate with Steiker. They write: 'Nothing in our argument is inconsistent with the claim that there is a deontological check on deliberate decisions to execute innocent people' (Sunstein and Vermeule 2005b, 855). Although these attempts to combine deterrence-oriented theories with retributivism might be criticized as inadequately motivated and principled, and although the distinction underpinning Hart's discussion might be impugned,[14] my rejoinders here proceed along a different route. I shall allow that those attempts succeed as far as they go, but I will argue that they cannot go far enough. They cannot eliminate the problem which they aim to dispel.

To see why the efforts to blend the deterrence-oriented rationale with retributivism are unavailing, we should concentrate on an issue that arises in Steiker's exchange with Sunstein and Vermeule: the issue of putting to death some or all of the members of a heinous murderer's immediate family (Steiker 2005, 776–8; Sunstein and Vermeule 2005b, 855). As Steiker aptly observes, there are solid grounds for thinking that a practice of punishing vile malefactors by both executing them and also killing their closest relatives will produce considerably greater deterrent effects than will a practice of simply executing the malefactors themselves. The former practice has actually obtained in quite a few countries governed by repressive regimes in the modern age (Steiker 2005, 777), and it obtained in sundry parts of the world during bygone times.[15] Not only is such a practice highly likely to be efficacious as a marginal deterrent, but in addition it will be utility-maximizing in many credible circumstances. It will admittedly give rise to some apprehension among the general citizenry, which has to be balanced against the salutariness of its deterrent efficacy. Similarly, it will of course inflict pain on the people who are directly affected; their distress must also be taken into account by utilitarians. Nonetheless, in many credible circumstances, the increase in utility due to the heightened deterrence will exceed the decrease in utility due to the heightened apprehension and the direct distress— especially given that the powerful deterrent efficacy of such a practice will mean that the occasions for the activation of it are quite few and far between. With reference to any actual or credibly possible societies in which such a practice will indeed be generally utility-maximizing, the deterrence-oriented proponents of capital punishment are committed by their utilitarianism to supporting the slaying of the close relatives of murderers as well as the slaying of the murderers themselves.

---

[14] See, for example, Hurka 1982, 647 n 1. Hart's distinction, between justifying a practice and justifying the application of that practice to some particular course of conduct, is also central to Rawls's 1955 essay. I do not share Hurka's reservations about that distinction.

[15] For one of the many Biblical passages in which miscreants are punished through the slaying of their close relatives as well as through the slaying of themselves, see Numbers 16:23–33.

Can those proponents evade that distasteful implication of their outlook by resorting to a retributivistic side-constraint? For two reasons, the answer to this question is negative. The first of those reasons is premised on the assumption that the specified side-constraint is indeed an offshoot of retributivism as a theory of punishment. Given that assumption, the side-constraint will not disallow the practice of killing the close relatives of murderers. After all, in the practice envisaged here, such killings are undertaken not in order to punish the relatives but in order to punish the murderers. When the family members are put to death, no one is claiming to hold them responsible for anything that they have done or failed to do. Rather, they are overtly being used as means for the punishment of their murderous kinsmen in an especially effective deterrence-oriented manner. They are being used as means in much the same way that the pets or other prized belongings of murderers would be used if those pets or other prized belongings were to be destroyed in order to punish the murderers. Just as the pets or belongings would not be punished by being subjected to destruction, so too the relatives are not punished by being slain. Like the destruction of the former, the liquidation of the latter is a technique for punishing murderers and thus for discouraging potential murderers from becoming actual murderers henceforward. Since the liquidation does not involve the punishment of anyone who is innocent, it does not contravene a retributivistic side-constraint.

To discern a second reason for answering negatively the question above, however, we should now abandon the assumption that the specified side-constraint is narrowly retributivistic. Let us assume instead that it is a more expansive deontological prohibition on the harsh treatment of anyone who has not actually committed a crime. Such a prohibition—which can be designated here as the 'Deontological Prohibition'—will cover the killings of murderers' relatives that have been discussed in the preceding paragraph, even though those killings are not correctly classifiable as punishments inflicted on the relatives. With such a side-constraint in place, the deterrence-oriented theorists may appear to have shielded their doctrine against the charge that it countenances the slaying of innocent people.

Any deterrence-oriented theorists who draw such a conclusion are being excessively optimistic. We can see as much by noting that a deterrence-oriented theory provides only an account of the role of punishments. For an account of criminalization—that is, for a specification of the modes of conduct that should be proscribed as criminal offences—the deterrence-oriented theorists have to turn to the general utilitarian framework in which their theory of punishment is located. In application to many actual or credibly possible societies, their utilitarian principles will entail the proposition that the close relatives of any murderer should be subjected to criminal liability for having failed to prevent him from engaging in his heinous crime(s). Any such move would greatly amplify the ordinary conception of what counts as being an accessory to a crime, by establishing that any close relatives of a murderer who were physically capable of averting his misbehaviour (through exhortation or coercion or betrayal or any other means) should be deemed accessories simply by dint of their not having averted it. However unwitting a relative's failure to prevent the misbehaviour may have been, utilitarian principles—in application to many actual or credibly possible societies—can call for the criminalization of that failure. When a utilitarian prescription along those lines is combined with a deterrence-oriented theory of punishment (itself an offshoot of utilitarianism), the upshot can credibly be the attachment of the death penalty to each close relative's non-prevention of a murder. The prospect of such a punishment will discourage the relatives of other potential murderers from being remiss or timid, and will more importantly provide the potential murderers themselves with additional very strong reasons for restraining their actions. Thus, although deeming people to be guilty of capital crimes for not having prevented their close relatives from engaging in murderous misdeeds will obviously give rise to quite widespread consternation and will cause pain to the people whose close relatives do commit murders, the disutility owing to the consternation and pain might well be surpassed by the gains in utility owing to the deterrence of murderous misdeeds. That balance of advantages over disadvantages is far from improbable, because the direness of the overall penalties for murder will tend to lower the incidence of murders significantly and will thus mean that those penalties are only quite seldom imposed. At any rate, if that balance of advantages over disadvantages does predictably obtain in many contexts in some society, the utilitarian accounts of criminalization and punishment will there generate the conclusion that the close relatives of any murderer should be held guilty of capital crimes for not having prevented him from wreaking havoc (if those relatives were physically capable of having prevented him in some way).

In the situation envisaged, the executions of the members of murderers' families are imposed upon the family members for their own criminal conduct and are thus veritable punishments. Accordingly, those executions are not disallowed by the Deontological Prohibition, which only forbids the harsh treatment of anyone who has not actually committed a crime. Thus, the deterrence-oriented theorists cannot rely on that prohibition as a side-constraint that will rule out executions of people who are innocent under any ordinary criteria for innocence and guilt. Although the Deontological Prohibition does improve upon the retributivistic side-constraint by excluding any executions of babies and young children and severely handicapped people (who would not be physically capable of thwarting the perpetration of a murder), it does not in all circumstances disallow executions of any other close relatives of murderers. Hence, the Deontological Prohibition is not sufficient to rescue the deterrence-oriented theorists from some of the noxious prescriptions that are entailed by their conception of punishment. When that conception is combined with a utilitarian account of criminalization—in keeping with the utilitarian allegiances of the deterrence-oriented theorists—it can in credible circumstances call for imposing capital punishment on people who are innocent under any ordinary standards for guilt and guiltlessness.

2.4.2.1.3. *Justifiable executions of innocents?*

In their debate with Steiker, Sunstein and Vermeule squarely address the question whether their focus on deterrence commits them to the proposition that some executions of innocent people (including the close relatives of murderers) are morally justifiable. As has already been noted, they respond in part by affirming that their arguments are consistent with a deontological side-constraint. Although they never straightforwardly endorse that side-constraint, they add that 'the killing of innocent people is a prima facie moral wrong,' and that '[w]e have hardly argued for execution[s] of innocent people' (Sunstein and Vermeule 2005b, 855). In addition, they approvingly invoke Rawls's reasoning and conclusions. However, the main point of interest at this juncture is that Sunstein and Vermeule also adopt an approach which we have not yet probed. That is, they declare that some executions of innocent people are indeed morally justifiable.

Having broached a deontological side-constraint (without unequivocally embracing it), Sunstein and Vermeule quickly go on to assert that 'almost all deontological views recognize a consequentialist override to deontological rules'. They continue: '[I]f the execution of an innocent person were genuinely necessary to save an exceedingly large number of people (10,000, 100,000, or 100 million?), we believe that the execution might well be justified, and we doubt that Steiker would disagree. For both consequentialists and deontologists, the killing of innocent people could be justified in some imaginable world' (Sunstein and Vermeule 2005b, 855). There are two chief ways in which these remarks by Sunstein and Vermeule can be construed, each of which is insurmountably problematic. Under one interpretation, their remarks articulate a mistaken understanding of the moral upshot of the dilemma to which they advert. Under a second interpretation, their comments correctly characterize that moral upshot; but, in stating the moral situation accurately, Sunstein and Vermeule would be abandoning the utilitarian moorings of their whole approach to capital punishment.[16]

To detect the ambiguity of the statements that have been quoted, we should focus on the notions of a 'prima facie moral wrong' and a 'consequentialist override' as well as on the assertion that 'the killing of innocent people could be justified'. As I have observed elsewhere (Kramer 1999a, 267–9; Kramer 2004, 290–1), the phrase 'prima facie' is itself construable in two quite divergent ways. On the one hand, it can mean 'presumptive' or 'on initial examination'. On the other hand, it can mean 'susceptible to being overtopped in importance by some competing factor'. According to the first construal, a prima facie moral wrong is something which appears to be such a wrong

---

[16] It is not entirely clear whether Sunstein and Vermeule adhere to utilitarianism or instead to some closely related variety of consequentialism. Any such difference is immaterial for all of my purposes in this chapter. I should note, incidentally, that Sunstein and Vermeule purport to be prescinding from debates between consequentialists and deontologists (Sunstein and Vermeule 2005a, 717–19). However, while putatively bracketing those debates, they in fact misrepresent deontological theories as consequentialist doctrines—in the manner criticized by Robert Nozick some decades ago (Nozick 1974, 28–33).

on initial inspection but which might turn out not genuinely to be a moral wrong when all things have been considered. According to the second construal, a prima facie moral wrong is a genuine moral wrong that might be exceeded in importance by a countervailing moral imperative.

Equally ambiguous is the notion of a consequentialist override. On the one hand, such an override can be understood as consisting in the defeat and consequent suspension or nullification of some deontological restriction by an extremely weighty public-welfare factor (Lenta and Farland 2008, 281). On the other hand, it can be understood instead as that which occurs when an extremely weighty and urgent public-welfare factor exceeds in moral importance a deontological restriction that is nonetheless still operative as a moral requirement.

Equivocal in largely the same way is the assertion that executions of innocent people can be justified. On the one hand, such an assertion might be declaring that executions of innocent people can sometimes be morally permissible. That is, it might be contending that such executions in some possible circumstances will not be in violation of any moral obligations. On the other hand, it might instead be declaring that dauntingly weighty moral obligations which in certain contexts require executions of innocents can exceed in ethical importance the potently stringent moral obligations which forbid any such executions. Construed in this latter way, the assertion would not be denying that executions of innocent people are always morally impermissible; it would simply be maintaining that those morally impermissible actions can in some imaginable circumstances be morally imperative.

Let us first assume, then, that Sunstein and Vermeule in their quoted remarks are holding that executions of innocent people are sometimes morally permissible because of the overwhelmingly large gains in public welfare that will ensue therefrom. While such a claim is a corollary of their general utilitarian outlook and is therefore obviously consistent with that outlook, it misrepresents the moral bearings of the executions that Sunstein and Vermeule envisage. Although the officials of a legal-governmental system are under moral obligations to safeguard the lives of citizens against dangers that are reasonably foreseeable and preventable, and although those obligations are extremely weighty when the dangers are immense, they do not cancel or eliminate any moral obligations with which they conflict. In particular, they never cancel or eliminate the officials' moral obligations to eschew the imposition of punishments (especially severe punishments) on innocent people. On a prodigiously rare occasion when a moral obligation of the latter type is overtopped in ethical importance by some countervailing moral obligations of officials to protect citizens against extraordinary dangers, the officials' obligation to avoid punishing any innocent person persists as such. Albeit the morally optimal course of conduct for the officials in the terrible circumstances is to act athwart that obligation, they will indeed be acting athwart it rather than acting permissibly. Sometimes—as in the situation evoked by Sunstein and Vermeule—a morally imperative course of conduct is morally impermissible. Though somebody faced with such a moral dilemma will

have acted correctly if he fulfils the weightier of the two conflicting moral obligations, he will have breached the less important moral duty and will thus have incurred
a further moral duty to remedy the situation in some way. Were he acting permissibly
by fulfilling the weightier duty, he would not incur any remedial obligation; yet,
precisely because he will not in fact be acting permissibly (even though he is acting
optimally), such an obligation will indeed be incurred.[17]

Of course, utilitarian theorists can allow that some measures which *resemble* genuine remedies should be undertaken by legal-governmental officials after certain
utility-maximizing executions of innocents. If the guiltlessness of a person subjected
to such an execution has somehow become known, and if the people in his society
do not themselves adhere to utilitarian ways of thinking, then the undertaking of a
remedy-resembling measure will most likely tend toward the maximization of utility through its alleviation of people's distress. Such a measure might be adopted with
full sincerity by the officials concerned, but utilitarian theorists have to perceive it as a
simulacrum of a genuine remedy. A veritable remedy constitutes an acknowledgment
that something wrong has been done. That is, it constitutes an acknowledgment that
some moral duty has been breached.[18] Utilitarians are obliged by their doctrine to
deny that any wrong whatsoever has been committed by legal-governmental officials
who execute an innocent person in circumstances where the execution is foreseeably
utility-maximizing. They are therefore obliged by their doctrine to deny that the
remedy-resembling measure broached above is genuinely remedial. Given that there
is no wrong to be rectified, a measure of that sort does not play any rectificatory role.
Such a measure will be applauded by utilitarian theorists if it tends toward the maximization of utility, but they will not view it as a way of correcting a wrong. In their
eyes, its only role is consolatory. It furnishes solace to people who deludedly think
that they or others have been treated impermissibly. A utilitarian theorist will maintain that, if legal-governmental officials are morally obligated to take any remedy-
resembling steps, they are so because they are morally obligated to make people feel
happy (in this case, by catering to people's misconceptions).[19] Such a theorist will

---

[17] This point is largely missed in Moore 1997, 719–24; and Tasioulas 2006, 304–5. I have discussed
moral conflicts, and the persistence of moral duties in such conflicts, at much greater length in Kramer
2004, ch 8; Kramer 2005; and Kramer 2009a, 117–26, 142–50. (Especially relevant is Kramer 2004, 280–5,
where I differentiate between strong permissibility and weak permissibility, and where I discuss the distinction drawn by some other philosophers between violations and infringements.) As I make clear in all
my writings that have just been cited, a moral wrong committed for the sake of avoiding a more grievous
moral wrong is heavily extenuated by the circumstances in which it is committed (unless those circumstances were themselves illegitimately brought about by the person who commits the wrong). Some
serious moral wrongs are not blameworthy.

[18] Thus, for example, a remedial obligation is different from an obligation to make a payment for
something that has been lawfully acquired (such as a meal consumed by a customer in a restaurant or a
plot of land acquired by a government through its power of eminent domain). A payment for something
lawfully acquired does not remedy a wrong that has occurred; rather, it averts the occurrence of a wrong.
See Kramer 2004, 286–7.

[19] If the remedy-resembling step is a simulacrum of compensation, then the utilitarians can favour
making it mandatory on the ground that requiring such a step will internalize the costs of governmental

contend that the obligation of the officials has nothing to do with any need for the righting of a wrong, since no wrong has occurred.

Utilitarianism's gainsaying of the reality of moral conflicts is to be rejected, for it entails the conclusion that absolutely any policy—the execution of innocent people, torture, genocide—is morally permissible so long as the utility-promotive considerations that support the policy are strong enough. We should recognize instead that someone faced with a moral conflict will have to act impermissibly regardless of what he does. If legal-governmental officials are ever confronted with a predicament in which they elect to breach their moral duty-not-to-execute-an-innocent-person in order to comply with some surpassingly important moral duties owed to the general public, they will be justified only in the sense that they will be pursuing the morally best course of action. They will not be justified in the sense of behaving permissibly. On the contrary, because any act of executing an innocent person is abidingly impermissible, the officials will incur a stringent remedial obligation if they ever carry out such an act. That obligation will be genuinely remedial, rather than a sop to people's delusions.

If Sunstein and Vermeule believe that the officials in the situation just described are acting permissibly, then they are obliged to accept that those officials will not incur any genuinely remedial obligations whatsoever by virtue of executing an innocent person. In regard to the moral bearings of the officials' actions, such an execution would be perceived by Sunstein and Vermeule as fundamentally on a par with the ordinary incineration of some garbage; neither the execution nor the incineration imposes a duty on anyone to experience regret or to express any genuine apologies or to carry out any other genuine remedies. If Sunstein and Vermeule believe that the execution of an innocent person can be justifiable in this sense, then they are cleaving faithfully to their utilitarian principles, but they are profoundly mistaken about the nature of moral conflicts.

Let us suppose instead, then, that Sunstein and Vermeule do not believe that executions of innocent people are ever morally permissible. When they say that deliberate executions of innocents can be morally justifiable in some truly terrible circumstances, they are simply maintaining that such executions in some such circumstances can be morally optimal. If their position is indeed along those lines, then it is morally tenable. However, it is at odds with their utilitarian allegiances. Utilitarianism leaves no room for genuine moral conflicts, since it insists that no foreseeably utility-maximizing pattern of behaviour is ever wrong in any respect. It acknowledges the occurrence of prima facie wrongs only in the first sense that was delineated above. That is, while allowing that some events or states of affairs initially appear to be wrong but turn out not to be wrong when all things have been considered, it does not

operations and will thereby help to ensure that those operations in the future do not go ahead unless their expected drawbacks are significantly exceeded by their expected benefits. Many theorists in the law-and-economics movement ascribe a non-remedial role of this type to awards of damages in tort law.

allow that any events or states of affairs are wrong if they foreseeably contribute to the maximization of utility. For utilitarians, wrong-making events or states of affairs are all and only those that do not foreseeably promote the maximization of utility; the utilitarian doctrine defines the very notion of wrongness exclusively by reference to that maximizing imperative. Consequently, in the scenario conjured up by Sunstein and Vermeule, the deliberate execution of an innocent person is not wrong at all under utilitarian principles. No officials who perform the execution will have incurred any genuinely remedial obligations whatsoever, nor will any such obligations be incurred by the legal-governmental regime on whose behalf the officials act. There are no genuinely remedial obligations, because there is no wrong to be rectified. Were the officials subsequently to apologize sincerely to the decedent's family, or were they to engage non-instrumentally in any other sort of remedial endeavour, they would be displaying moral confusion. Such is the conclusion to which a proponent of utilitarianism is committed.

Hence, if Sunstein and Vermeule do recognize the reality of moral conflicts, they will *pro tanto* be repudiating the general utilitarian theory that underpins their conception of capital punishment. If they choose instead to remain faithful to that theory, they will be committing themselves to the proposition that executions of innocent people are morally permissible whenever those executions foreseeably tilt the social balance—the balance of public-welfare advantages and disadvantages—toward the maximization of utility. If Sunstein and Vermeule seek to adopt some hybrid position involving what they take to be a deontological prohibition and a consequentialist override, they will confront a displaced version of the same dilemma. To pin down the nature of the consequentialist override, they have to say whether the triggering of the override will have rendered some executions of innocents morally permissible or whether instead it will merely have rendered those impermissible executions morally optimal. By coming to grips with the dilemma in the former way, Sunstein and Vermeule would be blinding themselves to the reality of moral conflicts and to the consequent impermissibility of some patterns of conduct that are nonetheless morally imperative. By coming to grips with the dilemma in the latter way, Sunstein and Vermeule would be renouncing the utilitarian tenets from which their deterrence-oriented rationale for capital punishment derives its fundamental purpose.

In sum, Sunstein and Vermeule cannot have things both ways. Either they abandon their utilitarian position in order to deal adequately with the problem of executions of innocents by recognizing that all such executions are morally wrong (however extenuated the gravity of the wrong might be in certain extreme circumstances of moral conflict), or else they cleave to their utilitarian principles and insist that some executions of innocents are not wrong in any respect. Their reliance on ambiguous phrases such as 'prima facie' and on ambiguous notions such as that of a consequentialist override does not eliminate the crux that confronts them and the unpalatable choice that awaits them.

2.4.2.2. Types of punishments

Another commonly voiced objection to deterrence-oriented theories of the death penalty is that such theories call for the imposition of punishments that are morally illegitimate in their severity (Jones and Potter 1981, 162–3). Indeed, as was mentioned earlier in passing, one aspect of the problems relating to innocent people can be classified also under this heading: the matter of executing the members of a murderer's family in order to punish the murderer. However, the present problem encompasses many other morally illegitimate punishments as well. If executions are efficacious as marginal deterrents, then executions preceded by prolonged and savage torture will almost certainly be even more effective. Likewise, if executions performed through relatively humane methods are efficacious as marginal deterrents, then executions performed through gruesomely brutal methods will almost certainly be more effective. In other words, contrary to what is often suggested in public discourse about the punishments that should be undertaken by a criminal-justice system in response to murders, the death penalty is not 'the ultimate sanction'. As Steiker aptly remarks: 'Death is an awesome and terrible punishment, but it is not in itself the worst punishment that we can inflict.'[20] Thus, the proponents of the deterrence-oriented rationale for the death penalty face the task of explaining why they are not also proponents of much more severe punishments.

Like the problem of executions of innocent people, this problem of morally illegitimate severity was pithily summarized by Hart: 'There are many different ways in which we think it morally incumbent on us to *qualify* or *limit* the pursuit of the utilitarian [deterrence-oriented] goal by the methods of punishment. Some punishments are ruled out as too barbarous or horrible to be used[,] whatever their social utility' (Hart 1968, 80, emphases in original). As Hart's comment makes clear, the challenge for deterrence-oriented theorists is to specify an upper limit of severity that does not rule out the death penalty.[21] They plainly cannot hope to find the justification for such a limit within the confines of their emphasis on deterrence, since that emphasis is precisely what gives rise to the need for such a limit. Considerations of deterrence militate in favour of the morally illegitimate punishments that have been broached above. Hence, if the deterrence-oriented theorists want to avoid being in the position of advocating the infliction of those wrongful punishments, they have to step beyond the boundaries of their rationale for the death penalty.

---

[20] Steiker 2005, 778. For some similar observations, see Markel 2009, 1175, 1203.

[21] This way of putting the matter is slightly simplistic. Rape and torture and amputation are morally illegitimate as punitive measures even though some varieties of them are less severe than capital punishment. Hence, although there is a strong correlation between the severity of punishments (at the top end of the scale) and the moral illegitimacy of punishments, the correlation between those two properties is by no means perfect. I can ignore this complication in my current discussion. In Chapter 6, where the deterrence-oriented rationale for capital punishment will have been superseded by the purgative rationale, I explain why torture is morally impermissible while the death penalty is morally permissible (in appropriate cases). As will become apparent, my explanation of that point is very different from the explanation offered in Davis 2002, 23–5.

2.4.2.2.1. Proportionality

In particular, those theorists cannot avail themselves of the fact that the punishments in a deterrence-oriented system of criminal justice will generally meet the requirement of proportionality that is usually associated with retributivism. That is, the punishments will be arranged in such a way that their severity is aligned with the seriousness of the crimes for which they are levied. Within a deterrence-oriented system, the requirement of proportionality is fulfilled not because of a focus on people's deserts but because of the nature of marginal deterrence. Given that especially serious crimes are more detrimental to the general well-being of a society than are less serious crimes, the need for deterrence is particularly pressing in connection with the former crimes. Yet, if the punishments for the especially serious crimes and the less serious crimes are the same (or, at least, are equal in severity), then *ceteris paribus* the deterrent effect will be no greater with regard to the former crimes than with regard to the latter. For example, if a penalty of ten years in prison is attached to burglary and murder alike, and if the probability of a culprit's being apprehended and convicted is the same for each crime, then *ceteris paribus* the latter crime will not be more effectively deterred than the former. To avoid such an undesirable upshot, a deterrence-oriented system of criminal justice will typically attach increasingly severe punishments to increasingly serious crimes. To a large extent, then, it will exhibit the feature of proportionality in its scheme of punishments.

Patently, however, the feature of proportionality in the schedule of punishments imposed by a deterrence-oriented system of criminal justice is not per se sufficient to vindicate the use of the death penalty. At most, an appeal to that feature simply indicates that the assigned punishment for a really serious crime such as murder should be significantly more severe than the assigned punishment for a much less serious crime such as shoplifting. An appeal of that sort does not establish that the penalty for the really serious crimes, within any system of criminal justice focused on deterrence, must be death. Furthermore, it does not even establish that—within a system of criminal justice focused on deterrence—gradations in the seriousness of crimes should always be accompanied by gradations in the severity of the punishments attached to those crimes. After all, marginal deterrence can be strengthened by increasing the likelihood of apprehension and conviction for the most serious crimes as well as by increasing the sternness of the sanctions that are levied for those crimes.

In short, the requirement or quasi-requirement of proportionality does not in itself go any way toward providing a satisfactory justification of the death penalty. Moreover, when it is fleshed out with other considerations of deterrence, it leads back to the very problem that is under investigation here: the problem of specifying an upper limit of punitive severity. Just as the requirement of proportionality is insufficient to ensure that any punishment as severe as the death penalty will figure among the sanctions in a properly functioning system of criminal justice, so too it is insufficient to exclude the far more brutal punishments that have been mentioned above. Conformity to the requirement of proportionality is fully consistent with the use of the especially grisly punishments, which can be imposed for crimes more serious than those for which the death penalty itself is imposed. Consequently, if the deterrence-oriented theorists want to distance themselves from those morally illegitimate punishments, they cannot remain content with invoking the requirement of proportionality. Though their doctrine generally commits them to that requirement, it also commits them to calling for gruesome punishments insofar as the systematic use of such punishments is maximally promotive of deterrence and utility.

2.4.2.2.2. *Utilitarianism*

A natural place for the deterrence-oriented theorists to seek refuge is the utilitarian foundation of their conception of punishment. Notwithstanding that a focus on deterrence favours the imposition of illegitimately brutal punishments in many credible circumstances, the broader utilitarian principles that undergird such a focus might be thought to militate against the use of such punishments. After all, those rebarbative sanctions will cause excruciating pain to the criminals who are subjected to them, and they will elicit consternation among many members of the public. They might also give rise to the phenomenon of brutalization, which was discussed earlier in connection with capital punishment. Those utility-diminishing effects have to be weighed against the utility-augmenting effects that are associated with the sanctions' lowering of the incidence of serious crimes. Utilitarians are likely to contend that, once we balance the former consequences against the latter, we shall recognize that the rebarbative punishments are unjustified. Thus, the utilitarian moorings of the deterrence-oriented accounts of capital punishment can supply the upper limit of severity that is not supplied by those accounts themselves—or so the deterrence-oriented theorists will be tempted to claim.

Unfortunately for those theorists, this latest tack is vulnerable to largely the same objections that were raised earlier in this chapter (in § 2.4.2.1.1) against the efforts of utilitarians to rebut the charge that they countenance executions of innocent people. In the first place, the claim that brutal punishments would not be justifiable on utilitarian grounds is far from compelling. Given the likely deterrent effects of such punishments, they could significantly reduce the incidence of serious crimes without being imposed very often. As a result, the drawbacks of those punishments—consisting in the pain which they cause directly and in the apprehension or dismay or brutalization which they cause more diffusely—might well be surpassed by their benefits, consisting in substantially lowered rates of murders and other very serious crimes. Undoubtedly, there are credibly possible worlds in which those punishments in various societies would indeed be utility-maximizing. As Sunstein and Vermeule themselves concede: 'Everything depends on what the facts turn out to be' (Sunstein and Vermeule 2005a, 734).

A second fatal weakness in the utilitarian defence of the deterrence-oriented conception of punishment is precisely that that defence makes everything hinge on what the facts (concerning people's propensities) turn out to be. As was stated earlier, the utilitarian response mistakenly treats an objection of principle as if it were an objection about probable consequences. Even if the utilitarian conjectures about the most likely balance of advantages and disadvantages were more plausible than they are, they would miss the point of the complaint that is being pressed here. As was underscored by the quotations from Hart and Dworkin in § 2.4.2.1.1, the key point is not that the utilitarians' surmises about people's inclinations and outlooks are implausible—though in fact those surmises are hardly compelling. Rather, the key point is that the moral legitimacy or illegitimacy of the shockingly grisly punishments does not depend on the details of those inclinations and outlooks, or on the resultant balance of public-welfare advantages and disadvantages. Even in the many credibly possible situations where that balance militates in favour of applications of those punishments, no such applications are morally legitimate.

As Hart rightly stated in the passage that was quoted earlier, the key values contravened by executions of innocent people are those of fairness and moral responsibility. With regard to the use of barbarous punishments (against people whom we can here assume to be guilty of heinous crimes), the values transgressed are somewhat different though overlapping. Of central concern in this context are the human dignity of the punished criminals and the moral integrity of the community in which the punishments are levied.

Opponents of capital punishment often invoke the human dignity of criminals as a basis for insisting that death cannot ever be an appropriate sanction. Given that this book will be arguing that death is an appropriate sanction in a limited range of cases, my invocation of the human dignity of criminals is obviously not an element of a stance against capital punishment. However, the issue here is not the legitimacy or illegitimacy of capital punishment *tout court*, but the legitimacy or illegitimacy of the gruesome modes of capital punishment that have been discussed (capital punishment preceded by savage torture and mutilation, and capital punishment carried out by especially grisly methods). In connection with that latter issue, the interrelated values of human dignity and moral integrity are dispositive. As understood here, the value of human dignity consists in the moral force of three fundamental features of human individuals: the capacity to feel intense pain; the capacity to undergo positive experiences; and the status of a rational agent who is capable of setting and pursuing objectives in ways that are far more sophisticated than the ways in which any other animals conduct themselves.[22] (Not every human being is possessed of deliberative capabilities, of course. Any human being not so possessed is endowed with human

[22] I am not denying that animals are themselves endowed with moral dignity as creatures capable of feeling intense pain and undergoing positive experiences and engaging in primitive reflection. They clearly are so endowed; the deliberate infliction of torture on animals is strictly forbidden and is something that sullies the moral integrity of anyone who stoops to it. However, the basis for the moral dignity of animals is not exactly the same as the basis for human dignity, and the moral constraints imposed by the former are therefore not exactly the same as those imposed by the latter. An exploration of the differences is well beyond the scope of this book.

dignity by virtue of his membership in a species for which rational and moral agency is the norm.) Because of the moral force of those elementary characteristics, human beings are constrained in what they can legitimately do to one another.

They are morally entitled to hold one another responsible as agents for benign or malign conduct, and, as Chapter 6 of this book will argue, they are morally entitled to put to death someone who has acted so wickedly as to defile the community in which he abides. When odious malefactors are held responsible for their misconduct in that fashion—through humane methods of execution after fair trials and appeals— they are treated in accordance with the value of human dignity which they have themselves so grotesquely flouted. By contrast, the savage torture of someone for the purpose of deterring others from committing serious crimes is neither a way of holding him responsible for his conduct nor a way of otherwise treating him in accordance with his human dignity. As has already been discussed in this chapter, deterrence-oriented punishments do not hold responsible the people on whom they are inflicted. Such punishments are entirely prospective in their orientation, and they can fully perform their assigned role in any number of contexts by being wielded against people who are mistakenly but very widely believed to be guilty. Moreover, insofar as those punishments include the wantonness of torture, they sully the community on whose behalf they are imposed.

Now, again, the point here is not that the unsparingly tortured and dismembered people are being used purely as means. Though they are certainly being used as means, they too may have benefited from the existence of a system of governance through which the incidence of very serious crimes is kept at a low level as a result of the use of ferocious punishments; if so, then they are not being treated *only* as means. Rather, the point is that the specific way in which they are being used as means is violative of their human dignity and is thus at odds with the moral integrity of the community that treats them in such a manner.

Here the focus should indeed lie on the moral posture of the community. Irrespective of the public-welfare advantages that may ensue from the deliberate subjection of someone to prolonged and excruciating pain that will culminate in his death, any such exploitation of the human capacity to feel intense pain is morally illegitimate. If legal-governmental officials acting on behalf of a community do exploit someone's pain-experiencing capacity in that fashion, they degrade the whole community by authoritatively eschewing all limits on the depravity with which they pursue the public weal. They bear out Finnis's complaint about the preparedness of consequentialists to do *anything* in the belief that it is morally permissible.

To be sure, if the subjection of someone to hideous torture culminating in his death were ever somehow knowably necessary in order to avert what Nozick described as 'catastrophic moral horror' (Nozick 1974, 30 n*), then the perpetration of the lethal torture would be morally optimal. The relevant legal-governmental officials would be morally obligated to carry it out, and that obligation would be morally weightier than their obligation not to do so. However, even under such outlandish circumstances, the torture would be a morally impermissible degradation of the community in which it occurs. In the dire and fanciful circumstances envisaged, the officials would have to commit a great wrong in order to prevent a much greater wrong; neither their perpetration of the torture nor their abstention from it would be a morally permissible course of conduct, and the latter would be an even graver wrong than the former.

Of course, what has been said here is the barest sketch of an account of human dignity and moral integrity. The moral impermissibility of torture is not one of this book's central concerns, because executions conducted on the basis of the purgative rationale do not involve any exploitation of the pain-experiencing capacity of human beings. Nevertheless, my sketchy remarks here have touched upon some of the key propositions that would have to be elaborated in a much more ample exposition of human dignity and moral integrity. Even the most repellent people who have committed the most appalling outrages are endowed with human dignity that sets moral constraints on how they can legitimately be treated. No community can retain its moral integrity if it shows itself willing to stoop to commensurate outrages by sweeping away all limits on the nature of its punitive responses to such people. Those limits are morally required not because the noxiously evil people's lives are of any positive worth, but because a community debases itself if it fails to accept that even such wicked people with lives of only negative worth are not to be subjected deliberately to torture or to butcherously agonizing methods of execution. Any such deliberate exploitation of a person's pain-experiencing capacity, even if undertaken for the furtherance of public security rather than out of sadism, is fundamentally at one with the worst type of evil (to be explored at much greater length in Chapter 6). Benign or putatively benign though the motives for a society's embrace of such evil may be, the failure to draw limits that exclude it is corrosive of the society's moral integrity.

Extreme utilitarians would disagree with my invocation of the values of human dignity and moral integrity, of course, but their dismissal of such values would simply highlight the turpitude of their extreme credo. Most deterrence-oriented theorists pay at least implicit tribute to those values as they try strenuously to explain why their conception of punishment does not lead them to condone monstrous torture or barbarous methods of execution. We have encountered several of their argumentative strategies already, and we shall examine some more of them presently. The powerful tug of the values of human dignity and moral integrity is felt even by theorists whose doctrine leaves no place for them. Thus, although a thorough exposition of those values is not feasible within the scope of this chapter,[23] their widespread appeal compensates to some degree for the terseness of the exposition here.

One point of clarification should be emphasized, before we move on. My remarks on human dignity and moral integrity have been propounding moral theses rather

---

[23] I say far more about them in a forthcoming book of mine, *Torture and Moral Integrity*. I also say some more about them in subsequent chapters of the present book, especially in Chapters 3, 6, and 7.

than empirical theses. More specifically, they have not resumed or extended my earlier discussion of brutalization. According to the social scientists who maintain that capital punishment produces brutalizing effects, the employment of such a sanction badly coarsens the moral sentiments of the people who live in some society where it is used. That sanction can therefore prove to be counterproductive, as the salutariness of its deterrent effects is offset by the perniciousness of its callousing effects. Accordingly, it can actually contribute to an increase in the incidence of serious crimes. Such is the claim of the aforementioned social scientists. Now, clearly, that claim is an empirical proposition about the observable impact of a certain practice on the behaviour of human beings. Despite the huge practical difficulties that beset the verification or disconfirmation of that proposition, it is in principle subject to empirical verification or disconfirmation. Hence, social scientists rather than moral philosophers are best equipped to assess the truth-values of any pronouncements on brutalization.

By contrast, my discussion of human dignity and moral integrity has been articulating moral propositions. On the one hand, the properties of human beings that have figured saliently in the discussion—the capacity of human beings to feel intense pain, their capacity to undergo positive experiences, and the status of such beings as rational agents who set and pursue objectives—are of course empirically ascertainable characteristics. On the other hand, my focus has lain not on those characteristics themselves, but on their moral import. Human dignity consists in that moral import rather than in anything that is detected empirically. Likewise, of course, the moral integrity of a community is a moral property rather than an empirical property. When I have referred to the degradation or sullying of a community's moral integrity, I have not been talking about the coarsening of people's moral outlooks (though, naturally, such an effect might also be occurring). Rather, such references have pertained to the erosion of a community's moral probity through the unscrupulousness of the community's interaction with irredeemably terrible human beings whose lives are of negative value and who nonetheless are possessed of human dignity. So understood, the degradation or sullying is a moral upshot rather than a social-psychological effect.

This point of clarification is advisable because Steiker does not sufficiently disentangle the empirical issue of brutalization from the normative issue of a community's moral integrity. On the one hand, she seems to be aware of the difference between those matters, and she writes about them at separate junctures (Steiker 2005, 786–9, 773–4). On the other hand, her brief comments about human dignity too often veer into making empirical claims about the psyches of people who inflict excruciating pain upon their fellow human beings. In those comments she writes, for example, that 'when the purposeful infliction of extreme suffering is yoked with emotions of righteousness and satisfaction, it will inevitably suppress our ordinary human capacities for compassion and empathy'. A few sentences later, she adds that 'the inherent moral satisfaction that attends the practice of punishment when it includes the infliction of...extreme forms of suffering does seem to permit, or even require, the weakening of important psychological constraints against brutality' (Steiker 2005, 773). An ancillary point worth noting here is that, whereas the first of these two quotations very boldly declares that the callousing of people's ethical sentiments will *inevitably* take place, the second quotation far more modestly declares that such a development seems to be permitted. More important in the present context is that the statement in each quotation adverts to a contingent social-psychological effect rather than to a moral upshot. Quite understandably, therefore, Sunstein and Vermeule are bemused by Steiker's 'dignity argument' (Sunstein and Vermeule 2005b, 855).

At any rate, Steiker's conception of human dignity is apparently somewhat different from mine; it appears to be focused partly on the social-psychological coarsening that worries the critics of brutalization. (Steiker apparently believes—correctly—that such coarsening is intrinsically bad and that it is intrinsically corrosive of any sound basis for punishing people.) Regardless, the general message here is that the values of human dignity and moral integrity as understood in this book are moral ideals rather than empirical phenomena. My recourse to those values in support of my rejection of the deterrence-oriented rationale for capital punishment is straightforwardly a moral stance rather than an exercise in armchair sociology or psychology.

2.4.2.2.3. *Retributivism to the rescue?*

Utilitarian principles provide no succour for any deterrence-oriented theorists who seek to shed their commitment to the notion that brutal executions preceded by shuddersome bouts of torture can be appropriate punitive measures in many credibly possible contexts. Consequently, those theorists might once again be inclined to turn to retributivism as a source of side-constraints. Having found no resources in their own theories for specifying suitable upper limits of severity past which any punishments cannot be morally legitimate, the proponents of the deterrence-oriented rationale for the death penalty might hope to find in retributivism the resources for specifying such limits. They might think that a hybrid theory can rescue them from the horrible implications of a monomaniacal pursuit of deterrence.

One problem with such a tactic is that the deterrence-oriented theorists would have to establish that the hybrid theory is principled and that it is not a desperately makeshift hodgepodge. However, we can put that problem aside. A far more formidable difficulty lies in the fact that the retributivists are in essentially the same quandary as the deterrence-oriented theorists. As will become evident in my next chapter, retributivism does not furnish any basis for fixing determinately a suitable upper limit on the severity and types of the punishments for which it calls. Although the specific reasons for the indeterminacy in retributivism are of course different from the reasons for the corresponding indeterminacy in the deterrence-oriented rationale, the gaps left by those two theories are homologous in all respects relevant to the present discussion. Indeed, as will be observed in Chapter 3, some retributivists and critics of retributivism are disposed to resort to deterrence-oriented theories in order to fill the very lacuna which some of the deterrence-oriented theorists aspire to fill by resorting to retributivism. In this game of mirrors, neither side ends up with a determinate specification of the requisite upper limit of severity.

2.4.2.2.4. *Sunstein and Vermeule on analogies*

Let us consider one final effort by deterrence-oriented theorists to shield their doctrine against the sorts of objections that have been raised in this discussion. In the article to which Steiker retorts, Sunstein and Vermeule anticipate the allegation that their focus on deterrence commits them to advocating the use of gruesome punishments. The gist of their reply should be quoted at length:

> Because arguments about policies such as capital punishment and torture are hostage to what the facts turn out to show in particular domains, slippery-slope arguments are disabled; instead of a slope, there is just a series of discrete policy problems. Support for capital punishment need not, by analogical reasoning or otherwise, commit policymakers to support for public floggings or punitive mutilation or other horrors. Nor is there any obvious mechanism that would push policymakers or citizens to adopt those other practices once they have adopted capital punishment. Not only is there no slope, there is no a priori reason to believe the ground slippery. [Sunstein and Vermeule 2005a, 734-35, footnote omitted]

This riposte to the anticipated allegation is misdirected in a number of respects. In the first place, there has been no suggestion here (or in most other critiques of deterrence-oriented arguments for capital punishment) that the answers to questions about the utility-maximizing tendency of capital punishment in a particular society are somehow determinative of the answers to questions about the utility-maximizing tendency of torture or any other horror in that society. On the contrary, as should be manifest from what has been said in this chapter, the social-psychological facts determining the utilitarian justifiedness or unjustifiedness of capital punishment in any given context do not settle the utilitarian justifiedness or unjustifiedness of torture or any other horrible practice in that context. Although many credibly possible worlds in which the death penalty is promotive of utility-maximization in some society are worlds in which the death penalty preceded by hideous torture is likewise promotive of utility-maximization in that society, there are many other credibly possible worlds in which the addition of hideous torture to the death penalty would not be promotive of utility-maximization in the specified society. This chapter has never suggested otherwise.

Nor has this chapter implied that the adoption of capital punishment on utilitarian grounds by legal-governmental officials will somehow inevitably dispose them to adopt a regimen of savage torture on similar grounds. Plainly, there is no 'mechanism' that irresistibly impels the adoption of the latter regimen whenever the institution of capital punishment has been embraced. Such matters of legal-governmental implementation are unmistakably contingencies rather than necessities.

Instead of voicing any of the complaints that are easily rebutted by Sunstein and Vermeule, this portion of the current chapter has argued in effect as follows. Like other deterrence-oriented theorists, Sunstein and Vermeule believe that capital punishment is both morally permissible and morally obligatory in any society where its net effect is to contribute to the maximization of utility by significantly deterring potential malefactors from perpetrating serious crimes. There are many societies in the actual world, or in credible counterfactual worlds, where capital punishment would produce such a net effect. Consequently, according to Sunstein and Vermeule, there are many societies—in the actual world or in credible counterfactual worlds— where capital punishment is both morally permissible and morally obligatory. Given as much, Sunstein and Vermeule are committed to holding that capital punishment through ferocious torture is morally permissible and obligatory in many societies in the actual world or in credible counterfactual worlds.[24] After all, in many of the societies in those worlds, the great deterrent efficacy of a practice of executing people through ferocious torture will outweigh the utility-reducing features of such an approach to punishment and will thereby promote the maximization of utility. That savage punitive practice can therefore satisfy Sunstein's and Vermeule's standard for moral permissibility and obligatoriness. If Sunstein and Vermeule do not wish to embrace that implication of their position, they will have to alter their understanding of what is sufficient for moral permissibility and obligatoriness. In so doing, they will have lost their basis for asserting that the death penalty is sometimes morally permissible and obligatory. Alternatively, they can cleave steadfastly to their understanding of what is sufficient for moral permissibility and obligatoriness, and they can thereby commit themselves to accepting that capital punishment through grisly torture is morally permissible and obligatory in many societies (in the actual world or in credible counterfactual worlds). Should they opt for that nettle-grasping approach, they will have confirmed the central contention in this portion of Chapter 2. That is, they will have confirmed that the putative justification for capital punishment propounded by deterrence-oriented theorists is antithetical to the value of moral integrity and is thus not a correct moral justification for anything.

2.5. A pithy conclusion

Although this chapter has not endeavoured to expose every weakness in the deterrence-oriented rationale for capital punishment,[25] it has sought to show that any

---

[24] Indeed, this point is largely conceded in Sunstein and Vermeule 2005a, 734: 'We accept this claim about what our hypothesis entails.'

[25] Sunstein and Vermeule deny the applicability of the act/omission distinction to the workings of a criminal-justice system. They sometimes query the very intelligibility of that distinction in application to those workings (Sunstein and Vermeule 2005a, 720–4, 749–50; Sunstein and Vermeule 2005b, 850). In so doing, they overlook the rigorous exposition of the act/omission distinction—put forward from a consequentialist perspective—by Jonathan Bennett (1981; 1995, chs 4–8). I discuss Bennett's exposition at length, with several further citations to his writings, in Kramer 2003, 324–36. Bennett's analysis can certainly be applied to the functioning of a criminal-justice system. Another issue raised by Sunstein

veritable justification for the use of such punishment will have to be found elsewhere. Still, nobody should be surprised that the deterrence-oriented rationale has over the years won numerous adherents. Although the deterrent efficacy of any punishments is never per se sufficient for the moral legitimacy of those punishments, and although not every morally legitimate punishment is efficacious as a deterrent, the function of deterrence is central to any system of criminal justice. No such system could endure for more than a brief period if most of its punishments were devoid of deterrent efficacy. Any satisfactory general theory of criminal law has to take account of deterrence as one of the chief desiderata promoted by criminal sanctions. However, the question in this chapter has not been whether the deterrence of wrongdoing is a major and salutary function of the general institution of punishment. Rather, the question has been whether the marginal deterrent efficacy (if any) of the death penalty is sufficient to justify in principle the use of such a penalty. To that question the present chapter has returned a negative answer.

and Vermeule but not addressed here is that of collective agency and intentions. Sunstein and Vermeule believe that attributions of mental states (including culpable intentions) to collective entities such as governments are 'metaphorical shorthand' (Sunstein and Vermeule 2005b, 850–1). In so maintaining, they disregard the large and rigorously argued literature in recent years on the topic of collective or corporate agency. For one of the many valuable contributions to that literature—quite a few of which had been published by the time of the appearance of Sunstein's and Vermeule's articles on capital punishment—see Pettit 2007.

3

Death and Retribution

To a greater extent than any of the other theories that have been enlisted in support of capital punishment, retributivism has been championed in a number of divergent and prominent forms. Although the sundry varieties of retributivism are consistent with one another and are frequently conjoined, and although each of them highlights the fundamental equality and moral responsibility of human agents, the focus of the argumentation differs from one variety to the next. This chapter will take account of the several principal renderings of retributivism, and will argue that none of them is adequate as a justificatory basis for the institution of capital punishment.

That conclusion about the inability of retributivism to justify the use of the death penalty is a proposition with which many proponents of retributivism would heartily agree. Indeed, as will become apparent, some of them adhere to the excessively strong view that retributivism and capital punishment are squarely incompatible. By contrast, this chapter will not maintain that the institution of capital punishment contravenes any tenets of retributivism. Rather, the problem that undermines a retributivistic justification of the death penalty is that any use of such a penalty for the realization of retributivistic ends is in violation of the Minimal Invasion Principle that was broached in Chapter 1.[1] Although the theses of retributivism do not themselves rule out the institution of capital punishment, they likewise do not *require* the introduction or retention of that institution. All the requirements laid down by the principles of retributivism can be fulfilled without any use of the death penalty. Consequently, given that the Minimal Invasion Principle provides that the pursuit of any public objective by a legal-governmental regime is morally illegitimate unless the regime employs the least severely invasive measures that are sufficient for the attainment of the specified objective, and given that the worthy purposes set forth in retributivistic conceptions of punishment are all realizable through the use of sanctions that are less severe than the death penalty, executions conducted on the basis of retributivistic principles are morally illegitimate.

---

[1] As should be clear, I am here invoking the Minimal Invasion Principle not as a tenet of retributivism but as an independently correct precept of political morality.

My discussion of retributivism will begin by considering briefly some central themes that run through most versions of the doctrine, and it will then delineate the most salient such versions. We shall proceed to ponder whether any of them can vindicate the practice of putting people to death for the commission of especially heinous crimes. Though the answer to that question will turn out to be negative (as has just been stated), some of the features of retributivism initially seem to point straightforwardly toward an affirmative answer. Hence, the target of this chapter's critique—retributivism as a rationale for the death penalty—is very far from being a straw man.

Even more plainly, retributivism as a general theory of punishment is no straw man. After having fallen into quite widespread disfavour during the first half of the twentieth century (Bedau 1978, 601–2; Berns 1979, 9; Braithwaite and Pettit 1990, 2; Davis 1972, 136; Dolinko 1991, 537; Dolinko 1992, 1623; Hampton 1992, 1659; Mabbott 1939, 152), that general theory has returned to rude health. Among philosophers and other scholars, retributivism with its deontological tenor now rivals the consequentialism of deterrence-oriented theories as the most influential contemporary approach to punishment; and among members of the public at large, the retributivistic ideals of desert and equality and moral responsibility resonate far-reachingly. Not only in the philosophical literature on punishment generally, but also in the philosophical literature more specifically on capital punishment, retributivistic positions have been espoused by many of the foremost theorists of criminal justice. Retributivism as a general theory of punishment has undergone some trenchant critiques (Bedau 1978; Dolinko 1991; Dolinko 1992; Shafer-Landau 1996; Shafer-Landau 2000), but the critiques have been undertaken precisely because that theory in its sundry forms has once again become such a potent presence in the thinking of philosophers about crime and punishment.

At any rate, although this chapter will expound most of the key ideas that inform retributivistic accounts of the purposes of punitive institutions generally, and although some of my critical remarks will cast doubt upon certain elaborations of those ideas, the chapter does not contest the merits of retributivism outside the context of debates over the death penalty. Only insofar as retributivistic theses are invoked in support of that penalty (or against it), do they come under attack herein. To be sure, when this chapter holds that retributivism is incapable of prescribing any exact degrees of severity that should mark a criminal-justice system's responses to wrongdoing, it will be pointing toward difficulties that extend beyond the specifics of capital punishment. All the same, given that my challenges to retributivism on that point would be endorsed by quite a few retributivists—who believe that their doctrine does not constitute a basis for prescribing any levels of punitive severity—the critique in this chapter should be understood as focused on a rationale for the death penalty rather than on a broader justification of punishment.

3.1. Some key themes

At a bare minimum, as we have seen intermittently in Chapter 2, retributivism maintains that nobody can ever legitimately be subjected to a punitive measure unless he or she has actually committed the type of wrong to which the prospect of such a measure has been attached in advance as a publicized sanction. Anthony Quinton among others has claimed that the defining tenet of retributivism is an insistence that 'it is necessary that a man be guilty if he is to be punished. . . . The essential contention of retributivism is that punishment is only justified by guilt' (Quinton 1954, 134). Construed along these modest lines, retributivism can serve as an array of side-constraints on the implications of other rationales for punishment.

Even when taken to be a fairly unambitious position of the sort just outlined, retributivism is plainly of considerable importance. Though retributivistic side-constraints cannot overcome all the weaknesses in the deterrence-oriented rationale for capital punishment, they can overcome or lessen some of those weaknesses (as we have beheld in Chapter 2). An insistence on the illegitimacy of any punishments in the absence of guilt is a significant moral advance over the preparedness of consequentialists to condone some executions of innocent people as morally permissible. Still, such an insistence on its own is manifestly insufficient to constitute a theory of punishment. For one thing, retributivism as a set of side-constraints is not sufficiently distinctive. It diverges of course from any consequentialist approach to punishment, but it is not distinguishable from other deontological accounts of punishment such as the purgative rationale for the death penalty. Hence, if retributivism is to be worthy of a separate chapter as a conception of punishment that is more than just an aspect of certain other such conceptions, it has to go beyond affirming that only the guilty can ever legitimately be subjected to punitive measures.

Moreover, the modest version of retributivism is too modest. Retributivism as a set of side-constraints that will limit punishment to the guilty is confined to playing a negative role. It cannot justify the imposition of any punishment; *a fortiori*, it cannot justify the imposition of the death penalty. Nor can it go any way toward indicating which types of conduct should be criminalized, or which types of punishments should be levied, or how severe those punishments should be. Indeed, retributivism as a mere set of side-constraints does not go the slightest way toward explaining why any punishments should ever be inflicted at all. Its only role consists in disallowing the subjection of innocent people to sanctions. Crucial though that role undoubtedly is, a full-blown theory of punishment must comprehend quite a bit more.

Fortunately for retributivists, they have in fact come up with an array of further ideas and concerns. Although the themes propounded by retributivists are developed by them in a number of different directions, some of those themes are common to nearly all of them. Perhaps most prominent among the common foci is the notion of desert.

3.1.1. Desert and moral responsibility

In its negative facet, of course, the notion of desert generates the side-constraints that we have just been pondering. It yields the conclusion that nobody can legitimately be punished unless he or she deserves such treatment by dint of having committed some misdeed(s) to which the threat of sanctions has been publicly attached. However, desert also plays a major positive role in the thinking of virtually all retributivists, who reason as follows. If some person deserves to be punished by virtue of having engaged in misconduct to which the threat of sanctions has been publicly attached by a morally worthy government, then, in the absence of special circumstances that would give rise to countervailing moral duties, the subjection of that person to punishment is morally legitimate. In the eyes of most retributivists, the subjection of that person to punishment is likewise morally obligatory (though the weight of the moral obligation is susceptible to being overtopped by the import of countervailing moral demands). For most retributivists, then, the property of desert serves not only to furnish *innocent* people with normative protection against the administration of sanctions but also—in the absence of special circumstances—to warrant the infliction of sanctions upon *guilty* people. Its positive role is that of a basis for appropriate impositions of punishments, even while its negative role is that of an array of side-constraints which forbid inappropriate impositions.

Desert is the chief component of the ideal of moral responsibility, which is central to just about every version of retributivism. When miscreants are punished for their violations of criminal-law mandates, they are being held responsible as agents for what they have done or omitted to do. In the absence of special circumstances, a failure to subject a miscreant to a sanction for such a violation is at odds with his moral responsibility and is thus at odds with the respect that is due to him as a moral agent. Of course, any typical malefactor who does elude apprehension and conviction will undoubtedly be delighted and will scarcely object to the fact that he has not been held responsible in accordance with his status as a rational agent. Nevertheless, that status is independent of his desires and of anyone else's desires. The incongruity between his nefarious actions and the absence of punitive consequences is demeaning to all his fellow citizens, since they should be interacting with him as an agent who is responsible for his conduct just as they are responsible for their conduct.

3.1.2. Human equality

This point about the interaction between evildoers and other human beings is directly connected to another central preoccupation of most retributivists: their emphasis on human equality. For most versions of retributivism, the essence of the wrong perpetrated by criminal conduct lies in the elevation of the criminal over his immediate victim(s) and over the public at large. As has already been indicated in Chapter 1, retributivists differ in the specific ways in which they cash out this general idea. We shall explore some of the principal variations in this chapter. However, the diversity of the affirmations of human equality should not obscure the extent to which the proponents of retributivism are at one in focusing on such equality.

According to those proponents, a crime disrupts the fabric of a society through the illegitimate self-indulgence of a criminal and through the consequent degradation of any direct victim(s) and of the society as a whole. Punishment inflicted upon the wrongdoer is essential for the restoration of a relationship of equality between him and others in his community, including of course his direct victim(s). It offsets the unfair advantage that he has gained over his fellows, and it vindicates the status of any victim as a right-holding agent who cannot permissibly be treated only as a means by anybody else. It likewise upholds the dispositive role of a society's legal-governmental institutions in determining authoritatively which types of conduct are to be eschewed by everyone within the society's ambit.

This emphasis on equality reveals that retributivism is tenable as a general theory of punishment only in application to some societies. If any of the legal mandates backed by criminal sanctions in some society are iniquitous—either because of what they require *in abstracto* or because of their tendency to sustain conditions of evil oppression on the level of concrete results—then many breaches of those mandates will not contravene the value of human equality in any morally problematic way. When somebody abstains from behaving abominably despite being legally required to behave in such a fashion, his conduct might well promote the realization of the value of human equality rather than detract therefrom. Thus, if we are to take seriously the retributivistic insistence on the value of human equality as a basis for the infliction of punishments, and if we are to conclude that that basis is comprehensively rather than very selectively operative within each jurisdiction where it prevails, we have to assume that any society to which the retributivistic conception of punishment applies is governed by a liberal-democratic regime with legal requirements that are morally legitimate.

Such a limitation on the scope of retributivism's justificatory force is not in itself problematic. After all, as has been remarked in Chapter 1 (and as will be explained more amply in Chapter 6), my purgative rationale for capital punishment is likewise tenable only in application to societies governed by liberal-democratic regimes. Moreover, like the purgative rationale for the death penalty, the retributivistic rationale for punishment can gain a purchase on societies that are governed by regimes which are imperfect in some respects. So long as a system of governance is sufficiently robust in its adherence to liberal-democratic ideals—even if it falls short in regard to some of those ideals, as does any such system in the actual world and in every credibly possible world—the community over which it presides can be a genuine moral community in which the value of human equality meaningfully reigns. Thus, the prominence of that value in the thinking of most retributivists does not mean that retributivism is a theory too fanciful or demanding to be of any relevance in a world where every society is marked by significant inequalities.[2]

3.1.3. Commensurateness, proportionality, and *lex talionis*

Central to most varieties of retributivism are some aspects or offshoots of the property of desert. Some retributivists perceive desert not only as a property that warrants the imposition of punitive measures, but additionally as a property that calls for those measures to be of certain types or to be at certain levels of severity.

3.1.3.1. Commensurateness

One requirement which many retributivists associate with desert is that of commensurateness. They contend that the appropriateness of any given punishment depends on its being commensurate in severity with the seriousness of the crime for which it is imposed. To be morally legitimate, a punishment—in the absence of special circumstances—must be condign in the sense that its burdensomeness fits the gravity of the situation that has been brought about by somebody's wrongdoing. If a sanction is too severe or too lenient for the crime in response to which it is levied, it will have failed to satisfy the requirement of commensurateness or fittingness. It will thus have failed to impose upon the offender the degree of hardship that he or she deserves.

3.1.3.2. Proportionality

Although the term 'proportionality' is often used to cover the property of commensurateness as well as the distinct though overlapping property that will here be designated by that term,[3] the two characteristics should not be run together. Neither of them is reducible to the other, and neither of them is entailed by the other. Whereas commensurateness is a cardinal phenomenon, proportionality is an ordinal phenomenon (Bedau 1978, 613; Dolinko 1986, 594 n 241; Dolinko 1992, 1636; Dolinko 1994, 506–10; Finkelstein 2002, 13; Gardner 1978, 1183–84; Nathanson 2001, 75–7; Reiman 1998, 72; Scheid 1995, 399–400; Schwarzschild 2002, 9; Shafer-Landau 1996, 307–8;

---

[2] Some philosophers have maintained that the limitations on the scope of retributivism's justificatory force are due to the emphasis of retributivists on desert and moral responsibility. See, for example, Murphy 1973, 231–43; Reiman 1985, 131–3; Reiman 1998, 125–8. Compare Weiler 1978, 316–18. As will become clear in Chapter 6's discussion of circumstances that can extenuate the gravity of heinous crimes, such a view of moral responsibility is highly problematic. Much more straightforward and solidly defensible is the proposition that the egalitarian tenor of the retributivistic justification for punishment confines the reach of that justification to liberal-democratic societies. Only in such societies has the ideal of human equality been significantly realized.

[3] See, for example, Bedau 1978, 603; Bedau 1985, 912, 914 n 128; Burgh 1982, 197–8; Davis 1996, 35; Dolinko 1994, 523 n 114; Edmundson 2002; Feinberg 1970, 116–17; Fish 2008; Gale 1985, 1011–12, 1015–16, 1020–1; Hampton 1998, 39; Hood 2009, 20; Kaplow and Shavell 2002, 301–3; Pearl 1982, 275 n 18; Pojman 1998, 19–20; Primorac 1982, 137; Primoratz 1989a, *passim*; Ridge 2004; Sorell 1987, 147; Von Hirsch 1978, 622; Waldron 1992, 47.

Shafer-Landau 2000, 201–2, 206; Tasioulas 2006, 292, 303; Van den Haag 1985b, 961, 962; Van den Haag and Conrad 1983, 38).

Proportionality as understood here has been briefly discussed in Chapter 2, in § 2.4.2.2.1. It obtains when the levels of severity of the punishments imposed by a legal-governmental system are aligned with the levels of seriousness of the crimes for which the punishments are inflicted, such that increases in the latter levels are always associated with increases in the former levels. The more serious a crime, the more severe the sanction that is imposed under a retributivistic schedule of punishments which meets the requirement of proportionality.

As has been stated, proportionality and commensurateness are to be kept distinct. The former property pertains to the comparative severity of punishments, whereas the latter property pertains to the absolute severity of each punishment. Sanctions can satisfy the requirement of proportionality without satisfying the requirement of commensurateness, and vice versa. The fact that compliance with the former requirement does not entail compliance with the latter is especially plain. If the bottom end of the scale of penalties in some criminal-justice system is too low, or if the top end is too high, then all the penalties can be arrayed in conformity to the requirement of proportionality while not a single one of them conforms to the requirement of commensurateness. Moreover, even if some of the punishments in the scale happen to meet that latter requirement, the remaining punishments can fail to meet it; their being arranged proportionately is hardly a guarantee that each of them will be commensurate in severity with the seriousness of the crime to which it is attached.

Perhaps less evident is that a criminal-justice system's conformity to the requirement of commensurateness does not guarantee its conformity to the requirement of proportionality. If we know that every sanction in such a system is commensurate in severity with the seriousness of the crime for which it is levied, we might be tempted to conclude that all the sanctions must be arranged in an order that exhibits strict proportionality. Such a conclusion, however, would be too quick. On the one hand, if the principle of commensurateness in application to each crime could single out a precise level of punitive severity as the only such level that is appropriate for that crime, and if there were no overall lower limit or upper limit of severity within the principle of commensurateness itself, then the satisfaction of such a principle would indeed entail the satisfaction of the principle of proportionality. On the other hand, the first of the two antecedents in the preceding sentence is plainly false, and the second antecedent is probably also false. Hence, we cannot detach the consequent.[4]

Quite untenable is the notion that one precise level of punitive severity is uniquely appropriate for any particular crime or for any type of crime. What the principle of commensurateness establishes is that a legitimate sanction for any particular crime

---

[4] In a conditional statement—a statement with the form 'If X, then Y'—the 'If X' clause is the antecedent, and the 'then Y' clause is the consequent. Detaching the consequent consists in drawing the conclusion 'Y' from the following two premises: 'If X, then Y' and 'X.'

or any type of crime must lie within some range of levels of severity (the upper and lower ends of which cannot be specified precisely). As a prominent contemporary retributivist has remarked: '[P]enalties must be chosen by the judge from a range. There is no...rationally determinable and uniquely appropriate penalty to fit the crime. Punishment is the [Thomist] tradition's stock example of the need for *determinatio*, a process of choosing freely from a range of reasonable options none of which is simply rationally superior to the others' (Finnis 1999, 103). The ranges of the apposite punishments for some crimes will overlap with those for other crimes that are more serious or less serious. Consequently, in a scheme of punishments that fully complies with the requirement of commensurateness, there can be some departures from the requirement of proportionality.

Moreover, the principle of commensurateness itself might well include an overall lower limit or upper limit of severity. That is, it might deem some range of very gentle sanctions to be appropriate for any crime beneath some low level of seriousness, or it might deem some range of very harsh sanctions to be appropriate for any crime above some high level of seriousness. If there is such an overall lower limit or upper limit within the principle of commensurateness, then once again the full satisfaction of that principle does not entail the full satisfaction of the principle of proportionality.

Before moving on, we should note that the requirement of proportionality is not unique to retributivism. Although some philosophers tend to write as if retributivism were the only account of punishment that calls for proportionality in the assignment of sanctions (Scheid 1995, 379), we have already seen in Chapter 2 that deterrence-oriented theories of punishment are similar to retributivism in that respect. As will become apparent in the next two chapters, the incapacitative and denunciatory rationales for punishment likewise generally require proportionality in the fixing of sanctions for various crimes. To be sure, the retributivistic basis for the requirement of proportionality differs from the bases for such a requirement in these other standard accounts of punishment. Theories that focus on deterrence or incapacitation or denunciation are consequentialist in their orientation, whereas retributivism in its primary form is deontological. Consequentialist theories that generally call for proportionality in the arranging of punishments will countenance departures therefrom whenever such departures are foreseeably serviceable for the realization of the ends upheld by those theories. By contrast, retributivism's insistence on proportionality is not similarly swayed by consequentialist considerations. Still, notwithstanding that that retributivistic insistence is oriented toward desert rather than toward consequences, and notwithstanding that it is therefore impervious to the consequentialist winds that buffet the other prevailing theories of punishment, it is paralleled by demands for proportionality—on alternative grounds—in those other theories. (Of course, one theory that does not involve any requirement of proportionality is this book's purgative rationale for the death penalty. Such a rationale is not a general account of punishment, but is instead a justification for only one type of sanction.

Accordingly, the issue of proportionally aligning punishments and crimes does not arise for the purgative rationale.)

3.1.3.3. *Lex talionis*

A doctrine commonly associated with retributivism by its opponents—and by some of its supporters[5]—is the *lex talionis*, which prescribes that like should be returned for like in any proper punitive response to wrongdoing (Bedau 1978, 611; Bedau 2002, 7; Dolinko 1986, 595; Finkelstein 2002, 13; Fish 2008; Gale 1985, 1012; Gerstein 1974, 78; Jones and Potter 1981, 165–7; Kaplow and Shavell 2002, 302–3, 306–7; Logan 2002, 1369; McCord 1998, 122; Mitias 1983; Murphy 1971, 166–7, 168; Oldenquist 2004, 335; Pearl 1982, 273, 275; Posner 1981, 208; Primorac 1982, 137–38; Primoratz 1989a, 12, 79–81, 85–94, 158–9; Pugsley 1981, 1514–16; Reiman 1985; Reiman 1998; Rubin 2003, 27–8; Shafer-Landau 1996, 299–301; Shafer-Landau 2000, 193–8; Symposium 2003, 153 [remarks by William Erlbaum]; Van den Haag and Conrad 1983, 22–4, 33, 38; Wilson and Herrnstein 1985, 496–7). Formulations of the *lex talionis* principle often resort to Biblical 'eye for an eye' language, but that wording tends to be more misleading than illuminating. It frequently elicits derision, as critics query whether such a principle demands that rapists be raped or that arsonists' houses be burned or that serial murderers be executed repeatedly or that blackmailers be subjected to blackmail. Proponents of the *lex talionis* principle are much better advised to employ the 'like for like' phraseology.

Most philosophers who write on these matters have construed the *lex talionis* as a quantitative principle, under which the severity of a punishment must be equivalent in degree to the seriousness of the crime for which the punishment is imposed. In other words, these philosophers have taken the *lex talionis* to be an especially demanding—and wooden—version of the principle of commensurateness. However, in an important article to which we shall return later in this chapter, Jeremy Waldron has persuasively submitted that the requirement laid down by the *lex talionis* principle is best understood as quite different from the requirements of commensurateness and proportionality (Waldron 1992). The *lex talionis* is fundamentally qualitative rather than quantitative. Its 'like for like' instruction indicates not that the magnitude of a crime's seriousness should be matched by the magnitude of a sanction's severity, but instead that the wrong-making features of a crime should be countered with a punitive response that partakes of cognate features. Like the requirements of commensurateness and proportionality, the *lex talionis* principle derives from the egalitarian impetus of retributivism (in ways that will be explored later). Unlike those requirements, however, the *lex talionis* is concerned with qualitative homologies rather than with quantitative equivalences. Elaborated in this fashion, the *lex talionis* is a far more robust principle than most philosophers have allowed. Nevertheless, as

---

[5] Some other supporters of retributivism have, for various reasons, disavowed the *lex talionis* as a principle of punishment. See, for example, Davis 1986; Davis 1991, 526–9; Hampton 1991, 406–9; Hampton 1992, 1690–1; Markel 2005, 412–13, 475–6; Markel 2009, 1204; Pugsley 1981, 1520 n 91; Van den Haag 1985a, 167; Van den Haag 1985b, 970; Van den Haag 1986, 1666–7. See also Moore 1995, 632.

we shall see—and as Waldron himself would agree—it cannot suffice to vindicate the use of capital punishment.

This brief preliminary discussion of the *lex talionis* should conclude by reiterating a point that was made in Chapter 1. Retributivism is often thought to be a doctrine of vengeance,[6] especially when it is associated with the *lex talionis*. Such a view of retributivism is mistaken, however, even though it is occasionally propounded by retributivists themselves. As Hugo Adam Bedau rightly remarks: '"Revenge" and "retribution" are not synonyms, nor is the latter merely a euphemism for the former.'[7] Retributivistic punishments qua retributivistic punishments, whether guided by the *lex talionis* or by the ideals of commensurateness and proportionality, are never grounded on feelings of hatred or vindictiveness. They are based instead on considerations of human equality and moral responsibility and human dignity (the moral responsibility of the perpetrators of crimes and the human dignity of their victims and of other people in their communities). Such punishments reaffirm the fundamental equality of all human beings, and hold the people in any jurisdiction accountable to their community in the event of their having acted athwart that equality. Far from giving vent to passions of furious animosity in a quest to 'get even', retributivistic sanctions aim to restore the patterns of human interaction that obtain when the ideal of equal dignity is upheld throughout a community. Any such sanction indeed expresses the perspective of the whole community, rather than solely or especially the perspective of an aggrieved person who has been directly wronged by criminal conduct. In that respect as in several others, retributivistic sanctions differ from acts of vengeance.

3.1.4. Punishment as communication

In many versions of retributivism, the communicative dimension of punishment is a central concern (Duff 2000; Feinberg 1970, 95–118; Hampton 1991; Hampton 1992; Markel 2005; Markel 2009; Matravers 1999; Primoratz 1989b; Tasioulas 2004, 114–15; Tasioulas 2006; Von Hirsch 1994). Especially in the vindicatory variety of retributivism that will be examined later in this chapter, a key role of the imposition of sanctions is to communicate to wrongdoers (and secondarily to the public at large) an affirmation of the dignity and equality of the wrongdoers' victims and of the wrongdoers'

---

[6] See, for example, Abernethy 1996, 423–4; Allen and Shavell 2005, 628–9; Berns 1979, 38–40; Braithwaite and Pettit 1990, 2, 5–7; Gardner 1978, 1177–8; Lempert 1981, 1185–7; Logan 2002, 1346–7; Massaro 1991, 1891–3; Menninger 1968, 204–6; Murphy 1991; Oldenquist 2004, 339–40; Pearl 1982, 273; Posner 1981, ch 8; Reiman 1985, 122 n 12, 125–6; Rubin 2003, 27–30, 40–1, 46–8; Symposium 2003, 157, 158–9 n 192 (remarks by William Erlbaum); Whitman 2003, 93–5; Wilson and Herrnstein 1985, 498.

[7] Bedau 1999, 49. For some other writings that distinguish between retribution and revenge, see Bradley 1999, 113–14; Davis 1972, 140; Dressler 1990, 1461–2; Finnis 1999, 102–3; Gardner 1978, 1183, 1184; Gerstein 1974, 76; Hampton 1991, 413–14; Hampton 1992, 1691; Hampton 1998, 39; Markel 2005, 410–11, 414, 424, 437–8, 462; Markel 2009, 1179–81, 1190–1; Moore 1995, 632–3, 638–52; Moore 1999, 67, 75–6; Nozick 1981, 366–70; Pojman 1998, 21; Pugsley 1981, 1514; Sorell 1987, 42–4; Tasioulas 2006, 296; Van den Haag 1990, 506, 507–8.

fellow citizens more broadly. Those values of dignity and equality, which have been implicitly or explicitly denied by criminals through their misconduct, are directly upheld by the subjection of the criminals to penalties. Consequently, the penalties communicate to those lawbreakers the norms of proper conduct which their misdeeds have flouted. Whether or not any particular offender accepts the message that is conveyed to him through the punitive measures that are inflicted upon him, the censorious message—underscoring the fact that he is neither fundamentally better nor fundamentally worse than his fellow human beings—will have been sent. The very communication of that reprobative message through the medium of punishment, to an offender capable of understanding it, will have rectified the wrong for which the punishment is imposed. Retributivism in its primary form is a deontological theory that prescribes such communication (and rectification) as an end that is morally worthy and imperative even if it does not yield any further salutary consequences. As Dan Markel writes: 'Retributive justice is thus understood as the good achieved by the use of the state's coercive power to communicate certain ideals to an offender convincingly determined to have breached a legitimate legal norm.' He later declares: 'The state's coercive measures communicate the norm of equal liberty under the law and they are directed to the person most in need of hearing it: the offender. This [retributivistic] theory reveals in part, then, how the practice of punishment is intelligible and attractive, apart from the other beneficial consequences that may contingently arise from its practice.'[8]

Still, albeit the communication of censure that reaffirms the basic equality of all the members of a community is a worthy end in itself, the communication achieves an additional morally valuable end if it generates an improvement in a particular offender's moral outlook. Thus, although retributivism is not to be confused with a consequentialist theory that posits the reformation of offenders as the guiding basis of punishment, the full fruition of the communications conveyed by retributivistic punishments does hinge on the occurrence of reformative improvements. In that regard, retributivism includes an ancillary reformative component. On the one hand, retributivistic sanctions can on their own terms be fully justified even if they do not elicit any improvements in the outlooks of the criminals on whom they are inflicted. Under the retributivistic rationale for punishment, a high likelihood of reformative success is not a necessary condition for the legitimacy of the imposition of any particular sanction. On the other hand, such success enhances the moral value of the reprobative message conveyed by any sanction. When the communication of that message through the levying of a punishment does induce a criminal to accept the principles of human dignity and equality which he has thitherto slighted, the message takes effect in the mind of the person to whom it is primarily addressed. An outcome of

---

[8] Markel 2005, 411, 432. Though Markel makes these points well, the deontological cast of his own version of retributivism is in fact ultimately embedded in a consequentialist framework. He is one of the retributivists to whom I have referred in note 6 of Chapter 1. I briefly criticize the consequentialist bearings of his theory later in this chapter (in § 3.3.2.1).

that sort is of great moral worth, even though neither its occurrence nor the likeli-hood of its occurrence is a necessary condition for the legitimacy of a retributivistic punitive measure. Any such measure does aim for an offender's internalization of the aforementioned principles, notwithstanding that the communication of an insistence on those principles is itself sufficient to justify the measure.[9]

3.2. Versions of retributivism

Though not all retributivists endorse every one of the themes summarized so far, those themes do figure saliently in most versions of the retributivistic account of punishment. Divisions emerge when the themes are fleshed out. The present sec-tion recounts the two principal renderings of retributivism that have been promi-nent in recent decades. However, nobody should infer that there is some tidy bifurcation in the ranks of retributivists. As will become plain, each side of the bifurcation is itself multifarious. Moreover, a theorist's allegiance to one side of the divide does not rule out his also being positioned on the other side. Because the differences between the two camps are largely matters of contrasting emphases, the ideas developed in either camp can be combined pretty straightforwardly with those developed in the other.

3.2.1. Desert-focused retributivism

Nearly every theory that can correctly be classified as a specimen of retributivism is concerned with the negative deserts of people who have engaged in wrongdoing. Here, however, the epithet 'desert-focused' will be reserved for retributivistic theo-ries that devote attention chiefly to the ways in which any malefactors gain through their self-indulgent noncompliance with the legitimate criminal-law mandates of their community. Precisely because a miscreant elevates himself above his fellows and his community when he contravenes just legal requirements in order to satisfy his own impulses and desires, the administration of punishment is necessary to offset the unfair advantage that he has seized. By offsetting that advantage, the punishment reasserts the ideal of human equality which the wrongdoer has implicitly or explic-itly denied through his transgression(s). In two respects, the imposition of a sanction brings the offender down to his proper level vis-à-vis the others in his society. First, by subjecting him to material hardships such as the loss of most of his freedoms, it serves in palpable ways to lessen the amenity of his everyday life. Secondly, it symbol-izes the downfall of his effort to place himself above his fellows through his indul-gence of his urges while most other people were exercising proper self-restraint, and it thereby conveys to him the impertinence of that effort. Both materially and com-municatively, then, a suitable punishment counteracts the disruption of fair social

---

[9] As will be seen, this ancillary reformative aspect of retributivism has sometimes been invoked against the proposition that capital punishment is consistent with retributivistic tenets.

relations that has been brought about by an offender's misdeed(s). It 'is the healing of a disorder—precisely an unjust inequality—introduced into a whole community by the wrongdoer's criminal choice and action' (Finnis 1999, 97).

Proponents of this version of retributivism have to specify the nature of the unjust inequality that has been generated by a criminal's misconduct. That is, they have to specify the nature of the unjust gain that has accrued to any wrongdoer simply by dint of his having acted athwart the terms of a morally worthy criminal-law mandate. Clearly, the relevant gain does not consist in one or more of the desiderata that can contingently be acquired through criminal endeavours, such as money or power or land or sexual gratification. Though many instances of criminal activity do endow their perpetrators with such goods, many other instances do not. (Consider, for example, bank robbers who have to abandon their loot as they begin to flee the scene of their dastardly venture.) Likewise, the relevant gain does not consist in feelings of pleasure or satisfaction resulting from the performance of a misdeed. Though many instances of criminal activity do elicit such feelings in their perpetrators, many other instances do not. Desert-focused retributivism aspires to offer a comprehensively applicable account of the grounds for inflicting punishments upon criminals within a liberal-democratic society; that aspiration will obviously go unfulfilled if the grounds adduced are in fact applicable to only some crimes. Hence, desert-focused retributivists who strive for comprehensiveness will need to look beyond the sorts of goods and feelings mentioned above—and so they have.

3.2.1.1. Freedom as the unjust gain?

Most problematic is the suggestion that the unjust gain accruing to every criminal resides in the inordinate freedom which he arrogates to himself through his law-breaking conduct. This line of thought has been most sustainedly developed by George Sher (1987, 74–90), but it has also won varying degrees of adherence from some other writers (Bradley 1999; Duff 1990, 16–17; Finnis 1972, 132; Finnis 1999, 98–9, 101; Markel 2005, 430; Markel 2009, 1186–7; Von Hirsch 1990, 266, 268). Even Russ Shafer-Landau, who objects to the line of thought, has acquiesced in certain key aspects of it.[10] Nonetheless, we should reject altogether the proposition that every violation of a criminal-law mandate bestows upon its perpetrator a quantum of extra freedom.

Sher takes as his point of departure a celebrated essay by Herbert Morris which is in many respects the fountainhead of modern desert-focused retributivism (Morris 1968). Under Morris's account of punishment, every criminal is said to have

---

[10]   Shafer-Landau 1996, 293, 302–3; Shafer-Landau 2000, 206. Much the same is true of Murphy 1994, 291. Likewise, Richard Burgh, who takes exception to desert-focused retributivism, nonetheless commits Sher's error in the second of the following two sentences: 'According to [Jeffrie] Murphy, the benefit received [by any criminal] is the renouncing of the burden of self-restraint, which a violation of the law entails. I take it that this is a benefit, because the offender now has a bit more freedom than those who undertook the burden of obeying the law' (Burgh 1982, 209).

gained an unfair advantage over others by violating some legal requirement(s) within a network of such requirements that are collectively beneficial for everyone. Seeking to build upon this account, Sher has to pin down the nature of the unfair advantage that is said to be conferred by every criminal course of conduct. He submits that that unfair advantage can best be explicated along the following lines: '[A] person who acts wrongly does gain a significant measure of extra liberty: what he gains is freedom from the demands of the prohibition he violates. Because others take that prohibition seriously, they lack a similar liberty. And as the strength of the prohibition increases, so too does the freedom from it which its violation entails.' Sher slightly later repeats his view that 'the most plausible way of understanding [a wrongdoer's unfair extra benefit] is as an extra measure of freedom from moral restraint,' and that a 'wrong-doer [through his misconduct] has unfairly gained an extra measure of freedom from moral restraint' (Sher 1987, 82, 83, 84).

These statements by Sher are unsustainable.[11] Under any tenable conception of freedom, it is not the case that someone who transgresses a legal mandate has thereby acquired freedom from its demands. Were Sher correct, then no violation of a law would ever be a violation, since a wrongdoer would become free of a law's require-ments precisely by virtue of having flouted those requirements. Only because a law-breaker does *not* become free of the demands of a legal mandate when he contravenes them, is his contravention classifiable as such. As David Dolinko pungently observes, 'there would be no basis for deciding to punish the wrongdoer if his criminal act had somehow repealed the prohibition it is alleged to violate' (Dolinko 1991, 548).

Sher does not improve his position when he focuses his remarks on moral restraints. Indeed, he worsens his position, for he appears to be relying on an assumption that will be briefly challenged later in this chapter: namely, the assumption that every-body in a society governed by a reasonably just regime is always under a prima facie moral obligation to comply with the terms of each of the morally justified legal man-dates introduced or retained by that regime. At any rate, the chief weakness that besets Sher's argument in application to moral constraints is the same as the weak-ness that besets the argument in application directly to legal mandates. No defensible conception of freedom would support the claim that someone who breaches a moral restriction has thereby freed herself from that restriction or from any other moral requirement. On the contrary, her breach is a breach exactly because she remains sub-ject to the violated restriction before, during, and after the occurrence of the viola-tion. If Sher's position were correct, then anyone could come to be free from a moral requirement simply by transgressing it, and thus no transgression would ever count as such (since the sheer fact of its having happened would negate its status as a con-

---

[11] My criticisms of Sher are prefigured by those in Dolinko 1991, 546–8 and in Dolinko 1994, 499–500. (In the latter work, the immediate target of Dolinko's censure is Michael Davis rather than Sher.) Dolinko's objections to Sher's analysis are recounted—but neither endorsed nor repudiated—in Davis 1996, 259.

travention). By murdering some person, anyone could liberate herself from a moral constraint against murdering that person.

The startling implications of Sher's analysis reveal the unsustainability of that analysis. Instead of becoming free from a moral restraint by doing what it forbids, an offender remains subject to that restraint, and she also incurs further moral obligations to remedy the wrong that she has perpetrated. Morally, her overall liberty is lower than before. Hence, the notion that a criminal gains an extra quantum of moral liberty whenever she commits an offence is very far indeed from the truth.

Sher cannot rescue his position by switching to a focus on physical freedom in contrast with deontic freedom.[12] That is, he cannot vindicate his analysis by concentrating on unpreventedness or abilities rather than on permissibility. Suppose that he were to be understood as claiming that a criminal always becomes physically free (that is, physically able) to commit an offense by dint of committing it, and that a criminal thereby acquires something which her law-abiding fellow citizens lack. Both of the theses in this revised claim are false.

Except in special cases, a miscreant who engages in a criminal act at some time t was physically free before t to engage in the specified act at t. Hence, the performance of a misdeed is not typically what endows a miscreant with the physical freedom to perform it; the performance is not typically what removes any physical obstacles to its own occurrence, since those obstacles were already absent. Accordingly, the first thesis in the revised claim posited above—the thesis that a criminal always becomes physically free to commit an offence by dint of committing it—is false.

Also false is the second thesis, and not only because of the falsity of the first thesis. Quite a few people in any society are physically free to engage in numerous modes of conduct that are criminally proscribed therein (even if they might be apprehended pretty quickly thereafter). Some people would of course be more adept than others at performing any of those modes of conduct, but it is certainly not the case that the only people able to perform any of them are the criminals who actually do so. People possess countless physical freedoms—including freedoms to carry out criminally forbidden acts—which they decline to exercise. Thus, the fact that a criminal has been physically free to commit a misdeed of some kind is typically not anything that sets her apart from most of the people in her society who do not commit any such misdeed.[13]

Defenders of Sher might contend that the physical liberty newly acquired by any wrongdoer is not the liberty to perpetrate the crime which she actually does

---

[12] 'Physical' is not here contrasted with 'mental' or 'psychological'. Rather, the sole contrast is with 'deontic' or 'normative'. Someone is not physically free to φ unless she is psychologically capable of φ-ing. On the distinction between physical freedom (including psychological freedom) and deontic freedom, see Kramer 2003, 60–75.

[13] The points in this paragraph and the preceding paragraph are missed by Don Scheid when he writes as follows: 'By breaking the law, [a criminal] makes for himself opportunities not available to law-abiding persons....[B]reaking a rule against embezzlement might create an opportunity for gaining an enormous sum of money, while breaking a law against jaywalking only creates the opportunity for realizing a very minor convenience of saving a few minutes' walking time' (Scheid 1995, 393–4).

perpetrate, but instead some further physical freedom that is engendered by the wrongdoer's exercise of her liberty to carry out the aforementioned crime. Such a retort would be misguided in two respects. First, the acquisition of some further physical liberty through the commission of a criminal misdeed is contingent rather than inevitable. For example, if Joe commits assault and battery against Julia and is then forcibly apprehended straightaway, he will have lost many of his erstwhile freedoms and will not have gained any additional freedoms. Secondly, even when a criminal does acquire some additional freedom-to-φ through his criminal misconduct, numerous law-abiding people in his society might also possess the freedom to φ. For instance, if Bruno kills his wife in order to be able to watch a football game on television in peace, the newly acquired freedom-to-watch-the-football-game-in-peace is something that he shares with any number of law-abiding people in his society. Thus, if defenders of Sher were to engage in the manoeuvre suggested at the outset of this paragraph, they would be failing to specify a way in which every criminal vests herself with some liberty that is not enjoyed by her law-abiding fellow citizens.

Defenders of Sher might try instead to shift the focus from a criminal's particular liberties to her overall liberty. That is, instead of maintaining that every criminal acquires some new freedom-to-φ as a result of indulging in misconduct, those defenders might submit that every criminal undergoes an increase in her overall liberty through her misconduct. Any such rejoinder, however, would be a non-starter. After all, there is no guarantee that a criminal will have acquired any new physical freedom-to-φ whatsoever as a result of carrying out this or that crime. Under some theories of freedom (such as that espoused in Steiner 1983), the absence of such a guarantee is itself sufficient to negate any guarantee of an increase in a criminal's overall liberty. Admittedly, under the theory of freedom for which I myself have argued at length elsewhere (Kramer 2003), the absence of a guarantee of the former type is per se not quite sufficient to preclude the existence of a guarantee of the latter type—because, under my theory, an increase in a person's overall freedom can be attributable to the replacement of an instance of unfreedom by a mere inability. In other words, somebody may have become freer overall if a particular inability of hers is no longer due to some action(s) or disposition(s) of some other person(s) but is now due decisively to natural limitations. Nevertheless, the notion that every perpetrator of a crime undergoes that sort of increase in her overall liberty by virtue of indulging in her criminal misconduct is fanciful. The occurrence of such an increase will be rare rather than inevitable. Consequently, an attempt to salvage Sher's argument by construing it as focused on every culprit's *overall* physical freedom—rather than on any *particular* physical freedom(s) of each culprit—will prove unavailing. Sher's argument does not withstand scrutiny when it is assessed in the light of any credible account of liberty.

3.2.1.2 The price of a licence

Michael Davis has been a prominent and astute exponent of desert-focused retributivism since the early 1980s. He has developed a piquant thought-experiment in an
attempt to pin down the nature and extent of the unfair advantage that is gained by
every criminal through his or her misconduct (Davis 1983, 743–5; Davis 1986, 258–60;
Davis 1991, 530–1; Davis 1996, 257–80). However commendably thought-provoking
Davis's exposition of the nature and extent of that unfair advantage may be, it is deeply
flawed—both in itself and in its relationship with another scheme proposed by Davis
for the assignment of punishments to crimes. On a number of points, my queries about
his analysis are broadly in line with those of several previous critics (Dolinko 1994;
Duff 1990, 3–17; Reiman 1998, 75–6, 85–6; Ridge 2004; Scheid 1990; Scheid 1995;
Shafer-Landau 1996, 303–4; Shafer-Landau 2000, 206–7; Von Hirsch 1990, 265–8).

Davis envisages an auction in which people can bid for licences to commit various crimes with impunity. The number of licences for each type of crime is limited
to reflect the exigencies of social cohesion. Because the especially serious crimes are
more disruptive of such cohesion than are crimes that are less serious, the licences for
each of the former kinds of crimes will generally be fewer than those for each of the latter kinds. 'The more serious the crime, the fewer the social order can tolerate, all else
equal' (Davis 1983, 744). People can submit bids for licences either because they wish
to commit the specified crimes or because they wish to lower the incidence of those
crimes by buying up the licences. When all the bids are in, the licences for each type of
crime will have been sold at a price that can be used as a benchmark for the assignment
of penalties to offences. 'A penalty is a fair price [for the commission of a crime] only if
it corresponds to what a license to do that crime would fetch on the open market.' Davis
makes clear that the correspondence to which he here refers is a matter of proportionality rather than of commensurateness: 'The correspondence is not equality but homol-
ogy, a relative correspondence. There is, after all, no decisive reason that the society
should choose this or that minimum of social order; nor is there any privileged rule for
converting dollars into years in prison, lashes of the whip, or the like' (Davis 1983, 745).

3.2.1.2.1. A first query

One major weakness in Davis's scenario of the auction is that it has to be supplemented
with some extremely dubious assumptions in order to shield it against sundry telling
objections. For example, in response to queries about the commission of unlicensed
crimes, Davis has to assume either that all such crimes will be punished in the same way
or that no unlicensed crimes of any sort will occur (Davis 1996, 272, 279 n 27). He disconcertingly explains his assumptions as follows: 'The point of the assumptions defining the market is to filter out irrelevant factors. If an argument [by a critic] reveals an
irrelevant factor, then I will try to filter it out' (Davis 1996, 278 n 27). When Davis fends
off objections to his model by amplifying it with outlandish assumptions, his claim that

the objections are concerned with 'irrelevant factors' is hardly reassuring. As Dolinko acridly retorts: 'Avoiding the punishment one would receive for an unlicensed crime is plainly the most important reason for buying a crime-licence in the first place. How, then, can Davis treat the differing punishments for unlicensed crimes as mere irrelevancies to be swept away by fiat?' (Dolinko 1994, 504–5, footnote omitted.)

3.2.1.2.2.   A second query

Another major weakness in the scenario of the auction is that the rankings generated by it do not coincide with any plausible scale of the seriousness of crimes. Davis somewhat blithely asserts that 'the demand for licenses is likely to increase with the seriousness of the crime'. In parentheses he adds: 'If that seems unlikely given moral constraints on potential buyers, ask yourself whether you would prefer to have a license to steal or a license to jaywalk' (Davis 1983, 744). Even if we were to accept these assertions by Davis entirely on their own terms, we would be well advised to note that they advert only to a likelihood rather than to any firmer correlation between the prices of the licences and the seriousness of the crimes. What is more, the assertions are not in fact convincing. Consider, for example, instances of murder that involve cannibalism. Such crimes are more serious than ordinary murders, and *a fortiori* they are more serious than acts of grand larceny. Yet the demand for licences to commit grand larceny will be far, far higher than the demand for licences to commit murders that involve cannibalism. Thus, even if the latter licences are substantially fewer in number than are the former, the strong likelihood is that the price for each of the licences to commit cannibalistic murder will be lower than the price for each of the licences to commit grand larceny. Accordingly, Davis has saddled himself with the conclusion that the punitive measures imposed for cannibalistic murder should be gentler than the punitive measures imposed for grand larceny.

Davis has saddled himself with a similar conclusion concerning cannibalistic murder versus ordinary murder. (I am assuming that a licence to commit cannibalistic murder cannot be employed to gain exemption from punishment for an act of murder that does not involve the perpetrator's consumption of the flesh of the victim.) Although the demand for licences to commit ordinary murder might be somewhat lower than the demand for licences to commit grand larceny, it will still be far higher than the demand for licences to commit cannibalistic murder. Moreover, the disparity between the number of licences to commit cannibalistic murder and the number of licences to commit ordinary murder will be significantly narrower than the disparity between the former number and the number of licences to commit grand larceny. Consequently, the strong likelihood is that the price for each of the licences to commit ordinary murder will be higher than the price for each of the licences to commit cannibalistic murder. Davis's version of retributivism thus has to call for the imposition of stiffer penalties in response to each instance of the former crime than in response to each instance of the latter.

The rankings that would emerge from Davis's auction are rendered problematic in further ways by the influence of factors that can weaken the correlations between the prices of licences and the seriousness of crimes. To discern a principal example of those factors, we should note that the licences in Davis's auction do not by any means guarantee that the holders thereof will be successful in their nefarious endeavours. In particular, the licences do not shield the holders from opposition to their pursuit of their misdeeds. As Davis writes:

A license bought at our auction guarantees only that if the holder commits the appropriate crime and is then captured, tried, convicted, and sentenced, she can hand in the license and be excused from punishment. The license pardons. It does not guarantee success (for example, that a thief will get to keep what she has stolen for more than an instant). [Davis 1996, 272]

Given that the possession of a licence does not exempt its owner from interference with his wrongdoing, the potential purchasers of the licences will—*ceteris paribus*—gravitate toward crimes that are less likely to be opposed and thwarted. 'All else equal, [a criminal] will prefer "easy pickings"' (Davis 1996, 270).

In any given society, crimes of various types can be stymied (by police officers or by private citizens) more effectively than crimes of other types, and not all the latter crimes are more serious than the former. Insofar as the more serious crimes are among those that can most effectively be halted or disrupted, the consideration adduced in the preceding paragraph will skew Davis's rankings in a perverse direction. To be sure, that consideration will prevail only *ceteris paribus*. Some of the more serious crimes that can quite effectively be thwarted are probably more lucrative for their perpetrators than are some of the less serious crimes that cannot so effectively be countered. In the mind of a rational miscreant who contemplates the commission of one of those former crimes, the greater lucrativeness would partly or fully offset the unappealingness of the greater vulnerability. Nevertheless, not all the perverse skewing of Davis's rankings will be offset in that fashion.

For instance, suppose that bank robberies can effectively be scotched (or, at the very least, can be made extremely perilous for their perpetrators) through the presence of a few armed police officers or security guards in the lobby of each bank. If every bank in some society has introduced such a precaution, then the bids within the hypothetical auction for licences to commit bank robberies in that society will tend to be very low. Suppose now that, in the same society, the crime of shoplifting is much less easily foiled. Employing the number of plain-clothes detectives required to avert most instances of that latter crime would be prohibitively expensive for any shop. Accordingly, the likelihood of one's being thwarted in one's efforts to steal goods from a shop is markedly lower than the likelihood of one's being frustrated in one's efforts to rob money from a bank. Furthermore, even a shoplifter caught in the act does not typically face nearly the same level of danger as a bank robber who is confronted with armed policemen or security guards. Hence, although the proceeds from a successful bank robbery will normally be considerably higher than the proceeds from a successful bout of shoplifting, that disparity can be wholly or largely offset in the minds of aspiring criminals by the other disparities just mentioned (concerning the probability of success and the level of hazard). Thus, with reference to the eminently credible society that is envisaged here, the bids in Davis's auction for licences to commit bank robberies might well be somewhat lower than the bids for licences to carry out acts of shoplifting. At any rate, there is a strong likelihood that the former bids will not be much higher (if at all higher) than the latter. Consequently, Davis is committed to the conclusion that the punishments for acts of shoplifting in the envisaged society should be approximately the same as the punishments for bank robberies. Such a conclusion is at odds with the retributivistic principle of proportionality.

What is more, this example with some slight modifications will reveal a further respect in which Davis's rankings can depart sharply from retributivistic principles. Suppose that, within the limits of the resources at the disposal of the merchants in some society S, the monitoring of customers is insufficient to stymie any act of shoplifting that is performed with at least a minimal degree of dexterity. The probability of success among the potential shoplifters in S is very close to 100 per cent. Therefore, nobody or virtually nobody in S would be disposed to bid anything in a hypothetical auction for licences to engage in the crime of shoplifting. There is no point to paying for a licence of that kind when thefts of items from shops can already be carried out with no negative consequences. In application to S, then, Davis's scenario of the auction generates the conclusion that no penalty should be assigned to the crime of shoplifting. Far from making the punishment fit the crime, Davis has supplied a justificatory procedure that removes the punishment for the crime.

3.2.1.2.3. A third query

Another major problem, pointed out by most of the previous critics of Davis who were cited near the beginning of my discussion of his work, is that the outcomes of his hypothetical auction do not tally with those of another procedure (a seven-step procedure) which he proposes for the attachment of penalties to crimes. Davis insists that the results of the auction converge with those of his seven-step procedure, but his insistences are unpersuasive. Incongruities between the two procedures complicate his desert-focused version of retributivism, since the seven-step procedure—despite its limitations, including its inability to justify capital punishment (as we shall see)—is a far more plausible method for assigning punishments to crimes than is the hypothetical auction. With his adoption of the seven-step procedure, Davis adumbrates a more sophisticated understanding of the notion that the object of punitive measures is to remove unfair advantages gained by criminals through their wrongdoing.

He outlines the seven-step procedure as follows:

1. Prepare a list of penalties consisting of those evils (*a*) which no rational person would risk except for some substantial benefit and (*b*) which may be inflicted through the procedures of the criminal law.
2. Strike from the list all inhumane penalties.

3. Type the remaining penalties, rank them within each type, and then combine rankings into a scale.

4. List all crimes.

5. Type the crimes, rank them within each type, and then combine rankings into a scale.

6. Connect the greatest penalty with the greatest crime, the least penalty with the least crime, and the rest accordingly.

7. Thereafter: type and grade new penalties as in step 2 and new crimes as in step 4, and then proceed as above. [Davis 1983, 736–7]

As many commentators have pointed out, the paramount problem for Davis is that this procedure does not gauge the same thing that is gauged by his hypothetical auction. Whereas the latter device is supposed to measure the value placed by potential criminals on the avoidance of penalties for the commission of various crimes, the seven-step method focuses on the fearsomeness of various crimes in the eyes of potential victims. Within each category of crimes envisaged by the seven-step procedure, the offences are to be ranked not according to the benefits which they bestow upon their perpetrators (however measured), but instead according to the assessments of those crimes by the people who might fall prey to them. As Davis writes: 'The least crime [within each category] is the one a rational person would prefer to risk (all else equal) given a choice between risking it and risking any other [crime] of that type; the next least is the one a rational person would prefer to risk given a choice between it and any other of that type except the least; and so on' (Davis 1983, 739). Since there are no reasons to expect that one's ranking of crimes by reference to their fearsomeness in the eyes of potential victims will match (or even come close to matching) one's ranking of crimes by reference to their benefits in the eyes of potential malefactors, there are no reasons to think that Davis's two methods for assigning punishments to crimes will tally. The two sets of rankings will probably converge at some points, of course, but they will diverge at numerous other points. Thus, even if we leave aside all the problems that afflict each set of rankings in isolation, the incongruity between the two sets is a difficulty that confronts anyone who hopes to draw upon Davis's work for guidance in the fixing of punishments.

Davis persistently defends himself against the charge of having presented two procedures that yield dissimilar sets of rankings, as he contends that the procedures will in fact arrive at the same results. However, his arguments on that score are far from compelling. He points out that the licences for each type of crime in his scenario of the auction are limited in ways that reflect the degree of apprehension felt by members of the public toward each type of crime. Similarly, the licences can be purchased by people who wish to keep aspiring criminals from using them. Moreover, given that a licence guarantees only an ultimate pardon rather than success in the commission of a crime, a society with a crime-licence auction can still aptly devote more resources to thwarting felonies than to thwarting misdemeanours (Davis 1996, 266–73). In all these ways, the outcomes of the hypothetical auction are shaped by the very anxieties of the public that are taken squarely into account under the seven-step procedure. Thus, Davis concludes, 'our imagined [auction] and the seven-step method each reproduce the structure underlying the other'. He confidently exclaims: 'Contrary to what critics claimed, we have no reason to expect the two procedures to produce inconsistent results. The two are alternate ways of doing the same thing' (Davis 1996, 269).

Albeit the factors highlighted by Davis do bring the hypothetical auction closer to the seven-step method, they are not nearly enough to reconcile the results of those two approaches in all contexts. What remains true is that the latter method ranks crimes by reference to their fearsomeness in the eyes of potential victims while the former device ranks crimes partly by reference to their attractiveness in the eyes of potential perpetrators. In a wide range of contexts, then, the two procedures will fail to converge.

Let us contemplate here a somewhat modified version of an example adduced by Don Scheid for a slightly different purpose (Scheid 1995, 394–5). Suppose that robbery is feared by the typical person considerably more than is securities fraud, even though the latter type of crime is generally more lucrative and physically less dangerous for its perpetrators. We can suppose that the chances of being stymied are approximately equal between these two kinds of crimes. We can likewise suppose that, in the hypothetical auction, the number of licences to commit robbery is roughly the same as the number of licences to commit securities fraud—since the greater fearsomeness of the former crime is counterbalanced by the greater economic costliness of the latter. Thus, in application to these credible circumstances, Davis's seven-step procedure will generate the conclusion that robbery is to be punished more severely than securities fraud, whereas his hypothetical auction will generate the conclusion that securities fraud is to be punished more severely than robbery. Of course, if the specified circumstances were to be tweaked suitably, the seven-step method and the hypothetical auction could be made to tally. However, the point is precisely that the reconcilability of the two procedures will be dependent on the contingencies of various situations. In a wide range of circumstances, the two methods lead to divergent results (and sometimes even to starkly opposed results, as in this paragraph's example).

3.2.1.2.4. A fourth query

Let us now ponder an even more sweeping objection to Davis's scenario of the auction for crime-licences. This objection, adeptly pressed by Scheid (1995, 395–7), contests the very coherence of Davis's scenario by showing that it has to presuppose the schedule of punishments which it is designed to establish. To see why the hypothetical auction is afflicted by vicious circularity, we should attend more closely to what the bidders in the auction are seeking to purchase.

When somebody bids in the auction for a licence to commit a crime of some kind, she is endeavouring to acquire a pardon that will enable her to avoid punishment for the perpetration of that crime. (Let us leave aside here the potential victims who bid for licences in order to prevent villainous people from obtaining them. Any complications arising from such bids will hardly rebound to Davis's benefit.) Thus, in addition to some important ancillary concerns such as the likelihood of one's being thwarted in one's criminality and the danger posed to oneself by one's undertaking of that criminality, two main factors will determine the size of anybody's bid for some licence: (1) the favourableness or unfavourableness of her attitude toward committing the type of crime that is covered by the licence; and (2) the importance to her of avoiding the sanctions that are attached to that type of crime.

My discussion so far has concentrated solely on the first of those main factors along with the ancillary concerns. That first main factor is indeed of great significance. If somebody is not at all disposed to engage in armed robbery, for example, he will not submit any bid for a licence to commit armed robbery. Similarly, if he is only weakly tempted to engage in armed robbery, he will not be willing to pay very much for such a licence. Still, weighty though those considerations are in influencing the size of a person's bid, the role of the second main factor enumerated above is also crucial.

Suppose that Marvin is quite strongly attracted to the prospect of carrying out an armed robbery. Before he can informedly submit a bid for a licence to commit such a crime, he needs to know the severity of the sanctions that will be avoided through his possession of the licence. If the likely term of imprisonment for somebody convicted of armed robbery is one week, then Marvin will be far less strongly disposed to expend large quantities of money on a licence than he will if the likely term of imprisonment for somebody so convicted is ten years. Thus, until Marvin knows the magnitude of the penalty from which he will be gaining an exemption through his purchase of a licence, he does not have any informed basis for deciding how much to bid. He does not know what he will be buying. A parallel point applies, naturally, to everyone else who is at all inclined to bid for any of the licences in Davis's auction. Information concerning the sanctions attached to each type of crime must be available to the parties who participate in the auction, if their bids are to be more than groundless conjectures. Without such information, the participants in the auction will not know what they are seeking to purchase.

Accordingly, before the parties in the hypothetical auction can reasonably bid for any crime-licences, they need to know the sizeableness of the penalties from which those licences will shield them. What is so problematic for Davis, of course, is that the parties' bids are supposed to serve as the basis for fixing the levels of those penalties. His scenario of the auction, despite its initial plausibility, has turned out to be incoherent.

3.2.1.3. Self-indulgence

More promising than either Sher's focus on freedom or Davis's scenario of an auction is the proposition that the gain accruing to every criminal by virtue of his or her wrongdoing consists in self-indulgence. Nevertheless, this proposition has to be construed carefully. Understood as a rather facile claim, the proposition is plainly unsustainable and has rightly been derided by critics of retributivism. Understood as a more subtle claim, however, the thesis concerning self-indulgence is the best means of upholding desert-focused retributivism as a credible theory of punishment. To be sure, such a theory is scarcely unproblematic and in particular is incapable of justifying the use of capital punishment (a fact that will not trouble most of the theory's proponents). All the same, it is considerably more powerful as a general theory of punishment than are any of the alternative varieties of desert-focused retributivism. Before we examine the preferable rendering of the thesis about self-indulgence, we should briefly probe the more dubious rendering for which it might be mistaken.

3.2.1.3.1. A manifestly unsustainable version of the thesis

When desert-focused retributivists contend that the unjust advantage gained by every criminal through his or her wrongdoing is self-indulgence, they might be understood as asserting that every criminal through his or her misconduct has forgone the disagreeable burdens of law-abidance that are borne by everyone else. According to such a thesis, the unfair gain arising from every instance of criminality consists in an escape from the hardships involved in hewing to legal requirements. While other people toil strenuously to comply with those requirements, a criminal indulges himself by laying aside such toil. Unlike his fellow citizens, he does not undertake the hard work of stifling the propensities to which the law forbids him to succumb.

When the proposition about the self-indulgence of criminals is elaborated along these lines, it is highly vulnerable to the sorts of objections that have been raised against it by Richard Burgh and David Dolinko and other critics of retributivism (Burgh 1982, 207–10; Dolinko 1991, 545–6; Murphy 1994, 290). They have pointed out that the vast majority of people are much less strongly inclined to engage in monstrous crimes such as cannibalistic murder than to undertake far milder crimes such as tax evasion or speeding or shoplifting. For nearly everyone, abstaining from the perpetration of cannibalistic murder is utterly effortless, whereas abstaining from the perpetration of the milder crimes just mentioned is often a matter of conscious self-discipline. Thus, if we were to accept the preceding paragraph's analysis of the unfair advantage that is gained by every criminal through his or her wrongdoing, we would be committed to the conclusion that somebody who performs an act of cannibalistic murder has thereby attained a much smaller unfair advantage than has somebody who drives above the speed limit or who understates his income on his tax return. Ergo, a cannibalistic murderer would deserve a much lighter sentence than would someone convicted of speeding or of tax evasion. Such a conclusion is patently ridiculous, and Burgh and Dolinko are right to dismiss it. If desert-focused retributivism is to be strengthened through its drawing of attention to the self-indulgence of criminals, such a reorientation cannot concentrate on the intensity of people's desires to commit misdeeds of various types.

3.2.1.3.2. *A tenable version of the thesis*

Instead of adverting to the greater or lesser intensity of people's proclivities to engage in sundry criminal activities, the advocates of desert-focused retributivism should advert to the gravity of those activities. By so doing, they will be addressing the extent to which those activities deviate from norms of law-abidingness and non-injuriousness. Subject to some qualifications that will be noted shortly, the extent of the deviation from those norms that is entailed by any given act of criminality is what constitutes the degree of self-indulgence that has been exercised by the culprit who has performed the specified act. The size of the deviation is the size of the unfair gain or advantage which the culprit has acquired simply by virtue of carrying out the crime that he has committed. Whether he has also benefited in other ways—by experiencing some feelings of gratification, for example—is neither here nor there, for the purposes of desert-focused retributivists. Any such additional benefits might appropriately be handled by non-punitive legal proceedings (restitutionary legal proceedings, for instance), but the punishments in a desert-focused system of criminal justice are designed to nullify the unfair gains that are intrinsic to criminal wrongdoing.

When somebody perpetrates a criminal act, he uses his body and other objects or persons in ways that are legally proscribed. His manoeuvring of his body and other objects or persons through regions of space is such as to be eschewed by everybody who wants to avoid contravening any legal requirements. By going ahead with such manoeuvring despite its forbiddenness, a criminal gains something valuable that is not likewise gained by any law-abiding citizen, and he thereby obtains an advantage over all law-abiding citizens. His manipulation of his body and other objects or persons through regions of space is valuable not because he relishes it (though, of course, many criminals do relish what they have done), but precisely because that manipulation of his body and other objects or persons is legally forbidden. Since he has not rendered his conduct legally permissible by securing a change in the law or by purchasing a special exemption from the requirement(s) which he has breached, his employment of his body and other objects or persons through portions of space has temporarily misappropriated those very portions of space. Because law-abiding citizens have not engaged in any similar misappropriations, he has placed himself at an advantage vis-à-vis them. That advantage obtains even if his criminal endeavours are thwarted and come to nought. Regardless of whether he gets and retains any other advantages from those endeavours, the aforementioned misappropriation is what sets him apart from law-abiding citizens and is what renders him liable to punishment. It is the gain intrinsic to every act of criminal wrongdoing.

The extent of that gain is determined not by the sizeableness of the portions of space that have been misappropriated, but by the gravity of the purposes to which they have been put.[14] The more seriously wrong those purposes are, the greater the value of the misappropriation. To see this point, we need to attend to the distinction between offer prices and asking prices. An offer price is the maximal amount that someone is able and willing to pay in order to acquire something, whereas an asking price is the minimum amount that someone would demand in return for transferring something to somebody else.[15] Among the many other shortcomings in Davis's scenario of the hypothetical auction is his assumption that the offer prices of the bidders for licences are the dispositive indicators of the value of the unfair advantages that are gained by criminals. Rather, the value of any criminal's misappropriation is determined by the asking price of the society in which his crime occurs. Of course, I am not here suggesting that anything akin to the scenario of the hypothetical auction should be reintroduced with a focus on asking prices rather than offer prices. That scenario suffers from too many major weaknesses to be worth reviving in any form. Instead, the point here resides simply in observing that there is quite a straightforward sense in which the portions of space temporarily misappropriated by a criminal are valuable. Had the criminal temporarily acquired those portions of space for his purposes through some sort of exemption-procuring payment that could meet the society's asking price, the acquisition would have cost him dearly indeed. In exactly that sense, the value of his misappropriation is given by the seriousness of his crime.

Indeed, with the shift from offer prices to asking prices, the version of desert-focused retributivism recounted here is quite close to Davis's seven-step method rather than to his hypothetical auction. On the one hand, *pace* the seven-step method, the objective seriousness of various crimes does not necessarily accord fully with the extent to which those crimes are respectively feared by members of the public. On the other hand, the seriousness will indeed correspond closely (even though not always fully) to the fear. At any rate, what is common to the seven-step procedure and the version of desert-focused retributivism just described is their recognition that the value of a criminal's unfair gain is to be gauged from a societal perspective rather than from the perspective of the criminal.

One notable feature of this reconception of desert-focused retributivism, indeed, is that it clearly differentiates criminal law from tort law by concentrating on the unfairness of any crime toward a society as an overarching unit. Though every crime that victimizes some individual(s) is of course directly harmful and unjust to any such individual(s), the injustice rectified in a desert-focused system of criminal law is that

---

[14] Although I refer to illegitimate purposes here and elsewhere in this discussion, my remarks are not confined to intentional wrongdoing. Criminality impelled by any culpable frame of mind is covered by my discussion.

[15] In quite a different context, the offer/asking distinction is explored at length in Kennedy 1981, 401–21. I myself have invoked that distinction in a context more closely relevant to the present discussion, in Kramer 1999b, 142–3.

which has been committed against the whole community whose normative protection of the victimized individual(s) has been flouted. When a criminal employs his own body and certain other objects or persons through regions of space in furtherance of his nefarious purposes, he contravenes that normative protection and thus perpetrates an injury against the community as a whole (irrespective of whether he succeeds, even briefly, in realizing his objectives). Punishment rectifies that injury by imposing on the wrongdoer a disadvantage—in the form of imprisonment or some other disciplinary measure—that counterbalances the valuable advantage which he has gained simply by dint of pursuing his criminal purposes. It counterbalances that advantage by resubordinating the criminal's wrongful ends to the community's proper ends.

Although John Finnis intermittently writes as if he were in agreement with Sher's misconceived account of the unfair advantage gained by every criminal, his overall exposition of that advantage is in fact along the lines elaborated here (Finnis 1972; Finnis 1980, 262–4; Finnis 1999). His exposition highlights the egalitarian impetus of desert-focused retributivism, as he affirms that the role of desert-focused punishments is 'to maintain a rational order of proportionate equality, or fairness, as between all members of the society' (Finnis 1980, 262). Despite his occasional lapses into Sher's language, Finnis usually makes clear that it is a criminal's self-indulgence—rather than some extra share of freedom supposedly accruing to a criminal—that constitutes the gain which is intrinsic to every offence and which is properly counteracted through punishment. As he writes: 'Punishment does not negate the crime, but it does negate, cancel out, the advantage the offender gained in the crime—the advantage not necessarily of loot or psychological satisfaction, but of having pursued one's own purposes even when the law required that one refrain from doing so' (Finnis 1999, 102). By reasserting the priority of a community's moral purposes over the malign purposes of a criminal, punishment restores the fair social arrangements that have been disrupted by the criminal's wrongdoing: 'What is done cannot be undone. But punishment rectifies the disturbed pattern of advantages and disadvantages throughout a community by depriving the convicted criminal of his freedom of choice, proportionately to the degree to which he had exercised his freedom, his personality, in the unlawful act' (Finnis 1980, 263, footnote omitted). Hence, the aim of punishment based on desert-focused retributivism lies in 'restoring equality between offenders and [the] law-abiding, and cancelling the wrongdoer's unfair profit (advantage over them)' (Finnis 1999, 102).

Again, the restorative role expounded here by Finnis is distinct from the restorative role of awards of damages in tort law. Damages are awarded against tortfeasors to compensate their immediate victims for the harms which those victims have suffered. By contrast, punishments—according to desert-focused retributivists—are imposed upon criminals to repair any serious disruptions of a society's moral order and to uphold the egalitarianism of its social and economic relationships. Though

the extent of the harm inflicted by a crime on any immediate victim(s) is a key deter-
minant of the crime's gravity and consequently of the magnitude of its damage to a
society's moral order, the punishment imposed in response to a crime is undertaken
on behalf of the entire society rather than specifically on behalf of the immediate
victim(s). Any such victim V stands to benefit from the subjection of the crime's
perpetrator to punitive measures, of course, but the benefit accrues to V in her status
as a member of a moral community rather than in her status as an immediate victim.
Every other member of the moral community benefits likewise, as the priority of the
community's upright purposes over the nefarious purposes of a criminal is reasserted.
Far from being a doctrine of revenge, desert-focused retributivism is a doctrine of
impersonal justice.

3.2.1.3.3. Some qualifications

If desert-focused retributivism is to partake of any credibility as an account of the
worthy purposes of punishment, it has to be qualified in a few important respects. For
one thing, its pertinence in application to any given society is dependent in two ways
on the realization of liberal-democratic ideals. First, as has already been remarked in
§ 3.1.2, the saliently egalitarian tenor of desert-focused retributivism confines its justificatory reach to liberal-democratic societies. Only in such a society is the ideal of
human equality realized sufficiently to render germane the proposition that punitive
measures serve to effectuate that very ideal.[16] Only in such a society do the citizens
form a moral community of the sort envisaged by desert-focused retributivists when
they ascribe to punishment the role of restoring a society's moral order.

Secondly, desert-focused retributivism as a theory of punishment has to be combined with a suitable liberal-democratic theory of criminalization, if it is to respond
adequately to objections that have been raised by critics of retributivism. For example, as Dolinko and Shafer-Landau have separately contended, desert is not in itself
the key to legal punishment; somebody can deserve to suffer for his or her misdeeds
even though the imposition of legal punishments for those misdeeds would be morally untenable (Dolinko 1991, 542–4; Shafer-Landau 1996, 289–92). Suppose that
Mark has callously jilted his long-time lover Jane for a younger woman or for some
other selfish reason. Although Jane may well feel devastated by her lover's abandon-
ment of her, and although Mark undoubtedly deserves to receive his come-uppance
for his unfeeling treatment of her, the subjection of him to criminal penalties for his
misbehaviour would be morally unsustainable—and not only because his conduct
has in fact violated no criminal prohibitions. Even if there were a criminal-law mandate forbidding the callous and selfish rebuffing of one's lover, neither the punishment
of Mark nor the punishment of anyone else under that mandate would be morally
appropriate. Desert-focused retributivism cannot in itself account for the moral illegitimacy of subjecting Mark or anybody else to punishment under the imagined

---

[16] For a suggestion along these lines, see Finnis 1980, 263 n 1.

mandate. To account for that point, a liberal-democratic theory of criminalization is needed. When the laws in a system of governance conform to the prescriptions of such a theory, Dolinko's and Shafer-Landau's worries about the gap between somebody's deserving to suffer and somebody's deserving to undergo legal punishment will have been accommodated and defused. In other words, a necessary condition for the satisfactoriness of desert-focused retributivism as an account of the worthy ends of punishment is that it be conjoined with a liberal-democratic theory of criminalization. Only when it is so conjoined, and only when the notion of negative desert which it invokes is understood to be trained solely on breaches of criminal-law mandates, does the doctrine of desert-focused retributivism adequately overcome the problem broached by Dolinko and Shafer-Landau.

A further qualification is needed, however. As elaborated so far, the doctrine of desert-focused retributivism appears to presuppose that everyone within the jurisdiction of a liberal-democratic regime is under a moral obligation to comply with each of the regime's legal mandates in all circumstances to which any such mandate is applicable. Yet, as I have argued elsewhere (Kramer 1999a, 285–7), there can be circumstances in which somebody does not have any ethical reason at all—much less any moral obligation—to comply with a particular benign legal mandate promulgated by a liberal-democratic regime. Hence, as a justificatory account of the role of punishment, desert-focused retributivism pertains only to situations in which people are indeed under moral obligations to comply with the terms of the benign legal mandates which they contravene.[17] Extended to a situation in which somebody is not under a moral obligation of that kind, desert-focused retributivism would call for the imposition of a punitive measure when no such measure is legitimate. Hence, if this species of retributivism is to retain credibility as a justificatory doctrine, its sphere of application must be delimited in the manner suggested here.

3.2.2. Vindicatory retributivism

As has been stated, the differences between the principal conceptions of retributivism are largely matters of divergent emphases. Like the desert-focused retributivists, the proponents of vindicatory retributivism believe that the punishment of offenders is morally warranted because of the negative deserts of those offenders. However, instead of concentrating on the unfair gains that have been amassed by criminals through their wrongdoing, the vindicatory retributivists concentrate on the deprivations undergone by the victims of the wrongdoing. For these latter theorists, institutions of punishment are the mechanisms whereby the rights and dignity of victims are

---

[17] In some contexts, such obligations can obtain simply because non-compliance with the terms of certain benign legal mandates would foster disrespect for the law generally (either on the part of the non-compliant person or on the part of other people). However, it is not the case that violations of such mandates always produce—or are always likely to produce—some effects of that kind or any other detrimental effects.

publicly reaffirmed. Those institutions are *pari passu* mechanisms of communication that forcefully admonish criminals about the wrongness of what they have done and about the contents of the fundamental moral principles which they have violated.

Vindicatory retributivism has emerged in a number of varieties. In some of those renderings, which can be labelled here as 'individualized,' the focus lies on the immediate victims of crimes as the parties whose rights have been most directly and egregiously transgressed. Given such a focus, the overall community comes to the fore only in connection with crimes (such as tax fraud) that involve the whole community as the immediate victim. In other renderings of vindicatory retributivism, which can be labelled here as 'society-oriented,' the focus lies not only on the immediate victims of crimes but also—and indeed chiefly—on the community in which the crimes have taken place. 'In criminal cases, the harm accrues to the public as well as to the class of victims who suffer the invasion of a particular interest.'[18] According to the society-oriented variant of vindicatory retributivism, the central purpose of punishment resides in the 'vindication of just laws and political authority' (Bedau 1985, 902). Elaborated in this latter fashion, vindicatory retributivism converges on nearly all points with the most plausible form of desert-focused retributivism that was expounded above in § 3.2.1.3.2. It should therefore be understood as subject to the same restrictions on its sphere of application.

3.2.2.1. Retribution is not revenge

This chapter has already emphasized that retribution does not amount to revenge. Still, that point should be reiterated here, since vindication is often confused with vindictiveness. For example, just after recounting the key thesis of the society-oriented variant of vindicatory retributivism in words which I have quoted above, Bedau goes on to endorse the characterization of that thesis as 'the Vindictive Theory of Punishment' (Bedau 1985, 902 n 91). Admittedly, given that Bedau believes that the aforementioned thesis 'does not express a purely retributive outlook' (Bedau 1985, 902 n 91), he does not there intend to equate retribution with vindictiveness. Still, we are much better advised to accept that vindication is a species of retribution and that it is to be distinguished from vindictiveness or vengeance.

When Joe engages in vindictive retaliation against Mary, his aim is to inflict pain on her in order to derive gratification from his knowledge that she is suffering in return for some past action of hers (or some past action by somebody closely identified with her). By contrast, when the officials in a vindicatory-retributive system of law punish Mary for a criminal wrong which she has committed against Joe, their aim does not consist in deriving gratification from their knowledge that she is suffering. Rather, the point of their punitive treatment of her is to reaffirm the dignity of Joe and the

---

[18] Fletcher 1999, 56. For similar pronouncements, see Bradley 1999, 106–8; Dressler 1990, 1453 n 31; Finnis 1999, 98 n 32; Kennedy 2000, 838 n 35; Markel 2005, 431 n 109, 433–5; Schwarzschild 1990, 500; Van den Haag 1985a, 166–7; Van den Haag 1985b, 970; Van den Haag 1986, 1667; Van den Haag 1990, 506, 507–8.

relationship of basic moral equality between him and her. If the vindicatory retributivism that informs the legal system is society-oriented, then the point of the officials'
punitive treatment of Mary is also—and principally—to reassert the authority of the
system and the primacy of its moral purposes over her self-indulgent purposes. Suitable
punitive measures levied against her uphold not only the equal dignity of Joe but also
the dignity of the whole community as a moral community. In any typical case, those
measures will cause Mary to suffer; however, the key to the process is not her suffering
but is instead the resubordination of her projects to the community's moral purposes.

To say as much, of course, is not to deny that Joe and other people might derive
gratification from Mary's suffering. Rather, what is denied is that the occurrence of
such gratification will ever figure among the objectives of any criminal-justice system
that is based solely on the principles of vindicatory retributivism. As will be seen in
Chapter 5, the occurrence of such gratification is instead among the aims of a criminal-
justice system that is based on the denunciatory rationale for punishment. Within a
system of criminal justice informed exclusively by the principles of vindicatory retributivism, any such occurrence is incidental to the aims of the system's punishments.

3.2.2.2. The communicative dimension

More than desert-focused retributivists, vindicatory retributivists lay great stress on
the communicative dimension of punishments. In their view, the primary recipient
of the message imparted by a punishment is the offender on whom the punishment
is inflicted. Both a punitive measure itself and the proceedings that lead up to its
imposition are designed to convey to an offender the priority of a community's moral
principles over his own nefarious inclinations. Such proceedings underscore the fact
that the law breached by the offender is worthy of compliance, and they thus draw his
attention to the unacceptability of his disrespect for the requirements of a legitimate
system of governance. Likewise conveyed is the message that any immediate victim of the offender's wrongdoing is possessed of human dignity equal to that of the
offender. In this respect, a punitive measure counteracts the message communicated
by a criminal's own conduct. By insisting upon values that are antithetical to those
which have informed a criminal's mistreatment of any victims, it pressingly draws the
criminal's attention to the rights that have been violated through such mistreatment.

Whether the primary recipients of the messages conveyed by institutions of punishment are responsive to those messages or not, the communication of appropriate
values to offenders is a worthy enterprise in itself. Nonetheless, as has been remarked
in § 3.1.4, the moral worth of the endeavour is enhanced in any particular case if the
communication to an offender does yield some reformative effect. If the vindicatory
tenor of the message imparted by a punishment is to take full effect, the acceptance
of it by the primary recipient—through processes of contrite reflection rather than
through processes of brainwashing—is crucial. Still, the sending out of a forcefully
vindicatory message to the person who has made such vindication necessary is vital
irrespective of that person's ultimate response.

At any rate, the messages communicated by vindicatory-retributive institutions of punishment are also addressed secondarily to another audience: namely, to the general public. Whether or not the commission of a criminal misdeed has become widely known, the misdeed has evinced an attitude of disdain or unconcern for the rights of any immediate victims and for the moral standards of the community in which it has been perpetrated. To counter adequately that expression of contempt or indifference on the part of a criminal, the punishment levied for the misdeed—along with the procedures that lead up to the infliction of the punishment—must reassert the dignity of any immediate victims and the primacy of the community's upright moral standards. By demonstrating that the wayward will of a miscreant is subordinate to the moral judgements articulated in a liberal-democratic regime's code of criminal law, the punishment rebuts the audacious claims that were implicit in the miscreant's breach of the law.

In two main respects, the communicative orientation toward the general public under a vindicatory-retributive system of criminal justice differs from the corresponding orientation under a denunciatory system. First, within a system of the former type, the communication to the general public is ancillary rather than primary. The primary recipients of the messages conveyed by a vindicatory-retributive system are criminal offenders, who stand in need of the correction which those censorious messages can effect. Ordinary members of the public already largely share the values that are reaffirmed by vindicatory-retributive punishments in a liberal-democratic society. Such people do not need any major correction or solidification of their general moral sentiments. Rather, what they need is reassurance that the shared values are being upheld by the legal-governmental institutions that are entrusted with the securing of those values in sundry practical settings. As Walter Berns writes: 'The law must respond to the deeds of the wicked, and the righteous must have confidence that the law will respond, and do so in an appropriate manner' (Berns 1979, 145–6). Punishments and the proceedings that eventuate in the punishments supply some key elements of the requisite reassurance.

Second is a closely related point. Within a vindicatory-retributive system of criminal justice, the communication to the general public (and also to the punished offenders, of course) is indeed vindicatory rather than denunciatory. It does not consist in expressions of revulsion that appeal to people's vindictive instincts. Rather, it consists in public demonstrations of the moral dignity of any immediate victims—whose rights are not to be violated without any untoward consequences for the violators—and in public demonstrations of the sway of the moral values that are enshrined in a society's criminal law. Instead of being aimed at inducing ordinary people to feel gratification in response to the suffering of criminals, the communicative dimension of vindicatory-retributive punishments is (partly and secondarily) aimed at inducing ordinary people to feel reassured that their common allegiance to certain moral values is reflected in the institutions that govern them. In the face of challenges to those values by malefactors, the aforementioned institutions reaffirm the moral ties that hold members of the general public together as a community.

3.2.2.3. A first objection to the communicative dimension of vindicatory retributivism

Some astute critics of vindicatory retributivism (especially of the individualized variety of that doctrine) have posed a number of objections to the communicative dimension of the theory. For example, Dolinko has doubted that the subjection of a criminal to punitive measures can plausibly be understood as affirming the equal moral dignity of any immediate victim(s) of the criminal's wrongdoing:

> How does it get across that the victim has evened the score and can now claim whatever mastery the wrongdoer can? It would seem, rather, that while the wrongdoer claimed 'superiority' by defeating the victim himself, a whole gang of partisans of the victim has now banded together and defeated the hopelessly outnumbered wrongdoer! Perhaps this conveys the message that society as a whole is the equal (or perhaps the master) of the wrongdoer, but it hardly seems an apt way of expressing the message that the victim, individually, is the wrong-doer's equal. [Dolinko 1991, 553]

It is worth noting here that Dolinko's queries on this score are applicable only to the individualized variant of vindicatory retributivism. Even in application to that variety of the doctrine, the queries are at best overstated. Vindicatory-retributive punishments reassert the equal human dignity of any immediate victims precisely by demonstrating that the victims enjoy the backing of their society's governing institutions. That backing is available to every other member of the public as well (including lawbreakers insofar as they themselves are victimized by other lawbreakers). Exactly because a victim is not left to his or her own devices but is instead supported by the mighty coercive power of a legal-governmental apparatus, a criminal's presumption of superiority over his victim is shown to be unfounded.

Roughly analogous is the situation of a soldier in the army of a technologically sophisticated country whose efforts are facilitated by highly refined equipment and by support teams that can wield overwhelming force. As a result of the materials and assistance available to each soldier, a relatively small group of men from the technologically advanced army can defeat a much larger assemblage of soldiers from the army of a country with primitive technology. Man per man, the former army is far more effective than the latter. Is the superiority of the soldiers in the former army somehow belied by the fact that they are backed up with much better equipment and support teams? On the contrary, the access of those soldiers to much better equipment and support teams is precisely what makes them superior to the soldiers in the poorly furnished army.

In the context of a liberal–democratic society, of course, the fundamental relationship between criminals and victims is that of equal human dignity rather than superiority. However, in some other germane respects, the scenario of the soldiers can shed light on the role of punishment in such a society. Just as a soldier is not demeaned or shown to be inferior by dint of his access to highly sophisticated equipment and assistance, so too the victim of a crime is not demeaned or shown to be inferior by dint of her access to the mechanisms of criminal justice which vindicate her status as a right-holder of equal human dignity. That very access, indeed, is what makes that status manifest. When a criminal presumes to treat his victim as if she were someone of lesser dignity or no account, the backing that she receives from legal-governmental institutions—backing that would have been comparably available to him if he had been a victim—is a public demonstration of the mistakenness of his attitude.

3.2.2.4. A second objection to the communicative dimension of vindicatory retributivism

Shafer-Landau, another perspicacious critic of retributivism in general, has mounted a further attack on the communicative aspect of vindicatory retributivism—again in response to Jean Hampton's individualized version of the theory. He writes as follows:

> [I]t remains unclear why the deliberate infliction of hard treatment on an offender is necessary to explain away the relevant message of inferiority. Why couldn't a very forcefully worded, publicly promulgated message from the bench be sufficient to do this? . . . What needs explaining is why a convict must be intentionally made to suffer. Hampton's explanation must take the form of showing how such an imposition is necessary to send the relevant moral message. [Shafer-Landau 2000, 196]

One shortcoming of this passage is its assumption that vindicatory retributivists hold that punitive measures necessarily involve suffering on the part of anyone who is penalized.[19] Although the imposition of such measures will normally give rise to suffering, the essential purpose of punishment is instead to resubordinate the will of each offender to the moral standards of his community. Punishment places the criminal and the victim back on an equal footing through that resubordination rather than through the inducement of suffering (though, as has been stated, punishment will indeed normally induce suffering).

In a situation involving a minor crime, a stern rebuke from a judge or from some other legal-governmental official (such as a policeman) can be sufficient as a means of re-establishing the priority of the community's moral order over the wayward impulses of a malefactor. Such a rebuke, in such a situation, can consequently be sufficient as a means of reaffirming the rights of any immediate victim that have been infringed through the commission of the minor crime. In a situation involving a more serious crime, however, a stern reprimand or any other merely verbal repudiation of a criminal's disdain for his victim would be hollow and self-defeating if it were unaccompanied by some more substantial punishment. A merely verbal response to a serious crime would convey to the wrongdoer the message that he can grossly violate somebody else's rights with virtually no untoward consequences for himself even though he has been apprehended. That message would imply that the

---

[19] For a sustained attack on that assumption, see Markel and Flanders 2010.

moral order of his community, which strictly forbids his misconduct, is subordinate to his self-indulgent propensities. Far from countering his expression of an attitude of superiority over his victim which he has conveyed through his serious mistreatment of her, the limpness of a mere reprimand would tend to corroborate his assessment. It would reveal that the status of the victim as a member of a putative moral community is hollow—because that status provides her with virtually no backing in the aftermath of a major transgression of the community's legal and moral standards that has immediately impinged upon her. She would be like a soldier whose equipment and support teams never arrive. If the resubordination of the wrongdoer to the community's moral order is to be effected and communicated, and if the status of the victim as a member of a moral community is to be meaningfully vindicated, then some much more weighty and tangible measures for restricting the wrongdoer's leeway are essential.

Of course, Shafer-Landau is correct if he simply wishes to emphasize that—even in connection with very serious crimes—there are some logically possible worlds in which the institutions of criminal justice can operate in a forcefully effective manner without imposing sanctions beyond mere rebukes or proclamations. As a matter of logical possibility, there can be worlds with communities in which the issuance of rebukes or proclamations is such a devastatingly shame-inducing method of punishment that it effectively incapacitates the villains against whom the rebukes or proclamations are directed. With reference to a community of that sort, the vindicatory retributivists might not need to call for any other methods of punishment. After all, in such a community, rebukes or proclamations carry (and are perceived as carrying) punitive weight akin to that of long-term imprisonment in the actual world. However, although a community along those lines is logically possible, it is markedly different from any liberal-democratic societies in the actual world. In liberal-democratic societies in the actual world, stark reprimands and pronouncements are woefully insufficient as responses to serious crimes—because the impacts of such measures are not nearly enough to resubject the wayward inclinations of the perpetrators of those crimes to the moral and legal frameworks of their communities. For the accomplishment of that vindicatory-retributive purpose of resubjection (the attainment of which is commended by retributivists as morally valuable even when it does not ultimately produce reformative or deterrent effects), some punishments that substantially curtail the liberty of serious evildoers are necessary. As Waldron has written:

If someone asks why these [retributivistic] messages cannot be conveyed by letter or over the telephone rather than through punishment, the response may be that the offender has already shown by his conduct that he has not internalized the message in any of its conventionally communicated forms, and we now have to abandon words and try to show him why such acts are wrong, in the most direct and powerful way, by getting him to experience them at the sharp end, so to speak. [Waldron 1992, 30]

3.3. Does retributivism disallow capital punishment?

Heretofore, this chapter has discussed retributivism as a general theory of punishment and has only occasionally adverted to its bearing on the matter of the death penalty. Henceforth, the focus of the chapter will lie on that very bearing. Whereas the tone of my discussion has hitherto been fairly sympathetic toward retributivism (albeit not always toward particular retributivists), much of the rest of this chapter will be far more wary. Whatever the virtues of retributivism as an overall rationale for punishment, it cannot succeed in justifying the imposition of the death penalty. Still, to maintain as much is not to reject retributivism altogether. After all, as has been remarked, many retributivists would themselves happily agree that their doctrine cannot justify the use of capital punishment. Indeed, quite a few retributivists would concur with the chief claim on which my critique of any retributivistic rationale for the death penalty will rely: namely, the claim that retributivism as a doctrine for assigning specific types or levels of punishments to specific types of crimes is marked by a significant degree of indeterminacy. Although some proponents of retributivism have sought to show that specific types or levels of punishments are uniquely commensurate with specific types of crimes, many other proponents have firmly eschewed any such aspiration. Hence, to quite an extent, this chapter will be drawing upon retributivism as a general theory in order to discredit retributivism as a justification of capital punishment.

I undertake the discrediting of that justification in the next main section of this chapter. In the present section, we shall first consider whether the tenets of retributivism are sufficient in themselves to disallow the use of capital punishment. Some retributivists such as Dan Markel have argued for just such a view of those tenets. This section of the chapter will seek to rebut that view and will contend that retributivism in itself is not sufficient to rule out the moral legitimacy of the death penalty.[20] Only in combination with the liberal-democratic Minimal Invasion Principle does retributivism militate against the institution of capital punishment. (Of course, given that retributivism is pertinent as a justificatory account of punishment only in application to liberal-democratic societies, and given that the Minimal Invasion Principle is a precept at the core of liberal democracy, the fulfilment of that principle constitutes a necessary condition for the legitimate implementation of the tenets of retributivism. Many retributivists might therefore be inclined to characterize the Minimal Invasion Principle as integral to a full-scale exposition of their doctrine. There is obviously no need for me to quarrel with anyone about that point. Rather, the claim here is that capital punishment is not disallowed by the tenets of retributivism when those tenets are considered in abstraction from the conditions for their legitimate implementation.)

---

[20] Some of Markel's worries about the alleged inconsistency between capital punishment and retributivism are focused on procedural matters. I defer any investigation of those matters until Chapter 7. In the present chapter, I focus only on his substantive queries.

3.3.1. Contrition precluded?

In his impressively nuanced endeavours to establish that the ideals of retributivism are inconsistent with the employment of the death penalty, Markel submits that an executed prisoner will have had no opportunity to undergo reformation by internalizing the principles of equal human dignity and moral responsibility that are communicated to convicts through the punishments in a vindicatory-retributive system of criminal justice (Markel 2005, 460–62). As Markel writes: '[T]hrough its use of coercive confrontation, retributive punishment communicates certain fundamental norms. And the communication is itself insufficient if the confrontational encounter fails to leave a chance for the offender to internalize and live by the ideals animating retribution (even if in a prison) during or after the encounter' (Markel 2005, 461). On the one hand, as has been stated several times, the punishment of a prisoner can be in full accordance with the ideals of vindicatory retributivism even if that prisoner does not actually undertake a process of reformation through salutary reflection and deliberation. Retributivism is a deontological theory rather than a consequentialist doctrine that takes the reform of convicts as an orienting goal. On the other hand, as has likewise been stated, the reform of a convict through his internalizing of the principles that are communicated to him is exactly what is encouraged by the imposition of punishments in conformity to the ideals of vindicatory retributivism. Hence, any type of punishment that closes off the very possibility of such reform is inimical to those ideals. As Markel declares: '[T]he reason for this restriction on the mode of punishment is to avoid pointlessness. In the way that an insult shouted to an offender in a language she does not understand is a pointless exercise, a punishment that leaves no opportunity for internalization grimly forecloses the reconstruction of the offender's self as moral agent and as citizen' (Markel 2005, 462).

Markel's argument would be persuasive in connection with a system of criminal justice where capital prisoners are executed only a few days after being arrested. Think, for example, of Claudio in Shakespeare's *Measure for Measure*. Although Claudio seeks earnestly to reconcile himself to death during the brief time between his sentence and his scheduled execution, the shallowness of the change in his outlook becomes apparent when he believes that his sister Isabella can spare him by sacrificing her chastity. Owing to the brevity of the span of time during which the ostensible alteration in his outlook occurs, the alteration never really takes root. Much the same would typically be true of reformative transformations in the mores of other capital prisoners. Internalizing the principles of moral responsibility and equal human dignity is a feat that almost always extends over a considerable period of time. If the interval between a capital sentence and an execution is very short, the internalization of those principles by a condemned convict will almost always be shallow rather than profound. An abrupt yet thorough Damascene conversion is not impossible, but it is very rare. Far more commonly, a deep-rooted transformation in the mores of an offender can only happen gradually. Thus, if capital trials are speedy and if death sentences are implemented posthaste, the institution of capital punishment that comprises those trials and sentences is in tension (if not outright conflict) with the communicative dimension and reformative aspirations of retributivism.

However, as Markel is well aware, the processes of capital punishment in the United States are in fact highly protracted. He points out that, among prisoners put to death in the United States in 2003, the average length of time between sentencing and execution was nearly eleven years (Markel 2005, 462 n 235). Moreover, although the intervals between sentences and executions in the United States are especially prolonged, the average period of time between arrest and execution—and even between sentencing and execution—will be quite lengthy in any country with the procedural safeguards that are characteristic of liberal democracies. Given as much, Markel is significantly exaggerating when he worries about the foreclosing of any opportunities for capital offenders to internalize retributivistic ideals. In virtually every case, there will be ample time for reformative reflection and deliberation by anyone convicted of a capital crime.

Markel himself anticipates the foregoing reply to his line of reasoning. He retorts as follows:

I recognize that the long period of time that often elapses between the conviction of an offender and the time of his eventual execution may weaken this argument. Offenders arguably have the time and opportunity to internalize the values animating [vindicatory retributivism] while waiting on death row. After all, as Samuel Johnson said, nothing concentrates the mind so wonderfully as the sight of the hanging gallows. But this reasoning is perverse, no? Executions, more likely than not, preclude opportunities for these moral norms to take root. During the time an offender is on death row, he constantly fears that today is the day death comes knocking, making it hard for him to actually lend much thought to the values animating retributive justice. [Markel 2005, 462, footnote omitted]

In the first half of this passage, Markel presents an apt riposte to his own argument. In the second half of the passage, he offers an ineffective rebuttal of that riposte. To the question which begins that rebuttal—'But this reasoning is perverse, no?'—the correct answer is 'no'. Not at all perverse is the notion that somebody condemned to death for a ghastly crime will have ample opportunities to engage in reformative reflection during the quite substantial span of time between the sentencing and the execution. Whether an evildoer will avail himself of those opportunities is a matter that may vary from case to case, of course. However, the sheer availability of those opportunities is independent of their being exercised.

In the closing half of the passage above, Markel tries to deny that opportunities for reformative reflection are indeed available to death-row convicts. In so doing, he propounds some unsubstantiated empirical conjectures. Moreover, even if those conjectures were more plausible than they are, they would not bear out the point which Markel needs to make at this juncture in his argument. He needs to establish that, whenever convicts are condemned to death, the prospect of being executed will somehow close off any opportunities for them to internalize the principles of moral responsibility and equal human dignity. Yet the empirical surmise at the end of the quoted passage merely maintains that taking advantage of those opportunities is difficult for a capital convict (more difficult, presumably, than for a convict sentenced to a punishment less severe than that of death). Even if such a surmise is correct, it does not point to any inconsistency between the communicative-reformative dimension of retributivism and the institution of capital punishment. It does not support the claim that the messages conveyed to capital offenders by their death sentences are pointless and are thus akin to complicated utterances spoken in a language that is unknown to the hearers thereof.

3.3.1.1. A first rejoinder by Markel

In a recent article, Markel insists that the period spent on death row by any capital convict is not satisfactory as an array of opportunities for the convict to internalize the values that animate vindicatory retributivism. He retorts as follows:

> [T]his reasoning is misplaced because it misunderstands the critical tracking between intention and causal action necessary for retributive punishment. To be clear: we do not create those delays in order to allow for that internalization; the delay occurs largely because of procedural wrangling... Thus, the execution cannot be a communicative punishment even if the confinement prior to the execution serves as time at which the defendant internalizes some of the correct values. For the reasons mentioned earlier about how the intentions must line up with the causal actions appropriately to create the correct social meaning, the confinement period is not a period that can reliably be said to serve communicative retributive purposes. [Markel 2009, 1196–7]

Markel is quite correct when he states that the long periods between sentences and executions in the present-day United States are due to protracted appeals and procedural wrangles. However, he is touching on a purely contingent feature of the practice of capital punishment in various American jurisdictions. The concern which he expresses would be fully met in any given jurisdiction if the officials responsible for designing and operating the system of capital punishment there were to introduce a span of time for reformative reflection and deliberation by each capital defendant. For every such defendant, after his appeals have been exhausted, a couple of years could be authoritatively set aside for his final ruminations. Because that length of time would deliberately be made available to each capital convict for reformative self-scrutiny, the intentions and causal actions of the officials would tally in support of the aspirations of vindicatory retributivism. Hence, although the passage above from Markel has highlighted a way in which the practice of capital punishment in the United States does not currently accord with the ideals of vindicatory retributivism, the modification broached here would eliminate the problem. By requiring every capital convict to spend a period in post-appellate contemplation, the officials who run a system of capital punishment would match their vindicatory-retributive actions with their vindicatory-retributive intentions.

3.3.1.2. The time of the punishment

Markel seeks to bolster his argument with the claim that any moral reform undergone by a convict on death row is pre-punitive rather than post-punitive:

[T]here has not yet been the punishment called for by the legislature in conjunction with the jury or judge—the death penalty. Because our intentions have to line up with our causal actions to convey the correct social meaning, we cannot use the defendant's post-conviction but prepunishment attitude as evidence of the intrinsic success of the communicative punishment; after all, the intended punishment has not yet been imposed. [Markel 2009, 1209]

Markel here adopts a tack which I shall criticize again in Chapter 7. That is, he treats the consummation of a punishment as if it were the whole punishment.

When a person is sentenced to death, he is more specifically sentenced to be detained until he is executed. Like the administering of a term of imprisonment, the administering of any instance of the death penalty is a process that extends over a considerable period of time. It culminates in the death of the convict, but it begins as soon as he becomes a convict and is sentenced to death. His incarceration on death row leads up to his execution but not to his punishment; rather, his incarceration on death row is itself a part of his punishment, which is consummated by his execution. Hence, contrary to what Markel suggests, the opportunities available for reformative self-searching between the pronouncement of a death sentence and the full implementation of that sentence are not pre-punitive. Those opportunities arise during the overall course of the administering of a punishment which eventuates in the death of the person on whom that punishment is inflicted.

Markel writes that 'the period of languishing on death row is not articulated by the legislature as the communicative punishment; rather, it is the adjudication followed by the actual execution that is intended to convey the condemnation and thereby serve as the punishment' (Markel 2009, 1209). Though an execution is of course the event that is pivotal in any process of capital punishment, it is the capstone of that process rather than the entirety thereof. To see why Markel's position should be rejected, let us suppose that Bruno is a convict who has been sentenced to death. After Bruno has spent ten years on death row, his sentence is commuted to a term of ten years of imprisonment, and he is released. As Markel would surely agree, nobody could plausibly claim that Bruno has not been punished at all for his crime. Such a claim would be absurd precisely because a period of incarceration on death row is in itself plainly punitive and condemnatory—even though that component of a capital convict's overall punishment gains its heightened significance from the execution that follows it. An execution is the climactic punitive step, rather than the sole punitive step, in the administration of any instance of the death penalty.

3.3.1.3. Post-punitive opportunities for reform

Markel submits that the death penalty is illegitimate because it 'deprives offenders of the ability to live [in accordance with correct moral] values day by day during and, if applicable, after their punishment,' and he asserts that a vindicatory-retributive system of criminal justice will have 'committed itself to a view that [any] punishment must leave some *opportunity* during and after the punitive encounter for the defendant to internalize why he is being punished so that he may do something with that rational understanding' (Markel 2009, 1200, 1212, emphasis in original). In each of these statements, Markel maintains that the legitimacy of any course of punishment hinges partly on the availability of opportunities for the internalization of correct moral values by an offender during the time when he or she undergoes the course of punishment. Now, on the one hand, such a standard is doubtless too stringent, since it appears to disallow both fines and short periods of incarceration as criminal sanctions; after all, the span of time between the pronouncement of a sentence and the payment of a fine or the completion of a short term of imprisonment is typically so brief as to furnish no meaningful opportunities for the internalization of salutary values. On the other hand, the standard just mentioned can go uncontested here. As has been argued in the preceding subsection, a process of capital punishment begins well before the blade of the guillotine has dropped or the lethal dose of chemicals has been injected. Thus, the opportunities available to a capital convict for the internalization of correct moral values during the lengthy interval between sentencing and execution are opportunities that obtain during his punishment.

What will be impugned here is a further suggestion in each of the statements quoted above: namely, the suggestion that the legitimacy of any course of punishment hinges partly on the availability of opportunities for the internalization of correct moral values by an offender *after* he or she has undergone the course of punishment. In the first of the two quoted statements, the 'if applicable' qualification removes any inconsistency between Markel's position and my own. However, there is no such qualification in the second of the quoted statements. Consequently, Markel is contending that no type of punishment is morally legitimate unless the people who undergo that type of punishment are ordinarily alive afterward. Such a contention denies the legitimacy not only of capital punishment but also of lifelong imprisonment-without-parole. The disallowance of lifelong imprisonment-without-parole as well as of capital punishment reveals that this contention by Markel is an ad-hoc stipulation rather than a genuine corollary of the tenets of vindicatory retributivism. After all, nobody can credibly maintain that someone who spends several decades in a term of lifelong imprisonment has been deprived of opportunities for rumination on the wrongness of the crime(s) that he has committed. Not at all incompatible with the communicative dimension of vindicatory retributivism is the imposition of such a term of imprisonment. Except in unusual circumstances where someone dies fortuitously soon after being incarcerated, anybody who serves such a term of imprisonment will have had ample time to reform himself by internalizing correct moral values.

Nearly as clear is that a convict sentenced to death will have ample opportunities to reform himself. In a liberal-democratic system of criminal justice, the interval for appeals will itself be protracted. On top of that interval, in a system of criminal justice informed by the principles of vindicatory retributivism, would be the period set aside for post-appellate contemplation of the kind which I have discussed in § 3.3.1.1 above. In such a system, then, capital offenders would be treated 'in a manner that…invites them to participate in the correct values of moral responsibility and equal liberty'. Any such offender would be treated as 'someone whose response matters to us' (Markel 2009, 1212). In short, although I will presently argue that the employment of the death penalty on vindicatory-retributive grounds is illegitimate, the reasons for the illegitimacy have not been correctly identified by Markel. Contrary to what he maintains, there is no inherent inconsistency between the application of that penalty and the emphasis on reformative communication in vindicatory retributivism.

3.3.2. Human dignity revisited

Markel further claims that the use of capital punishment is at odds with any due respect for human dignity and is therefore at odds with retributivism. He understands the notion of human dignity along the following lines: 'That dignity is the exalted moral status that all human life possesses by virtue of human existence itself. At least with respect to punishment, it is fair to define dignity as the value that attaches to human existence by virtue of the distinctly human capability for acting in accordance with autonomy and reason' (Markel 2005, 465). In this initial formulation, Markel's conception of human dignity is especially problematic and is markedly different from my own conception which was sketched in Chapter 2 (§ 2.4.2.2.2). Whereas my conception pertains to limitations on the ways in which any human being can legitimately be treated, Markel's conception pertains to the value of human existence. Markel's conception, at least as it is stated here, lends itself to a consequentialist interpretation. Indeed, it closely resembles the consequentialist version of retributivism which Cass Sunstein and Adrian Vermeule quite easily accommodate within their own consequentialist approach to the matter of capital punishment.[21] So construed, Markel's conception of human dignity does not erect any principled barrier to the moral legitimacy of the death penalty. On the contrary, as Sunstein and Vermeule repeatedly suggest, a consequentialist version of retributivism can readily be invoked in support of the institution of capital punishment (on the basis of empirical assumptions about the marginal deterrent efficacy of such punishment).

Markel's wording in his initial attempt to specify the nature of human dignity is matched by his later concurrence with Sunstein and Vermeule on

---

[21] In note 16 of Chapter 2, I criticize Sunstein and Vermeule for recasting deontological theories (including retributivism) as consequentialist doctrines.

several important points (Markel 2005, 469–73), most of which I have impugned in Chapter 2. Nevertheless, although Markel embeds his retributivism in a consequentialist framework, he goes on to articulate an understanding of human dignity that is deontological within its own confines. He submits that 'we ought to forbear from executions because we want to protect the dignity of the offender as well as that of the polity in whose name the punishment is imposed,' and he declares that his 'thinking about dignity places limits on how we punish' (Markel 2005, 466–7). Revealingly, however, Markel immediately turns to the example of torture in order to try to explain why capital punishment is in conflict with the human dignity of anyone who is executed:

For example, consider why we ought not [to] torture offenders for even the most brutal crimes. As [Jeffrie] Murphy trenchantly observes, '[s]ending painful voltage through a man's testicles to which electrodes have been attached, or boiling him in oil...are not human ways of relating to another person. [The offender] could not be expected to understand this while it goes on, have a view about it, enter into discourse about it, or conduct any other characteristically human activities during the process—a process whose very point is to reduce him to a terrified, defecating, urinating, screaming animal.' [Markel 2005, 467, quoting Murphy 1979, 233]

Markel's quotation from Jeffrie Murphy captures vividly why the use of torture is always morally impermissible, in line with what I have maintained in Chapter 2. However, as was contended in that earlier chapter, the inconsistency between torture and human dignity is not per se a basis for concluding that capital punishment likewise contravenes human dignity.

Markel squarely disagrees: 'The reason torture is wrong helps explain why executions are wrong: it removes the possibility that punishment will comport with the respect for dignity qua autonomous personhood that animates (at least in part) retributive punishment.' He adds that such a 'failure of respect for human dignity degrades the offender and the punishing agent,' and he approvingly quotes Austin Sarat's assertion that the use of capital punishment in a liberal democracy 'contradicts and diminishes the respect for the worth or dignity of all persons that is the enlivening value of democratic politics' (Markel 2005, 467, quoting Sarat 2001, 16–17). Markel concludes: 'Opposition to the death penalty arises, then, not only because of our fundamental commitment to respect the basic dignity of the offender, notwithstanding his past offense, but also [because of our commitment to] our own dignity' (Markel 2005, 468, footnote omitted).

On some points, of course, Markel's conception of human dignity and my own conception are in harmony. Like Markel, my discussion of human dignity in Chapter 2 has stressed the importance of the sophisticated autonomy of most human beings as agents who can reason and deliberate about their sundry objectives; and, like him, Chapter 2 has emphasized that people who violate the human dignity of others will thereby have degraded themselves. In some salient respects, however, his conception of human dignity is problematic. Let us here consider two main points.

3.3.2.1. The exploitation of pain

Though Chapter 2's discussion of human dignity has highlighted the moral significance of the fact that most human beings are capable of reflection and deliberation, it has also highlighted the moral significance of their capacity to undergo positive experiences and their susceptibility to intense pain. Markel omits that last-mentioned feature in his exposition of human dignity, yet it is central to the force of the passage which he quotes from Murphy. As that passage adeptly underscores, the distinctive aim of torture resides in exploiting a human being's susceptibility to intense pain in order to overwhelm her normal faculties of reasoned reflection and self-control. Whether torture is administered as a form of punishment or as a means of extracting information (or cooperativeness) or indeed as a means of sadistic entertainment, it proceeds by temporarily or permanently squelching someone's personhood through the deliberate manipulation of her proneness to experience agony. That characteristic of torture is what Murphy trenchantly brings to the fore. Yet that very characteristic is absent from the imposition of capital punishment through humane methods of execution. Capital punishment does of course permanently extinguish the personhood of any executed offender, but—when properly administered—it does not trade at all upon an offender's proneness to experience agony. Any discomfort inadvertently caused during an execution is incidental to the object thereof, which is to terminate a life rather than to induce excruciating pain for instrumental or sadistic reasons. In precisely that regard, the death penalty differs from torture and is consistent with human dignity.

Defenders of Markel might retort that the deliberate termination of a healthy person's life outside the context of an emergency or a military conflict is inherently violative of human dignity, or they might retort that—even if considerations of human dignity are momentarily put aside—there is never any adequate justification for such a termination. We shall ponder the first of these two potential retorts in the next subsection. For the moment, let us concentrate on the latter of them. Insofar as that latter riposte amounts to the claim that 'there is no retributivist argument available in favor of executions' (Markel 2005, 472), it will be endorsed by this chapter. Retributivism's doctrines do indeed lack the moral and philosophical resources to justify the use of capital punishment, and, in combination with the Minimal Invasion Principle, those doctrines in fact yield the conclusion that such punishment is morally illegitimate unless some satisfactory alternative justification is available. Hence, the decisive question is whether any adequate alternative justification is indeed available.

Chapter 6 of this book will argue that the purgative rationale for the death penalty is a satisfactory justification, in that such a rationale establishes that executions can be both morally legitimate and morally obligatory in appropriate contexts. Markel, of course, does not address the purgative rationale at all. (In that respect, he is like virtually every other contemporary philosopher or jurist who writes on capital punishment.) However, there is no need for a discussion of the purgative rationale in this chapter, since

Markel himself explicitly states that certain deterrence-oriented considerations can justify putting people to death. He denies that 'there could never be a reason to undertake an execution for the purpose of saving innocent lives,' and he declares that 'saving lives could...be used to justify an execution (even of an innocent)' (Markel 2005, 472, 473, footnote omitted). On the one hand, Markel correctly insists that 'executions occurring for the purpose of saving innocent lives would not be permitted under a retributivist framework because no account of retribution purports to justify punishment for that purpose' (Markel 2005, 473). On the other hand, as the previous quotations in this paragraph reveal, he believes that executions can be morally permissible—even if the people sentenced to death are themselves innocent—when there is compelling evidence that the executions will save innocent lives through strong marginal deterrent effects.[22] Hence, although he is in a position to deny that any such compelling evidence has emerged, he is hardly in a position to maintain that there cannot ever be any adequate justification for the deliberate termination of a healthy person's life.

Of course, as should be evident from Chapter 2 (particularly from § 2.4.2.1.3), I disagree with Markel about executions based on deterrence-oriented considerations and especially about executions of innocents. The infliction of capital punishment on innocent people is always morally impermissible. My invocation of his stance on that matter is not an endorsement of the stance, for the dialectical situation does not require any such endorsement. Rather, I have invoked his views here simply in order to show that he has already conceded that there can in principle be an adequate justification for deliberately terminating the life of a healthy person outside the contexts of emergencies and military strife. Quite unproblematic is my disagreement with his grounds for accepting the proposition that there can sometimes be such a justification; after all, Chapter 6 will provide alternative grounds for accepting that proposition.

3.3.2.2. The death penalty and moral responsibility

Let us now examine the other retort that might be advanced by Markel or his defenders. Are executions inherently violative of human dignity? Notwithstanding his belief that executions of innocents on consequentialist grounds can be morally permissible in extreme circumstances, Markel thinks that retributivistic principles entail an affirmative answer to this question. Recall that, in one of the statements quoted above, he asserts that the death penalty 'removes the possibility that punishment will comport with the respect for dignity qua autonomous personhood that animates (at least in part) retributive punishment' (Markel 2005, 467). Yet, apart from adducing

---

[22] I am assuming that, when Markel writes that such executions can be justified, he is using the term 'justify' and its cognates in the first of the two senses which I have specified in § 2.4.2.1.3. In other words, he is contending that such executions can be morally permissible. This interpretation of his wording is supported by his explicit assertion elsewhere that torture can be morally permissible in extreme circumstances, and also by his assimilation of justified executions of innocents to other governmental actions that save some lives at the expense of others: 'At that point, we are interested in saving innocent lives[,] and society frequently requires the sacrifice of some innocent lives for the preservation of many when there is conclusive evidence that this will be the net effect' (Markel 2005, 473).

the analogy to torture which I have controverted, he provides no basis for his insistence that capital punishment is inconsistent with human dignity. His line of thought
appears to be that, because an execution involves the deliberate and permanent discontinuation of a person's rational faculties, it is incompatible with any profound
respect for human agency. Such a line of thought runs up against the fact that, under
the purgative rationale for capital punishment, the particularly heinous offenders
who undergo executions are sentenced to death precisely because they as agents have
committed iniquities which make their lives defilingly evil. The moral responsibility
of such offenders is affirmed rather than negated when they are put to death.

Markel acknowledges that some retributivists have also believed that capital punishment is the only means of holding the worst criminals responsible for their atrocities. In a footnote, he writes: 'I recognize that not everybody agrees that human
dignity is necessarily degraded through execution. Van den Haag, for example,
observed that some philosophers, such as Kant and Hegel, might think "execution,
when deserved, is required for the sake of the convict's dignity"' (Markel 2005, 468
n 256, quoting Van den Haag 1986, 1669). Markel's response to such retributivists is
curious: 'Nonetheless, one can insist that the claim that executions degrade human
dignity is self-evident, while also acknowledging that its self-evidence is not apparent to everyone' (Markel 2005, 468 n 256). In support of this comment, Markel in his
footnote includes a citation to Finnis's discussions of the property of self-evidence.
For Finnis, however, the property of self-evidence consists in non-derivativeness or
irreducibility; a self-evident proposition is axiomatic or foundational, in that its truth
or knowability is not dependent on the truth or knowability of any other proposition
of the same type (Finnis 1980, 31–34, 66–69). Hence, Markel is to be understood here
as contending that the inconsistency between human dignity and capital punishment
is a bedrock matter of morality and that it is therefore not derivative of any deeper
moral principles.

When Finnis observes that some self-evident propositions are not recognized as true
by certain people, he follows Aquinas by explaining that 'while some propositions are
self-evident to "everyone", since everyone understands their terms, other propositions
are self-evident only to "the wise"' (Finnis 1980, 32). Now, Markel is not supercili-
ously suggesting that he himself is one of 'the wise' and that the retributivists whom
he opposes are benighted. Even so, his claim about the bedrock status of the supposed
inconsistency between capital punishment and human dignity is itself implausible.
Whether or not there is any such inconsistency—and I of course believe that there is
not, so long as executions are conducted on the basis of the purgative rationale in appropriate contexts—we should scarcely credit the notion that such a matter is fundamental
rather than derivative of deeper moral principles (specifically the principles that account
for the property of human dignity). Important though the issue of capital punishment
is, it does not reside at a foundational level in the domain of morality.

Let us close this discussion by noting that Markel's quotation above from Sarat, in
which we are told that the death penalty 'contradicts and diminishes the respect for the

worth or dignity of all persons that is the enlivening value of democratic politics', is potentially a source of confusion. By using the terms 'worth' and 'dignity' appositionally, Sarat's pronouncement implies that those words are interchangeable and that the properties denoted by them are equivalent. To be sure, there is no canonically uniform pattern of usage among philosophers; the terms 'worth' and 'dignity' are sometimes used synonymously. Nonetheless, we are best advised not to run those two words together. We should distinguish between them in order to distinguish carefully between the property of moral worth and the property of human dignity. Even somebody whose continued existence is defilingly evil—and whose life is therefore worse than worthless—is possessed of human dignity. Human dignity attaches to a person regardless of what he has done. It is not a product of his moral responsibility, and is not lost or lessened by his perpetration of misdeeds. By contrast, the worth of a person (or the worth of his life) is determined by what he has done. If what he has done is monstrously evil, then the worth of his life is strongly negative.

3.4. Can retributivism justify capital punishment?

We now arrive at the main topic of this chapter. My long exposition of retributivism has laid the groundwork for the present section's conclusion that retributivistic precepts cannot justify the imposition of the death penalty. Those precepts cannot establish that the imposition of such a penalty is ever morally obligatory or morally legitimate. Hence, anyone who favours capital punishment will have to seek an alternative justification.

As has been argued in the preceding section, retributivism does not in itself rule out the legitimacy of capital punishment. However, because the satisfactory fulfilment of the demands of retributivism never requires the use of such punishment (as opposed to less severe sanctions), those demands do not support the proposition that the realization of a major purpose of government depends on that use. Consequently, in combination with the Minimal Invasion Principle, retributivism generates the conclusion that the institution of capital punishment is morally illegitimate unless some non-retributivistic purpose of government can justify it.

Because this section of the chapter will be arguing that the imposition of the death penalty is not necessary for a society's conformity to the requirements of retributivism, there is no need here for me to consider whether those requirements are sufficiently weighty to justify capital sentences. We can assume, at least *arguendo*, that they are sufficiently weighty. Accordingly—so we can assume—if the satisfaction of retributivism's distinctive precepts were indeed dependent on the institution of capital punishment, the introduction and retention of that institution would be morally obligatory and morally permissible. With that assumption in place, then, the key question to be addressed is whether the aforementioned precepts do indeed call for capital punishment. This section of the chapter will deliver a negative answer to that question. In the course of arguing that capital punishment is not required by any retributivistic doctrines, this section will rebut a number of lines of argument that might be marshalled against my stance.

3.4.1. The views of retributivists

Some proponents of retributivism, most famously Immanuel Kant, have contended that retributivistic ideals do call for the imposition of the death penalty in certain cases. However, the most obvious reason for querying such a position is that countless retributivists have rejected it. Though some retributivists have gone too far by submitting that capital punishment is inconsistent with the aspirations of retributivism, most have simply maintained that those aspirations are fully consistent with the *absence* of such punishment. They have denied that the ideals of retributivism—desert, human equality, moral responsibility—ever single out specific types or levels of sanctions as uniquely appropriate for specific types of crimes. They have denied that the principles of proportionality, commensurateness, and *lex talionis* ever single out specific types or levels of sanctions in that manner. They have consequently denied that the use of the death penalty is ever required in a retributivistic system of criminal justice.

Admittedly, the advocates of moral principles do not necessarily understand those principles correctly. What the values of desert and moral responsibility and human equality require is not determined by what any retributivists believe them to require. Still, when we are surrounded by so great a cloud of witnesses—who include many of the most sophisticated champions of the doctrines of retributivism—we should take very seriously their insistence that nothing in retributivism demands the employment of the death penalty for any crime(s). At the very least, the myriad expressions of that insistence place an onerous burden of proof on anybody who wants to justify the institution of capital punishment by reference to retributivistic principles.

Let us contemplate a few examples of the pronouncements by eminent retributivists concerning the inability of their theory to prescribe specific types or levels of punishments for specific types of crimes. Finnis lays stress on that inability, in a passage that was partly quoted earlier in this chapter:

> [P]enalties must be chosen by the judge from a range. There is no 'natural' measure of punishment, that is to say, no rationally determinable and uniquely appropriate penalty to fit the crime. Punishment is the [Thomist] tradition's stock example of the need for *determinatio*, a process of choosing freely from a range of reasonable options none of which is simply rationally superior to the others. So there is no 'natural,' i.e. rational, requirement that murder, even the most atrocious, be punished capitally. [Finnis 1999, 103]

In much the same vein, though perhaps even more emphatic, is the following remark by Gerard Bradley: 'The centrality of retribution to understanding punishment does not mean that retribution includes premises which lead, by deduction or by compelling inference, to specific forms and degrees of punishment for particular offenses. Quite the contrary is the case: retribution as the justifying aim of punishment does not dictate any specific form or degree of punishment' (Bradley 1999, 114–15). Bradley indicates that, because of the limited determinacy of retributivism as a doctrine for assigning punishments to crimes, there is ample room for variations in the assignments among jurisdictions or within a single jurisdiction over time: 'Even if retribution were the *sole* aim of punishment, sentences imposed upon convicted criminals would vary from place to place. They would depend upon the free choices of those responsible for design and administration of the criminal justice system, and would rightly reflect, to some extent, the customs of the local population' (Bradley 1999, 115, emphasis in original).

Markel expounds a similar view as he counters the objections of critics of retributivism who adopt the 'position that a retributivist who gives a justification for *why* we have institutions of punishment also instructs society *how much* to punish. . . . But the *why* punish question is distinct from the *how much* to punish question[,] and there is no retributivist doctrine that states we should punish as much and as harshly as we seem to be doing in America today' (Markel 2005, 412, emphases in original). In his rejoinder to these critics, he asserts that 'the nature of the justification for punishment may constrain the range of responses a state may apply to a criminal, but it does not determine the sentencing outcome' (Markel 2005, 413). He later goes even further—indeed, somewhat too far—by declaring that 'retributivism cannot determine which range of punishments is commensurate with a given offense. Retributivism, after all, need not purport to be a comprehensive theory of criminal justice, and thus should not be expected to dictate whether driving under the influence should be penalized by a sentence of a suspended driver's license or twenty years imprisonment' (Markel 2005, 475 n 278). Markel connects these general remarks to the matter of capital punishment, which is his principal concern: 'For a retributivist to insist upon capital punishment is to move away from the question of why punishment is justified to the questions of how much punishment is deserved and how much punishment the state should impose. . . . Under [vindicatory retributivism], there is a capacious range of punishments that a state may impose after democratic and reasoned deliberation' (Markel 2005, 477). When these passages are considered in combination with the Minimal Invasion Principle, they make clear that Markel's arguments purporting to reveal certain points of incompatibility between retributivism and the institution of capital punishment—arguments that were impugned in § 3.3 above—are superfluous. An insistence on the limited determinacy of retributivism as a doctrine for attaching specific kinds or levels of sanctions to specific kinds of crimes is sufficient to ground the conclusion that retributivistic ideals can never serve to justify the employment of the death penalty. The reason why those ideals can never serve in such a justificatory role is not that they are in themselves inconsistent with the use of capital punishment. Rather, the reason is that they never *require* the use of such punishment in preference to the use of certain less severe sanctions. Given that the death penalty is only ever legitimate within a liberal democracy, and given that the Minimal Invasion Principle is a central tenet of liberalism, the fact that retributivistic ideals never require the employment of the death penalty is sufficient to disqualify them from underpinning any ascription of moral legitimacy to that penalty.

Andrew Oldenquist joins the chorus of retributivists with some rhetorical questions:

[W]hile it often is easy to compare two crimes and judge one worse than the other, this says nothing about what punishment either warrants. Retributive justice has calibration problems: When we slide a scale of punishments past a scale of crimes, how do we know where to stop, that is, how do we know how much punishment fits a given degree of accountability? How, then, do retributivists know punishments shouldn't stop short of capital punishment? [Oldenquist 2004, 338]

Oldenquist presently supplies answers to his rhetorical questions: 'It does not follow from the acceptance of retributive punishment that we must accept the death penalty. How much and what kind of punishment a person deserves doesn't automatically fall out of a retributive system' (Oldenquist 2004, 340). Oldenquist's position on the matter thus closely resembles that of Michael Moore, who writes as follows:

[R]etributivism is sometimes identified with a particular measure of punishment such as *lex talionis*, an eye for an eye..., or with a kind of punishment such as the death penalty. Yet retributivism answers a question prior to the questions to which these could be answers. True enough, retributivists at some point have to answer the 'how much' and 'what type' questions for specific offenses, and they are committed to the principle that punishment should be graded in proportion to desert; but they are not committed to any particular penalty scheme nor to any particular penalty as being deserved. Separate argument is needed to answer these 'how much' and 'what type' questions, *after* one has described why one is punishing at all. It is quite possible to be a retributivist and to be against both the death penalty and *lex talionis*, the idea that crimes should be punished by like acts being done to the criminal. [Moore 1995, 632, emphasis in original]

This chapter will shortly contest Moore's assumption that the *lex talionis* is a highly determinate criterion for punishment. However, the main point here is his germane insistence that retributivism does not prescribe specific types or levels of penalties for specific types of crimes. On that point—both in its general application and in its more concrete application to capital punishment—Moore, of course, concurs with a host of his fellow retributivists.

Robert Pugsley is another such retributivist, as he casts doubt upon Kant's prescription for assigning punishments to crimes: 'The [Kantian] "principle of equality" demands rigid application of the *lex talionis*, a part often mistaken for the whole of retributivism. There are convincing arguments for the impossibility of achieving anything close to such a finely calibrated punishment scheme' (Pugsley 1981, 1514). Pugsley concludes: 'It would seem that Kant's own ambitious requirements for the practical determination of moral desert (including that, presumably, for murder) do not admit of being fulfilled' (Pugsley 1981, 1515). Like Moore, Pugsley overestimates the determinacy of the *lex talionis*. Furthermore, he once or twice seems to suggest that the difficulties besetting the so-called principle of equality might be due to epistemic constraints rather than to the limited determinacy of any such principle itself. Still, he is right to agree firmly with the 'conclusion that retribution does not in fact *require* the death penalty' (Pugsley 1981, 1507, emphasis in original).

Joel Feinberg also initially dwelt on some formidable epistemic and practical difficulties, but then he even more strongly proclaimed that 'the judgments required [for comprehensively matching the severity of punishments to the seriousness of crimes] are not merely "difficult"; they are in principle impossible to make'. He declared that 'reasonable men not only can but will disagree in their appraisals of comparative blameworthiness, and there appears to be no rational way of resolving the issue'. He asserted that '[c]ertainly, there is no rational way of demonstrating that one criminal deserves exactly twice or three-eighths or twelve-ninths as much suffering as another,' and he derided any version of retributivism in which 'the amounts of suffering inflicted for any two crimes should stand in exact proportion to the "amounts" of wickedness in the criminals' (Feinberg 1970, 117). Lest these pronouncements might seem too sweeping or dismissive, Feinberg went on to observe more mildly that 'the degree of disapproval expressed by [a] punishment should "fit" the crime only in the unproblematic sense that the more serious crimes should receive stronger [punishment-conveyed] disapproval than the less serious ones' (Feinberg 1970, 118).

Now, with this assemblage of passages from the writings of prominent retributivists, I am obviously not implying that the proponents of retributivism are unanimous in rejecting the notion that their doctrine can attach punishments to crimes with quite a high degree of determinacy. Some contemporary retributivists do subscribe to that notion. Instead of trying to deny or obscure that evident fact, this subsection has aimed to make clear that many leading advocates of retributivistic ideals are at one with many critics of retributivism in insisting that those ideals cannot properly be invoked for the purpose of specifying the quantum of punitive severity that fits each type of crime.

3.4.2. On the limited determinacy of retributivism

Although the ranking of crimes by reference to their seriousness and the ranking of punishments by reference to their severity are endeavours that will be marked by numerous lacunae—and although the idea of ascribing cardinal values to the sundry crimes and punishments is preposterous—the principal source of the limits on the determinacy of retributivism as a doctrine for assigning punishments to crimes is the task of bringing the rankings together. None of the principles of retributivism can link those rankings in a manner that is more than very rough. In each case, the links will have presented at least as many problems as they resolve.

3.4.2.1. Commensurateness to the rescue?

Somebody who hopes to vindicate retributivism as a theory that can prescribe specific sanctions for criminal misdeeds is likely to resort to the requirement of commensurateness. Under that requirement, as we have seen, the severity of a punishment must match the negative desert of a miscreant if the punishment is to be morally legitimate. What determines the negative desert of the miscreant, of course, is the seriousness of the criminal misdeed which he or she has committed. (Retributivists, both vindicatory and desert-focused, differ among themselves in their cashing out of the property of seriousness. Some of them concentrate on the harm caused by a criminal offence; others focus on the culpability of the outlook with which such an offence is undertaken; and still others concentrate on both harm and culpability as determinative factors. I shall henceforth take the last of these three positions for granted, but my critique of any retributivistic rationale for the death penalty does not depend on that choice. My critique's challenge to the determinacy of retributivism will stand regardless of how the seriousness of crimes is cashed out.)

An invocation of the requirement of commensurateness in the present context would be an instance of wishful thinking, rather than a genuine means of salvaging the determinacy of retributivism. If that requirement could really single out some specific type or level of punishment as uniquely appropriate for each specific type of crime, then retributivism would indeed be fully determinate as a doctrine for answering the 'how much' question broached by Moore. However, the problem is that the antecedent of the conditional in the preceding sentence is fanciful; thus, although the conditional is true, its consequent cannot be detached.

3.4.2.1.1. Going too far

On the one hand, Shafer-Landau in his powerful attack on retributivism goes too far when he proclaims that the property of desert is thoroughly indeterminate, as he espouses a thesis of 'nihilism about moral desert: the view that there is no fact of the matter about what sanction(s) a wrongdoer morally deserves for his offense' (Shafer-Landau 2000, 191, italics removed). Were Shafer-Landau's extreme position true, then all ascriptions of deserts to people would be false. False, for example, would be a statement asserting that a sentence of lifelong imprisonment is far harsher than what an ordinary jaywalker deserves, and also false would be a statement asserting that a sentence of two days in prison is far lighter than what a sadistic mass murderer deserves. Yet the evaluation of either of those statements as false is outlandish. As Shafer-Landau himself readily acknowledges, 'many plausible judgments about cases seem to imply that there are morally deserved punishments' (Shafer-Landau 2000, 192). His acknowledgment should be approached with caution. If he is suggesting that the judgements about the jaywalker and the mass murderer (or any other plausible judgements about wrongdoers' negative deserts) seem to imply that there are uniquely suitable punishments for the offences about which the judgements are articulated, then he is incorrect. Those judgements neither imply nor seem to imply a thesis of unique suitability, and the people who utter or endorse the judgements are therefore not committed to any such extravagant thesis. If Shafer-Landau is instead suggesting that the statements about jaywalkers and mass murderers respectively imply that any punishment beyond a vaguely defined range would be unfitting for the offence of jaywalking and that any punishment beyond a vaguely defined range would be unfitting for the offence of mass murder, then he is correct. However, his suggestion can then be happily accepted by anybody who utters either of those statements, for he is pointing to a perfectly sensible implication of each of them.

When Shafer-Landau delineates his extreme position, he indicates that he is not criticizing retributivists for their inability to specify a uniquely appropriate type or level of punishment for each type of criminal offence. He recognizes that such an objection would be pointlessly captious: 'It would be unfair to claim that [a thesis affirming the requirement of commensurateness] is true only if there is, for some crimes, a precise number of days in jail that was *the* deserved legal sanction. There is nothing in principle problematic about allowing for a range of sanctions that "fit the crime"' (Shafer-Landau 2000, 191, emphasis in original). In other words, his complaint is not about the vagueness of the concept of moral desert: 'My argument...does not rely on an appeal to the vagueness of the notion of desert, where vagueness is understood to characterize properties that are embeddable in sorites paradoxes' (Shafer-Landau 2000, 212 n 4). Acknowledging that '[w]e can allow for some indeterminacy in the sentencing correlations [between punishments and crimes],' he immediately adds: '[B]ut at some point we must ask whether moral desert is giving us any guidance at all' (Shafer-Landau 2000, 191). Expanding on these remarks about vagueness, Shafer-Landau sets his sights on the target of his critique: 'Were considerations of moral desert capable of specifying a determinate range of sanctions (e.g., one to three years in jail), that would be sufficient to fend off my concerns. My view, however, is that moral desert fails to do even this' (Shafer-Landau 2000, 212–13 n 4).

In the last of these quoted comments, Shafer-Landau imposes an unreasonable burden upon his retributivistic opponents, for he is in effect insisting that they must overcome second-order vagueness. Retributivists can forswear Shafer-Landau's nihilistic position without thinking that there is a determinately demarcated range of suitable punishments (much less a uniquely suitable punishment) for any crime. They should do as I did in the penultimate paragraph above, by maintaining that the range of suitable punishments for any crime is itself vaguely delimited. In so doing, the retributivists will simply be contending that moral desert is like any other vague property. Desert's vagueness—second-order as well as first-order—does not preclude its reality and does not entail that there is never any fact of the matter concerning whether a punishment is deserved or undeserved. As Scheid pertinently writes: 'Although desert claims are by nature quite vague, they do carry some content' (Scheid 1995, 407).

Moreover, retributivists can reject Shafer-Landau's nihilism about moral desert while allowing that there might not be even vaguely demarcated ranges of fitting punishments for some crime-types *in abstracto*. Shafer-Landau devotes particular attention to the crime-type of impersonating a policeman. He asks: 'Does the impersonator deserve a few weeks, a year or a couple of years in jail?' He supplies a sceptical answer to his question: '[T]here...does not appear to be any way to know whether the impersonator morally deserves eighty, eight hundred or eight thousand days behind bars, or even whether some amount of jail time is the appropriate kind of punishment to impose in the first place' (Shafer-Landau 2000, 191). With regard to the general crime-type of impersonating a policeman, retributivists need not disagree with Shafer-Landau. They can accept that, because the harm and culpability associated with that crime-type are so heavily dependent on the concrete ways in which it is instantiated, there is no delimited range of punishments—not even a vaguely delimited range—for that crime-type *in abstracto*. Only when the context of any instance of that general crime-type is filled in, can a vaguely defined range of punishments be deemed suitable for the particular instance. For the general crime-type itself, there is no such range. At any rate, whether or not a concession along those lines is correct in application to the crime-type of impersonating a policeman, the concession can be made by retributivists who look askance at Shafer-Landau's nihilism about moral desert. They can give a very wide berth to his nihilism without being committed to the proposition that *every* general type of crime is linked to a vaguely demarcated range of fitting punishments.

3.4.2.1.2. *Against uniqueness*

On the other hand, although Shafer-Landau goes too far, he is right to join many retributivists in emphasizing that the property of desert or the requirement of commensurateness is never sufficient to single out some specific level of punitive severity as uniquely appropriate for some specific type of criminal wrongdoing. Because the property of desert and the requirement of commensurateness are vague, the most that they can ever do is to select some vaguely defined range of levels of punitive severity as appropriate for this or that specific type of criminal wrongdoing. To underscore how limited the selectivity of the requirement of commensurateness is, the present subsection will take as its point of departure a somewhat disconcerting feature of Shafer-Landau's discussion.

While pressing his nihilistic case against the determinacy of the requirement of commensurateness, Shafer-Landau swerves repeatedly between ontological concerns and epistemic concerns. His swerving is to some degree evident from the quotations above, where he shifts from (1) proclaiming that there is no fact of the matter concerning desert to (2) complaining that considerations of desert do not provide any guidance. To be sure, this swerving is not entirely unmotivated. Shafer-Landau believes that the best explanation for the absence of any guidance from considerations of desert is precisely that there is no fact of the matter concerning desert. In the sentences immediately preceding his proclamation of his nihilism, he states the explanatory connection explicitly: 'If we assume that criminals deserve to suffer, we will still want to know how much they deserve to suffer, and in what way. I don't believe that we can ever know this. My suspicion is that we are in the dark on this matter because there is no determinate kind or amount of suffering that a criminal morally deserves' (Shafer-Landau 2000, 191). Still, although Shafer-Landau's veering between an ontological orientation and an epistemic orientation is far from unmotivated, his *explanandum* and *explanans* should be transposed. Shafer-Landau adduces our inability to know that any specific level of punitive severity is uniquely appropriate for any specific type of crime, and from that very inability he explanatorily infers that no specific level of punitive severity is ever uniquely appropriate for any type of crime. That is, he seeks to explain an epistemic limitation by reference to ontological lacunae. We should proceed in the other direction, albeit with due circumspection.

As I have argued elsewhere at some length (Kramer 2009a, 51–6, 98–9), a moral question to which no correct answer can ever be known is a moral question to which there is no correct answer. Of course, the existence of correct answers to moral questions is not dependent on their being *known*; it is, however, dependent on their being *knowable*.[23] Were the correct answers to various moral questions strictly unknowable even by agents who deliberate in optimal conditions for moral reflection, some basic ethical values such as fairness and moral responsibility would be undermined. As a matter of moral necessity,[24] then, the correct answers to sundry moral questions are always knowable even though many of them at any given time may be unknown.

Hence, if nobody can ever know that some level of punitive severity is uniquely fitting for a given type of criminal misconduct, there indeed is no level of punitive severity that is uniquely fitting for that type of criminal misconduct. Now, for every type of criminal misconduct, we in fact are strictly unable to know that some level of punitive severity is uniquely suitable as a response. To know that some level is uniquely suitable, we would have to be epistemically justified in believing so; yet, with reference to every type of criminal misconduct, no such justification is available. Notwithstanding the nihilistic exaggeration to which Shafer-Landau resorts, he is correct in maintaining that there is no justification-conferring basis in moral epistemology for us to declare that a term of five years in prison—as opposed to, say, three years or four-and-a-half years or six years—is the uniquely suitable form of sanction for burglary or some other type of crime. Any ascription of unique suitability would amount to a ludicrously unfounded stipulation rather than a solidly justified knowledge-claim.

Note that this discussion is focusing on our ability to know pre-conventional moral deserts, by reference to which we can assess any sentencing guidelines that are legislatively or judicially formulated within a particular legal system. As Shafer-Landau remarks, many retributivists hold that 'sentencing guidelines are morally justified only in so far as they accurately capture moral desert claims that [are morally prior to] the guidelines themselves' (Shafer-Landau 2000, 192). Within the workings of a just legal system, some level of punitive severity can be legislatively or judicially singled out as appropriate for every one of the instances of some crime-type. If the seriousness of those instances as such instances is not significantly variable, and if the level of punitive severity singled out is toward the lower end of the vaguely demarcated range of levels that would be pre-conventionally fitting for the type of crime in question,

---

[23] The only partial exceptions to this generalization are some moral questions with empirical elements (such as a question about the moral status of some actual instance of conduct). To some such questions, the correct answers can be unknowable because certain aspects of the empirical matters to which the questions pertain are unknowable. What can never be unknowable, however, are the contents and the non-empirical implications of basic principles of morality.

[24] For a discussion of the nature of moral necessity, see Kramer 2009a, 157–61.

then the selected measure of punishment can be uniquely fitting within the particular legal system. Its unique suitability within that system is knowable. In that respect, the institutionally defined moral/legal deserts of people differ markedly from their pre-conventional moral deserts which many versions of retributivism seek to capture. Whereas a just legal system's specification of the punishment to be imposed for the perpetration of a certain type of crime can render that punishment uniquely appropriate within the system, the pre-conventional requirement of commensurateness does not ever single out any specific level or type of punishment as uniquely proper.

As has been submitted, one key reason for insisting that that pre-conventional requirement does not ever single out any specific level of punitive severity as uniquely suitable is that we can never be epistemically justified in claiming that there is such a level. Whereas we can know whether the sentencing guidelines in a just legal system have prescribed some specific measure of punishment for a given type of crime, and whereas we can know (through moral reflection) whether the prescribed measure is within the vaguely delimited range of sanctions that satisfy the pre-conventional moral requirement of commensurateness, we can never know that that range is not a range at all but is instead only a single measure. Because nobody can ever be epistemically justified in thinking that the spectrum of pre-conventionally commensurate sanctions for this or that crime is confined to one unique level of punitive severity—that is, because any assertion which represents a pre-conventional spectrum as one level is an arbitrary stipulation rather than a credible and warranted judgment—there is indeed a vaguely demarcated pre-conventional spectrum for each crime, rather than a single talismanic point.

In short, like any other vague requirement, the pre-conventional requirement of commensurateness can disallow many possibilities but can never pick out any one possibility as the sole legitimate option. Retributivism's insistence on effecting a proper match between the seriousness of a crime and the severity of a punishment should not be construed as an insistence on locating a singularly legitimate level of severity. The retributivistic insistence always allows a range of sanctions. Proponents of the death penalty cannot rightly hope to vindicate that penalty by alleging that it is the only type of punishment that conforms to the deserts of the worst offenders.

3.4.2.2. Proportionality

Given that the principle of commensurateness cannot ever call uniquely for the death penalty (as opposed to some less severe sanction) in response to any crime, the advocates of that penalty might attempt to have recourse instead to the principle of proportionality. However, as should be clear from my discussion of proportionality in Chapter 2 (as well as my earlier discussion of it in this chapter), any such attempt will prove to be unavailing. On the one hand, hardly anybody on either side of the debates over the moral legitimacy of capital punishment denies that the most serious crimes should be punished most severely and that the less serious crimes should be punished less severely. On the other hand, that very widely endorsed premise is not sufficient to sustain a conclusion in favour of capital punishment. Like the principle of commensurateness, the principle of proportionality is consistent with the use of the death penalty; yet each of those principles can likewise be satisfied without any use of such a penalty. Because the requirement of proportionality is consistent with the absence of capital punishment (in favour of various less severe sanctions such as lifelong imprisonment-without-parole), it cannot successfully be invoked by the supporters of executions. When those supporters draw upon a requirement which generates the conclusion that the death penalty is dispensable, they cannot overcome the hurdle of the Minimal Invasion Principle.

As Chapter 2 has emphasized, the paramount problem faced by the advocates of capital punishment who hope to rely on the principle of proportionality is that that principle does not establish what the most severe punishment within any legal system should be. It establishes merely that, whatever the most severe type of sanction employed by any particular legal regime is, that type of sanction should be imposed for the most serious crimes and not for lesser crimes. A requirement of that kind is obviously consistent with the absence of the death penalty in any particular jurisdiction, and is frequently recognized to be so (Bedau 1978, 613; Bedau 1993, 188; Bedau 2002, 7; Bradley 1999, 115; Dolinko 1986, 595–6; Dolinko 1994, 507–8, 515–22; Finkelstein 2002, 13; Gale 1985, 1032; Gardner 1978, 1183–4; Primoratz 1989a, 89; Pugsley 1981, 1522; Reiman 1985, 120; Scheid 1995, 399–400, 404–9; Schwarzschild 2002, 9; Shafer-Landau 1996, 303–4; Shafer-Landau 2000, 204, 206; Symposium 2003, 129 [remarks by Robert Blecker]; Van den Haag and Conrad 1983, 38, 42, 44).

How, then, might the supporters of capital punishment seek to avail themselves of the principle of proportionality? Davis has suggested that that principle can vindicate the institution of capital punishment in a jurisdiction where the sanction of lifelong imprisonment-without-parole is already imposed for crimes that are not as serious as some other offences—such as mass murder, or murder through torture—that might be committed within the jurisdiction.[25] Such an argument is unsuccessful, however, for at least three reasons.

In the first place, as Davis himself is well aware, the principle of proportionality in application to the hypothesized circumstances can yield the conclusion that the use of lifelong imprisonment-without-parole as a sanction for any crimes below the level of the most serious is morally illegitimate.[26] If lifelong imprisonment-without-parole is the most severe punishment that can legitimately be inflicted, then the employment

---

[25] Davis 1996, 114–15; Davis 2002. Along the same lines is Van den Haag 1986, 1666 n 17. For a largely similar argument that also draws on the retributivistic ideal of moral responsibility, see Sorell 2002, 33–4. As can be inferred from the critique of Sorell's argument in Shiffrin 2002, his appeal to the value of moral responsibility is vulnerable to broadly the same objections as those that can be raised against his appeal to the principle of proportionality.

[26] See Davis 1996, 122–3. Davis, however, seems to take the view that the use of lifelong imprisonment-without-parole for crimes below the level of the most serious is socially inexpedient rather than deeply illegitimate. His own opposition to the death penalty is based explicitly on grounds of social expediency; see Davis 1996, 3–4. For a broadly similar approach to the issue of the death penalty, see Laudan 2006, 57–61.

of that sanction for crimes less serious than mass murder or murder through torture is a violation of the principle of proportionality and is consequently illegitimate. Accordingly, in a jurisdiction where that sanction is so employed, any people positioned to influence the situation are morally obligated to take reasonable steps to introduce more lenient sanctions for the lesser crimes. Such is the conclusion to be drawn if no punishment more severe than lifelong imprisonment-without-parole is morally legitimate. In other words, the situation envisaged by Davis cannot be invoked to settle the moral status of capital punishment within the jurisdiction where that situation obtains. Which conclusion we should draw from that situation in light of the requirement of proportionality—the conclusion that punishments more severe than lifelong imprisonment-without-parole should be imposed for the most serious crimes in the relevant jurisdiction, or the conclusion that punishments less severe than lifelong imprisonment-without-parole should be imposed for the lesser crimes in that jurisdiction—is a matter that depends on the general moral status of certain severe sanctions such as capital punishment. No message in favour of the death penalty can be derived from Davis's scenario, unless we assume that capital punishment is morally legitimate. An assumption that affirms the moral legitimacy of such punishment, however, would beg the question by taking for granted one of the principal points which the scenario (in combination with the requirement of proportionality) has to establish.

A second objection is very closely related to the first. As is evident from my delineation of Davis's seven-step procedure in § 3.2.1.2.3 above, his whole discussion of the ranking of punishments is framed by the exclusion of punishments that are inhumane. Hence, the principle of proportionality as Davis himself understands it is insufficient ever to support the institution of capital punishment unless that principle is supplemented by a thesis affirming the humaneness of such punishment. A thesis of the latter sort is extrinsic to any of the major principles of retributivism. Thus, the proponents of retributivism who wish to champion the institution of capital punishment will have to look beyond their theory in order to address the question of inhumaneness.

Strangely, Davis adopts a stance of moral relativism when he grapples with that question. He submits that the key factor which determines the humaneness or inhumaneness of any given type of sanction in each society is the prevailing public sentiment in that society (Davis 1996, 34–40, 51–2; Davis 2002, 24–5). If a punitive technique is widely viewed by the members of some community as unacceptably cruel or brutal, then the technique is inhumane within that community and is therefore not something that can legitimately be employed therein. Contrariwise, if a punitive technique is widely viewed by the members of some community as not unacceptably cruel or brutal, then the employment of the technique within that community is not inhumane and is thus legitimate there. As Davis summarizes his criterion for inhumaneness: 'So, a penalty is inhumane (in a particular society) if its use shocks all or almost all; humane, if its use shocks at most a few; and neither clearly humane nor clearly inhumane, if its use shocks many but far from all' (Davis 2002, 24). Now, the present book is not the place for a sustained critique of

Davis's moral relativism on the issue of punitive humaneness. Having elsewhere undertaken a critique of moral relativism on a much broader scale (Kramer 2009a, 30–6, 38–46), I shall confine my remarks here to pointing out that Davis's criterion for humaneness and inhumaneness yields the conclusion that even the most grisly methods of punishment are humane in a community whose members are morally too obtuse to recognize the objectionableness of those methods (Edmundson 2002, 42). Prolonged torture, boiling in oil, executions of the close relatives of convicts, burning at the stake, systematic dismemberment, crucifixion, feeding to piranhas, the gouging out of eyes, and any number of other gruesome punitive measures are humane in certain actual or credibly possible communities, according to Davis's way of thinking. Albeit this conclusion to which Davis has committed himself is not logically incoherent, it is morally outlandish and is to be rejected for moral reasons. As Dolinko rightly contends, Davis's account of inhumaneness implies that there is 'no meaningful way of asking whether [any appalling method of punishment] might be excessive even if most [members of a community] approve of it' (Dolinko 1986, 596 n 252). Fortunately for the proponents of retributivism, nothing in their general theory commits them to Davis's moral relativism. They do need to address the matter of inhumaneness, and they need to look beyond the ambit of retributivism itself in order to deal with that matter; but they do not need to weaken their theory grievously by tying it to any variety of moral relativism. Still, the chief point to be noted here is that Davis's effort to justify capital punishment on the basis of the principle of proportionality is dependent on a satisfactory account of inhumaneness, which Davis has not provided.

Thirdly, even if the preceding two objections are put aside, no conclusion about the moral status of capital punishment in any jurisdiction will follow. Davis assumes that the only morally legitimate sanction more severe than lifelong imprisonment-without-parole is the death penalty. Such an assumption is untenable. Though punishments involving torture or amputation or rape are never morally legitimate, some legitimate punitive measures that fall between lifelong imprisonment-without-parole and the death penalty are available. Those measures consist in various deprivations that can be imposed on the worst or most unruly convicts (McCord 1998). Most obvious among those deprivations is a state of solitary confinement, which can itself be of different degrees of prolongedness. Some additional deprivations are the elimination or sharp curtailment of any communications with family members and other people in the outside world; strict limits on the variety and tastiness of the meals served; and the removal or stringent restriction of a prisoner's access to books and magazines and newspapers and radios and other means of entertainment. In a legal regime where the sanction of lifelong imprisonment-without-parole is imposed for some crimes that are below the level of the most serious, each of these techniques for intensifying the severity of that sanction can enable the regime to satisfy the requirement of proportionality without putting anyone to death. Hence, even if retributivists were to take for granted that the imposition of lifelong imprisonment-without-parole for some crimes below the level of the most grave is itself morally legitimate, they could not safely rely on the principle of proportionality in order to draw any conclusions about the moral status of the death penalty. Davis errs in presuming otherwise.

3.4.2.3. *Lex talionis*

Many retributivists distance themselves from the *lex talionis* (as was noted earlier), but some continue to embrace it. Moreover, as has already been suggested, the principle of *lex talionis* when properly understood is a far more creditable precept than it might initially seem. Thus, we need to ponder whether that precept supports the proposition that the institution of capital punishment is necessary for the fulfilment of retributivism's ideals. If the *lex talionis* does not support that proposition, then nothing in retributivism requires the use of capital punishment—in which case, given the sway of the Minimal Invasion Principle, nothing in retributivism renders the use of capital punishment morally legitimate.

At first glance, the principle of *lex talionis* appears to call for the employment of the death penalty against murderers. It maintains that the retributivistic ideal of equality is realized only when the punishments levied for various crimes are such as to inflict upon the perpetrators the same sorts of harms that they have inflicted upon their victims. Given the type of harm that a murderer inflicts upon his victim, retributivists who uphold the *lex talionis* may be inclined to think that the death penalty is the only sanction that can return like for like. Kant famously drew just such a conclusion: '[I]f [anyone] has committed murder, he must *die*. In this case, no possible substitute can satisfy justice. For there is no *parallel* between death and even the most miserable life, so that there is no equality of crime and retribution unless the perpetrator is judicially put to death' (Kant 1970, 156, emphases in original). Some more recent retributivists have echoed Kant's sentiments. Igor Primorac, for example, has written as follows: '[T]here is only one truly equivalent punishment for murder, namely death....[T]here is nothing equivalent to the murderous destruction of a human life except the destruction of the life of the murderer' (Primorac 1982, 138). Primorac declares that 'the crime of murder...calls for the literal interpretation of the *lex talionis*' (Primorac 1982, 137).

To perceive why these pronouncements are unsustainable, we should examine two sophisticated and highly sympathetic discussions of the *lex talionis* by two opponents of the death penalty: Jeffrey Reiman and Jeremy Waldron. Though each of them allows that the *lex talionis* standard is consistent with the use of capital punishment, each of them denies that such punishment is ever rendered morally obligatory by that standard. Alternative sanctions can satisfy the *lex talionis* precept. In combination with the Minimal Invasion Principle, this conclusion about the absence of moral obligatoriness is sufficient to establish that the *lex talionis* cannot vindicate the institution of capital punishment in any jurisdiction. Since every other tenet of retributivism is likewise unable to furnish the requisite vindication, any retributivistic rationale for the death penalty will have foundered.

3.4.2.3.1 Reiman on retribution and equality

Reiman thought-provokingly argues at some length, with reference to Kant and Hegel, that the *lex talionis* is a worthy component of retributivism because it gives expression to the basic retributivistic values of human equality and moral responsibility (Reiman 1985, 121–6). He elaborates a version of vindicatory retributivism, according to which the central role of punishment is to reaffirm the rights and equal human dignity of the victims of crimes. In addition, punishments in conformity to the *lex talionis* serve to uphold the moral responsibility of the perpetrators of crimes, by visiting upon them the patterns of human interaction to which they have implicitly committed themselves through their choices as rational agents to engage in criminal misdeeds. Punitive institutions that deem those miscreants to have committed themselves to such patterns of human interaction are in turn grounded on a precept of human equality, since 'a rational agent only implicitly authorizes having done to him action similar to what he has done to another, if he and the other are similar in the relevant ways' (Reiman 1985, 124–5). For Reiman, with his inspiration from Kant and Hegel, moral responsibility and human equality are intertwined.

Though Reiman's attempt to expound the justificatory underpinnings of the *lex talionis* as a wide-ranging criterion for punishment is open to challenge in a number of respects—most of which will not be apparent from my synopsis in this subsection, where I deliberately play down those aspects of his discussion—my concern here is solely with his remarks about the bearing of the *lex talionis* on the matter of capital punishment. Reiman maintains that, although the use of capital punishment against murderers is consistent with the *lex talionis*, it is not thereby rendered morally obligatory. For one thing, the *lex talionis* sometimes calls for punitive measures that are both non-obligatory and straightforwardly impermissible as violations of human dignity (Reiman 1985, 126–8). As countless opponents of the *lex talionis* principle have contended, a practice of sentencing rapists to be raped and torturers to be tortured is morally illegitimate regardless of what that principle might seem to prescribe. More important, even when a punishment that returns like for like is not at odds with the values of human dignity and moral integrity, it is not morally obligatory. It is deserved but not required, since any suitably harsh alternative punishment can be substituted for it. For example, lifelong imprisonment-without-parole—perhaps in solitary confinement or in other austere conditions, for the worst murderers—can serve the vindicatory and egalitarian purposes of punishment in response to acts of murder just as well as can the death penalty (Reiman 1985, 130, 131).

In other words, Reiman arrives at the conclusion that the aforementioned purposes of the *lex talionis* can be fulfilled in connection with each crime by any sanction that falls within a relevant range of levels of punitive severity. He indicates that those purposes fix the vaguely delimited bottom end of each such range: '[W]e fall below the bottom end and commit an injustice to the victim when we treat the offender in a way that is no longer compatible with sincerely believing that he deserves to have done to him what he has done to his victim'. As Reiman slightly later adds, 'the alternative punishments must in some convincing way be comparable in gravity to the crimes which they punish, or else they will trivialize the harms those crimes caused and be no longer compatible with sincerely believing that the offender deserves to have done to him what he has done to his victim and no longer capable of impressing upon the criminal his equality with the victim'. As has been noted, Reiman believes that a lifelong term of imprisonment clearly falls within the spectrum of punishments that are retributivistically appropriate for the crime of murder: 'I cannot see how a sentence that would require a murderer to spend his full natural life in prison . . . can be regarded as anything less than extremely severe and thus no trivialization of the harm he has caused' (Reiman 1985, 128, 129, 131).

Reiman goes on to argue that capital punishment should be eschewed because it is morally on a par with torture as an uncivilized type of sanction (Reiman 1985, 134–42). That portion of his discussion patently diverges from this book's observations on human dignity and moral integrity—observations in which I distinguish between the blanket illegitimacy of torture and the legitimacy of capital punishment in certain cases. However, what is important here is not the direction in which Reiman develops his thesis that punishments for murderers which fall short of the death penalty can amply fulfil the ends of retributivism (ends that are the fundaments of the *lex talionis*). Rather, what is important is that thesis itself. Because the underlying purposes of retributivism and the *lex talionis* can be realized without any use of the death penalty even for the worst murderers, a retributivistic rationale for capital punishment cannot overcome the obstacle laid down by the Minimal Invasion Principle. Even in application to the worst murderers, some sanctions less severe than the death penalty can fulfil the same retributivistic ideals that would be fulfilled by the use of that penalty; consequently, the doctrine of retributivism does not warrant the conclusion that the institution of capital punishment is the least severe means for the attainment of a major public purpose. It therefore does not support the conclusion that that institution is ever morally legitimate.

3.4.2.3.2. *Waldron on returning like for like*

Waldron's article on the *lex talionis* is philosophically the most perceptive treatment of the topic heretofore. Unlike most other theorists who have written about the *lex talionis* principle, Waldron does not regard that principle as a version or ramification of retributivism's requirement of commensurateness. Instead, as was mentioned earlier, he contends that the 'like for like' principle is qualitative rather than quantitative in its orientation. Whereas the requirement of commensurateness calls for a (rough) quantitative correspondence between the seriousness of a crime and the severity of the punishment levied for that crime, the *lex talionis* calls for qualitative homologies. As Waldron states, it 'requires the act of punishment to exhibit some or all of the wrong-making features of the offense, some or all of the characteristics on which its wrongness supervenes' (Waldron 1992, 37). Though the egalitarian impetus behind the *lex talionis* is fundamentally the same as that behind the requirement of commensurateness, these two ways of giving effect to that impetus are not identical; nor is either of them identical to the requirement of proportionality.

Waldron fixes upon the wrong-making features of offences because only those features account for the fittingness of sanctions as responses to the offences. No supporter of the *lex talionis* seriously maintains that all the properties of each offence—including all the morally irrelevant properties—must be reproduced in the punitive measure that is imposed on the offender. For example, the fact that a criminal misdeed occurred on a Tuesday would not lead any serious proponent of the *lex talionis* to hold that the punitive response to the misdeed must occur or commence on a Tuesday. Moreover, even certain properties of an offence that do possess some moral relevance would not have to be reproduced in a punishment that fully satisfies the *lex talionis* principle. For example, notwithstanding that a murder carried out by strangulation might be morally more serious than a murder carried out by poisoning, the *lex talionis* does not demand that the perpetrator of the murder be strangled rather than executed in some other manner. After all, even the classical wording of the *lex talionis* as 'an eye for an eye' or 'a life for a life' specifies only the injurious or lethal result of a criminal misdeed, rather than the manner in which that result has been brought about.

In either of two main ways, a defender of the *lex talionis* principle can seek to rule out the death penalty as an appropriate type of punishment. In the first place, some types of punishments are ruled out by even the most robust champions of that principle such as Kant. Like every other moral philosopher who deserves to be taken seriously, Kant was opposed to any punitive practice of raping rapists or torturing torturers (Waldron 1992, 38 n 27, 40–1). To respect the human dignity of an offender and to preserve the moral integrity of a system of governance and its officials, such a system must eschew punitive techniques of the sorts just mentioned. Consequently, under any morally defensible version of the *lex talionis*, not all the wrong-making features of acts of rape and torture will be reproduced in the punishments that are inflicted upon the perpetrators of those acts.

Now, as has been argued more than once in this book, the death penalty is not morally on a par with torture or rape as a punitive measure that violates an offender's human dignity and sullies a punisher's moral integrity. Hence, the exclusion of torture and rape from the repertoire of punishments authorized by any morally defensible version of the *lex talionis* does not perforce translate into the exclusion of the death penalty from that repertoire. Still, what is of key importance in Kant's disallowance of those types of sanctions is his manifest recognition that the moral force of the *lex talionis* standard—the moral force that it derives from the values of human equality and moral responsibility—depends on the meshing of that standard with other major moral values. Under the *lex talionis*, that is, the wrong-making properties of criminal misdeeds are to be paralleled by the properties of a criminal-justice system's punitive responses to those misdeeds only insofar as the paralleling does not run athwart any moral values that bear upon the matter. Accordingly, proponents of capital punishment who wish to rely on the *lex talionis* in support of their position will have to establish that the use of such punishment does not run athwart any other moral values. They cannot take for granted, on the basis of the *lex talionis*, that all the wrong-making characteristics of murders will be matched by characteristics of the sanctions that are justifiably levied upon murderers.

Of even greater significance for this chapter is a second way in which the critics of the death penalty can resist the invocation of the *lex-talionis* principle in support of such a penalty. As Waldron points out, any recourse to that principle must distil the wrong-making features of a crime that are to be reproduced in the sanction imposed on the person who has committed the crime. Even the 'eye for an eye, life for a life' formulation comprises such a distillation, however crude and laconic it may be. Now, whenever the wrong-making features of a crime are explicitly or implicitly distilled for the purpose of undertaking a punitive response, a choice has to be made about the degree of abstraction or concreteness with which those features are to be encapsulated. For example, in the crude Biblical formulation just mentioned, the wrong-making features are specified quite concretely but not so concretely as to indicate the manner in which an eye has been lost or a life has been extinguished. Any other explicit or implicit distillation of a crime's wrong-making properties must likewise proceed at some level of abstraction or specificity, and the level is not predetermined by those properties themselves.

How, then, is the correct level of abstraction or specificity determined? Waldron addresses this question as an epistemic matter: '[E]lements of the offense can be understood in more or less abstract terms. The level of abstraction we choose will be [based on] our sense of what ultimately matters in our reckoning something an offense, our sense of finally why it is wrong.' He states similarly that, 'in specifying the wrong-making characteristics of the offense, we will be guided by our best sense of what made the action wrong in the first place' (Waldron 1992, 37). Though these pronouncements are unexceptionable and illuminating, the question of the correct level of abstraction or concreteness can more fruitfully be addressed as a matter of underlying values.

When the wrong-making features of a crime are to be distilled for the implementation of the *lex talionis*, the proper degree of abstraction or specificity is fixed by the basic moral values—human equality and moral responsibility—that underlie the *lex talionis* and endow it with moral force. Choices in the characterization of any such features are to be made with reference to those values. That is, the characterization, along with the punishment for which it calls, should be such as to reaffirm the fundamental equality between the offender and everyone else in the jurisdiction (including of course the immediate victim, if there is indeed an immediate victim of the particular offence). *Pari passu*, it should be such as to uphold the moral responsibility of the offender by accurately capturing the gravity of his or her misconduct.

As can be inferred from my earlier remarks about the vagueness of the property of desert, the ideals of human equality and moral responsibility—and the principle of *lex talionis* which they sustain—are vague. In application to each type or instance of crime, they allow the imposition of any sanction within a vaguely delimited range or array. This vagueness is manifested in the *lex talionis* through the differing levels of abstraction with which the wrong-making properties of a crime can suitably be encapsulated. Those differing levels militate in favour of differing types of sanctions, any one of which is appropriate as a society's punitive response to the crime in question. Any one of those sanctions is an apt means of reaffirming the value of human equality, which has been contravened by the commission of the crime.

Though Waldron's discussions of the crime of murder will prove here to be in need of some modification, they admirably make clear the importance of the level of abstraction in the distillation of a crime's wrong-making characteristics. Waldron centres his discussions on questions about why the crime of murder is wrong, but his points can equally well be understood as addressing questions about how punishments should reflect the basic equality between offenders and victims. A lengthy quotation is warranted here:

Someone may try to push us to a level of [higher] generality.... 'What makes an act of killing wrong? What is it about killing that makes it something that one should not do?' Suppose, for example, that I deliberately injure someone in a way that is calculated to deprive them of consciousness and reduce them to the state of a living vegetable, from which medical science is incapable of awaking them. Isn't that as bad as killing, and in roughly the same way? In which case, the bad thing about a killing is not that it involves the infliction of what clinicians define as death, but that it disrupts and terminates the conscious self-direction of one's life. From this point of view, the fact that clinical death is involved may seem as [tenuously relevant] as the fact that shooting [rather than strangulation or poisoning or stabbing] is involved.

If anyone takes that line, it may alter his views on what is appropriate punishment for murder. The aim will be to perform as punishment an action calculated to disrupt and terminate the conscious self-direction of the prisoner's life. Such punishment may be something other than capital punishment as we understand it: putting the prisoner into an irreversible coma, for example, or certain forms of very highly restrictive confinement. Of course, this new approach does not *preclude* execution (any more than focusing on [death rather than death-by-shooting] precluded the use of firing squads). But it may give us other alternatives for punishing murder, just as states may choose among various forms of execution. [Waldron 1992, 36]

Waldron presses this point again when he slightly later discusses Kant's insistence on the unique suitability of the death penalty for murderers. He submits that an opponent of Kant's position 'might concede that the killing aspect is all-important in the wrongness of murder, but he might propose . . . that we understand the wrongness of killing in terms that are a little more abstract in character. Why is killing wrong? Because it radically disrupts an autonomous life. Very well, then let us radically disrupt the autonomous life of the offender' (Waldron 1992, 41–2). Having broached a characteristic that might account for the wrongness of every murder, Waldron proceeds by way of a question to adumbrate the implications of the *lex talionis*: 'Does this mean we have to kill [the offender]? It depends on whether or not we have available some other punishment that shares this abstract feature with acts of killing' (Waldron 1992, 42).

As has been indicated, Waldron's attempt to pin down the key wrong-making property of the crime of murder is in need of modification or amplification. His account, as it stands, cannot explain the wrongness of an act of murder that is committed against someone who is afflicted by profound dementia or profound mental retardation. Any human being who suffers from one of those maladies is devoid of the ability to lead an autonomous life. Thus, if we fix upon the termination of the conscious self-direction of a person's life as the aspect of a murder that determinatively accounts for its wrongness, we shall have left ourselves unable to say why the murder of a senile human being or of a mentally retarded human being is wrong. Clearly, then, the diagnosis of the wrongness of murder which Waldron proposes is not satisfactory.

Instead of focusing on a murder's termination of the victim's conscious self-direction of her life, we should focus on its irreversibly complete termination of any opportunities for the victim to undergo future positive experiences. That latter feature is correctly predicable of the murder of a retarded or senile person, and is even correctly predicable of the murder of a thoroughly comatose person. (Notwithstanding that the condition of a thoroughly comatose person may be irreversible on the basis of current medical technology, there remains a minute chance—so long as she is still alive—that future breakthroughs in such technology will enable her to regain at least a meagre capacity to undergo positive experiences. Once she is no longer alive, that minute chance will have come to an end.) A murder's irreversibly complete termination of any prospect of future positive experiences can obviously be reproduced in a legal-governmental system's punitive response through the execution of the perpetrator, but it can also be reproduced through a sentence of lifelong imprisonment-without-parole in drably austere conditions of solitary confinement. If the irreversibility of the murder is to be reproduced adequately in the punitive response, the sentence of lifelong-imprisonment-without-parole will have to be insusceptible to commutation by any executive or judicial official. Indeed, the insusceptibility to commutation might even be entrenched in a constitutional provision. (Of course, if compelling evidence of a convict's innocence were to come to light, the sentence of lifelong imprisonment-without-parole could be quashed. The terminability of the sentence in that respect is straightforwardly consistent with its blanket insusceptibility to commutation.)

In short, even the strand of retributivism that is most favourable for supporters of capital punishment cannot establish that the use of such punishment is morally obligatory. Any morally tenable rendering of the *lex talionis* principle does allow the use of capital punishment but does not require it. Even when the *lex talionis* is understood to call for the reproduction of the wrong-making features of a crime in any appropriate punitive response to that crime, it leaves room for the sentencing of murderers to punishments that fall short of the death penalty. The basic moral values which endue the *lex talionis* with its moral force will have left such room. Consequently, given that the *lex talionis* never renders the institution of capital punishment morally obligatory, and given that the Minimal Invasion Principle prescribes that any public purposes are to be pursued only through the least restrictive legal-governmental measures that can satisfactorily achieve those purposes, the *lex talionis* cannot successfully be invoked in support of capital punishment. Because some sanctions less severe than the death penalty can fulfil the demands of the *lex-talionis* standard, the Minimal Invasion Principle does not allow any legal-governmental system to employ that penalty on the basis of that standard. It permits only the employment of the less severe sanctions.

Let us note, in conclusion, that this discussion of the *lex-talionis* precept has not watered down that precept in any way. Just as the traditional 'eye for an eye' formulation does not water down the *lex-talionis* standard at all by abstracting from the specific manner in which an eye has been lost, my abstraction from some of the specificity of death in my account of the wrongness of murder has been aimed at giving full effect to the *lex talionis*. I have pursued that aim by singling out the central feature of death that has to be reproduced in a criminal-justice system's punishment for murder if the punishment is to conform to the fundamental moral values which underlie the *lex talionis* precept. Every application of that precept has to address the matter of abstraction and specificity. As has been contended, the correct way of addressing that matter is to select the level(s) of abstraction that will optimally realize the aforementioned moral values. That criterion for the selection of some level(s) of abstraction in the devising of a punitive response to any sort of crime will generate a distillation of wrong-making features that can be satisfactorily matched by any one of an array of sanctions. When the crime under consideration is that of murder, one of the sanctions in the relevant array is the death penalty. However, since that array will also include lifelong imprisonment-without-parole, the Minimal Invasion Principle does not countenance the use of the death penalty on retributivistic grounds. Retributivists who champion the *lex talionis* are obligated by the Minimal Invasion Principle to favour lifelong imprisonment-without-parole, rather than capital punishment, for murderers.

In other words, in reaching the conclusion just stated, this discussion has gone through exactly the kind of reasoning that is involved—implicitly or explicitly—whenever the *lex talionis* is properly applied. Far from diluting the 'like for like' standard, my reflections here on its implications for the death penalty have done precisely what is necessary in order to bring it to bear on the matters which it addresses.

3.5. A concluding rejection of scepticism

This chapter, throughout its second half, has argued against any retributivistic rationale for the death penalty by maintaining that the ideals of retributivism do not ever determinately require the use of that penalty. Because those ideals do not require such a sanction, they in combination with the Minimal Invasion Principle do not permit it. What should be emphasized in closing is that my claims about the limited determinacy of retributivistic ideals do not have anything to do with moral scepticism. Moral sceptics insist that there are never any determinately correct answers to moral questions. Having elsewhere criticized at length the pronouncements of such sceptics (Kramer 2009a, 87–106), I have scarcely embraced them here.

My highlighting of the limitedness of retributivism's determinacy might somehow seem to resemble the proclamations of sceptics who purport to detect rampant indeterminacy in the domain of morality. However, any such resemblance is very tenuous and superficial indeed. In the first place, even if this chapter had argued that matters of desert and commensurateness and proportionality are thoroughly indeterminate, it would not thereby have denied the existence of determinately correct answers to countless other moral questions. Let us keep in mind, for example, that Shafer-Landau—who does contend that matters of desert are thoroughly indeterminate—is one of the premier contemporary moral realists. Scepticism about one area of moral enquiry is hardly tantamount to scepticism about morality generally.

Even more important, this chapter has decidedly not concurred with Shafer-Landau's nihilistic dismissal of the value of desert. On the contrary, his extreme position has undergone sustained criticism herein. While affirming that questions about the implications of vague touchstones such as desert and commensurateness and proportionality do not lend themselves to uniquely correct answers, I have hardly submitted that those touchstones are completely open-ended and that 'anything goes'. What this chapter has sought to underscore is the limitedness—rather than the absence—of determinacy in a certain area of political morality. To any question about what would constitute a pre-conventionally deserved or commensurate or proportionate punishment in some context, multiple answers will be correct; but, at the same time, a myriad of intelligible answers will be incorrect. Limited determinacy is limited *determinacy* as well as *limited* determinacy. In sum, even with reference solely to the chief principles of retributivism (and leaving aside the rest of morality), this chapter has distanced itself from any variety of moral scepticism. The fact that my critique has dwelt on the partial open-endedness of retributivism's precepts is no indication whatsoever of rampant indeterminacy in this area of political morality.

4

Death as Incapacitation

Although the incapacitative rationale for capital punishment has not received nearly as much scholarly attention as the deterrence-oriented and retributivistic rationales, it is quite often invoked in popular debates over the issue (where it is frequently run together with the deterrence-oriented justification). In any case, this rationale has to be considered separately, for it propounds a distinctive set of considerations in favour of putting the worst criminals to death. Its fortunes do not stand or fall with those of any of the other commonly advanced rationales for the death penalty. Still, notwithstanding the distinctiveness of the incapacitative justification, and notwithstanding the uniqueness of some of the problems to which it gives rise, a few of the principal points that tell against it are broadly similar to several of the pitfalls that bedevil certain other arguments in support of capital punishment. Given the strongly consequentialist character of the incapacitative line of thought, we should hardly be surprised to find that its weaknesses overlap with those which afflict other consequentialist approaches to the matter of the death penalty.

4.1. The general doctrine

As has been stated in Chapter 1, the central idea in the incapacitative rationale for the imposition of capital punishment is that thugs who are strongly disposed to engage in savage murders are too dangerous to be kept alive. Even if such people are apprehended and convicted and incarcerated, the likelihood of their continuing to commit mayhem (or of their inspiring others to commit mayhem) is unacceptably high. They can slaughter their fellow convicts or the guards in their prisons, and—through communications carried to people outside—they can direct nefarious doings far beyond the confines of the walls that immure them.[1] Moreover, so long as they are

---

[1] 'There are only two grounds on which the death of a citizen might be held to be necessary. First, when it is evident that even if deprived of his freedom, he retains such connections and such power as to endanger the security of the nation, when, that is, his existence may threaten a dangerous revolution in the established form of government' (Beccaria 1995, 66–7). Cesare Beccaria, of course, was an opponent of the death penalty. However, in the foregoing passage he appeared to endorse the incapacitative rationale for that penalty, at least in application to high-profile political subversives with numerous followers. His general conception of the purpose of punishment was unmistakably incapacitative as well as deterrence-oriented: 'The purpose [of punishment], therefore, is nothing other than to prevent the offender from doing fresh harm to his fellows and to deter others from doing likewise' (Beccaria 1995, 31).

alive, there will abide some probability of their escaping from those confines. Only if they are executed will they cease to pose a clear and present danger to everyone around them and to the wider community. Jeremy Bentham, usually associated with a deterrence-oriented perspective on punishment, delivered a classic statement of the incapacitative justification for the penalty of death:

The most remarkable feature in the punishment of death, and that which it possesses in the greatest perfection, is the taking from the offender the power of doing further injury: whatever is apprehended, either from the force or cunning of the criminal, at once vanishes away; society is in a prompt and complete manner delivered from all alarm. [Bentham 1962, 444 (bk II, ch 12, § 1)]

4.1.1. Punishment as incapacitation

Like the other standard rationales for the death penalty, the incapacitative rationale derives from a general theory of punishment. Although putting someone to death is a singularly thorough way of incapacitating him, all or nearly all other punishments can likewise correctly be understood as means of reducing the abilities of convicts. When a monetary fine is imposed, it lessens the resources at the disposal of the person who has thereby been punished, and it consequently removes his ability to pursue various combinations of projects that could have been pursued with the forfeited resources. *Pro tanto*, it incapacitates that person from engaging in activities which he might wish to undertake. Even more obviously incapacitative is a term of imprisonment. Somebody locked in a cell is plainly deprived of countless opportunities that would otherwise be available to him. Though he might still be able to interact with the outside world in certain respects through intermediaries, his effectiveness in realizing his objectives in that wider world will patently be lowered by his confinement. Somebody sentenced to a period of monitored service in his community will also undergo a curtailment of his overall ability to act in sundry ways, though of course the curtailment will not typically be as sharp as that produced by a term of incarceration.

In liberal-democratic legal systems, warnings or rebukes by legal-governmental officials (such as policemen) are generally alternatives to punishment. However, there can be legal systems in which the issuance of warnings or rebukes is itself standardly a form of punishment imposed on people who have been convicted of certain crimes. In a system where a warning or a rebuke is indeed a punishment rather than an alternative thereto, the speech-act in question might carry a significant debilitating effect on the person to whom it is addressed. As was noted in § 3.2.2.4 of Chapter 3, there can exist societies in which the warnings or reprimands issued by legal institutions are so intensely shame-inducing or despondency-eliciting as to be psychologically incapacitating to quite a high degree. Nevertheless, although such societies are logically possible, they bear little resemblance to liberal-democratic societies in the actual world. In the legal

institutions of liberal-democratic societies in the actual world, the use of warnings
or rebukes as punishments is not directly incapacitating to any appreciable degree.
Largely for that reason, such speech-acts in liberal-democratic societies in the
actual world are typically alternatives to legal punishments; they do not typically
amount to such punishments in themselves.

Still, considerably less fanciful are societies—mostly illiberal societies—in
which the issuance of warnings or reprimands is *indirectly* incapacitating to a high
degree, through the reactions of other people. Even in a society where such effects
occur, any typical warning or reprimand by legal-governmental officials will not
directly incapacitate the person who undergoes it; but numerous other people in
his society will shun him and will thereby significantly lower his opportunities
to pursue his economic livelihood and to engage in any of countless projects.
Accordingly, a public reprimand or warning can be a potent punitive infliction in
such a context.

Certain other measures quite commonly used as legal punishments in some jurisdictions are imposed primarily in order to elicit shame and humiliation (Kahan 1996,
630–52), yet they too indirectly reduce the opportunities open to the people who are
punished. For example, offenders are sometimes required to wear luridly coloured
wigs or garish clothing while they undertake monitored service in their communities.
They are sometimes required to display signs in front of their houses to announce their
criminality, or they are required to wear shirts emblazoned for the same purpose. In
the past, and in illiberal societies today, offenders have been branded (with the scarlet
letter 'A,' for example), and their ears have been clipped. With these and other shame-
inducing punitive techniques, legal-governmental officials in some jurisdictions
aim principally to mortify offenders. However, like the warnings and reprimands
described in the last paragraph, such techniques likewise influence the behaviour of
other people toward the offenders. When ordinary citizens are alerted by one or more
of those techniques to the fact that someone has been convicted of a crime—perhaps
an especially unsavoury crime such as paedophilia—most of them will respond by
distancing themselves from the person or even by persecuting him. His opportunities
for gainful employment and for pursuing various other activities will consequently
be diminished considerably. Like other sanctions that have commonly been used as
punishments in the past and present, then, shame-eliciting sanctions are incapacitative
as well as humiliating.

Indeed, as should be apparent from Chapter 3, the incapacitative effects of sanctions are of major importance even for conceptions of punishment that do not take
incapacitation to be the central justificatory purpose of punitive institutions. For
example, when retributivists ascribe to punishment the role of resubordinating the
projects of offenders to the moral frameworks of their communities, the resubordination is presumed to occur through the imposition of measures that significantly curtail any opportunities for offenders to contravene the moral values that are upheld by

the legal-governmental institutions in their communities. Each such punitive measure temporarily or permanently limits the ability of an offender to prioritize his own
heinous urgings over the moral and legal restraints of his community, and each such
measure thereby communicates to him the misconceivedness of his priorities. So, at
any rate, the proponents of retributivism maintain (with reference to liberal democracies). In sum, although retributivists shrink from the consequentialist orientation of
incapacitative theorists, their conceptions of punishment overlap in some substantial
respects. While retributivists impute to punishment the morally worthy purpose of
repairing crime-engendered disruptions in the egalitarian fabric of a society, they
readily accept that the repairs occur by way of incapacitation.

Hence, arguments in favour of capital punishment that concentrate on its
lethally incapacitating force are applying a general exposition of the role of punishment to the peculiar problems posed by hoodlums who are especially dangerous
(because of their sadism or because of their cold-blooded indifference toward the
lives and basic well-being of other people). Some elements of that general exposition figure quite saliently in the main competing accounts of punishment as well.
Still, the emphasis on promoting public security through the incapacitation of
wrongdoers—rather than through the deterrence of potential wrongdoers or through
the denunciation of wicked conduct—is unique to the incapacitative conception
of criminal justice. Accordingly, although some of the vices of that conception are
similar to some of the vices of other consequentialist approaches to punishment,
the incapacitative rationale also partakes of weaknesses that are due to its distinctive
preoccupations.

4.1.2. Incapacitation is not tantamount to deterrence

Given what has just been said about the distinctiveness of the incapacitative rationale's preoccupations (and of some of its shortcomings), we should note carefully
the differences between that rationale and certain other understandings of the point
of punishment. Let us begin with the deterrence-oriented approach, which resembles the incapacitative approach in its consequentialist concern with promoting the
public weal through the enhancement of public security. Despite that conspicuous
point of similarity, these two accounts of punishment—and specifically of capital punishment—diverge in a number of respects (Allen and Shavell 2005, 630–2;
Bedau 1993, 177, 179–80; Berns 1979, 89–90, 100; Bradley 1999, 117–18; Gale 1985,
981, 984–5; Lempert 1981, 1189; Oldenquist 2004, 335; Sorell 1987, 42; Sunstein and
Vermeule 2005a, 715–16).

4.1.2.1. Four differences

First, whereas the deterrence-oriented rationale for the death penalty is focused on
evoking fear in people other than the offenders who are executed, the incapacitative

rationale is focused on permanently eliminating those offenders themselves. Deterrence-oriented executions do not achieve their assigned purpose unless they frighten potential murderers into complying with laws that prohibit murder. By contrast, executions conducted on the basis of the incapacitative justification can fully accomplish their assigned purpose even if nobody is frightened by them and indeed even if hardly anybody is aware of them.

A second difference is very closely related to the first. Each rationale implies certain conditions for the appropriateness of executions. Under the incapacitative rationale, the imposition of the death penalty is justified only if an offender is lethally and inveterately dangerous. Under the deterrence-oriented rationale, contrariwise, the dangerousness of executed offenders is an irrelevant consideration. What matters under that latter rationale is the likelihood that executions will serve more effectively than any alternative modes of punishment to deter potential murderers from becoming actual murderers. That likelihood does not hinge on the extent of the actively homicidal peril that would have been posed by the continued existence of each criminal who is put to death. Conversely, the extent of the actively homicidal peril that would have been posed by the continued existence of each such criminal—and thus the question whether the incapacitative rationale has called for putting each one to death—will not hinge on the likelihood that any given executions are more effective than alternative sanctions in deterring members of the public from resorting to murder.

To be sure, the difference just highlighted can become blurred in some cases. Suppose, for instance, that the leader of a criminal gang is extremely dangerous even while incarcerated, and that the incapacitative justification for capital punishment therefore demands that he be executed. Suppose further that the execution of him will not only deprive his subordinates of the direction and inspiration that they receive from him, but will also frighten them into desisting from many of their nefarious activities lest they in turn be subjected to the death penalty. Indeed, if the gang leader is especially prominent throughout the jurisdiction, the execution of him might be likely to produce deterrent effects on the members of other criminal gangs as well. In these circumstances, the dangerousness of the continued existence of the gang leader is due partly to the fact that the termination of his existence through the implementation of a death sentence will deter the commission of quite a few serious crimes. Even in application to a case of this sort, however, the incapacitative rationale and the deterrence-oriented rationale diverge as importantly as they converge. For example, were the gang leader to die abruptly of a heart attack while serving a sentence of life-long imprisonment, the ends sought by the proponents of the incapacitative rationale for capital punishment would be at least partly realized. No longer would the gang leader be directing and inspiring his subordinates to carry out wicked crimes. By contrast, the ends sought by the deterrence-oriented supporters of capital punishment would remain unrealized in the aftermath of such a contingency; the marginal deterrent effects of an execution would not materialize, given that no execution ever occurred.[2] (Of course, there can be circumstances in which the continued existence of some person P is dangerous only in the sense that the non-occurrence of his execution will result in the non-occurrence of deterrent effects that would have ensued if the execution had taken place. If P is genuinely not significantly dangerous in any other respect, however, the correct conclusion to be drawn is that the incapacitative rationale for capital punishment does not in itself apply to his situation. Whereas the deterrence-oriented justification of capital punishment calls for executions on the ground that they tend to induce fear in people who are inclined to commit capital crimes, the incapacitative justification calls for executions on the ground that the executed evildoers themselves will no longer be capable of perpetrating such crimes either on their own or through their associates. Given that P is *ex hypothesi* disinclined or unable to commit any further such crimes, the incapacitative rationale does not militate in favour of putting him to death.)

A third dissimilarity between the deterrence-oriented theory and the incapacitative theory pertains to the matter of specific deterrence.[3] Under neither theory is specific deterrence an objective that is to be achieved through capital punishment. However, the underlying reasons for that common position diverge between the two theories. Under the deterrence-oriented rationale, the peculiarities of capital punishment are the factor that explains why specific deterrence is not an aim of such punishment. Because anyone who undergoes an execution is no longer in a position to comply with the law—on the basis of fear or on any other basis—the notion of specific deterrence in application to such a person is simply out of place. Under the incapacitative justification, the reason for the exclusion of specific deterrence as an end to be pursued through capital punishment is not focused on the peculiarities of such punishment; rather, the exclusion stems from the fact that neither specific deterrence nor general deterrence is pursued through any sanctions under the incapacitative account of punitive institutions. Instead of being imposed to frighten people into refraining from exercising their abilities to contravene legal requirements, incapacitative sanctions are imposed to remove some or all of those abilities. This difference between the incapacitative approach and the deterrence-oriented approach is overlooked by theorists who use the phrase 'specific deterrence' and the term 'incapacitation' interchangeably.[4]

A further, closely connected dissimilarity between those two approaches is also linked to a matter of linguistic usage. In ordinary discourse, the phrase 'crime prevention' is quite often used indiscriminately to cover alike the incapacitating

---

[2] An exception to this generalization can arise in a situation where the officials of the relevant criminal-justice system dissimulatingly persuade members of the public that the gang leader's demise is due to his having been executed.

[3] As was remarked in Chapter 2 (§ 2.1), specific deterrence consists in a sanction's eliciting of fearful law-abidingness on the part of the person who has undergone the sanction.

[4] For some examples of this conflation, see Greenberg 1986, 1676 n 36; Kahan 1999, 425, 469. For correctives, see Bedau 1993, 179–80; Bradley 1999, 117–18.

effects and the deterrent effects of sanctions (and also to cover anticipatory measures such as the installation of locks and alarms). In fact, however, only the incapacitating effects of sanctions—along with anticipatory steps such as the installation of locks and the hiring of armed security guards—veritably prevent crimes. People who are deterred from committing a crime of some kind are not thereby prevented from committing it; rather, they are frightened into declining to commit it even though they are mostly *un*prevented from committing it. Although the incapacitative effects and the deterrent effects of sanctions both tend to lower the incidence of crimes (*ceteris paribus*), they do so by different routes. Insofar as punishments succeed in incapacitating the malefactors on whom they are inflicted, they render impossible the commission of certain crimes by those malefactors. Insofar as punishments succeed in deterring would-be criminals from perpetrating certain crimes, they incline such people not to avail themselves of any opportunities to perpetrate those crimes. Incapacitation operates by removing or averting possibilities, whereas deterrence operates by altering people's all-things-considered dispositions. Given this important difference between deterrence and incapacitation or prevention, Thomas Hurka goes astray in the following passage by implying that those two phenomena are equivalent:

[Governments] are never permitted to inflict punishments which infringe rights that are more important than is necessary to *prevent* further violations of the right which they are enforcing. If two punishments will be equally effective in *deterring* violations of this right, they have a duty to impose the less severe punishment; and if no punishments will be effective in *deterring* violations, they have a duty to impose no punishment at all. [Hurka 1982, 657, emphases added]

4.1.2.2. A missed distinction: some closing remarks and examples

Of course, despite my underscoring of the dissimilarities between incapacitation and deterrence, nobody should infer that those two types of punitive effects are somehow incompatible. The deterrence-oriented account of punishment is perfectly consistent with the incapacitative account, and the two of them are frequently combined. Rather than suggesting that they are somehow mutually exclusive, my discussion here has simply endeavoured to accentuate their distinctness.

The ease with which the distinctness of incapacitation and deterrence can get obscured is evident from some comments by Dan Markel concerning the use of the death penalty against convicts who commit murders in prison while serving lifelong terms of incarceration: 'Various commentators suggest that it is only the threat of death that keeps these convicts from killing prison guards or other prisoners. Executing these prisoners arguably reduces risks that they will murder, rape, or assault others in prison, or outside should they escape (or be released early)' (Markel 2005, 471, footnotes omitted). In the first of these two quoted sentences, Markel is referring to the deterrent force of the death penalty. When that penalty is threatened as a measure to be inflicted on every convict who commits a murder while in prison for life, it can serve—with greater or lesser effectiveness—to deter the commission of any such murder. In the second of the two quoted sentences, by contrast, Markel is referring to the incapacitative effects of executions. In that sentence, as becomes especially plain in an attached footnote where he adverts to recidivism among murderers, his focus lies on putting people to death because of the risks which they pose. Whereas the first sentence in the quotation is concerned with the *deterrence* of murders through the threat of the imposition of capital punishment, the second sentence is concerned with the *prevention* of murders through the actual application of such punishment. Yet Markel conveys the impression, probably unwittingly, that the second sentence is a straightforward elaboration of the first. Anyone attuned to the differences between incapacitation and deterrence should not be misled. Fully consistent though incapacitation and deterrence are, they are not identical to each other.

Let us look briefly at one further example of a sophisticated theorist who does not properly come to grips with the distinction between deterrence and incapacitation. Carol Steiker first stumbles in the same manner as Hurka when she asserts that her opponents 'suggest that if the death penalty can *prevent*—through incapacitation of the offender or general deterrence—the loss to murder of even one innocent life, then it is a morally justified or perhaps even morally required penal response' (Steiker 2005, 752, emphasis added). Contrary to what Steiker implies here, only incapacitation prevents certain crimes. As has already been indicated, deterrence averts certain crimes not by preventing them but by disinclining people to engage in them. It alters people's all-things-considered propensities instead of removing their opportunities. (Some readers might retort that, in ordinary parlance, the term 'prevent' quite frequently means no more than 'avert' or 'bring about the non-occurrence of'. For example, members of the public in the United States are often admonished to prevent forest fires by avoiding any careless uses of incendiary materials while camping. For years, the slogan associated with the US Forest Service was 'Only you can prevent forest fires'. Given these patterns of everyday linguistic usage, so the retort would go, my insistence on the distinction between prevention and deterrence is captious and misconceived. Any such retort, however, would itself be misguided. Though the verb 'prevent' in the Forest Service's motto does mean 'avert' or 'bring about the non-occurrence of', it is referring to conduct that renders the ignition of a fire physically impossible by excluding the conditions that are physically necessary for combustion to occur. Hence, the employment of 'prevent' in that motto is unexceptionable, whereas the employment of 'prevent' to refer to conduct that involves dissuasion or discouragement rather than outright preclusion is inapposite. If theorists are to capture accurately the differences between incapacitation and deterrence, they should not be grouping together those phenomena under the heading of 'prevention.')

More puzzling is a second misstep by Steiker, which occurs when she is contrasting the practice of capital punishment with a practice of killing kidnappers or terrorists in emergency situations in order to rescue their captives. She writes: 'In the context of criminal punishment, by contrast, the punishment itself is never directed solely or even primarily at the cause of the danger; rather, the substantial net savings of lives results from the deterrent effect that the punishment will have on the future actions of other people' (Steiker 2005, 783–4). This pronouncement sweeps aside the incapacitative rationale for punishment altogether, as it asserts in effect—without any substantiation—that no punishments are ever undertaken in accordance with that rationale. Within the terms of the incapacitative justification for the death penalty, there is a fairly close analogy between the execution of an extremely dangerous convict and the shooting of a kidnapper or terrorist. Though the danger posed by a captor to his hostages is usually more pressingly urgent than the danger posed by an incarcerated convict to his potential victims, the general reason for putting to death the convict (according to the incapacitative rationale) is the same as the general reason for shooting the captor. In each case, a murderous thug is killed because his continued existence would have gravely imperilled the lives and basic well-being of other people. Indeed, with that general reason in mind, some theorists have suggested that the incapacitative role of punishment can best be understood as a form of collective self-defence (Bradley 1999, 118; Kennedy 2000, 858).

Steiker appears to assume that the only consequentialist rationale for capital punishment which concentrates on saving lives is the deterrence-oriented rationale. When the distinction between incapacitation and deterrence is duly observed, the untenability of any such assumption becomes manifest. Of course, the reason for her addressing herself solely to the deterrence-oriented justification might instead be that she takes for granted the moral unsustainability of the incapacitative justification of the death penalty. If so, then her underlying belief about that latter justification is correct; but the correctness of the belief should scarcely be taken for granted. Any satisfactory critique of the incapacitative rationale must advance arguments against it, instead of disregarding it or assuming it away.

4.1.3. Incapacitation is not tantamount to retribution or denunciation

Whereas the incapacitative justification for capital punishment and the deterrence-oriented justification are both consequentialist approaches that take the saving of lives as their chief objective (albeit by significantly different routes), the incapacitative justification and the retributivistic justification in its primary form are on opposite sides of the consequentialism/deontology divide. As Ernest van den Haag, among many others, has remarked: 'When retributive, punishment is an end in itself, satisfying a moral requirement. It is not a means to any material end, as are rehabilitation and incapacitation' (Van den Haag 1990, 506). Indeed, as we shall see, some of the most problematic features of the incapacitative approach to capital punishment are the ways in which it deviates from the deontological tenor of retributivism.

Given that the incapacitative account differs so markedly from retributivism, the two doctrines have seldom been conflated. To be sure, each of them is egalitarian in some sense. Retributivism is egalitarian in the respects that have been expounded in Chapter 3. An incapacitative approach to capital punishment is egalitarian in a thinner sense, in the manner of the utilitarian theory wherein it is usually embedded. That is, under the incapacitative approach, everyone's basic interests in life and well-being are weighed alongside the corresponding interests of everyone else; nobody's interests are excluded. Under that approach, the balance of interests will sometimes militate in favour of executing somebody because of the extreme dangers that he poses to other people.

Still, although the incapacitative rationale and the retributivistic rationale for the death penalty are both egalitarian in certain ways, the egalitarianism of each is different in nature from that of the other, and there are hardly any additional affinities between the two doctrines. We should scarcely be surprised that, whereas the distinction between incapacitation and deterrence often gets missed, the distinction between incapacitation and retribution is almost never overlooked.

Also notably divergent are the incapacitative rationale and the denunciatory rationale for capital punishment. Notwithstanding that those two justifications are both consequentialist in their orientation, the methods which they respectively advocate are strikingly different and are thus not easily mistaken for each other. While the denunciatory conception of punishment emphasizes the communicative role of sanctions as public expressions of revulsion and indignation, the incapacitative rationale for the death penalty—like the purgative rationale—does not ascribe any significant communicative role to executions. It perceives the imposition of the death penalty as a means of removing grave dangers rather than as a means of communicating messages to offenders or to the general public. Of course, the conducting of executions on incapacitative grounds is perfectly consistent with the issuance of announcements of the executions in order to reassure members of the general public that they are being properly safeguarded. Such announcements will presumably be routine in virtually any system of criminal justice that does conduct executions on incapacitative grounds. Still, the occurrence of the executions themselves is what suffices for the fulfillment of the ends prescribed by an incapacitative justification. Those ends are accomplished through the elimination of extremely dangerous hoodlums, even in the quite unlikely event that all or most members of the public are unaware that the hoodlums have been eliminated.

Other aspects of the denunciatory theory, directly connected to its communicative dimension, are likewise unparalleled in the incapacitative rationale for capital punishment. Uncombined with other justifications, the latter rationale is not concerned with improving the moral sentiments of the citizenry in a jurisdiction, nor is it concerned with channelling vindictive impulses through institutional forms in order to satisfy and defuse those impulses. Its only concern, on its own terms, is the removal of grave dangers. Naturally, that concern can be conjoined with the preoccupations of the denunciatory theorists; there are no inconsistencies that would preclude such a conjunction, and indeed the incapacitative role of executions is rarely articulated in isolation from other roles which the executions can and should perform. All the same, notwithstanding the manifest compatibility of the incapacitative rationale and the denunciatory rationale for the death penalty, those two consequentialist doctrines are irreducibly distinct.[5] Hence, as this chapter now turns to probe the shortcomings of the incapacitative justification, we should be alert to the peculiarities of that justification as well as to its affinities with the other consequentialist rationales for capital punishment.

4.2. The fatal shortcomings of the incapacitative justification

Quite beyond any reasonable doubt is the proposition that some incarcerated murderers are lethally dangerous individuals who pose extreme risks to everyone around them and sometimes to people far outside the walls of their prisons (Allen and Shavell, 630–2; Gale 1985, 991–2; Markel 2005, 470–1; McCord 1998, 27; Van den Haag 1990, 508–9). The incapacitative account of capital punishment correctly diagnoses a problem. What remains to be seen is whether that account's prescription for dealing with the problem is morally defensible.

4.2.1. Moral responsibility swept aside

One major shortcoming of the incapacitative rationale for the death penalty is that, on its own terms, it discounts the significance of moral responsibility (Davis 1996, 6, 17). It deals with dangerously violent people as if they were wild animals or rabid dogs, instead of dealing with them as moral agents who are responsible for their misdeeds. It focuses not on what they have done but on what they are very likely to do in the future; the latter rather than the former is the determinative basis for their subjection to capital punishment. Highly doubtful, then, is whether executions conducted for the sake of incapacitating extremely dangerous people are properly classifiable as punishments at all.

Indeed, as Chapter 1 has remarked, an especially disconcerting feature of the incapacitative justification for the death penalty is that it does not make its applicability conditional on the occurrence of misdeeds. If a strong person is perdurably disposed to commit carnage, and if there are solid grounds for knowing of his disposition, then the incapacitative rationale calls for putting him to death irrespective of whether he has actually carried out any serious crimes. In other words, that rationale can efface the role of moral responsibility altogether. Not only does it prescribe the imposition of the death penalty by reference to what a dangerous person is very likely to do rather than by reference to what he has done; in addition, it can sometimes prescribe that penalty for such a person even though he has not yet done anything seriously amiss. (Of course, usually the best indicator of the dangerousness of any particular person is the destructive conduct in which he has already engaged. However, even when someone has not yet carried out such conduct on any appreciable scale, there can be

---

[5] Their distinctness is blurred by Walter Berns when he applies the label of 'general prevention' to the effects of the denunciatory workings of a criminal-justice system. See Berns 1979, 143, 145, 149, 152. Berns adopts that phrase from Andenaes 1974, chs I and II. Andenaes himself used it chiefly to refer to the deterrent, retributive, and denunciatory effects of criminal-justice systems.

enough alternative indicators of his dangerousness to constitute a solid basis for the imposition of the death penalty under the incapacitative rationale. Though alternative indicators are not usually sufficient on their own to confirm that some person is extremely and irredeemably dangerous, they can occasionally be so. Whenever they are, the incapacitative rationale for the death penalty is applicable to the person in question.)

As will be recalled from Chapter 2, the deterrence-oriented justification of capital punishment likewise calls in certain circumstances for putting people to death even though they have not committed any criminal misdeeds. Virtually any consequentialist account of the institution of capital punishment will give rise to the problem of executions of innocents in some form or another. However, the specifics of the problem as it arises under the incapacitative justification are quite different from its specifics under the deterrence-oriented justification.

For one thing, as has already been observed, the linchpin of the incapacitative rationale—the trait of extreme dangerousness—is per se irrelevant within the deterrence-oriented account. Under the incapacitative approach, the sole decisive reason for executing someone in spite of his not having perpetrated any serious misdeeds is that his murderous inclinations will gravely endanger other people if he is kept alive. Such a reason is per se not a reason at all under the deterrence-oriented rationale for the death penalty. According to that latter rationale, the only reason for ever putting an innocent person to death is that the execution of the person will be efficacious as a marginal deterrent.[6] Given that such an execution can be effective as a marginal deterrent even if the person put to death is not genuinely dangerous, the deterrence-oriented theorists' standard for prescribing executions of innocents is extensionally as well as intensionally different from the incapacitative theorists' standard.

Closely connected to the foregoing point is a further dissimilarity between the deterrence-oriented approach and the incapacitative approach. Whereas the deterrence-oriented rationale for the death penalty will support executions of innocent people only in situations in which the innocence of those people is generally unrecognized (at least by members of the public at large), the ends pursued by the incapacitative rationale can be attained through executions of people who are widely known not to have committed any serious crimes. Only when innocent people are very widely thought to have committed heinous crimes, and only when the likelihood of the uncovering of their actual innocence is extremely low, will executions of those people promote the ends sought by the deterrence-oriented justification of capital punishment. Only in such circumstances can the executions be lastingly effective in deterring members of the public from perpetrating serious crimes. By contrast, no widespread errors of perception are necessary for the applicability of

---

[6] With an eye toward the readability of my prose, I have formulated this point along act-utilitarian lines only. It can easily be formulated along rule-utilitarian lines as well.

the incapacitative justification to the situation of an innocent but extremely dangerous person. Even though nobody mistakenly believes that the person in question is
guilty of any serious crimes, the incapacitative rationale will call for executing him
if his murderous proclivities gravely imperil the people around him. Because that
rationale aims for the removal of homicidal dangers rather than for the provision of
fear-based incentives to members of the public to refrain from misbehaviour, the fact
that no such incentives will be engendered by an execution of the sort just mentioned
is not an obstacle to the applicability of the incapacitative rationale. Incapacitative
considerations militate in favour of some executions that are irreconcilable both with
the objectives of deterrence-oriented theorists and with retributivism's insistence on
guilt as a necessary condition for the legitimacy of any punitive infliction.

Of course, the citizenry in a liberal-democratic society will very likely not acquiesce in such executions. Undeceived about the innocence of the admittedly dangerous people who are to be executed, members of the public in any enlightened polity
will not long tolerate a practice of putting those people to death. However, insofar
as the citizens of a liberal-democratic country do baulk at such a practice, the proper
basis for their doing so is that they *pro tanto* reject the incapacitative rationale for the
death penalty; they would err if they based their objections instead on the notion
that that rationale does not call for the envisaged executions. In any event, unless the
popular consternation about the executions has become so intense that the conducting of them will produce a net diminution in a society's overall utility, the incapacitative rationale (along with the utilitarian theory in which that rationale is usually
embedded) will indeed call for them. In that respect, as has been indicated, the problem of the massacre of the innocents under the incapacitative justification for capital
punishment differs significantly from that problem under the deterrence-oriented
justification. When the innocence of someone is widely known, the deterrence-
oriented rationale for capital punishment does not prescribe the execution of him,
because such an execution will not produce any deterrent effects. In other words,
the deterrence-oriented rationale is inapplicable in such circumstances. By contrast,
when the innocence of a shuddersomely dangerous person is widely known, the incapacitative rationale will still call for the execution of him. That latter rationale is
applicable rather than inapplicable, because the absence of any deterrent effects does
not detract from its applicability. Hence, when an execution of such a person on incapacitative grounds is in the offing, any query about its propriety should be a query
about the propriety of those grounds themselves rather than about their scope.

Let us consider a final aspect of deterrence-oriented executions of innocents that
distinguishes them from any such executions under the incapacitative rationale. As
was argued in Chapter 2, deterrence-oriented considerations will frequently militate
in favour of executing the close relatives of malefactors even if the relatives have not
done anything wrong (beyond their not having averted the crimes perpetrated by the
malefactors). Now, unless the relatives of vile criminals are themselves extremely dangerous, the incapacitative rationale for the death penalty will never militate in favour

of executing them. Neither as a means of punishing the vile criminals nor as a means of punishing the relatives for not having averted the wrongdoing of those criminals, would putting the relatives to death ever be prescribed by the incapacitative rationale. To that extent, though only to that extent, the problem of executions of innocents under the incapacitative rationale is less troublesome than under the deterrence-oriented approach.

4.2.2. More on moral responsibility

In the preceding subsection, we have looked at the ways in which the incapacitative account of capital punishment fails to treat moral responsibility (for very serious crimes) as a necessary condition for the legitimacy of any imposition of such punishment. We should now note that the general incapacitative conception of punishment likewise does not treat moral responsibility as a *sufficient* condition for the legitimacy of any sanctions whatsoever. Not only will that conception sometimes call for executions of people who have as yet committed no crimes; in addition, and conversely, it sometimes militates against the infliction of *any* punishments upon people who have committed heinous crimes. More specifically, it calls for exonerating any criminal who poses no threat of any serious violations of the law in the future.

Suppose for example that Paul has brutally murdered a number of people and that, over the course of several years, he undergoes a thorough conversion and becomes deeply repentant. He is now resolutely undisposed to commit any further misdeeds. His contrition leads him to turn himself over to the relevant law-enforcement authorities. If the authorities are guided by an incapacitative conception of the role of punishment, and if they are aware of the sweeping transformation that Paul has undergone in his ethical outlook, they will conclude that he should not be punished at all. Not only would the execution of Paul be unwarranted under the terms of the incapacitative rationale for the death penalty; what is more, any sanction of any type would be unwarranted under the terms of the general incapacitative account of punishment. His having perpetrated several grisly murders is relevant under those terms only for evidentiary purposes; that is, his having perpetrated those murders is strong evidence of his character and of the danger that he consequently poses to other people. However, given that the strength of that evidence has been exceeded (*ex hypothesi*) by the strength of the contrary evidence of the comprehensive change in his character, the past murders fall away under the incapacitative theory of punishment. Legal-governmental officials who take their guidance exclusively from that theory will focus on what Paul is likely to do in the future. (As has been stated, what he has done in the past is relevant under that theory only as evidence of what he is likely to do in the future.) Given that Paul no longer poses any threat to other people, the aforementioned legal-governmental officials will decide against subjecting him to any sanctions whatsoever.

In sum, with regard to the value of moral responsibility, the incapacitative approach to punishment is doubly problematic. It calls for the execution of some people who have undisputedly not yet committed any serious crimes, and it calls for the wholesale acquittal of some people who have undisputedly committed vile murders. Under the incapacitative approach, moral responsibility is neither a necessary condition nor a sufficient condition for the imposition of sanctions.

4.2.3. The hurdle of the Minimal Invasion Principle

Like the general incapacitative theory of punishment, the incapacitative rationale for the death penalty is inconsistent with the value of moral responsibility. Even more damaging is the inconsistency of that rationale with the Minimal Invasion Principle. Although the prevention of extremely dangerous thugs from wreaking havoc is undoubtedly a legitimate and important objective to be pursued by any liberal-democratic government (indeed, by any government), the fulfillment of that objective does not require the use of capital punishment in preference to some less severe sanctions. Consequently, the administration of such punishment on incapacitative grounds is in contravention of the Minimal Invasion Principle and is therefore morally illegitimate.

Capital punishment is not necessary for the incapacitation of extremely dangerous offenders, because highly restrictive modes of incarceration can also incapacitate those offenders effectively (Bedau 1993, 179; Bedau 1999, 51–2; Gale 1985, 1017; Lempert 1981, 1189; Markel 2005, 471; Sorell 1987, 42, 83; Van den Haag 1968, 280). Since the highly restrictive modes of incarceration are less severe punishments than the death penalty, the Minimal Invasion Principle obligates any proponent of the incapacitative rationale to advocate them in preference to executions. Indeed, in some cases, the requisite incarceration does not even have to be lifelong in its duration. Some people who are extremely dangerous during their adolescence and during the subsequent few decades—either because of their own strength and depravity or because of the willingness of their associates to commit mayhem at their behest—can safely be released when they have become elderly and feeble and when any erstwhile cronies of theirs have died or become enfeebled. Hence, even the punishment of lifelong imprisonment-without-parole on incapacitative grounds will sometimes be violative of the Minimal Invasion Principle.

Like retributivism, the incapacitative account of the role of punishment is not per se inconsistent with the use of the death penalty. As is evident, the administration of capital punishment is a formidably effective means of preventing noxious thugs from wreaking havoc in the future. Moreover, the elements of retributivism that have seemed to some philosophers to be incompatible with any use of the death penalty—retributivism's ancillary reformative aspect and its emphasis on moral responsibility and human dignity—are not similarly elements of the incapacitative account. Nonetheless, although there is no inconsistency between the institution of capital punishment and the incapacitative conception of sanctions, the invocation of that conception as a basis for such punishment is indeed inconsistent with a major liberal-democratic principle. Because alternative sanctions of lesser severity can fully realize any legitimate incapacitative ends, the employment of the death penalty in pursuit of such ends is always impermissible under the Minimal Invasion Principle.

As has been observed in Chapter 3, some versions of retributivism prescribe that murderers (or, at any rate, the worst murderers) should be imprisoned in austere conditions of confinement to minimize their opportunities for pleasurable experiences. For proponents of the incapacitative approach to punishment, grim drabness in the confinement of extremely menacing convicts is not essential. Crucial instead are two other factors: the isolation of such convicts from their fellow prisoners, from prison guards, and from people in the outside world; and the foreclosing of opportunities for escapes. So long as those two factors are secured, there is no additional requirement of stark austerity that has to be met for the realization of incapacitative aims. Drabness is to be imposed only insofar as is necessary to maintain the isolation of a menacing offender and to close off any opportunities for him to free himself from his incarceration.

Admittedly, there can never be any absolutely fail-safe guarantees that a dangerous prisoner in solitary confinement will not somehow manage to escape or otherwise cause mayhem and carnage. After all, the isolation of such a person will have to be interrupted for intermittent searches of his cell, for urgent medical or dental care (since the withholding of such care—in circumstances where it is badly needed—would amount to a form of torture and would thus be morally impermissible), and occasionally for other purposes. Furthermore, there is no absolutely foolproof way of ensuring that a crafty and murderous thug will remain immured for years while he is desperately keen to break loose. Nonetheless, especially with the development of the so-called supermaximum prison facilities in the United States and elsewhere,[7] the likelihood of seriously untoward incidents can be reduced to an extremely low level. With the use of constant surveillance through closed-circuit monitoring in the cell of each inmate in those facilities, and with the adoption of a myriad of precautions for the infrequent occasions when direct contact with any such inmate is necessary, the officials in supermaximum penitentiaries can virtually eliminate the ability of even the most dangerous prisoners to wreak havoc. Such measures are expensive, but, because they are needed only for the most violently refractory prisoners, the implementation of them is not extravagantly unaffordable. Such techniques of incarceration are a realistic alternative to executions. Thus, given that those techniques amply fulfil the incapacitative objectives that could also be fulfilled through the death penalty, and given that they are less severe than that penalty (despite their unpleasantness), a champion of the incapacitative conception of punishment is obligated by the Minimal Invasion Principle to favour supermaximum imprisonment over executions for the most unruly offenders. Capital punishment administered on the basis of incapacitative concerns is morally illegitimate.

---

[7] For some overviews of the development of supermaximum prison facilities in the United States, see Ferrier 2004, 294–6; Kurki and Morris 2001; McCord 1998, 95–104; Ward 1999. For a stridently unsympathetic account, see Gawande 2009. Of course, I am not here endorsing every aspect of the supermaximum facilities in the United States or in any other country.

4.3. Conclusion: irreparable damage

As has been stated, the insurmountability of the hurdle laid down by the Minimal Invasion Principle is more damaging to the incapacitative rationale for capital punishment than is the inconsistency of that rationale with the value of moral responsibility. Whereas the latter problem can to some degree (though only to some degree) be overcome through the supplementation of a general incapacitative theory with retributivistic side-constraints, there is no comparable buttressing that can rescue the incapacitative rationale for the death penalty from its clash with the Minimal Invasion Principle. Though the concerns of incapacitative theorists about the perils posed by murderously recalcitrant convicts are well-founded and pressing, they are not sufficient to vindicate the institution of capital punishment.

5

Death as a Means of Denunciation

Notwithstanding that the denunciatory rationale for the death penalty is rarely espoused by contemporary philosophers in isolation from other rationales, some strands of it do figure saliently in both philosophical debates and popular debates over the morality of executions. Moreover, the denunciatory rationale has enjoyed a distinguished history, as its development has unfolded through the writings of major thinkers such as James Fitzjames Stephen and Emile Durkheim.[1] Though it can initially seem pugnacious or unsavoury as it draws upon primal emotions of hatred and revenge in its justification of the institution of capital punishment, it in fact presents some powerful moral considerations in favour of that institution. Its chief concerns together form an impressive case for putting the worst criminals to death. That consequentialist case is what will come under scrutiny in this chapter.

5.1. The general denunciatory theory of punishment

Like each of the other commonly propounded rationales for the death penalty, the denunciatory rationale is an offshoot of a general account of punishment. More than any of the other major conceptions of punishment, the denunciatory conception highlights the communicative dimension of sanctions. It attributes to sanctions the purpose—the morally worthy purpose—of expressing the attitudes of hatred and revulsion that are felt by law-abiding people toward the criminal misdeeds for which the sanctions are levied. Punitive institutions are centered on that very purpose, as they are the standing means of communicating forcefully those attitudes of hostility in response to wrongdoing.

In the eyes of the denunciatory theorists, the primary recipients of the messages conveyed by punishments are members of the public at large. Whereas retributivists maintain that the principal recipients of the messages of reprobation conveyed by punishments are the offenders who undergo the punishments and who are in need

---

[1] Durkheim's account of the role of punishment is contained principally in the second chapter of Durkheim 1933.

of such messages, the proponents of the denunciatory approach concentrate instead on the sentiments of ordinary people. In three major respects, punishments that give expression to public outrage can salutarily influence those sentiments.

In the first place, such punishments will tend to inform and reinforce people's jaundiced attitudes toward serious misbehaviour. When offenders are subjected to sanctions that manifest those attitudes, the moral inclinations of ordinary people are confirmed and strengthened. By expressing the hostility which the members of the public feel toward patterns of misconduct, denunciatory punishments solidify that very hostility. The wielding of legal sanctions more firmly entrenches the moral convictions that underlie and animate the sanctions. In so doing, furthermore, it tends to refine those convictions by helping to ensure that people's animosity toward wrongdoing is pertinently directed. Denunciatory punishments, as communicative acts, perform a function of education and purification as well as a function of consolidation. While reinforcing people's deep-seated moral sentiments, such punishments also guide those wrathful sentiments toward appropriate objects of indignation.

A second main salutary effect of the imposition of denunciatory sanctions is linked to the passion of revenge. Criminal wrongdoing, especially when it involves serious harm to individual victims, tends to elicit the antipathy of the public not only toward the wrongdoing itself but also toward the person responsible for it. Members of the public are apt to wish to 'get even' with the miscreant who has prioritized his own noisome urges over the moral and legal restraints to which he and they alike are subject. He has shown contempt for his immediate victim(s) and also for the whole community whose normative protection of the victim(s) he has contravened. Consequently, particularly if the crime is unsavoury and violent, some ordinary people may be inclined to indulge in private acts of retaliation. By giving vent to the impulses of outrage and vindictiveness felt by many members of the public, denunciatory punishments satisfy and thus defuse those impulses. Such punishments obviate private acts of vengeance, as they enable people to 'get even' vicariously through the workings of a system of criminal justice. Denunciatory sanctions, therefore, curb private violence by channelling the potentially disruptive instincts of hatred and revenge through institutional forms. As Stephen famously proclaimed: '[Criminal law] regulates, sanctions, and provides a legitimate satisfaction for the passion of revenge....The criminal law stands to the passion of revenge in much the same relation as marriage to the sexual appetite' (Stephen 1863, 99).

Closely related to what has just been said is a third benign consequence of the administration of denunciatory punishments. Such punishments foster the solidarity of a community not only by damping down the occurrence of private exploits of retaliation against criminals, but also by strengthening a community's sense of its own identity in opposition to the wrongdoers who seek to defy it. When a community responds collectively and forcefully to criminal misdeeds that challenge its fundamental values, it contributes to the forging of its own identity through the differentiation of itself from its enemies. As Andrew Oldenquist contends: 'It is doubtful that members of a [community] could possess common values and a common way of life if they were totally lacking in indignation and censure at threats and affronts to their way of life....Without taking proportional [punishment] in grave cases a society undermines public confidence that it takes itself and its values seriously' (Oldenquist 2004, 336, 338). Though the passions of hatred and revenge can be destructively unruly when they are left to roam freely, they can be forces for social cohesion when they are properly marshalled and directed through a society's mechanisms of punishment. As Joseph Kennedy writes in his summation of Durkheim's understanding of punitive institutions: 'Punishment's core function [according to Durkheim] was to maintain social cohesion by affirming the moral order by which upright people lived their lives' (Kennedy 2000, 835).

Now, if the denunciatory theory of punishment is to be credible at all as an exposition of the morally worthy purposes that are served by a system of criminal justice, its scope has to be understood as subject to restrictions that are similar to those which circumscribe the scope of retributivism. Claims by the denunciatory theorists about the purification of citizens' moral outlooks and the defusing of vindictive sentiments and the fostering of social cohesion would lack any moral credibility if they were applied to societies in which the odiously unjust mandates of evil regimes are enforced through the mechanisms of the criminal law. Hence, the denunciatory theorists' claims are to be construed as applying only to societies governed by liberal-democratic regimes with laws that are largely fair and reasonable. Even within such societies, the sole relevant contexts are those in which people are under moral obligations to comply with the prevailing laws. Only with reference to those contexts can the denunciatory theory partake of any credibility.

5.1.1. Denunciation versus deterrence

In some manifest respects, the denunciatory account and the deterrence-oriented account of punishment resemble each other. Each of them is a consequentialist theory that concentrates on reducing the incidence of crimes by using punishments to shape the outlooks of members of the public appropriately. Each theory ascribes key importance to the communicative dimension of sanctions, as the proponents of each theory maintain that the central role of sanctions is to convey messages to the general citizenry. Furthermore, each of these two conceptions of punishment is premised on some controversial empirical theses concerning the effects of punitive institutions on people's thinking.

Nonetheless, despite the foregoing similarities between the denunciatory approach and the deterrence-oriented approach, the divergences between them are at least as salient and numerous (van den Haag and Conrad 1983, 36–37). Whereas the point of deterrence-oriented sanctions is to frighten potential criminals into refraining from misbehaviour by leading them to worry that they too will be subjected to sanctions if they indulge in the misbehaviour, the point of denunciatory punishments is not focused on the emotion of fear. Instead, as has been remarked above, the point of the latter punishments is to strengthen and refine the existing moral convictions of people, which are presumed to be oriented toward law-abidingness already.

Reinforced and purified through exposure to denunciatory sanctions, those moral convictions can be admirably robust. People who harbour such convictions might well stand in little need of the provision of fear-based incentives for compliance with legal requirements. Of course, the provision of such incentives in order to back up people's moral convictions is typically very valuable; denunciatory theorists can and do recognize that many sanctions are efficacious as deterrents, and they can favour such sanctions partly on that ground. Still, although deterrence and denunciation are obviously compatible, they are not equivalent. Spreading fear among people is not the same as honing their moral compunctions about wrongdoing. (This point about the distinctness of deterrence and denunciation can easily get lost when theorists invoke ambiguous notions such as 'internal controls.'[2])

Other aspects of the denunciatory conception of punishment are even more distant from anything in the deterrence-oriented conception. When denunciatory theorists contend that the imposition of sanctions is salutary partly because it averts private acts of retaliation—in that it vents and thus allays the feelings of vindictiveness which people will naturally experience in response to serious wrongdoing—those theorists are making claims that have no counterparts in deterrence-oriented accounts of punishment. Likewise, when the denunciatory theorists declare that publicly institutionalized expressions of revulsion in reaction to criminality will help to cement a community's sense of its own identity, they are making claims that have no real counterparts in deterrence-oriented accounts. To be sure, if we ascend to a sufficiently high level of abstraction, we can assimilate all the pronouncements of the denunciatory theorists to those of the deterrence-oriented exponents. For example, we can note that all such pronouncements are consequentialist (Hart 1968, 74). In that very general respect, denunciatory considerations and deterrence-oriented considerations are to be placed together in contradistinction to the deontological concerns of retributivists. However, once we move to a somewhat more fine-grained level of analysis, we can detect a number of notable dissimilarities between those two sets of consequentialist considerations.

Of course, some of the dissimilarities will be less clear-cut in practice than they are in theory. No mean feat, for example, is the task of distinguishing in practice between law-abidance that is due to moral reservations and law-abidance that is due to fears about sanctions. Given the intensity of the quarrels among social scientists over the extent to which the administration of various sanctions (such as the death penalty) is responsible for limiting the incidence of various crimes, we can hardly expect much agreement among those social scientists on the question whether any crime-lowering effects of sanctions are attributable to denunciation or to deterrence (or to both). Still, notwithstanding the practical difficulties of differentiating between denunciatory efficacy and deterrent efficacy, the distinction between the two at a theoretical level

---

[2] See, for example, Abernethy 1996, 393, 407 n 159; Berns 1979, 137–9; Davis 1996, 11–12; Gale 1985, 995–6; Goldberg 1974, 68–9; Kahan 1999, 444; Logan 2002, 1358; Van den Haag 1968, 282, 287 n 1.

is straightforward. An understanding of sanctions as expressions of ethical revulsion that solidify citizens' law-abiding moral sentiments is very different from an understanding of sanctions as exemplary inflictions that promote obedience to the law through fear.

5.1.2. Denunciation versus retribution

Though the denunciatory conception of punishment and the deterrence-oriented conception are quite often run together, the denunciatory conception is more often conflated with retributivism. That latter conflation may initially seem puzzling; after all, the denunciatory theory of punishment is strongly consequentialist, whereas retributivism in its primary form is deontological. Nevertheless, the frequency of the conflation is not really so surprising, since it is due to the frequency with which retributivism itself is mischaracterized (even occasionally by some retributivists).

As has been observed in Chapter 3, many critics and some supporters of retributivism have deemed it to be a doctrine of revenge. They have mistakenly supposed that the retributivistic aim of resubsuming the activities of offenders under proper moral and legal restraints is an aim of 'getting even' with the offenders. Chapter 3 has explained at some length the erroneousness of such a supposition. What should be added here is that the mistaken association of retribution with revenge has often been articulated in ways that assimilate retributivism to the denunciatory understanding of punishment.

For example, Hugo Adam Bedau, an astute critic (and sometimes a wary proponent) of retributivism, has written as follows: 'Some retributivists believe that we want to punish the guilty, or want to be assured that someone will undertake to punish them, because in that way we purge ourselves of feelings of vicarious resentment; and that, where we are ourselves the victims of crime, we want the offender punished out of revenge' (Bedau 1978, 608). In the same essay, Bedau goes on to maintain that some 'retributivists try to justify the practice of punishment by appeal to the socially cathartic, purgative, expiatory *effect* that the practice of punishment is alleged to have,' and he likewise criticizes 'the currently…popular [view] that the system of punishment is justified by its authoritative role in denouncing as wrong the harmful conduct made liable to punishment—a dubious version, perhaps of a retributive justifying general aim' (Bedau 1978, 616, emphasis in original). These quoted remarks largely efface the distinction between the deontological preoccupations of retributivists and the consequentialist preoccupations of denunciatory theorists. Worth noting here is that Bedau does not cite any of the so-called retributivists whom he has in mind while he makes these statements. At any rate, the concerns which he ascribes to some unidentified retributivists are in fact among the chief concerns of denunciatory theorists. For the latter theorists rather than for retributivists, the socially cathartic role of punishment—its role in cleansing away the miasma of noxious vindictiveness from a community by dealing firmly with the offenders whose misdeeds have given rise to vindictive anger—is of central importance.

Of course, there are some genuine resemblances between the retributivistic conception of punishment and the denunciatory conception. Each theory highlights the communicative dimension of sanctions, and, although the communicative role envisaged by each theory is quite different from that envisaged by the other, those roles are sometimes formulated in ways that blur the dissimilarities between them. Consider, for instance, George Fletcher's remark that a certain species of retributivism—which Fletcher seeks to distinguish from the deterrence-oriented account of punishment—has presented the imposition of sanctions as 'an effort to secure social protection by supporting the basic norms prohibiting criminal behavior rather than by frightening people into compliance' (Fletcher 1999, 54). Fletcher's statement is inscrutable. It might be encapsulating the account of punishment advanced by many vindicatory retributivists, or it might instead be encapsulating the account advanced by denunciatory theorists. Though the reference to 'secur[ing] social protection' strongly suggests that the denunciatory theory is what Fletcher has in mind, the passage in which his statement occurs—where he speaks of punishment as 'vindicat[ing] the legal order, or the norm prohibiting the [criminal] conduct' (Fletcher 1999, 54)—suggests instead that vindicatory retributivism is what he is discussing. In any case, the difficulties in pinning down the referent of Fletcher's remark are indicative of a certain degree of overlap between retribution and denunciation.

Nevertheless, despite the shared emphasis on the communicative dimension of sanctions, the denunciatory approach and the retributivistic approach are irreducibly divergent.[3] Under the former approach, the principal addressees of the messages communicated by legal sanctions are the members of the general public. Under retributivism, contrariwise, the principal addressee of the message communicated by any legal sanction is the offender who undergoes the sanction. According to the denunciatory theory, the message conveyed to the general public by the imposition of a legal sanction is that hatred and revulsion are appropriate emotions to be felt in response to the wrongdoing for which the sanction has been levied. According to retributivism, by contrast, the message conveyed to an offender by the imposition of a legal sanction is that his misconduct has self-indulgently contravened basic moral and legal requirements to which he was and is subject. Under the denunciatory conception of punishment, the practice of conveying messages to the general public through the imposition of legal sanctions is justified insofar and only insofar as it tends to lower the incidence of criminal misbehaviour and private vendettas (and thereby tends to promote the public weal by enhancing the security of people's lives and belongings). Under retributivism, no such consequentialist justification is necessary or apposite; the communication of condemnatory messages to offenders through the imposition

---

[3] The non-equivalence of those approaches is recognized in Dressler 1990, 1451–2; Feinberg 1970, 100–1; Gale 1985, 988 n 41; Gardner 1978, 1207; Gerstein 1974, 76; Gey 1992, 106–8; Markel 2005, 439–40; Markel 2009, 1175–6, 1179–82; McCord 1998, 40–1; Pugsley 1981, 1506; Sigler 2003, 1183–4; Sorell 1987, 124, 157–8; Steiker 2005, 773. It is largely or altogether missed in Berns 1979, 144–6; Gardner 1978, 1190, 1197, 1208–10; Greenberg 1986, 1677; Hampton 1992, 1684; Logan 2002, 1347, 1368–9; Note 2001, 1614; Oldenquist 2004, 338.

of legal sanctions is worthy in itself as a practice that gives effect to values of human equality and moral responsibility.

In sum, notwithstanding the centrality of the communicative aspect of punishments in retributivistic theories and denunciatory theories alike, their respective elaborations of that communicative aspect differ greatly. Moreover, the contrasts recounted in the preceding paragraph—especially the final contrast, pertaining to the consequentialism/deontology divide—will prove to be linked to still further divergences between the two types of theories. In particular, the denunciatory conception differs from retributivism in being vulnerable to some of the general problems that also afflict other consequentialist approaches to punishment. Its vulnerabilities in that regard will become apparent presently.

5.2. The denunciatory theory as a rationale for capital punishment

When the general denunciatory theory of sanctions has been brought to bear upon the most heinous crimes, it has often been thought to call for the imposition of capital punishment. Central to the denunciatory theory as a rationale for capital punishment is the idea that the goals of the theory cannot be realized in response to an especially vile crime except through the execution of the perpetrator. If somebody has committed a ghoulish murder, for example, the only punitive reaction sufficiently severe to express a society's revulsion—so the argument runs—is the death penalty. Consequently, only such a penalty can adequately reinforce the moral sentiments of the citizenry in the aftermath of such an atrocity. Similarly, only the death penalty can satisfy the urge for vengeance that will be felt by ordinary citizens (including citizens who are imprisoned for less rebarbative crimes). If any punishment more lenient than death is imposed, those citizens will be inclined to take the law into their own hands. In addition, any gentler punishment will be insufficient as a means of bracing the identity of the community in which the terrible crime has occurred. Such a crime poses a grave challenge to the community's cohesion; to bolster that cohesion in opposition to the community's dire enemies, nothing less formidable than the death penalty will suffice.

In short, when theorists support executions on denunciatory grounds, they appeal to all the chief objectives of the general denunciatory conception of punishment. That conception, with its emphasis on the hatred and revulsion that should be felt toward criminality, would appear to be well suited to the task of addressing the most serious violations of the law that are perpetrated in any jurisdiction. Nevertheless, it will prove to be irredeemably problematic in its application to that task. Some of the shortcomings in the denunciatory rationale for capital punishment are ramifications of problems that vitiate the general denunciatory theory of sanctions, and some are peculiar to the matter of the death penalty. In the rest of this chapter, we shall examine those shortcomings in turn.

5.3. The unsustainability of the denunciatory theory

With its consequentialist bearings, the denunciatory approach to punishment—and specifically to capital punishment—unsurprisingly turns out to be afflicted by some of the difficulties that also plague the incapacitative and deterrence-oriented approaches. Let us begin with some empirical problems before we move on to ponder the moral drawbacks of the denunciatory approach.

5.3.1. Empirical murkiness

As a consequentialist justification of capital punishment, the denunciatory rationale has to rely on certain empirical claims for its operativeness. That is, its applicability to the actual world presupposes that the executions which it prescribes are likely to produce the orderliness-enhancing results which it commends. Denunciatory theorists maintain that executions of the malefactors who are responsible for shockingly nefarious crimes will (1) strengthen and purify the moral sentiments of members of the general public, (2) satiate the lust for retaliation that might otherwise drive members of the public to engage in private acts of vengeance against the malefactors, and (3) reinforce a community's solidarity and identity in stark opposition to the miscreants who pit themselves against its fundamental values. Now, if the denunciatory theorists are to show that their rationale for the death penalty is applicable to any community in the actual world, they will have to adduce empirical evidence of connections between the aforementioned executions and the triad of consequences enumerated here. Since the relevant connections would be causal, the empirical evidence must pertain to what happens in the absence of any executions as well as to what happens in their presence; that is, the connections and evidence must be such as to support an array of germane counterfactuals.

To establish the existence of causal links between denunciatory executions and the first of the consequences listed above, denunciatory theorists might hope to draw upon some of the studies by deterrence-oriented theorists which appear to confirm that executions marginally lower the incidence of murders. Denunciatory theorists would then have to present further studies to show that the marginal murder-inhibiting effects of executions are due principally to the solidification and purification of people's moral outlooks rather than principally to deterrence. Each of these two steps toward the empirical substantiation of the denunciatory theorists' position would be formidably problematic. We have already seen in Chapter 2 the thicket of controversy and inconclusiveness in which the deterrence-oriented theorists are caught when they try to confirm empirically the efficacy of executions as means for marginally reducing the incidence of murders. To say the least, the denunciatory theorists are no better positioned than the deterrence-oriented theorists to provide any conclusive empirical verification of the efficacy of executions in that respect. At least as daunting for the denunciatory theorists is the challenge of demonstrating that any murder-inhibiting effects of executions are chiefly ascribable not to deterrence but to the reinforcement and refinement of citizens' moral dispositions. To rise to that challenge, the denunciatory theorists would have to undertake far-reaching surveys of people's moral attitudes in societies which resemble one another in most respects but which differ in regard to the employment or non-employment of capital punishment. The surveys would have to be designed to distinguish carefully between fear-based inhibitions and moral compunctions. Likewise, they would have to ascertain the extent to which any of those moral scruples have been influenced by the occurrence or non-occurrence of executions. Suffice it to say that no such surveys have ever been carried out. Hence, the empirical presuppositions of the denunciatory rationale for the death penalty are even shakier than those of the deterrence-oriented rationale.

Also troublesome for the denunciatory theorists is the task of confirming that executions tend to satiate the vindictive feelings that are harboured by ordinary people toward the worst murderers. At the very least, those theorists will have to conduct empirical studies to ascertain the incidence of private acts of retaliation against the worst murderers and their relatives in societies which resemble one another in most respects but which differ in regard to the employment or non-employment of capital punishment. To be sure, if the private acts of retaliation include attacks by fellow convicts, the notion that the empirical studies will disclose some relevant causal connections is not wildly implausible. At any rate, such a notion is not implausible if the alternative to capital punishment in a given jurisdiction is imprisonment without solitary confinement. Still, as will be remarked near the end of this chapter, the greater frequency of attacks by fellow convicts in jurisdictions without capital punishment would not weigh in favour of the introduction of such punishment. Hence, even if this empirical issue can be resolved in line with the denunciatory theorists' assumptions, it will not vindicate their conclusions.

A final empirical matter for the denunciatory theorists is especially murky. To ascertain whether the absence of capital punishment in a jurisdiction tends to attenuate a community's sense of its identity and its general cohesion, the denunciatory theorists would have to marshal some wide-ranging empirical surveys of the attitudes of people toward their communities in several jurisdictions that do impose the death penalty and in several jurisdictions that do not impose it. Such surveys would somehow have to control for a multitude of variables that bear on the attitudes in question, in order to try to pin down the influence of the presence or absence of capital punishment. Suffice it again to say that no such surveys have ever been conducted. Pronouncements by denunciatory theorists on the solidarity-enhancing effects of capital punishment are, at best, wholly conjectural.

In short, any defence of the denunciatory rationale for the death penalty would have to substantiate the three major empirical propositions on which the operativeness of that rationale rests. The difficulties of verifying the first and third of those propositions are overwhelming. There is no realistic likelihood that any empirical studies to test rigorously those two propositions will be carried out; and, even if such studies were to be undertaken (*mirabile dictu*), their findings would almost certainly prove to be as intractably contentious as the outcomes of the studies conducted by deterrence-oriented theorists. As for the second of the denunciatory theorists' three empirical presuppositions—concerning the satisfaction and defusing of vindictive hostility—it might lend itself more readily to empirical testing. Moreover, in jurisdictions where the worst criminals are not placed in solitary confinement when imprisoned, the results of the testing might turn out to tally with what the denunciatory theorists have assumed. However, as has already been remarked, the substantiation of the second empirical assumption of those theorists (with regard to such jurisdictions) would not contribute to their case for the institution of capital punishment. Thus, each of the main empirical presuppositions of the denunciatory rationale is either unconfirmably speculative or justificatorily unfruitful.

5.3.2. When perceptions do not match reality

My critique of the immorality of the denunciatory rationale for capital punishment can begin with the familiar problem of the execution of innocent people.[4] In respect of that problem, the predicament of the denunciatory theorists is closely similar to the quandary of the deterrence-oriented theorists. That is, whenever some person *P* is widely but mistakenly believed to have committed a ghastly murder, and whenever the mistakenness of that belief is very unlikely to become known, the denunciatory rationale for capital punishment will be applicable to *P*'s situation and will call for his execution. Each of the objectives pursued by that rationale will be furthered by such an execution. Because the widespread perception of *P* as an iniquitous murderer will have aroused strong feelings of revulsion and hatred among many members of the public, the sentencing of him to death will be an unmistakably forceful expression of his community's attitude toward his ostensible misconduct. It will thereby strengthen the salutary moral sensibilities that lead people to feel outrage over the atrocity which is imputed to him. The imposition of the death penalty will also significantly lower the likelihood that any of those outraged people will resort to private acts of retaliation against *P*, and it will thus promote the tranquility and orderliness of the whole community. Putting him to death, moreover, will foster the cohesion of the community and its sense of identity by starkly differentiating it from someone who is believed to be irredeemably opposed to its fundamental values. In short, the execution of *P*—and of anyone else who is pervasively though erroneously believed to be guilty of a heinous crime—can contribute potently to each of the desiderata which a denunciatory system of criminal justice strives to realize. Within the rationale that underpins such a system, there is no basis for distinguishing between the execution

---

[4] In my discussion of this problem, I take for granted—purely *arguendo*—the correctness of the denunciatory theorists' empirical presuppositions.

of P and the execution of someone who is genuinely guilty of a grotesque murder. Denunciatory goals can be amply served through executions of innocents.

Of course, the problem of the massacre of the innocents under the denunciatory rationale for capital punishment is an offshoot of a broader problem in the general denunciatory theory of punishment. Whenever any person Q is very widely but falsely thought to be guilty of a crime of any magnitude, and whenever the falsity of the attribution of guilt to Q is very unlikely to be unearthed, the denunciatory conception of punishment will call for the infliction upon him of a sanction that will appropriately express the disfavour of the community toward his putative misconduct. Just as deterrence-oriented theorists are committed by their doctrine to favouring the punishment of Q in order to discourage other people (and perhaps also Q himself) from committing any further crimes like the one imputed to him, so too the denunciatory theorists are committed by their doctrine to favouring the punishment of Q in order to realize their distinctive goals. For the proponents of each theory, Q's actual innocence is something that matters only inasmuch as it is likely to come to light. So long as the perception of Q as guilty is likely to persist, the subjection of him to sanctions will be required on deterrence-oriented grounds and denunciatory grounds just as much as will the punishment of a truly guilty person who is widely thought to be guilty. The problem of the execution of innocents, under the denunciatory rationale for the death penalty, is but one manifestation—an extreme manifestation—of this vice that runs throughout the general denunciatory conception of punishment.

5.3.2.1. Denunciation versus incapacitation

As has been indicated in the preceding two paragraphs, the denunciatory theorists are in much the same plight as the deterrence-oriented theorists with regard to their countenancing of the imposition of sanctions (including the death penalty) on some innocent people. Given the similarities between the difficulties encountered by the denunciatory theorists and those encountered by the deterrence-oriented theorists, and given that the difficulties faced by the latter theorists are quite different from those faced by incapacitative theorists (as Chapter 4 has recounted), the problem of the massacre of the innocents as it arises under the denunciatory rationale for capital punishment is significantly different from that problem as it arises under the incapacitative rationale. For one thing, whereas the execution of an innocent person is prescribed by the denunciatory rationale only if the person is widely believed to be guilty of a nefarious slaying, the execution of an innocent but extremely dangerous person is prescribed by the incapacitative rationale even if everybody knows that the menacing person has not yet committed any crimes. No cognitive deficiencies need be involved in the triggering of that latter rationale against someone who is guiltless. In a closely related vein, the basis for any execution of an innocent person diverges between the two theories. Under the incapacitative rationale for the death penalty, the factor that decisively justifies an execution of an innocent person is his durably lethal dangerousness. Under the denunciatory rationale, that factor is never in itself a basis for an execution. Instead of focusing on what an innocent person is inclined to do in the future, the denunciatory rationale focuses on what he is generally thought to have done in the past. Egregious misconduct in the past—ascribed to him widely though erroneously at present—is what calls for the execution of him now under the denunciatory rationale, whether or not he would be capable of engaging in any wicked misconduct hereafter. (Although the standard applied by the denunciatory theorists for prescribing the execution of innocent people is extensionally as well as intensionally different from that applied by the incapacitative theorists, the extensions of the two standards can of course overlap. Someone erroneously blamed for committing a ghastly murder might be a lethally dangerous maniac notwithstanding the unfoundedness of the blame attached to him for that particular crime.)

In yet another respect, the denunciatory theorists are similar to the deterrence-oriented theorists—and different from the incapacitative theorists, to say nothing of retributivists—in their countenancing of executions of innocents. As was observed in Chapter 2, the deterrence-oriented justification of capital punishment often militates in favour of executing the close relatives of heinous murderers. Much the same is true of the denunciatory justification, though of course the grounds for putting the relatives to death are different from the deterrence-oriented grounds. Under the denunciatory rationale, the relatives of a vile criminal should be executed whenever such a step will be an especially effective expression of the revulsion and hatred that are felt toward the criminal and his iniquities. In such circumstances, putting to death the relatives will be highly serviceable for the realization of the objectives that are associated with the denunciatory approach to punishment.

As Chapter 2 has argued, the incorporation of retributivistic side-constraints into the deterrence-oriented rationale for capital punishment will not rescue that rationale from its countenancing of death sentences for the close relatives of people who have committed wicked crimes. Again, much the same is true in connection with the denunciatory rationale. If the side-constraints are prohibitions on any practice of punishing innocent people, they are consistent with executions of murderers' relatives—since those executions are conducted to punish the murderers rather than the relatives. The executions epitomize the sense of loathing that is felt by the relevant community toward the evil murderers and their misdeeds rather than toward the relatives. If the side-constraints are instead broader deontological prohibitions on any practice of subjecting innocent people to severe detriments, the utilitarianism that underpins the denunciatory conception of punishment can be invoked in support of criminalizing the remissness of any vicious murderer's relatives (namely, their non-prevention of the murderer from carrying out his homicidal endeavours). In such circumstances, the executions of the relatives will be expressive of the revulsion felt by members of the public toward the relatives' own criminal conduct. Accordingly, however the limits imposed by the aforementioned side-constraints may be construed, a denunciatory practice of putting to death the close relatives of murderers can stay within those limits. In that respect, the denunciatory rationale for capital punishment is morally no better than the deterrence-oriented rationale and is worse than the incapacitative rationale.

5.3.2.2. A problem of principle

Nothing in this discussion of the wielding of sanctions against innocent people has suggested that the levying of sanctions on such people will be inevitable in a denunciatory system of criminal justice or even that it will be highly probable. Any claims about the probability of such an upshot will be subject to numerous empirical contingencies (concerning, for example, the ease or difficulty with which the guiltlessness of various innocent people can become uncovered). Instead of speculating about what is highly probable, this discussion has adverted to what is plainly possible—and to what is wrong in principle, regardless of its likelihood or unlikelihood. In any system of criminal justice that operates in accordance with the denunciatory conception of punishment, there is an abiding possibility that some innocent people will be executed in furtherance of the goals that are integral to such a conception. Provided that such people are widely believed to be guilty of heinous crimes, and provided that their guiltlessness is likely to remain undiscovered, executions of them will be deemed legitimate by the terms of the denunciatory rationale.

Of course, there is an abiding possibility of the imposition of sanctions upon innocent people in any system of criminal justice, regardless of whether a system is operated in pursuit of denunciatory objectives. If a system of criminal justice *SCJ* is morally upright, however, any sanctions imposed on innocent people therein are morally illegitimate under the terms of *SCJ*'s own principles. In other words, not only would the infliction of a punishment upon an innocent person derive from cognitive errors on the part of *SCJ*'s legal-governmental officials (and many citizens); in addition, such an infliction would be classifiable as a moral transgression under the exact principles to which those officials adhere when they run *SCJ*. In a system of criminal justice that is operated in accordance with the tenets of the denunciatory theory, by contrast, the imposition of a sanction upon an innocent person is classified by those tenets as morally correct if the person is widely and persistently believed to be guilty of a crime in regard to which the sanction is an appropriate expression of outrage. That is, the tenets of the denunciatory theory purport to justify morally the punishing of innocent people in sundry actual or possible situations.[5] One reason for the moral untenability of that theory is its stance on this very matter.

---

[5] I am of course using 'justify' in the first of the two senses that were distinguished in § 2.4.2.1.3 of Chapter 2. In other words, the tenets of the denunciatory theory purport to establish that the punishing of innocent people in sundry actual or possible situations is morally permissible.

5.3.3. Inverted proportionality and surreptitious crimes

If the denunciatory theory is to be credible as an account of the purposes of pun-ishment, it will have to prescribe an array of sanctions that collectively conform to the requirement of proportionality. Under that theory, the most severe punishments (such as the death penalty) should be reserved for the most serious crimes, while sanctions that are less and less severe should be imposed for crimes that are less and less serious. Because the gravest crimes are those that should elicit the most resound-ing denunciations, they are the crimes that should trigger the harshest sanctions in a system of criminal justice that is based on the tenets of the denunciatory theory. Yet, given some of the objectives that are commended by that theory, a denunciatory scale of punishments can in certain respects be the opposite of what is enjoined by the requirement of proportionality.

5.3.3.1. Reinforcement of moral outlooks

Consider, most notably, the goal of shoring up and refining the moral sentiments of ordinary citizens in the aftermath of a crime. Crimes that are especially rebarba-tive, such as cannibalistic murder, are least likely to entice ordinary people or to alter their sense of right and wrong. More than any punishments ever could, the disgust and horror felt by ordinary people in response to such crimes will strengthen their disinclination to engage in any comparable wrongdoing themselves. Their aversion to shuddersomely grotesque iniquities will decidedly not be weakened by the occur-rence of the iniquities, and will therefore not stand in need of reinforcement through the imposition of harsh legal sanctions. Hence, if one of the central points of punish-ment is to supply such reinforcement, we should *pro tanto* conclude that sanctions for the vilest crimes are barely needed at all. As Richard Lempert understatedly writes with specific reference to the penalty of death:

> Normative validation through exemplary punishment has never actually been shown to exist, and murder, particularly the kind of murder that results in the death penalty, is so generally disapproved of at all levels of society that there is little a priori reason to believe that the death penalty must be substituted for life imprisonment to drive home the message that murder is wrong. [Lempert 1981, 1191]

Lempert has here drawn too modest a conclusion from what he has said. Not only are there few grounds for thinking that the death penalty itself is essential as a means of solidifying the aversion of the general public toward horrifically brutal murders. What is more, there are few grounds for thinking that *any* severe penalty is necessary for that purpose.

Of course, in combination with my remarks in § 5.3.1 above, the opening portion of Lempert's statement along with his slightly later insertion of the phrase 'a priori' should induce circumspection in my current discussion. Although I am here taking exception to a moral shortcoming of the denunciatory account of punishment, I am relying on some empirical claims in so doing. While no empirical studies have been conducted (or are ever likely to be conducted) to confirm the empirical presuppositions of denunciatory theorists, it is also true that no such studies have been conducted to refute those presuppositions. Studies of the latter sort are no more realistically on the horizon—even a very distant horizon—than are studies of the former sort. In the absence of data from any systematic surveys, this discussion must appeal to commonplace experience for the plausibility of its empirical assertions. Any readers can judge for themselves whether the repugnance of ordinary people toward cannibalistic murder (for example) would be apt to diminish if the perpetrators of such a repellent crime were punished quite leniently. Far more plausible is the hypothesis that ordinary people would be particularly outraged and sickened by the indulgence with which the culprits have been treated. Ordinary moral sentiments concerning cannibalistic murder are not precariously in need of any bolstering. Thus, insofar as the role of punishments is to furnish such bolstering, the infliction of heavy punishments is superfluous in connection with the most repulsive crimes. (Denunciatory theorists will undoubtedly contend that the considerations just broached are offset by what is required for the fulfillment of another goal of theirs: the goal of defusing people's inclinations toward private acts of vengeance. As will be remarked shortly, such a reply is correct as far as it goes. However, the very point of this discussion of inverted proportionality is to show that the objectives of the denunciatory theorists are often not mutually reinforcing. Those key objectives quite often point in different directions.)

If someone doubts the veracity of the empirical claims advanced in the preceding couple of paragraphs, he or she can construe my comments as focused on a possible world—closely similar to the actual world—with reference to which those claims are true. So focused, my complaint is that one of the chief objectives of the denunciatory theory does not support the requirement of proportionality in application to that nearby possible world. In any event, let us recall that the burden of proof in debates over the death penalty always rests on people who support such a penalty in preference to less severe sanctions. Accordingly, given that the empirical assertions in the last couple of paragraphs are highly credible, the burden lies on denunciatory proponents of the death penalty to counter those assertions with findings from empirical studies that would somehow support contrary empirical claims. As has already been suggested in this chapter, such a burden of proof cannot ever realistically be discharged.

Successfully concealed crimes are even more problematic for the denunciatory theorists than are grotesquely repellent crimes that do not entice any ordinary citizens. If a crime has been kept hidden so that nobody apart from the perpetrator (and perhaps the victim) is ever aware of it, then its occurrence will not have posed any challenge to the moral outlooks of ordinary citizens. Consider for instance the murder of Fortunato by Montresor, the narrator of Edgar Allan Poe's short story 'The Cask of Amontillado.' So stealthily and cleverly was the murder carried out that it remained permanently undiscovered. As a consequence, its occurrence did nothing to shake the moral sentiments of the citizenry in the surrounding community. Contemplating such a crime, the denunciatory theorists have to conclude that there was no reason for punishing Montresor; his successful concealment of his misdeed rendered his impunity morally appropriate. In other words, a corollary of the denunciatory theory is that the complete absence of any punishment will be morally justified whenever a crime has been kept hidden skillfully. The point here, of course, is not simply that the lack of any available evidence would render procedurally unsustainable all attempts to convict and punish Montresor for his crime (a crime that was unknown to any other living person). All attempts to convict and punish him would indeed be untenable on procedural grounds, but—in the eyes of the denunciatory theorists— the absence of any sanctions against him was also morally justified on substantive grounds. The withholding of such sanctions was substantively justified, according to those theorists, because his murder of Fortunato had not produced the sort of harm which the imposition of sanctions is designed to remedy. There were no substantive grounds for punishing him, just as there were no procedural grounds. In fact, there were no substantive grounds because of the specific way in which there were no procedural grounds. Adept furtiveness effectively exonerates a criminal, under the tenets of the denunciatory theorists. No matter how serious a criminal misdeed may be, and no matter how ruthlessly it may be perpetrated, the malefactor responsible for it can—through such furtiveness—remove any substantive basis for the infliction of sanctions. He will have kept himself from causing any untoward consequences of the kind that would be counteracted by denunciatory sanctions.

5.3.3.2. The defusing of vindictive impulses

As has been suggested by the preceding subsection's observation that ordinary members of the public will tend to be infuriated if the perpetrators of vile crimes are treated leniently, the second main objective of the denunciatory theorists does not bring about inversions of the principle of proportionality in the same way as their first objective. Vindictive sentiments among members of the public will generally increase in tandem with the gravity of any crimes that are known to have been committed. Accordingly, the punishments levied for the most atrocious crimes will have to be especially severe if ordinary people with their sentiments of vengeance are to be mollified and if private acts of retaliation are thus to be averted. Consequently, unlike the goal of strengthening and purifying the moral outlooks of citizens, the goal of satisfying and defusing people's vengeful impulses does not lead to the conclusion that the most disgusting crimes should be punished lightly. On the contrary, as has just been stated, it leads to the conclusion that the punishments for such crimes should be particularly severe—in accordance with the requirement of proportionality. Still, the point here of my discussion of especially sickening crimes is precisely to reveal that the three main objectives of the denunciatory theory are often not tidily aligned with one another. In application to such crimes, those objectives militate in favour of sharply divergent punitive responses.

Moreover, although the second chief concern of the denunciatory theorists does not invert the principle of proportionality as crazily as does their first concern, it too generates preposterous implications concerning the treatment of carefully concealed crimes. Surreptitious crimes do not elicit any vindictive hostility in anybody, because no one has become aware of their occurrence. Ergo, crimes perpetrated with sufficient stealthiness do not produce any detrimental effects of the sort which a denunciatory system of criminal justice is seeking to undo through the administration of punishments. Hence, there are no substantive grounds—as well as no procedural grounds, of course—for the imposition of any sanctions upon someone who has carried out a well-hidden crime. Even if the crime in question is an instance of cannibalistic murder, the perpetrator through his furtiveness has managed to avoid doing anything that will arouse feelings of vengeful antagonism in members of the public. Under the tenets of the denunciatory theory, therefore, he has managed to avoid doing anything that warrants his being punished. On substantive grounds as well as procedural grounds, then, the impunity of his crime is morally justified according to those tenets. By performing his misdeed (perhaps a heinous misdeed) with sufficient craftiness, the wrongdoer has effectively exonerated himself legally—not only in the sense that he has incurred no punishment, but also in the sense that the absence of any punishment is morally appropriate. Even if the procedural snags are left aside, the very purpose of punishment would not be served by the imposition of any sanctions upon the wrongdoer. Such, at any rate, is the conclusion to which the denunciatory theorists have committed themselves.

5.3.3.3. The consolidation of a community's identity

The final principal goal of the denunciatory theorists—the goal of tightening a community's bonds of solidarity and enhancing the sense of its identity that is held by its members—is as disconcertingly unsupportive of the requirement of proportionality as is their first principal goal. As has already been argued, many of the most horrific crimes (such as instances of cannibalistic murder) will be singularly unenticing in the eyes of ordinary people and will thus not typically give rise to a need for harsh punishments in order to stiffen the moral convictions of people against such crimes. Much the same is true in connection with the ties of solidarity that unite people as a community. In response to a revelation of some hideous crime, those ties will tend to harden as people in the affected community are brought together by their common revulsion and their common sense of animosity toward the perpetrator of such a heinous offence. If a lenient penalty is levied for an offence of that kind, a shared reaction of outrage will tend to unite citizens all the more firmly. Their recognition of themselves as a community is dependent far more on the attitudes which they share—and which they correctly perceive themselves as sharing—than on the stringency of the sanctions that are imposed by their system of criminal justice. Indeed, as has just been suggested, the inordinate gentleness of those sanctions will typically reinforce the solidarity of citizens as they join with one another in a common state of indignation and fury. (Note that here, and throughout my discussions of inverted proportionality, I am referring to crimes that are handled by a system of criminal justice in an ongoing liberal-democratic society. My comments are largely inapplicable to the sort of situation that arises when a town or village is thoroughly overrun by the depredations of an occupying army or by the murderous rampages of a band of marauding rebels. Neither the denunciatory theory nor my critique of it is aimed at addressing the occurrence of community-shattering onslaughts.)

Now, plainly, the foregoing paragraph has propounded a number of interrelated empirical assertions. Equally plainly, those assertions do not derive from any systematic empirical studies conducted by me or by anybody else. In the absence of such studies, the empirical claims put forward here are grounded in commonplace experience rather than in social science. Any reader who dissents from my empirical assumptions should take the preceding paragraph to be focused on a nearby possible world rather than on the actual world. So understood, my objections to the denunciatory theory are assailing its implications for that possible world.

With regard to the prospect of cleverly hidden crimes, the denunciatory theorists' third objective is as troublesome as their first two objectives. When a crime is performed with sufficient furtiveness to ensure that it never becomes known to anyone apart from its perpetrator (and perhaps its immediate victim), it will not pose any threat to the feelings of solidarity that are harboured by the members of a community toward one another and toward their assemblage as a whole. If people are completely unaware that a crime has been committed, their sense of allegiance to their community will be entirely unaffected by it. Consequently, the crime has not produced any harm of the type which a denunciatory system of criminal justice would seek to repair through the imposition of a sanction. Because of his craftiness in concealment, the perpetrator of the crime has not done anything that impairs a community's cohesion. He has not done anything that detracts from the extent to which people collectively identify themselves as a community. Under the principles of the denunciatory theory, then, there is no substantive basis—nor any procedural basis, naturally—for the wielding of a sanction against him. Even if the denunciatory theorists prescind from all the procedural obstacles that block the conviction and punishment of the perpetrator, they have to conclude that he has been treated in a morally impeccable fashion.

5.3.4. No upper limit

Like the deterrence-oriented theorists, the denunciatory theorists are committed to the view that punishments much more severe than any humane version of the death penalty can be morally legitimate in various circumstances. Prolonged and savage torture, systematic dismemberment, boiling in oil, executions of close relatives, and crucifixion are among the sanctions that can be countenanced as morally legitimate by the denunciatory conception of punishment. To be sure, the requisiteness of such odious punitive measures under the principles of the denunciatory conception is not inevitable with reference to any particular society. The matter in every case will depend on a host of considerations relating to the moral sentiments and other attitudes of the citizenry in each jurisdiction. Still, if the salutary moral dispositions of the people in some society are precarious and are responsive to the functioning of the system of criminal justice that operates therein, and if the punishments needed to bolster those dispositions are ferocious, and if a practice of inflicting such punishments for that purpose will increase the overall well-being of people in the society despite the pain and apprehension which the practice engenders, then the use of the excruciating punishments in the specified society will be deemed by the denunciatory theory to be both morally legitimate and morally obligatory.

Of course, the conditional statement at the end of the preceding paragraph contains three antecedents, and the factors specified in those antecedents might obtain only in possible societies that are quite remote from any liberal-democratic society in the actual world. My current objection to the denunciatory theory does not hinge on any claims about what is actual or probable. Rather, the objection is adverting to the clear possibility of a liberal-democratic society in which the factors specified in those antecedents obtain. With reference to such a possible society, the denunciatory account of punishment favours the employment of brutally inhumane sanctions against criminals. That is, it favours the employment of morally illegitimate sanctions.

In other words, the criticism here pertains to a matter of principle rather than to something that is likely in practice. My animadversions in this subsection are not a warning about a probable upshot in the actual world, but are instead an exposure of the inability of the denunciatory theory to provide a moral justification for the imposition of any sanctions. With reference to the possible society envisaged above, the denunciatory theory requires the use of outrageous punishments that are morally illegitimate everywhere. Hence, the sheer fact that the tenets of the denunciatory theory have prescribed some sanction is not a sufficient condition for the moral legitimacy of that sanction; if some type or instance of punishment is indeed morally legitimate in a given context, its being so is due to considerations other than the fact that it is the type or instance of punishment for which the denunciatory theory calls.

This point is of great significance in debates over the moral legitimacy of capital punishment. After all, each of the commonly propounded rationales for such punishment has sought to maintain that the imposition of the death penalty is sometimes both morally obligatory and morally legitimate. What we have seen here is that, even if the denunciatory conception of punishment does prescribe the infliction of such a penalty in any particular situation, it does not thereby establish that the infliction is morally legitimate. A punishment's tendency to further the goals that are associated with the denunciatory theory is never sufficient in itself for the legitimacy of the punishment. Accordingly, even if the denunciatory theorists can show that executions in some circumstances would strongly further those goals, they will not yet have shown that the executions would be morally legitimate.

In its inability to set any upper limit for the severity of the punishments which it advocates, the denunciatory theory resembles the deterrence-oriented theory (as was suggested at the outset of this subsection). Each of the two theories, in application to many credibly possible societies—whether or not any of those possible societies are actual—will call for the use of sanctions that are morally illegitimate. Consequently, neither of those theories has adduced any considerations that suffice to justify morally any type or instance of punishment; if the sets of considerations respectively associated with those theories were sufficient to justify types and instances of punishment, then neither theory would ever require impermissible sanctions. Ergo, the invocation of denunciatory objectives as a justification for the death penalty is otiose. Though the administration of such a penalty in certain contexts may well be morally legitimate (as my next chapter will be arguing), the source of the legitimacy lies beyond the concerns and desiderata to which the denunciatory theorists draw attention.

5.3.5. The minimal invasion principle afresh

While the foregoing objections are enough to discredit the denunciatory rationale for capital punishment, this chapter will close with one further line of attack. Like most of the other standard justifications for capital punishment, the denunciatory rationale transgresses the Minimal Invasion Principle. It prescribes a mode of punishment that is more severe than alternative modes that can equally well fulfil the objectives which the denunciatory theorists laud.

What those theorists need to contend when purporting to justify capital punishment is that their sentiment-solidifying and vengeance-defusing and solidarity-bolstering goals cannot adequately be realized in some contexts by any sanction less severe than that of death. Now, in order to impugn the denunciatory theory in its strongest form, my discussion here will put aside the queries in § 5.3.3 about that theory's partial inversion of the requirement of proportionality. Let us assume, for present purposes, that the attainment of each desideratum pursued by the denunciatory theorists will require that the most severe punishments in a system of criminal justice be levied in response to the most sickening crimes. Can this concession to the denunciatory theorists—granted here purely *arguendo*—be parlayed by them into a successful vindication of the death penalty? Because of the Minimal Invasion Principle, the answer to this question is negative.

In many respects, the violations of the Minimal Invasion Principle by the denunciatory rationale for capital punishment are similar to those by the retributivistic rationale, and my rejoinders to the denunciatory rationale on this point will to some degree be reminiscent of my rejoinders to Michael Davis in § 3.4.2.2 of Chapter 3. However, because the denunciatory approach to punishment is consequentialist whereas the retributivistic approach is deontological, my current critique—unlike my riposte to Davis—has to draw on some empirical assumptions. Although those assumptions are of course not incontestable, they are highly plausible; given that the burden of proof in any debate over the death penalty rests on the people who advocate that penalty, my plausible empirical assumptions will stand unless the denunciatory proponents of capital punishment can somehow disconfirm those assumptions with data that are the products of systematic empirical studies.

The key point that tells against the denunciatory rationale is that the principle of proportionality is never sufficient in itself to establish the moral legitimacy of capital punishment (or indeed of any other type of punishment). What the precept of proportionality ordains is that greater and greater levels of law-transgressing malignity should be met with greater and greater levels of punitive severity. Accordingly, the harshest sanctions imposed by a system of criminal justice are to be reserved for the gravest misconduct. Such a requirement, however, does not go any way toward determining what the harshest sanctions should be. The principle of proportionality can be fulfilled by a system of criminal justice that employs the illegitimately barbarous modes of punishment that have been touched upon in § 5.3.4. Since those modes of punishment are morally impermissible even when administered within a schedule of sanctions that conforms to the requirement of proportionality, that very requirement has to be supplemented by a standard that fixes the maximal legitimate level of punitive severity. Conversely, the principle of proportionality can likewise be fulfilled by a system of criminal justice that does not employ the death penalty or any other sanction that is harsher than some modest term of imprisonment. Thus, given that the sway of proportionality within a system of criminal justice is never a sufficient condition for the moral legitimacy of any punishments, and given that the inclusion of the death penalty in a scheme of sanctions is not a necessary condition for that sway, a denunciatory defence of such a penalty must invoke something more than the requirement of proportionality.

Naturally, denunciatory theorists will resort to the goals which they seek to realize through the administering of proper punishments. They will contend that capital punishment is essential for the achievement of those goals in the aftermath of any hideous crimes, and they will therefore affirm that the use of such punishment in response to such crimes is fully consistent with the Minimal Invasion Principle. Now, of course, such a retort by the denunciatory theorists will run aground on the problem recounted in § 5.3.4; even if some type or instance of punishment is indispensable for the realization of denunciatory objectives, that fact alone is never a sufficient condition for the moral legitimacy of the type or instance of punishment. However, let us put that problem aside in order to concentrate instead on the question whether the death penalty is indeed an indispensable means for the attainment of the desiderata which the denunciatory theorists pursue.

A number of philosophers and jurists have rightly answered that latter question negatively. David Dolinko, for example, has written as follows:

As for normative validation [that is, the solidification of moral sentiments through the denunciatory force of punishments]: even if the crimes for which society reserves its harshest and most feared penalty are thereby rendered especially odious to most people, why should this effect be weaker in a society whose harshest and most feared penalty is (say) life without parole than in one that employs the death penalty?[6]

[6] Dolinko 1986, 589 n 220.

Mary Ellen Gale has made a cognate observation: 'If the principle of parsimony [namely, the Minimal Invasion Principle] applies to denunciation, one may contend that killing murderers to denounce their crimes is not the least burdensome or the least painful way of informing the public that murder is wrong' (Gale 1985, 1018 n 131). John Conrad has opined along similar lines: '[I]f serious crimes are leniently punished, then the system [of criminal justice] is in poor working order and its value in support of morality is impaired. In this sense, the justification of punishment offered by Durkheim is funda-mental to the continuing maintenance of a moral society. Nothing in that justification entails the infliction of death on criminals' (Van den Haag and Conrad 1983, 49).

These pronouncements by Dolinko and Gale and Conrad are pertinent in application to any of the three main goals of the denunciatory theorists. Their pertinence becomes especially evident when we keep in mind a point that has been highlighted at more than one juncture in Chapter 3 (and also, for a different purpose, in Chapter 4). There are many techniques, not involving torture or rape or amputation at all, by which the unpleasantness of a lifelong term of imprisonment-without-parole can be intensified. In connection with the perpetrators of the vilest crimes, the employment of some of those techniques—such as solitary confinement and the sharp curtailment of access to news-papers or other means of entertainment—can be highly serviceable for the realization of the denunciatory theorists' objectives. If the conditions of lifelong detention for the worst offenders are grimly austere and are known by members of the public to be grimly austere, then the sentencing of such offenders to those conditions can serve to denounce their hideous crimes as forcefully as would the sentencing of them to death. By con-demning a monstrous prisoner to a life of drab isolation, a system of criminal justice will have emphatically expressed the sense of revulsion felt by members of the public toward his grotesque misconduct and will thus have underscored the correctness of their moral sentiments. It will likewise have satisfied any vindictive impulses that might be harboured by them, and it will consequently have obviated any private acts of retaliation. Similarly, by so starkly dissociating the nefarious convict from the community in which he has wrought havoc, a sentence of lifelong imprisonment-without-parole in solitary confine-ment will have reinforced the whole ethos that binds the community together as such.

Some remarks by Tom Sorell nicely illustrate the importance that should be attached by denunciatory theorists to toughening the conditions of imprisonment for the worst offenders in any jurisdiction—and to publicizing the bleak austerity of those condi-tions. In a critical assessment of some arguments by the former US Supreme Court Justice William Brennan against the death penalty, Sorell retorts forthrightly: 'Brennan is on even weaker ground in claiming that imprisonment can serve as effectively as execution for the expression of outrage at a heinous crime. This invites the protest, expressed by many who are in favour of the death penalty, that prison conditions are too good for villains who have murdered or violently assaulted the helpless and innocent' (Sorell 1987, 115). Sorell quotes a complaint by the erstwhile British parliamentarian Arthur Lewis about the luxuriousness of prisons in England, and he offers the follow-ing comment: 'The fact that it is far-fetched to say that prison conditions are relatively luxurious is beside the point. If Lewis and other people believed that imprisonment was too light a sentence, then imprisonment was simply not as good a way of expressing his and other people's outrage as execution' (Sorell 1987, 115–16). Sorell's observations make clear that there are strong reasons for denunciatory theorists to insist on joylessly drab conditions of confinement for the gravest offenders in any society, and that there are likewise strong reasons for such theorists—and legal-governmental officials—to apprise ordinary people of the grimness of those conditions. Sorell himself is responsive to just such measures. He quotes from Amy Edwards's account of the stern regime for prisoners in England during the late nineteenth century, and he writes:

> Lewis's criticism of [the laxity of] British prison conditions in 1982 cannot conceivably be made against the regime Edwards describes.... And while it was probably more severe than it had to be for its intended purpose, namely, to deter and exact retribution for non-capital crimes, it would not strike everyone—it would not strike Lewis presumably—as excessive for the villains and criminals he thought should be "put down" for their killing. [Sorell 1987, 117]

Having initially aligned himself with Lewis against the likes of Brennan in an apparent defence of the denunciatory rationale for capital punishment, Sorell here switches to the other side. He thereby reveals that the role of such punishment in furthering denunciatory objectives can equally well be performed by a bleak regime of incarceration for the most wicked offenders.

Since terms of lifelong imprisonment-without-parole in conditions of solitary drabness are less severe punitive measures than are executions, and since such terms of imprisonment for the most evil criminals can help to realize the goals of denunciatory theorists as effectively as can executions—if the dreariness of the conditions of imprisonment is publicized adequately—the denunciatory theorists are obligated by the Minimal Invasion Principle to disfavour the institution of capital punishment and to advocate instead (for the most evil criminals) the type of incarceration described here. Of course, as has been readily acknowledged, this conclusion rests partly on some empirical assumptions about the reactions and inclinations of ordinary people in liberal democracies.[7] Let us close by noting how the credibility of one of those assumptions is greatly enhanced by the line of argument in this subsection.

Recall that the denunciatory theorists' concern about private acts of retaliation against nefarious murderers can be understood to encompass the prospect of such acts by fellow convicts. As was stated in § 5.3.1 above, the likelihood of attacks by fellow convicts against the perpetrators of gruesome murders is quite high in any jurisdiction that not only lacks capital punishment but also lacks solitary confinement for especially despicable criminals. Hence, if the lone alternative to capital punishment were lifelong imprisonment without solitary confinement, my invocation of the Minimal Invasion Principle would be somewhat dubious in relation to the aforementioned concern of the denunciatory theorists. They could reply that the only available alternative

---

[7] Only liberal democracies are relevant, because—as was remarked in § 5.1 above—the denunciatory theory is morally credible as an account of punishment only in application to liberal-democratic regimes.

to the death penalty is a type of sanction that does not satisfactorily avert acts of vindictiveness within prisons.

In my discussion heretofore, solitary confinement for vile murderers has been presented as a means of intensifying the disagreeableness of the incarceration in which they will spend their lives. As such a means, solitary confinement contributes to the realization of each of the denunciatory theorists' objectives. However, as should now be evident, the use of solitary confinement for the worst offenders is important also as a means of thwarting other convicts from gaining access to them. By eliminating such access, solitary confinement for the most rebarbative offenders will again contribute to the realization of the denunciatory theorists' revenge-averting objective; it helps to ensure that that objective is fulfilled inside a penal system as well as in the outside world.

Thus—as has been indicated in § 5.3.1—even if some empirical studies discover that the incidence of attacks by fellow convicts against the most odious offenders in jurisdictions that lack capital punishment is higher than in jurisdictions that impose such punishment, a discovery of that kind will not militate in favour of the introduction of the death penalty. Instead, it will militate in favour of the introduction of solitary confinement for the especially odious offenders. From a denunciatory perspective, such confinement is an appropriately unpleasant mode of punishment for them and is also the best means of stymieing assaults on them by other prisoners. Lifelong imprisonment-without-parole in solitary confinement for the worst criminals is as effective as the death penalty in advancing all three of the denunciatory theorists' goals; and because the use of such imprisonment is feasible in any jurisdiction, the Minimal Invasion Principle disallows the institution of capital punishment insofar as that institution is grounded on the tenets of the denunciatory theory. Lifelong imprisonment-without-parole in solitary confinement is a less severe alternative that can equally well yield all the desiderata which the denunciatory theory extols.

5.4. Concluding reflections

For more than one reason, then, the denunciatory rationale for the death penalty is untenable as a basis for the conducting of executions. If the practice of capital punishment in a society is founded on that basis, it is morally illegitimate. To say as much, of course, is not to say that the concerns of the denunciatory theorists are unworthy of being taken seriously. On the contrary, those concerns are genuinely weighty, and a system of criminal justice in a liberal-democratic society should seek to address them satisfactorily. However, any pursuit of the denunciatory theorists' objectives cannot morally justify the practice of capital punishment. No more than the other standardly proffered rationales for the death penalty, can the denunciatory rationale establish that executions of the perpetrators of atrocious crimes are morally legitimate and obligatory. My next chapter will endeavour to fill that justificatory gap.

6

The Purgative Rationale for Capital Punishment

From Chapter 2 onward, we have witnessed the failings of the four most frequently championed rationales for the institution of capital punishment. Those rationales have turned out not to be veritable justifications of that institution at all, as each of them runs athwart some major principles of political morality. Their contraventions of those principles are instructive for the present chapter, where this book turns from a 'negative' ground-clearing orientation to a 'positive' justificatory orientation. That is, the array of criticisms advanced in Chapters 2–5 can alert us to the pitfalls that must be avoided by any sustainable justification of the death penalty. If the purgative rationale for the use of that penalty is to withstand scrutiny—in other words, if it is genuinely to establish that executions in some contexts are morally obligatory and morally permissible—it will have to steer clear of the fatal shortcomings that have undone the other rationales.

Most notable among those shortcomings are transgressions of the Minimal Invasion Principle. Every standardly propounded rationale for the death penalty is unable to show that such a penalty is the least severe means for realizing the objectives that are integral to the rationale. An inability to show as much, against the background of the Minimal Invasion Principle, is tantamount to an inability to show that the institution of capital punishment is ever morally obligatory or morally legitimate. Thus, if the purgative rationale for such punishment is to succeed, it will have to confirm that no sanctions less severe than the death penalty can ever bring about the purgation for which it calls.

Another problem that afflicts most of the commonly invoked justifications of capital punishment—specifically the deterrence-oriented, retributivistic, and denunciatory justifications—is that they cannot set any principled upper limit on the severity of the sanctions which they prescribe. In application to many credibly possible societies (some of which might be actual), those justifications countenance the imposition of barbarous punishments that are always morally illegitimate. Accordingly, the considerations respectively adduced by deterrence-oriented theorists and retributivists and denunciatory theorists in support of capital punishment and other sanctions are not sufficient to establish that executions, or any other punitive measures, are morally permissible.

Hence, if the purgative rationale for the death penalty is to succeed, it will have to discountenance any barbarous punishments. It will have to maintain that no sanctions more severe than the death penalty are ever required under its terms, and it will have to explain why the differences between executions and those more severe sanctions are sufficient to render the executions morally legitimate.

In short, the purgative rationale has to contend that neither anything more nor anything less than the imposition of the death penalty on heinous offenders is serviceable for the fulfilment of the moral values that are upheld by the rationale. As Chapter 1 has indicated, my exposition of the purgative rationale will indeed argue for such a conclusion. In addition, however, the exposition will need to insist upon a firm link between punishment—including capital punishment, of course—and guilt. Apart from retributivism, each of the frequently espoused rationales for the death penalty severs the connection (in many a credibly possible case) between the subjection of a person to sanctions and the actual moral responsibility of the person for any crimes. One key reason for rejecting each of the consequentialist justifications of capital punishment is precisely that each of them does away with moral responsibility as a precondition for the legitimacy of any punitive infliction. Ergo, if the purgative rationale for the death penalty is genuinely to vindicate the use of that penalty, it will have to align itself with retributivism in reaffirming the role of moral responsibility as such a precondition. Only by always disallowing the punishment of innocent people can the purgative rationale forswear the morally damning commitment of consequentialists to the prioritization of perceived guilt over actual guilt.

In all these respects, the purgative rationale for capital punishment can succeed where the other rationales have foundered. As Chapter 1 has observed, the death penalty is the only type of sanction that is ever required under the purgative rationale, and it is the gentlest type of sanction that can realize the objectives of that rationale. Because of the latter point, the purgative justification for capital punishment does not violate the Minimal Invasion Principle; and, because of the former point, that justification never calls for any brutally inhumane sanctions. In other words, because purgation in the relevant sense cannot be achieved through any sanction that is lighter than the imposition of the death penalty, the employment of that penalty on the basis of the purgative rationale is in compliance with the Minimal Invasion Principle. It is the least severe means for the attainment of a pressing public end. Similarly, because purgation in the relevant sense never necessitates anything more than the termination of a defilingly evil offender's life in the most humane manner possible, the purgative justification for capital punishment sets an unwavering upper limit on the severity of the sanctions which it demands. Untainted by any approbation of ferociously illegitimate punishments, that justification can rightly profess to adduce considerations that are sufficient to vindicate morally the imposition of the death penalty. Furthermore, the purgative rationale never supports the execution of an innocent person. Under that rationale, the only morally legitimate and morally obligatory executions are those which put to death people whose lives are defilingly evil. If someone has not committed any iniquities, then he or she remains firmly outside the sway of the purgative justification for capital punishment. Within that sway, the value of moral responsibility is unswervingly respected.

Not only does the purgative justification surmount the moral hurdles that have tripped up the most frequently adopted approaches to capital punishment; what is more, the operativeness of its moral force within the actual world does not hinge on any controversial empirical claims (for which it cannot offer any substantiation). Unlike the deterrence-oriented and denunciatory approaches, then, the purgative rationale does not have to propound or presuppose any unverified empirical conjectures. Though every process by which a system of criminal justice brings that rationale to bear upon some particularly repulsive crimes is of course dependent on the ascertainability of the facts of those crimes, the applicability of the rationale itself is dependent on moral principles rather than on large and unconfirmed empirical propositions.

Hence, the purgative justification for the death penalty does not succumb to the moral vices or the empirical snarls that undermine the standard justifications for that penalty. Still, the virtues of the purgative rationale are indeed virtues only if the rationale itself is tenable as a ground for the institution of capital punishment. The task of this chapter is to maintain that purgative considerations do constitute such a ground.

6.1. The execution of Achan

As Chapter 1 has stated, the *loci classici* of the purgative rationale for capital punishment are numerous passages in the Bible. As was also suggested in the opening chapter, one probable reason why contemporary philosophers of punishment have ignored the purgative rationale is that they believe it to be inseparable from the hobgoblins of Biblical superstition. This chapter, in agreement with the hostility of many such philosophers toward religious doctrines, will seek to re-elaborate the purgative justification along strictly secular lines. Nonetheless, we can best begin by pondering one of the Biblical passages in which the purgative rationale for the death penalty figures saliently (though the notion of purgation is not directly and explicitly invoked). By mulling over the gist of this passage, with attention also to several of its extraneous elements, we can discern the chief features of the purgative rationale that must thereafter be reconceived and defended in purely secular terms.

Consider, then, the plight of the Israelites in the seventh chapter of the Book of Joshua. Having conquered the city of Jericho after their renowned marches around its walls, the Israelites prepare with confidence for an equally glorious triumph over the city of Ai. When the Israelites' warriors attack Ai, however, they are routed. Joshua, their leader, beseeches God for assistance. God replies by informing him that 'Israel has sinned; they have transgressed my covenant which I commanded them; they have taken some of the devoted things; they have stolen, and lied, and put them among their own stuff' (Joshua 7:11). The devoted things were the riches of Jericho that had been plundered after the conquest of that city. Nearly all of those riches were supposed to be destroyed in a devotional sacrifice to God, as a means of acknowledging His role in leading the Israelites to their victory. Because one of the Israelites has taken some of the booty for himself instead of including it in the mound of things to be immolated as a tribute to God, the wrath of the Almighty has descended upon the people of Israel. They are now helpless before their enemies. God tells Joshua that he must ascertain who has misappropriated some of the devoted things and that he must then execute the miscreant forthwith: 'And he who is taken with the devoted things shall be burned with fire, he and all that he has, because he has transgressed the covenant of the Lord, and because he has done a shameful thing in Israel' (Joshua 7:15). Joshua undertakes a divinely guided investigation that quickly identifies the culprit as Achan of the tribe of Judah. Having been adjured by Joshua to confess, Achan readily avouches that he has stolen from the devoted things a beautiful mantle, two hundred shekels of silver, and a bar of gold. After Joshua has verified that the pilfered items are indeed in Achan's tent, he chillingly carries out the sentence of the Lord:

And Joshua and all Israel with him took Achan the son of Zerah, and the silver and the mantle and the bar of gold, and his sons and daughters, and his oxen and asses and sheep, and his tent, and all that he had; and they brought them up to the Valley of Achor. And Joshua said, 'Why did you bring trouble on us? The Lord brings trouble on you today.' And all Israel stoned [Achan] with stones; they burned [Achan and his family] with fire, and stoned them with stones. And they raised over him a great heap of stones that remains to this day; then the Lord turned from his burning anger. [Joshua 7:24–26]

6.1.1. The extraneous features

Although the dismal story of Achan illustrates nicely the main elements of the purgative rationale for the death penalty, those elements have to be disentangled from other features of the story that are distracting or misleading. By understanding why some of the latter features are distracting or misleading, we can better grasp the purgative rationale itself.

6.1.1.1. Excessive severity and the massacre of the innocents

Perhaps most obvious among the distracting aspects of the narrative is that, under any credible moral reckoning, Achan's misdeed is not iniquitous at all. (It is certainly far less grave than the systematic butchery of the people of Jericho that has been perpetrated by the Israelites at God's behest when they conquer that city.) Some punishment may be appropriate for Achan, but capital punishment—on purgative grounds or any other grounds—is markedly inapposite. If my elaboration of the purgative rationale is to be morally tenable, it will have to eschew the barbarous superstition that could lead someone to believe that the imposition of the death penalty is an apt response to Achan's peccadillo. Neither the wounded pride of a deity nor the wrongness of the crime of theft is any basis whatsoever for putting a person to death.

Another shocking facet of the story is the destruction of Achan's sons and daughters. Even if Achan himself had committed a crime of such turpitude as to warrant his subjection to capital punishment under the purgative rationale, the slaughter of his sons and daughters would still have been wholly unjustified morally. (We can assume here that the sons and daughters have not committed any iniquities of their own. There is no suggestion in the Biblical narrative that they are put to death for any of their own doings.) Given that Chapters 2 and 5 have reproached the deterrence-oriented theory of punishment and the denunciatory theory for countenancing the practice of executing the close relatives of murderers, the present chapter will hardly be putting forward a theory that favours such a practice. On the contrary, the Biblical doctrine of visiting the iniquity of the fathers upon the children is inimical to the ideal of moral responsibility and is thus itself morally odious.[1] This point is of great importance within my exposition of the purgative rationale for capital punishment, because that rationale affirms that the continued existence of someone who has perpetrated hideous atrocities is such as to defile the community in which he or she abides. Though the phenomenon of defilement will have to be explicated later, what should be emphasized now is that that phenomenon does not involve anything at odds with the ideal of the moral responsibility of individuals.

6.1.1.2. Collective responsibility versus defilement

Closely related to what has just been said is another clarification that should be entered straightaway. As is indicated by the first of my quotations from the story of Achan, God imputes collective responsibility for Achan's theft to the Israelites. Instead of declaring that an Israelite has sinned by stealing some devoted things, God declares that 'Israel has sinned'. Now, although the notion of collective responsibility can be entirely appropriate in many contexts—including some contexts in which extravagantly heinous misdeeds have been committed—it is distinct from the notion of defilement. Notwithstanding that the phenomenon of collective responsibility and the phenomenon of defilement are perfectly compatible, the existence of either does not entail the existence of the other.[2] On the one hand, if grotesque atrocities are perpetrated by people in positions and circumstances that warrant the attribution of the atrocities to the collectivities on behalf of whom those people are acting, then both collective responsibility and defilement are operative; the atrocities are misdeeds for which there is collective responsibility, and the continued existence of the people who ordered or performed those grotesque misdeeds

---

[1] For expressions of this Biblical doctrine, see Exodus 20:5, 34:6–7; Deuteronomy 5:9. In some later parts of the Bible, the doctrine is stoutly repudiated. See Deuteronomy 24:16; Ezekiel 18:1–20.

[2] For some important recent accounts of collective or corporate responsibility, see Kutz 2000; Pettit 2007. For a fine collection of philosophical essays on the topic, see French and Wettstein 2006. As is probably apparent already, defilement is itself a variety of collective responsibility. Hence, when my present discussion poses a contrast between collective responsibility and defilement, it is really drawing a distinction between two types of collective responsibility: namely, collective responsibility for some original iniquities versus collective responsibility for subsequently keeping alive the perpetrators of those iniquities.

is such as to defile the communities in which they abide. On the other hand, however, most of the iniquities that fall under the purgative rationale for capital punishment are not committed by people acting on behalf of communities. Most such iniquities are performed in defiance of the mores and legal requirements of the communities in which they occur. Consequently, there is no collective responsibility for the commission of those shockingly evil crimes. For instance, when Ian Brady and Myra Hindley tortured and sexually assaulted and murdered several children in northern England in the early 1960s, they were scarcely acting on behalf of the residents of the municipalities near which their horrors took place. As far as can be told from the narrative of Achan and the devoted things, his crime—though incomparably less grave than the outrages perpetrated by the Moors Murderers—is likewise at odds with the prevailing attitudes and laws of his community. No more than Brady and Hindley has he been acting in a position of legal-governmental authority that would warrant an ascription of his misconduct to the people of Israel as a whole. Hence, when God articulates just such an ascription, He exhibits a dearth of moral and philosophical acumen.

This point about the distinction between defilement and collective responsibility was overlooked not only by God but also to a large degree by Immanuel Kant, in a famous passage of his *Metaphysics of Morals* where he went some distance toward adumbrating the purgative rationale for the death penalty:

Even if civil society were to dissolve itself with the consent of all its members (for example, if a people who inhabited an island decided to separate and to disperse to other parts of the world), the last murderer in prison would first have to be executed in order that each should receive his deserts and that the people should not bear the guilt of a capital crime through failing to insist on its punishment; for if they do not do so, they can be regarded as accomplices in the public violation of justice. [Kant 1970, 156]

Kant's terse remark is expressive of his retributivistic outlook, but, when construed quite sympathetically, it also gestures toward the purgative justification for capital punishment. However, the chief shortcoming of the passage is that it does not differentiate sufficiently between defilement and collective responsibility. Though the language of the passage is slightly ambiguous—in the original German as well as in the English translation—Kant strongly suggested that a failure to execute a vile murderer would render a community collectively responsible for the murderer's atrocities. Members of the community would in effect become accomplices to those atrocities, or so Kant apparently thought. Any suggestion by him along those lines was misconceived. Except in situations where malefactors have acted in positions of legal-governmental authority that render their heinous doings attributable to the communities on whose behalf they have exerted their powers, the communities do not bear any collective responsibility for those doings. The continued existence of a perpetrator of several grisly murders will have morally sullied the community in whose jurisdiction he resides, but it does not saddle that community with responsibility for the murders themselves. His being kept alive (past the period necessary for a fair trial and any concomitant appeals) is wrong not because it somehow retroactively makes the community a participant in his wreaking of carnage, but instead because it constitutes the community's failure to respond appropriately to the carnage. That is, instead of mysteriously becoming guilty of the original heinous misdeeds along with the culprit responsible for them, the community becomes guilty of the ancillary misdeed of declining to execute someone whose very survival calls into question the moral ties that hold the community together as such.

Of course, the passage from Kant's text can be read more generously (perhaps at the expense of exegetical accuracy for the sake of philosophical and moral clarification). If the passage is so read, we can detect in it a prefiguration of the purgative rationale that does separate defilement from collective responsibility. Rather than assuming somewhat woodenly that his phrases 'guilt of a capital crime' and 'accomplices in the public violation of justice' are references to collective responsibility for some original wrongdoing, we can construe them as references to the defilement of a community that ensues when the perpetrator of the wrongdoing is kept alive. In other words, Kant might be taken to indicate that the guilt deriving from crimes of great turpitude can pertain not only to the commission of the crimes but also to the inadequate addressing of them. Likewise, he might be taken to indicate that complicity in some iniquities can arise not only from proximate participation in them but also from the moral tarnishing that results when a community's resources are devoted to sustaining the existence of a perpetrator of the iniquities. When the quoted passage is interpreted in this more sympathetic fashion, we can conclude that Kant recognized that the role of punishment in application to the most hideous crimes is purgative rather than retributive (or rather than solely retributive). We can thereby conclude that he managed to stay away from conflating the phenomenon of defilement and the phenomenon of collective responsibility. Whether or not such a conclusion is exegetically defensible, it is morally and philosophically refreshing.

6.1.1.3. Some further extraneous features

Another feature of the story of Achan that is extrinsic to the purgative rationale for capital punishment is the brutality of the methods of execution. We are told that Achan and his family are burned with fire and stoned with stones. These cruel and primitive methods of putting people to death do not have any place in a system of criminal justice that is oriented toward the purgative rationale. (Naturally, the purgative justification differs in that regard from the deterrence-oriented justification, which countenances burning and stoning in any contexts where those techniques of punishment are maximally promotive of deterrence and of broader utilitarian goals.) What the purgative rationale for capital punishment seeks in any relevant case is the termination of a vile offender's life in order to avert the besmirching of his society by the continuation of his existence. Given the sway of the Minimal Invasion Principle, then, capital punishment administered on the basis of the purgative rationale must employ the most humane methods of execution that are available. Harsher techniques for ending offenders' lives would not be any more effective in furthering the important public purpose—the purgative purpose—which the institution of capital punishment is designed to fulfil. Consequently, the employment of any of the harsher techniques would contravene the Minimal Invasion Principle and would thus contravene the tenets of liberal democracy. Since the purgative rationale for capital punishment is itself possessed of moral force only insofar as it meshes with those tenets, it does not leave any room for cruelty. It does not leave any room for burning and stoning as punitive measures.

An additional facet of the Biblical account that should be ignored—or interpreted metaphorically—is the way in which the defilement of the Israelites by the continued existence of Achan leads to their suffering of a military debacle. That magical element of the story is integrally connected to the notion of a presiding deity who ensures that moral vices are attended by military defeats or other material setbacks. Such hocus-pocus does not play any role in the purgative rationale for the death penalty when that rationale is re-elaborated from a secular perspective. Though the defilement of a community that stems from its keeping repulsively evil criminals alive might be accompanied by military fiascoes or other physical afflictions such as earthquakes, any such hardships undergone by the community are coincidental. The phenomenon of defilement is a moral state or condition; outside the realm of religious mythology, the conjunction of that moral state or condition with military disasters (or other calamities) is purely fortuitous.

A final aspect of the story of Achan that might be misleading is the fact that his crime—his misappropriation of some of the booty of Jericho for himself—is an ongoing wrong rather than a completed wrong at the time when his guilt is exposed. His initial theft is completed, of course, but his withholding of the devoted things for his own pleasure is a wrong that persists to the point at which he is condemned. Some of the grotesque crimes that fall under the ambit of the purgative rationale for capital punishment are likewise ongoing wrongs, but many are not. Many hideous crimes, such as most instances of cannibalistic murder, have been completed when their perpetrators are eventually caught. Nothing in the purgative rationale limits its reach to evildoers who are still carrying out their iniquities at the time of their apprehension.

6.1.2. The gist of the purgative rationale

Despite the several elements in the narrative of Achan that are misleading or distracting, the narrative encapsulates the gist of the purgative rationale for the death penalty. What such a rationale maintains is that, among the countless crimes committed in any jurisdiction, some are so iniquitous that the continued existence of the thugs responsible for them is a blot on the moral order of the community in which those thugs are kept alive. Sparing such criminals from execution is wrong, for their lives are of negative value. So long as they survive (past the time necessary for fair legal proceedings against them), they sully any community with which they are associated. Just as the Israelites were all tainted by the continuing existence of Achan, a community is tainted—in other words, its moral integrity is lessened—by the continuing existence of anyone who has perpe-trated some especially hideous crimes and who is within the jurisdiction of the commu-nity or otherwise specially connected to it. To avert or remove that taint, a community must devote some of its resources to terminating the life of such an offender.

If this rationale for capital punishment is to be morally and philosophically respect-able, it will have to be supported by an account of the nature of evil and an account of the nature of defilement. What distinguishes misconduct that is merely wrong from misconduct that is evil? When is misconduct so evil as to imbue the life of its perpetrator with defilingness? Why does the prevention or eradication of a com-munity's defilement necessitate the execution of a vile offender (rather than, say, the banishment or lifelong imprisonment of him)? What circumstances, if any, mitigate the gravity of wicked conduct to the point where the imposition of the death penalty is inappropriate under the purgative rationale? These are some of the key questions which this chapter will address.

For the endeavour of addressing those questions, the Biblical story of Achan provides only very limited guidance. As has already been noted, for example, the Biblical conception of evil—whereby misconduct is deplored as evil if it is disrespect-ful toward God—is woefully unhelpful. Equally unilluminating is the notion that Achan's defilement of the Israelites was due to his having aroused God's fury, which was placated only by the termination of Achan's life. In a philosophically tenable exposition of the purgative rationale for capital punishment, the defilingness of the life of anyone responsible for great evil is a moral property that has nothing to do with the provocation of a deity's ire. Expounding the nature of that moral property with-out any reference to a deity is a task upon which the Bible sheds no light. (Indeed, as Chapter 1 has remarked, even contemporary philosophy does not shed much light upon that task. Because the phenomenon of defilement is so widely viewed as indis-severable from theistic doctrines, it has rarely been taken very seriously by modern-day philosophers. In that respect, as well as in some other respects, it differs from the phenomenon of collective responsibility.)

Still, although the narrative of Achan does not help very much in answering the questions that have to be tackled below, it does provide an apt orientation for my unfolding of the purgative justification of the death penalty. Notwithstanding that we should ignore many of the specifics of the narrative, we should heed its central message. In other words, we should recognize that the atrocities of an individual can sometimes lead his whole community to be tarnished through the very continuation of his life.

6.2. The nature of evil

On the one hand, the set of evil actions is substantially larger than the set of extrava-gantly evil actions, and the latter set is what is directly relevant to the purgative justi-fication of capital punishment (because only somebody responsible for extravagantly evil misconduct is within the scope of that justification). On the other hand, an understanding of the distinctiveness of evil conduct is obviously prerequisite to an understanding of the distinctiveness of extravagantly evil conduct. Thus, we need to come to grips with the nature of evil. We can best do so by mulling over several issues that have received attention from some of the other philosophers who have written on this topic.[3]

6.2.1. The underlying states of mind

All evil conduct is wrong,[4] but, plainly, not all wrong conduct is evil. For one thing, as I have argued at length elsewhere (Kramer 2004, 249–94; Kramer 2005), some wrong actions are non-culpable in that they arise from outlooks that are not blameworthy in any respect. Such actions are wrong and thus give rise to remedial obligations, but they are not products of faulty states of mind such as negligence or recklessness or heartlessness or sadistic malice. No such faultlessly wrong action is wicked. Moreover, even among the countless wrongs that do stem from blameworthy outlooks, most are not evil. Numerous wrongs are committed through negligence. Although some negligent wrongs are extremely harmful (as will be remarked later), none of them is properly classifiable as wicked. Carelessness is a vice, and it can lead to horrifically injurious consequences in some settings; but the gravity of the culpability of a careless action, even when calamitous results ensue therefrom, is not sufficient to render the action evil.

With regard to the factor of culpability, then, evil actions are distinguishable from other wrong actions. Certain blameworthy states of mind disjunctively underlie instances of evil conduct, and those states of mind do not ever include mere negligence. Two caveats should be entered straightaway. First, the evil-inducing mentalities occur in multitudinous concrete forms; wickedness is a variegated phenomenon. Secondly, although every evil action arises from heartlessness or extreme recklessness or sadistic malice, not every instance of conduct that derives from one of those frames of mind is evil. On the contrary, the status of any such instance of conduct as wicked

---

[3] I have benefited from the philosophical literature on evil—which is much more ample than the philosophical literature on defilement—notwithstanding my disagreements on a number of points with most of the contributions to the literature (and notwithstanding that my own reasons for enquiring into the nature of evil are quite different from those of other philosophers). Especially helpful for my purposes is Garrard 1998. Among the other writings that have been valuably illuminating in various ways are Baumeister 1997; Benn 1985; Card 2002; Card 2008; De Wijze 2002; De Wijze 2009; Gaita 1991; Garrard 2002; Kekes 1990; Kekes 2005; McGinn 1997, 61–91; Midgley 1984; Milo 1984; Morton 2004; Russell 2007; Steiner 2002. Throughout this chapter I use the adjectives 'evil' and 'wicked' interchangeably, and I likewise use interchangeably the nouns 'evil' and 'wickedness'.

[4] As Stanley Benn suggests, someone can be an evil person without having engaged in evil conduct: '[S]omeone who was fully conscious and rational but also completely paralyzed and aphasic, who spent his life hating everyone about him, rejoicing in their misfortune, wishing them ill, and reveling in malignant fantasies, would be a wicked person who did no wrong at all' (Benn 1985, 796). My focus here lies on evil conduct because the evil people with whom this chapter is ultimately concerned are those who have engaged in such conduct.

is dependent both on the substance of the underlying outlook and on the severity of the harm to which the conduct is connected. With these caveats in view, let us briefly consider each of the potentially evil-producing states of mind.

6.2.1.1. Sadistic malice

If someone is motivated by sadistic malice, he derives pleasure (usually involving thrilled excitement) from somebody else's suffering. Now, apart from people who strangely deny the existence of evil altogether, hardly anyone will contest the proposition that some evil misdeeds emanate from the sadistically malicious impulses of the perpetrators of those misdeeds. Indeed, because that proposition is so obviously correct, it can easily be taken too far. Quite tempting to some philosophers is the notion that every evil act is underlain by sadistic malice,[5] and similarly tempting is the notion that every act prompted by sadistic malice is evil. However, both of those notions should be resisted.

On the one hand, many paradigmatic instances of evil conduct are indeed products of sadistically malicious urges. In discussions of evil, references to the persecution of Jews and gypsies during the Nazi era are commonplace, and one reason for the frequency of such references is that the Nazi-era persecutors were so buoyantly gleeful in response to the anguish of their victims. Their derivation of pleasure from the agony that they were inflicting on the Jews who had fallen into their clutches is a particularly shuddersome aspect of their brutality. It is undoubtedly a major factor behind the unhesitatingness of numerous philosophers and other people in classifying that brutality as evil. On the other hand, however, we shall be construing the category of evil actions too narrowly if we confine it to actions that stem from sadistic malice. Contempt for the humanity and basic well-being of people can manifest itself in alternative ways that are sometimes equally vicious, as will be argued shortly in my remarks on the other evil-producing motivations. Those alternative motivations too can induce someone to view other human beings as his playthings of whom he may dispose as he pleases. Though the sadistic onslaughts against Jews during the Nazi era (or against Tutsis during the Rwandan genocide or against intellectuals during the reign of the Khmer Rouge in Cambodia) are rightly taken to be paradigms of evil misconduct, they do not exhaust the field.

Before we proceed to ponder whether every instance of sadistically malicious conduct is wicked, we should note another limitation that ought not to be imposed on any theory of evil. As is suggested by the examples in the preceding paragraph, evil actions that ensue from sadistic malice are often associated with racism or misogyny or religious bigotry or Communist zealotry or other odious ideologies. When the

---

[5] This notion is the central theme of Steiner 2002, which is criticized in De Wijze 2009 and retracted in Steiner 2009, 253–4. It also figures saliently in McGinn 1997, 61–91, though at one juncture McGinn acknowledges that evil is typically understood more broadly than his analysis implies (1997, 66–7).

mind of someone is warped by one of those poisonous ideologies, he will be inclined to dehumanize certain people and will thus be disposed to take pleasure in their misery (Glover 1999, 35–6 *et passim*). Nonetheless, although those noxious creeds have kindled innumerable acts of sadistic malice, we should not make the mistake of thinking that every such act has been impelled by somebody's adherence to one or more of those creeds. Sadistic impulses are sometimes not in need of such stimuli to any significant degree, yet the horrific acts produced by those impulses are still wicked. Thus, a theory of evil should recognize the possibility of the occurrence of sadistically malicious misdeeds that are linked only tenuously if at all to politically significant doctrines of hatred.

Is every instance of sadistically malicious conduct properly classifiable as evil? The answer to this question is clearly negative, for, although culpability is a key factor in the status of evil conduct as such, it is not the sole factor. In particular, if an instance of conduct is not connected to the genuine infliction of grievous harm,[6] it does not amount to an evil course of action. Suppose for example that Leonard attends a film (such as 'Psycho' or 'Dracula') that depicts purely fictional incidents of carnage, and suppose that he experiences a sense of thrilled delight and titillation when he witnesses the gruesome murders that are portrayed in the film. Such a mode of conduct is unsavoury, but it falls well short of being evil. Of course, the situation would be different if the film were a documentary—about the Holocaust, for example—and if the grisly murders represented in it were known by Leonard to be genuine. If he were to experience a *frisson* of elation and pleasure while watching such murders in the knowledge of their authenticity, his spectatorial conduct would be a low-level form of evil.

Even when a sadistically malicious mode of conduct is directly connected to the infliction of genuine harm, the harm itself—that is, the harm intended as well as the harm that actually results—may be too slight to warrant any attribution of wickedness. Numerous pranks carried out by teenagers and undergraduates are sadistically malicious, but the harms inflicted by most of them are too slight to support any allegations of evil. Mischievousness, unless taken to extremes, is not evil. In many contexts, indeed, it is no more than mildly wrong. Nor is *Schadenfreude* evil in most ordinary contexts. In most such contexts, the misadventures on which the sensation of *Schadenfreude* fastens are amusing rather than ghastly. When someone avers that that sensation in application to such misadventures is wicked, he is stretching the notion of wickedness beyond the breaking point.[7]

---

[6] The property of being connected to grievous harm, which I will invoke quite frequently in my remarks on the potentially evil modes of culpability, will be explicated in § 6.2.2 when I turn to consider the factor of harmfulness.

[7] I here disagree with McGinn 1997, 69. The inadequacy of the thought-provoking analysis which McGinn undertakes is revealed partly by the fact that he is committed to classifying the sensation of *Schadenfreude* as evil without discriminating among the different contexts in which that sensation can be experienced.

In short, although perhaps every action prompted by sadistic malice is at least mildly wrong, not every such action is evil. Sadistic malice is undoubtedly a dangerous frame of mind, and its more sinister manifestations are truly horrific. However, its tamer manifestations, focused on minor harms, cannot credibly be classified as wicked. Only an implausibly puritanical account of evil would lump together the sadistic pranks of undergraduates with the murderous exploits of Ian Brady or of the guards in Nazi concentration camps. (This chapter will return later to the factor of harmfulness in determining whether conduct is evil or not.)

6.2.1.2. Heartlessness

Whereas sadistic malice is a state of mind in which someone derives pleasure from the sheer fact of causing or witnessing other people's adversities, heartlessness is a frame of mind in which someone's lack of inhibitions about causing or witnessing other people's adversities is due to his regarding their woes as instrumentally gratifying (rather than as inherently gratifying). Heartlessness is the frame of mind that characterizes a steely contract killer or hit man who murders his targets with ruthless efficiency while not deriving any sadistic relish from their deaths. Like a depravedly sadistic murderer, an icy contract killer shows disdain for the humanity and basic well-being of his victims. He interacts with the victims as if the only relevant consideration in his treatment of them were the satisfaction of his own wishes and needs. However, he wields his god-like power of life and death over them not because he experiences sadistic glee in response to their discomfiture, but simply because their deaths are the means of advancing his own selfish ends. Their deaths do not elicit in him any sense of bloodthirsty elation, but they likewise do not cause him any consternation. In that respect, his attitude toward his extinguishing of human lives is similar to the feelings of an ordinary person about her own crushing of a plastic cup. Contemplating the deaths of his victims in abstraction from the consequences thereof, the contract killer feels neither exhilaration nor dismay but instead blank indifference (Morton 2004, 59–60).

Like a sadistic murderer, a cold-hearted contract killer wants to bring about the death of any person whom he has targeted. Were he to fail to bring about the death of such a person, and were he to know of the failure of his efforts, he would conclude that his principal objective in undertaking those efforts had not been realized. Similarly, a cold-hearted torturer seeks to induce excruciating pain in his victims. Were he to discover that one of those victims had not experienced anything more unpleasant than mild discomfort, he would conclude that his aim in subjecting that person to a certain type of treatment had not been accomplished. Even though the torturer might not harbour any sadistic impulses—that is, even though his demeanour might consist solely in stern unfeelingness rather than in sadistic zest—he resembles a sadist in that he endeavours deliberately to inflict agonizing pain on the people who are unfortunate enough to come under his control.

When a heartless frame of mind is connected to the infliction of severe harms such as murder and torture, the actions which it underlies are evil. Like sadistic malice, such a frame of mind—connected to the infliction of those gross harms—is incompatible with an elementary regard for other people as rational agents and as creatures whose basic interests include the avoidance of intense pain and the undergoing of positive experiences. Again like sadistic malice, heartlessness is often engendered by the influence of noxious ideologies and bigotries such as Nazism and racism and misogyny and anti-Semitism and Communism (Glover 1999; Morton 2004, 79–80, 112; Staub 1989). People whose minds are in thrall to such odious ways of thinking will be inclined to view certain other people as subhuman and will thus tend to feel no sense of fellowship or sympathy toward them. Still, just as myriad acts of sadistic malice do not originate from people's adherence to bigoted ideologies, so too many acts of heartlessness do not originate from such a source. An indurate personality can result from self-absorption as readily as from immersion in hate-mongering creeds. Most contract killers carry out their murders on the basis of relentless greed and self-devotion rather than on the basis of politically pregnant prejudices.

Indeed, an arresting account of the role of self-absorption in the perpetration of heartless iniquities is to be found in Hannah Arendt's book on the trial of Adolf Eichmann. When discussing the *Einsatzgruppen* (the mobile mass-murder units that operated under the direction of the German SS, principally in Eastern Europe), Arendt wrote in part as follows:

[T]he murderers were not sadists or killers by nature; on the contrary, a systematic effort was made to weed out all those who derived physical pleasure from what they did...Hence the problem was how to overcome not so much their conscience as the animal pity by which all normal men are affected in the presence of physical suffering. The trick used by Himmler—who apparently was rather strongly afflicted with these instinctive reactions himself—was very simple and probably very effective; it consisted in turning these instincts around, as it were, in directing them toward the self. So that instead of saying: What horrible things I did to people!, the murderers would be able to say: What horrible things I had to watch in the pursuance of my duties, how heavily the task weighed upon my shoulders![8]

Arendt's book in its broader themes can alert us to another important point about heartlessness in the commission of evil misdeeds. When heinous activities are performed under the auspices of a large organization such as a nation-state, numerous people are involved at varying levels of proximity and in varying capacities. Whether or not the knowingly involved people within the lowest ranks of an organization's bureaucracy are behaving evilly, the people (such as Eichmann) who manage large-scale atrocities from the upper ranks are thereby perpetrating great evils. Among such people in their official capacities, heartlessness is a common frame of mind. Because they are not usually present at the bloodletting for which they issue general or specific orders, they can distance themselves mentally from the graphic horrors of what they are commanding. Moreover, by concentrating their attention on their own advancement within their organization (as Eichmann did), and perhaps also by cleaving to

---

[8] Arendt 1963, 105–6. A portion of this passage is quoted (for a slightly different though related purpose) in Morton 2004, 80, 113–14.

a noisome ideology that circulates throughout the organization, the upper-level administrators can steel themselves against any misgivings that might otherwise have beset them. Heartlessness among such people is fostered by the formality and antiseptic remoteness of the bureaucratic setting in which they work, and by the competitive in-fighting that prevails there.

6.2.1.2.1. *Heartlessness without evil*

As was argued earlier, not every instance of sadistically malicious conduct is evil. Likewise, not every instance of heartless conduct is evil. Indeed, the range of heartless but non-evil actions is broader than the range of sadistically malicious but non-evil actions. Consider an example that was broached earlier. If someone watches a film or television programme about the Holocaust or the Rwandan genocide, and if she derives sadistic pleasure from the atrocities that are depicted in it, then *pro tanto* her frame of mind is evil. By contrast, if someone watches such a film or programme and reacts with stony detachment when witnessing the atrocities, then his frame of mind is clearly wrong but is not quite gravely culpable enough to be evil. Although he plainly should have been moved and appalled, his unconcern is morally obtuse rather than evil.

When the harm to which a heartless attitude pertains is minor, the conduct underlain by that attitude is not evil. Suppose for example that Fred is walking briskly toward the terminal in an airport where he needs to obtain his boarding pass for his flight. He is not in any danger of being late for his flight, but he is impatient to reach the terminal and the ticket counter. As Fred is striding along, an elderly man in front of him is struggling with some luggage. The man politely and diffidently asks Fred for a bit of assistance. Were Fred to stop in order to help the man, he would be delayed for a couple of minutes but would still have ample time to get to the terminal. Nevertheless, he brushes past the man without a word of consolation or apology, and he continues his steady progress toward the terminal. Though he derives no pleasure from the man's distress, he feels entirely unmoved by it. In the circumstances, his own convenience is the sole thing with which he is disposed to concern himself. Now, in this situation, Fred's heartless conduct is undoubtedly wrong but is not evil. Because the harm inflicted by his behaviour is far from grievous, the behaviour itself is boorish and vexingly self-centered rather than wicked.

A plethora of further examples could be adduced to establish the same point: not every instance of callous and harmful conduct is evil. Although heartlessness tied closely to the perpetration of iniquities such as torture and murder and rape is indeed evil, heartlessness connected to much less egregious harms is always at least mildly wrong but is not evil. To be sure, such a frame of mind is inconsistent with a proper level of solicitude for the well-being of other people (and of other animals, if such creatures are involved). Moreover, if the paucity of solicitude derives from some hateful prejudice, it is an evil mentality. However, when there is no connection to the infliction of major detriments, that evil mentality has not impelled any conduct that is itself so vicious as to be evil. Discourteous rebuffs animated by unconcern are not on a par ethically with murder or torture or rape that is animated by unconcern.

6.2.1.2.2. Heartlessness with some qualms

This discussion may have conveyed the impression that the culpable attitude of heart-lessness is an all-or-nothing property. In fact, however, no such impression has been intended. If a generally icy attitude of impassivity is mixed with a few small twinges of regret or sympathy, it is still a potentially evil frame of mind (Garrard 1998, 58). On the spectrum between a warmly solicitous demeanour and a thoroughgoing lack of benevolence, there reside a number of possible outlooks that are sufficiently close to the latter end of the spectrum to be properly classifiable as heartless. Such outlooks, if connected to terribly injurious attacks against other people, are evil notwithstanding that they contain small traces of misgivings.

Consider, for example, Lady Macbeth. With chillingly ruthless importunity, she urges her husband to commit regicide against their supposedly honoured guest Duncan. She unflinchingly overcomes Macbeth's reservations, with her insults and impassioned exhortations. Having implored the forces of darkness to '[m]ake thick my blood, [s]top up th' access and passage to remorse, [t]hat no compunctious visitings of nature [s]hake my fell purpose,' she famously announces to her husband the implacably fierce reso-luteness of her evil ambition: 'I have given suck, and know [h]ow tender 'tis to love the babe that milks me; I would, while it was smiling in my face, [h]ave pluck'd my nipple from his boneless gums, [a]nd dash'd the brains out, had I so sworn as you [h]ave done to [the murder of Duncan]' (*Macbeth*, I.v.43–46; I.vii.54–59). Ferocious though these utter-ances are, Lady Macbeth later fleetingly reveals that she has not been entirely success-ful in ridding herself of compunctions. While waiting for Macbeth to return from his slaying of Duncan, she fears that he may have botched the endeavour, and she wishes that she had performed the task on her own. She feels a need to justify to herself her deci-sion to entrust her husband with the enterprise of regicide: 'Had [Duncan] not resembled [m]y father as he slept, I had done't' (*Macbeth*, II.ii.12–13). Having acknowledged this vestige of sympathy that remains in her soul, she straightaway resumes her stance of murderously unremitting ambition. When Macbeth comes back from his assassination of Duncan, he looks down at his bloody hands and exclaims: 'This is a sorry sight.' Lady Macbeth retorts with heartless vehemence: 'A foolish thought, to say a sorry sight' (*Macbeth*, II.ii.18–19).

Lady Macbeth's conduct in goading her husband to murder their royal guest is evil irrespective of the fact that her generally unwavering sternness is tinged by a few small streaks of humaneness. Her demeanour is heartless despite those passing scruples, and its connection to a horrific crime renders it deeply wicked. In the case of Lady Macbeth, as in numerous other cases, ruthless callousness that falls somewhat short of completely unalloyed callousness is potently productive of wicked deeds.

These reflections can shed light on a matter that has received attention from some of the other philosophers who have addressed the topic of evil: namely, the question whether the distinction between evil conduct and merely wrong conduct is qualitative or quantitative

(De Wijze 2002; Garrard 1998; Garrard 2002; Russell 2007; Steiner 2002). That point of controversy, to which we shall return later in this chapter, now appears to be rather misleading. Though the question is normally taken to be posing mutually exclusive alternatives, the only tenable position on the matter is that the distinction between evil actions and merely wrong actions is both qualitative and quantitative. The correctness of such a position is evident from my whole discussion of the potentially evil modes of culpability.

On the one hand, the category of evil actions is qualitatively distinct from the category of merely wrong actions, because the modes of culpability that underlie the respective actions are divergent. Every instance of evil conduct is underlain by sadistic malice or heartlessness or extreme recklessness, whereas not every instance of merely wrong conduct is underlain by one of those modes of culpability. As has already been remarked, some wrongs are non-culpable, and many culpable wrongs are simply negligent. Of course, the category of mere wrongs does also include some instances of conduct that are sadistically malicious or heartless or recklessly indifferent. However, because that category further comprises all instances of conduct that are negligent and some instances of conduct that are non-culpable, it is qualitatively distinct from the category of evil conduct.

On the other hand, as should now be evident, the modes of culpability that disjunctively underlie evil actions are themselves vague properties (in the technical philosophical sense of being embeddable in sorites paradoxes).[9] That is, each of them is differentiated from a more benign type of outlook through a series of fine gradations, none of which is a talismanic point of transition between the benign type and the potentially evil type. For the present discussion, the relevant spectrum lies between the property of benevolence and the property of heartlessness. Though the contrast between those two properties is starkly qualitative, it is also quantitative; each property shades into the other through an indeterminate region of borderline cases. There is no magical point of transformation at which the trait of benevolence has abruptly flipped into being the trait of heartlessness, or vice versa. One brief twinge of sympathy or regret does not convert an attitude of overall heartlessness into an attitude of solicitude, nor do two brief twinges produce such an effect; and so on. Yet, although there is no precise tipping point, a spectrum of minute quantitative gradations does lie between benevolence and heartlessness. Hence, the stark qualitative contrast between them is also a quantitative contrast (like the contrast between day and night, which shade into each other through the indeterminate regions of dawn and dusk). Qualitative differences between vague properties are constituted by quantitative spectra. Thus, with regard to the factor of culpability, the distinctiveness of evil conduct vis-à-vis merely wrong conduct is neither solely qualitative nor solely quantitative but both qualitative and quantitative. As will be seen later, a similar conclusion is warranted with regard to the factor of harmfulness.

---

[9] I discuss vagueness at some length—with citations to the relevant philosophical literature—in Kramer 2007, 36–7, 70; and 2009a, 109–13, 260–1. I have also dealt with it in § 3.4.2.1 of Chapter 3 above.

6.2.1.2.3. Heartlessness with seemingly good intentions

Some instances of evil conduct that emanate from heartlessness (perhaps with mild misgivings) are motivated by considerations that might at first glance seem to be morally worthy. Suppose for example that the leaders of a repressive autocracy deem their crowded country to be overpopulated.[10] They therefore resolve to perpetrate genocide in a certain region of the country in order to free up space for the hordes of citizens who live in other regions. Now, although the objective of relieving the pressures of overpopulation might be morally worthy in the abstract, this concrete way of pursuing such an objective is iniquitous. Even if the leaders who order the genocide and the officials who implement it do feel some reservations about their butcherous course of action, they are heartless in that they go ahead with that course of action despite the overwhelming moral reasons against it. Like Pharaoh in the Book of Exodus, they proceed with hearts hardened against the compelling considerations that militate unequivocally in favour of their desisting.

Eve Garrard (1998, 49–58) has adroitly delineated the nature of the evil in this sort of situation. She maintains that the perpetrator of an evil act 'silences [in his own mind] the reasons against doing the act, which reasons are themselves metaphysical silencers, and where the agent's reasons for doing the act are members of the class of considerations which are in this case metaphysically silenced' (Garrard 1998, 55). When Garrard refers to metaphysical silencing, she means that certain 'considerations...ceas[e] to be [moral] reasons in the presence of certain kinds of contrary requirements' (Garrard 1998, 52). In other words, a factor that typically is endowed with some positive moral weight will be devoid of any such weight—and will therefore not be a veritable moral reason at all—in any context where it is constitutively connected to the perpetration of some atrocity. In such a context, the metaphysically silenced factor is not to be balanced as a favourable element against the appalling features of the atrocity in some peculiar cost/benefit analysis. Given that a metaphysically silenced factor is deprived of all moral force, it should count for nothing in any such analysis.

In the scenario of the repressive autocracy, the iniquitous aspect of the autocracy's policy for dealing with the perceived problem of overpopulation is constitutive of the policy's beneficial aspect. That perceived problem has been addressed only because there are fewer people at the end of the implementation of the policy, and there are fewer people at that juncture only because a myriad of other people have been butchered. Neither of the two instances of 'because' in the preceding sentence denotes an instrumental-causal relationship. Rather, each of them denotes a constitutive relationship. The fact that the problem has been addressed is constituted by the fact that the people have been butchered. Let us designate the former fact as 'F2' and the latter as 'F1.' In that event, F1 amounts to F2. That is, in combination with all the prevailing circumstances other than any causal laws, F1 logically entails F2.[11] Because

---

[10] In Kramer 2004, 241–3, I discuss some similar examples for a different purpose.

[11] I have expounded this understanding of constitutive relationships in Kramer 2003, 280.

those two facts are inseparable in this fashion, the seemingly salutary effects and the iniquitous effects of the autocracy's population-control policy cannot correctly be balanced against each other as if some good results and some horrific results have simply occurred in tandem. Instead, the seemingly good results have occurred only because they are constituted by the occurrence of the horrific results (in the sense just indicated). Consequently, there is no room for the purportedly benign aspect of the policy to possess an independent moral status—a favourable moral status—by reference to which we can weigh that aspect against the policy's horrendous features. As Garrard suggests, that putatively benign aspect has been deprived of all reason-giving force by its unity with the horrendous features. It has been metaphysically silenced.

Hence, if the leaders of the repressive autocracy pursue their programme of space-clearing genocide, they are acting on the basis of an objective that has been metaphysically silenced by its inseparability from the overwhelming considerations against the pursuit of such a programme. Heartlessly undissuaded by those considerations, the autocrats seek an ostensibly worthy objective that in fact is devoid of any positive moral weight. Their policy of genocide is deeply evil, as they inflict grievous harm for the sake of that thoroughly vitiated objective.

6.2.1.2.4. *Heartlessness, moral conflicts, and mitigation*

In the foregoing scenario of genocide, the vile aspects of the autocracy's policy are constitutively inseparable from the ostensibly laudable aspects. In each of many other actual or possible contexts, however, the negative features and the positive features of some course of action are not similarly inseparable. Those features might be instrumentally linked, for example. When the morally contrasting elements of a course of action are indeed co-occurrent rather than constitutively inseparable, the situation comprising them can amount to a moral conflict. That is, the person engaging in the course of action might be faced with a choice between a moral obligation to φ and a moral obligation not to φ.[12] If so, then the person is unable to avoid committing a wrong. If he recognizes his predicament and is not himself to blame for having come to be in it, then the gravity of his breach of either moral duty is mitigated by the fact that that breach has been necessary in order to avoid a violation of the other duty. In such circumstances, his chosen course of action may well not be wicked even if it would have been wicked had he undertaken it in the absence of any moral conflict.

Consider, for example, the decision by President Harry Truman of the United States to drop atomic bombs on the Japanese cities of Hiroshima and Nagasaki. (Although I believe that my account of the circumstances of his decision is historically

---

[12] I have discussed moral conflicts in a number of my past writings. See, for example, Kramer 2004, ch 8; 2005; 2009a, 117–26; 2009b. Though I will here be emphasizing the extenuative force of moral conflicts, I agree with a partly countervailing point of moral psychology that has been emphasized by Adam Morton: 'There is a general connection between moral dilemmas and evil in that moral dilemmas arise when the normal filters [against behaving wrongly] exclude all one's actions, so that to act at all one has to suspend the filters, thus opening the possibility of doing something evil' (Morton 2004, 144).

accurate, nothing here hinges on its accuracy. Anyone who disagrees with me about the historical facts can take the scenario in this paragraph as a sheer thought-experiment.) In light of the truculent determination of the Japanese War Cabinet to continue fighting, President Truman was confronted with a choice between undertaking an invasion of the Japanese mainland and dropping the atomic bombs. No mere demonstration of the power of the new weapon through the dropping of an atomic bomb on an uninhabited island in the presence of Japanese witnesses would have sufficed to obviate an invasion of the mainland. That is, no such demonstration would have induced the War Cabinet to desist from full-scale hostilities. Had an invasion of the Japanese mainland taken place, several million people—Allied soldiers, Japanese soldiers, and Japanese civilians—would have perished. Thus, given the circumstances, and given that a surrender by the Allies to the Japanese would have been morally the worst of all the feasible outcomes, Truman had to decide between two repellent options: (1) killing as many as 200,000 Japanese civilians by dropping the atomic bombs on Hiroshima and Nagasaki, and (2) launching an invasion of Japan that would have resulted in the deaths of vastly more Japanese civilians and Allied soldiers and Japanese soldiers. With the circumstances as they were, and with the responsibilities of his office incumbent upon him, Truman was under a moral duty to drop the bombs and under a moral duty not to drop them. He could not avoid committing a serious wrong.

Although the decision to drop the atomic bombs was in violation of a moral duty and was therefore wrong, it was not evil. Indeed, because it was reached and implemented in order to fulfil an even more pressing moral duty, it was morally the best thing to do in the dire situation. While Truman's breach of his moral duty-not-to-drop-the-bombs gave rise to countless remedial obligations, the gravity of his wrong was heavily mitigated by the role of his decision in averting an even worse moral catastrophe. The concept of evil is not applicable to his breach.

Yet, had Truman deliberately ordered the slaying of tens of thousands of people in circumstances where he was not fulfilling any major moral obligation by so doing, his conduct would have been profoundly evil. After all, his conduct—though doubtless undertaken with compunctions—was heartless in that he steeled himself to set in train the intentional annihilation of many tens of thousands of civilians. Given that the heartless frame of mind was connected to the production of severe harm on a massive scale, the conduct underlain by the heartlessness would have been a paradigmatic instance of wickedness in the absence of any mitigating factors. By contrast, in the presence of the mitigating factors that bore on Truman's decision, his conduct was not wicked at all (even though it involved the commission of serious moral wrongs).

Hence, the example of Truman's momentous course of action serves to underscore the importance of extenuative considerations within any account of evil. In the presence of such considerations that are of sufficient moral weight, wrongs that would otherwise have been evil are lessened in their gravity to the status of mere wrongs (albeit serious wrongs). In the presence of extenuative factors that are of sufficient moral weight, a wrong does not partake of the contemptuous attitude—a contemptuous attitude toward some other human being(s) as properly subject to destruction or severe harm for one's own nefarious purposes—that lies at the heart of evil.

To discern as much is in effect to discern another reason for maintaining that the distinction between evil conduct and merely wrong conduct is quantitative as well as qualitative. Although the assignment of cardinal values to mitigating factors is not usually feasible, the extenuative force of such factors can lend itself to ordinal rankings (no doubt with some gaps). That force is a scalar property, which exists by degrees. Indeed, in the scenario of Truman and the atomic bombs, the extenuative force is largely a function of the numbers of deaths and severe injuries to be averted. Thus, given that the mitigatingness of exigent circumstances varies quantitatively, and given that such mitigatingness can sometimes make the difference between the wickedness and the mere wrongness of a given pattern of behaviour, that difference is not exclusively qualitative. It is a qualitative divide that emerges from quantitative gradations.

6.2.1.3. Extreme recklessness

Sadistic malice and heartlessness are not the only states of mind that can impel evil conduct. In addition, some acts underlain by attitudes of extreme recklessness toward the lives and basic well-being of other people are evil. Suppose, for example, that Wilbur—a sane man of ordinary intelligence—fires a submachine gun repeatedly at a large crowd of people who are standing at quite a short distance from him. He does so not because he wants to murder or injure anyone, but simply because he wants to see whether he can shoot multiple rounds of bullets directly at a large crowd without hitting anyone. (Perhaps he is a guard in a concentration camp who wishes to relieve himself of boredom.) Were he somehow miraculously to avoid hitting anyone, he would not feel that he had failed in his objective. On the contrary, his objective is to fire multiple rounds of bullets at the crowd without killing or injuring anyone. When his shots in fact slay and wound many people and terrify many more, he does not derive any sadistic gratification from the carnage and panic. He might even be mildly dismayed by what has happened, with the thought that his carefree frolic has gone awry. Moreover, although he might instead feel indifference without any pangs of dismay, he has not deliberately set out to inflict severe harm on other people; thus, whether or not he experiences any chagrin after his fatal volley of shots, his outlook diverges significantly from that of a contract killer or that of a heartlessly homicidal member of the *Einsatzgruppen*. Hence, if we are to recognize that the massacre by Wilbur is evil—as we emphatically should—we shall likewise have to recognize that not every evil action is impelled by either sadistic malice or heartless deliberateness. Some evil actions are underlain instead by recklessness of the sort that is exhibited to an extraordinary degree by Wilbur.

Wilbur's reckless fusillade is evil because it causes severe harm and because the frame of mind that leads to it is utterly at odds with a proper level of respect and concern for other people. Although Wilbur has not acted with the aim of murdering or injuring anyone, he has treated other individuals as his playthings by shooting squarely and deliberately in the direction of a large crowd with a submachine gun. His treating other people in that manner is not done for sadistic pleasure, but the selfish insouciance with which he imperils them for no good reason is due to his attaching far greater importance to his own whims and antics than to their lives and basic well-being. Though his exertion of a god-like power of life and death over the people in the crowd is not undertaken with murderous intentions, his blithe wielding of that power ensues from his unconscionable prioritization of himself over others. Because that prioritization is directly connected to the perpetration of mass slaughter, it is an evil outlook that has prompted an evil course of conduct.

6.2.1.3.1. *More realistic examples*

As presented here, the scenario of Wilbur and the crowd of people may seem somewhat fanciful. Would a sane adult of ordinary intelligence really engage in a massacre so frivolously? The scenario is indeed pretty far-fetched—unless, as has already been suggested, Wilbur is a guard in a concentration camp who has arrogantly opted for a horrific diversion from his tedium—but the peculiarity of the example helps to make more vivid its general point, and that general point is applicable to situations that are much more credible.

Consider, for instance, a member of a criminal gang (Mario) who sprays bullets from a submachine gun at a member of a rival gang (Jeff) while the latter is standing amidst a crowd of people who have no connections with any criminality. Frenzied firing from a submachine gun will almost certainly slay some of the people in Jeff's vicinity, even though they are not the targets of the firing. Mario knows perfectly well that such an outcome will almost inevitably result from his indiscriminate hail of bullets, but he goes ahead with his rampage all the same. If he miraculously misses every bystander and hits only Jeff, he will scarcely conclude that he has failed in his mission. Rather, he will conclude that he has succeeded brilliantly. If (as is far more likely) he instead kills several of the bystanders along with Jeff, he will feel pleased about Jeff's death and will feel wholly impassive or slightly regretful about the deaths of the bystanders. He will still conclude that his mission has succeeded, for the demise of Jeff is his sole objective. In comparison, the deaths of the bystanders are a minor concern at most; Mario has not sought those deaths, but he cares little if at all about his not having managed to avoid them.

Mario's slaughter of the innocent bystanders is an evil act impelled by extreme recklessness. Though that slaughter (in contrast with the slaying of Jeff) has not been one of his goals, it is something which he has been knowingly unconcerned to avoid in the process of ensuring that his goal—the demise of Jeff—is attained.[13] Moreover,

---

[13]   Though Michael Moore does not address this example, his remarks on another example—involving someone who shoots down an airplane in order to collect on an insurance policy that covers only

unlike Wilbur's escapade, Mario's massacre is far from fanciful. It in fact closely resembles many a gangland shooting in which a volley of shots is fired sweepingly in order to ensure that some targeted person is felled. When other people too are slain by the volley, their deaths are the products of a recklessly evil action. (The death of the targeted person is the product of a heartlessly evil action.)

Racing on the roads in automobiles is another activity in which the occurrence of evil conduct underlain by extreme recklessness is quite common. When young men drive their cars at high speed with wanton hazardousness (by positioning themselves in the wrong lane or by lurching from lane to lane) in order to assert their virility vis-à-vis other drivers, and when as a consequence they collide catastrophically with oncoming cars, the fatalities which they cause are products of recklessly evil actions. The young men have not sought to collide with those oncoming cars; the chief point of their menacingly perilous exploits is to force other vehicles to give way in desperation. When the other vehicles do give way and when collisions are thus averted, the reckless daredevils hardly feel that their objectives have been thwarted. Quite the contrary. Thus, on the occasions when collisions do occur, they are attributable to extreme recklessness rather than to their having been heartlessly intended. Extreme recklessness of this sort is an evil frame of mind that generates evil conduct. Toying in extraordinarily dangerous ways with the lives and basic well-being of other people for one's own excitement—though admittedly without taking the *destruction* of their lives and basic well-being as one's aim—is a quintessentially evil enterprise.

6.2.1.3.2. *Recklessness without evil*

As should be evident, not all actions marked by extreme recklessness are evil. For one thing, some reckless conduct does not impinge significantly on the well-being of anybody apart from the person who is undertaking the conduct. If somebody without a family or other dependents is climbing a steep mountain by himself in a knowingly foolhardy though exciting fashion, then his deliberate placing of himself in severe danger is extremely reckless but is not evil. Although he commits a wrong against himself by treating his life and basic well-being with so little concern, the wrong which he commits is not evil. (If he were married, then he would certainly be wronging his family quite seriously by climbing a mountain so rashly. Even in such circumstances, however, his grossly irresponsible subjection of himself to mortal danger would fall short of being evil.)

Furthermore, many instances of extremely reckless conduct that do impinge directly on other people's interests are nevertheless not evil. If the risks engendered by such conduct pertain to minor harms, then the conduct is wrong without being evil. For example, suppose that Alan is cooking a meal for several other people, and

---

the plane and not the passengers—make clear that he would classify Mario's slaying of the bystanders as heartlessly intentional. See Moore 2007, 53. Nonetheless, given how I have expounded the notions of heartlessness and recklessness, actions that produce confidently foreseen but undesired harms are to be classified here (with regard to those harms) as reckless rather than as heartless.

that he inadvertently drops a substance into the pot of soup which he has prepared. He realizes what he has done, and he knows that the substance very often induces mild gastrointestinal maladies in people who consume it. Nevertheless, because he does not wish to serve a meal without soup, and because he likewise does not wish to go to the trouble of preparing a batch of soup afresh, he decides to leave things as they are. He does not tell any of his guests what has happened, as he presents a big bowl of soup to each of them. Now, whether or not each of the diners does indeed become ill, Alan has plainly committed a wrong against each of them by acting in such a reckless fashion. However, equally plainly, the wrong does not amount to an instance of evil. Because the harm to which his extreme recklessness has subjected his guests is minor, the wrong which he has committed against them is too slight to be classified together with iniquities such as Mario's slaughter of innocent bystanders (in § 6.2.1.3.1).

Countless other examples could be marshalled to illustrate this same point. Extreme recklessness is a wrongful state of mind which, insofar as other people are likely to be affected by it, is inconsistent with any proper level of respect and concern for them. Alan's recklessness, like Mario's, is just such a wrongful state of mind. However, because the hazard associated with Alan's recklessness is far from terrible, his conduct is wrongful without being evil. Much the same goes for many other instances of extremely reckless conduct.

6.2.1.3.3 *The qualitative/quantitative distinction again*

Like the properties of heartlessness and sadistic malice, the property of recklessness is embeddable in sorites paradoxes. Qualitative contrasts between recklessness and various other properties are constituted by quantitative divergences comprising myriads of fine gradations. Particularly worthy of attention here is the qualitative difference between recklessness and negligence.

On the one hand, the difference between recklessness and negligence is indeed qualitative. Both negligent conduct and reckless conduct give rise to risks, but the risks engendered by the former are inadvertent whereas the risks engendered by the latter are knowingly hazarded.[14] Largely for that reason, extreme recklessness is a mode of culpability that can underlie evil actions, whereas no merely negligent conduct—however harmful its consequences—is rightly classifiable as evil. (Adam Morton offers what might seem to be a counterexample to my claim here about negligent conduct. He characterizes the following instance of evil behaviour as 'an act of callous negligence': 'A driver is returning home when a vagrant falls drunk off a bridge and strikes the windscreen of her car. Instead of stopping, she drives home with the man still embedded in the windscreen, goes indoors to satisfy her drug habit, and does not return for several hours, by which time he has bled to

---

[14] A closely related point is that the risks engendered by reckless conduct are typically more acute than those engendered by negligent conduct. However, that difference is quantitative (or predominantly quantitative) rather than qualitative, and it obtains typically rather than always. Thus, for my present purposes, the difference stated in the text is more important.

death' [Morton 2004, 118]. Morton's characterization of the driver's behaviour as an instance of negligence is unsustainable. Unless the driver is woefully retarded in her mental functioning to the point of not being fully responsible as an adult, her failure to seek or provide assistance in a timely fashion is reckless rather than negligent. Through her omission, she has knowingly hazarded an acute risk that her behaviour will lead to the death of someone else in her proximity. Her conduct is evil because of the connection between her callous recklessness and that death.)

On the other hand, the qualitative contrast between recklessness and negligence is structured quantitatively by a spectrum of outlooks among which the minute differences run from fully confident awareness to completely inattentive unawareness. Along that spectrum is a vaguely demarcated region in which the sundry borderline outlooks are neither determinately reckless nor determinately negligent. Yet, although that region and the outlooks within it partake of indeterminacy, the outlooks beyond it toward each end of the scale are determinate in character; each of those latter outlooks is determinately a specimen of recklessness or determinately a specimen of negligence. The qualitative difference between recklessness and negligence is sustained by the actuality or possibility of those determinate specimens. Hence, to the question whether the negligence/recklessness dichotomy is qualitative or quantitative, the only tenable answer is that it is both qualitative and quantitative.

Consequently, given that the distinction between recklessness and negligence is in part a distinction between a state of mind that can impel evil actions and a state of mind that never per se underlies evil actions, the conclusion just reached is in effect a conclusion about the nature of evil. Once again, that is, we find that the debates over the qualitative or quantitative character of the division between evil conduct and merely wrong conduct are somewhat misconceived. Whenever a person's conduct is evil, it is underlain by one or another of the three modes of culpability that have been explored in this chapter (sadistic malice, heartlessness, extreme recklessness). Because each of those modes of culpability is a vague property that diverges quantitatively as well as qualitatively from a vague property that is relevantly opposed to it, the divide between evil actions and merely wrong actions is itself quantitative as well as qualitative. Someone who characterizes that divide as only qualitative or only quantitative is not adequately coming to grips with the ways in which vague properties are differentiated.

6.2.2. The factor of harmfulness

As has just been remarked anew, every instance of evil conduct is impelled by one of the three culpable states of mind mentioned above. In that respect, evil conduct differs qualitatively from merely wrongful conduct, for only some instances of the latter are impelled by those states of mind. However, evil conduct also differs from merely wrongful conduct in that all instances of the former involve very serious harm whereas only some instances of the latter involve such harm. Though not every wicked misdeed actually results in the infliction of grave detriments, every wicked misdeed is connected to such detriments in some repugnant manner. Let us begin this discussion of the factor of harmfulness, then, by considering the sorts of connections between culpability and harm that can warrant the classification of various instances of conduct as evil.

6.2.2.1. Connections between culpability and harm

Any paradigmatic instance of evil conduct involves some major detriment as the desired or knowingly hazarded consequence of the conduct. For example, when a sadistic criminal murders or mutilates or tortures other people for the gratification of his own perverse impulses, the appalling harms which he inflicts upon them are the intended and enjoyed effects of his endeavours. His victims would not have undergone those harms if he had not undertaken his gleeful endeavours. Similarly, when a steely contract killer unflinchingly liquidates the people who are his targets, or when a tyrant heartlessly decimates his opponents, the deaths and devastation are the desired consequences of his actions. His hapless victims would not have died if he had not carried out his merciless bloodletting. Evil conduct impelled by extreme recklessness is somewhat different, in that the detrimental effects of the conduct are not desired. Those effects are not what an extremely reckless person has been aiming to bring about. However, he has knowingly and gratuitously run a risk (typically a very high risk) that those effects will materialize, and they would not have materialized if he had not engaged in his irresponsible behaviour. Thus, although the deaths or other serious adversities that flow from his behaviour are not desired, they have been knowingly hazarded, and their occurrence is directly due to the behaviour whereby they have been hazarded.

In any paradigmatic instance of evil conduct, then, severely injurious consequences that actually ensue are desired or knowingly risked, and the conduct itself is a direct and necessary condition for the occurrence of those consequences. We should now examine some evil courses of conduct that deviate in certain limited respects from the paradigms. Of course, as has been stated, any instance of evil conduct is underlain by sadistic malice or heartlessness or extreme recklessness. However, the connection between the underlying culpability and the infliction of serious harm can be less straightforward than in the paradigmatic cases of evil.

6.2.2.1.1. Failed attempts and unmaterialized risks

If a person driven by sadistic malice or by heartlessness has been unsuccessful in his attempt to harm some innocent human being(s) grievously, his attempt is evil in spite of its fruitlessness (Card 2002, 22). For example, suppose that Felix plans to kidnap Alice in order to subject her to rape and torture and murder for his sadistic pleasure, and suppose that his effort to abduct her is thwarted by a bystander or policeman. Even though his endeavours have come to nothing and have not injured Alice (who, we can assume, never becomes aware of his evil designs), Felix—in his external behaviour as well as in his thoughts and desires—has regarded her as his plaything who can be made to undergo agony for his amusement. His sadistically malicious outlook is connected to the lethal abuse of her as the desired outcome of his actions. Because of that connection between his depraved frame of mind and the infliction of terrible harm upon Alice, his conduct is evil.

Similarly, if a ruthless terrorist shoots a missile at an ascending airplane in an attempt to murder everyone aboard, his action is iniquitous even if he misses his target. In his behaviour as well as in his mind, he has regarded the lives of the passengers and the crew as things of which he can dispose in order to further his grim cause. Notwithstanding that he has failed to kill or injure anyone, the deaths of all the passengers and crew members are connected to his heartless state of mind as the desired outcomes of his exploit. Because of that connection between his pitiless outlook and mass slaughter, his conduct is evil despite its bootlessness.

Just as a failed attempt to commit mayhem is typically evil, so too is an instance of extremely reckless conduct that does not actually result in the horrific consequences that have been knowingly hazarded. Let us think back to my account of Mario's slaying of Jeff, a member of a rival gang. Suppose that, although Mario sprays a host of bullets from a submachine gun in the direction of Jeff who is standing nearby amidst many other people, he miraculously misses everyone (or everyone other than Jeff). Given that Mario has not been endeavouring to kill the bystanders, their survival does not constitute a failed attempt on his part. Instead, it amounts to the non-materialization of an overwhelmingly high risk which he has knowingly run. Ethically, however, the non-materialization of the risk is on a par with the failure of an attempt. That is, the conduct of Mario—in relation to the bystanders, and also in relation to Jeff—is deeply evil in spite of his somehow not having brought about all the horrific consequences that were almost certain to follow from his frenzied firing of bullets. Because his extreme recklessness is connected to the bystanders' deaths and wounds as highly likely and knowingly hazarded effects of his shooting, his actions in application to the bystanders are wicked even though no deaths or wounds have ultimately ensued.

In sum, a failed attempt to bring about some result is evil if a successful attempt to bring about that result would be evil, and reckless conduct involving unmaterialized risks is evil if the same conduct with materialized risks would be evil. However, a caveat should be entered here. Nothing in the last few paragraphs is meant to suggest that the failure of an attempt or the non-materialization of a risk does not make any ethical difference. Though the topic of moral luck is a large matter that lies mostly beyond the ambit of the present book,[15] this chapter will later submit that the failure of an attempt or the non-materialization of a risk can make the difference between evil conduct and extravagantly evil conduct. That is, the failure of an attempt or the non-materialization of a risk can make the difference between a crime for which a

---

[15] The seminal works on the topic are, of course, Nagel 1979 and Williams 1981. For a very helpful overview of the issues, see Nelkin 2008. For an important collection of essays on the topic (including the classic pieces by Nagel and Williams), see Statman 1993.

long term of imprisonment is appropriate and a crime for which the imposition of the death penalty is appropriate. Thus, although the failure of an attempt or the non-materialization of a risk does not bear on the question whether the attempt or the incurring of the risk should be classified as evil, it does bear on the matter of defilement that is central to the purgative rationale for capital punishment.

6.2.2.1.2. Overdetermined harm

As has been stated, a paradigmatic instance of wickedness involves conduct by someone that is itself a necessary condition for the infliction of grievous harm on somebody else. However, there are many actual or possible instances of wicked conduct that bring about grievous harms which would have been brought about—or which are brought about—by independent causes. Suppose for example that two contract killers are hired by a businessman to murder the chairman of a rival company. As the chairman emerges from his home with his family, he and they are sprayed with bullets by each of the hired thugs. Now, suppose that the shots from either of those thugs would have been sufficient to murder everybody at whom the shots are fired. Thus, even if only one or the other contract killer had been on the scene, the deaths of the chairman and his family would have occurred exactly when (or almost exactly when) they do occur. Hence, neither killer has engaged in actions that were a necessary condition for the slaughter of the chairman and his family; had either killer been absent, or had his gun misfired, the slaughter would have gone ahead smoothly without his deadly contribution.

In this scenario, each of the contract killers—to say nothing of the businessman who hires them—has engaged in evil conduct. Admittedly, in the highly likely event that the bullets from one killer have reached the victims slightly before the bullets from the other (rather than at exactly the same instant), only the former killer has caused the victims' deaths. The shots from the other thug have been pre-empted as causes by the slightly earlier shots.[16] Still, although the second killer has not caused the deaths which his bullets would have caused if they had not been pre-empted, the connections between the deaths and his own heartless conduct are amply sufficient to render that conduct evil. He wants the chairman of the rival company to die, and he icily does what is necessary to ensure that such an outcome occurs. In so doing, he displays lethally reckless indifference toward the lives and basic well-being of the members of the chairman's family. The wickedness of his own murderous conduct has not been mitigated one whit by the fact that his fellow assassin has fired slightly more quickly.

---

[16] For a discussion of pre-emptive causation, see Kramer 2003, 295–309, 343–6. I am relying in this paragraph on the NESS criterion for causation, under which some event or state of affairs C is a cause of some other event or state of affairs E if and only if C is physically necessary for the sufficiency of a set of actual conditions that are together physically sufficient for the occurrence of E. For a discussion of the NESS criterion and its many complexities, see Kramer 2003, 277–303.

As should be evident, this scenario of overdetermination is a special case of a failed attempt. Although the result desired by the second gunman has come about, and although he has done what is necessary to ensure that it does come about, he himself is not the person who has caused its occurrence. In that very limited respect, his attempt has failed. This scenario of overdetermination is likewise a special case of an unmaterialized risk. Although the second killer has behaved with grotesque recklessness by shooting in the direction of the members of the chairman's family, and although the effects made overwhelmingly likely by his reckless indifference have indeed come about, he himself is not the person who has caused the occurrence of those effects. In that very limited respect, the risk engendered by his conduct has not materialized.

Hence, we can draw a conclusion here that closely resembles one of the principal conclusions in the preceding subsection about failed attempts and unmaterialized risks. When an action that is aimed at producing some result has been pre-empted from causing that result, or when an action that recklessly gives rise to an acute risk of some result has been pre-empted from causing that result, the action is evil if it would have been evil in the absence of the pre-emptive cause. Being deprived of causal efficacy by the presence of a pre-emptive cause does not make any difference to the status of an instance of conduct as evil.

Does being deprived of causal efficacy in that manner make any difference to the status of an instance of conduct as *extravagantly* evil? In other words, if an action that is aimed at producing some result has been pre-empted from causing that result, and if the action in the absence of the pre-emptive cause would have been extravagantly evil, is the action extravagantly evil (rather than non-extravagantly evil) in the presence of the pre-emptive cause? The answer to this question depends partly on the nature of the pre-emptive cause.

In the scenario presented here, the pre-emptive cause is the shooting of bullets by the first contract killer, who is working closely in collaboration with the second killer. His shooting causes the deaths of the victims in a manner qualitatively indistinguishable from the manner in which the second gunman's shooting would have caused them. In such circumstances, where the second gunman has indeed carried out his frenzied volley of shots, the moral status of his action is unaffected by the occurrence of the pre-emptive cause. If that action would have been extravagantly evil in the absence of the pre-emptive cause, it is extravagantly evil also in the presence thereof.

In many other possible scenarios, however, the occurrence of a pre-emptive cause can make the difference between evil conduct and extravagantly evil conduct. Such an effect will be particularly evident when the pre-emptive cause is a natural force that brings about the deaths of any victims in a manner significantly different from the manner in which some evil action would have unfolded. Let us consider, as an example, a modified version of the scenario that has just been discussed. Suppose that a contract killer is waiting at the home of the chairman of the rival company, with the firm intention of spraying the chairman and his family with bullets as soon as they emerge from the house. Suppose further that, a few moments before the chairman and his family would have sought to go outside, a lightning bolt or a meteor strikes the house and causes it to collapse devastatingly. Everyone inside is killed. Consequently, just as the contract killer is poised to fire, he finds that he does not need to do so. The general results which he would have caused—the deaths of the chairman and the family members—have been pre-emptively caused by a force of nature. Moreover, the manner in which those general results have ensued is significantly different from the manner in which they would have ensued if the lightning bolt or meteor had not struck. Thus, notwithstanding that the general results sought by the contract killer have come about, his situation here is much closer to that of an ordinary failed attempt than was the situation of the second gunman in the original version of the scenario. Accordingly, although the behaviour of the contract killer in this modified scenario is evil, it is not extravagantly evil. Whereas the death penalty might well have been warranted if the killer had shot the chairman and his family in the absence of the lightning bolt or meteor, such a penalty is not warranted in the aftermath of that pre-emptive cause.

Many other examples of pre-emptive causation could be adduced, in which the effects of the pre-emptive causes—with regard to the distinction between evil conduct and extravagantly evil conduct—would be intermediate between the extremes illustrated by the two versions of the scenario of the chairman's demise. Among the sundry considerations that bear on the matter are the nature of the pre-emptive cause; the length of the interval between the occurrence of the pre-emptive cause and the actual or intended occurrence of the causally pre-empted action; the links (if any) between the pre-emptive cause and the person performing the causally pre-empted action; the extent to which the person performing the causally pre-empted action has proceeded in his endeavour; and the similarity or dissimilarity between the way in which some harmful result has been pre-emptively caused and the way in which it would have been caused if the pre-emptive factor had not been present. No detailed examination of those considerations is necessary here. For the purposes of this chapter, we can simply note that the foregoing list suggests that the matter of distinguishing between evil conduct and extravagantly evil conduct can be knottily complicated in many concrete situations. After all, the complexities that arise from overdetermination are only one array of problems that affect such a distinction, yet those complexities themselves are richly multifaceted.

6.2.2.1.3. Attenuated links

As has been stated, any paradigmatic instance of evil conduct is a direct condition—as well as a necessary condition—for the affliction of somebody else with severe harm. The property of directness, as it is invoked here, often involves physical proximity but is a normative property. It pertains to the extent of one's moral responsibility for the occurrence of some severe harm. Anyone who has fatally stabbed or shot or beheaded somebody else is directly responsible for the death and suffering, but so too is anyone who has ordered the murder. A Soviet or Nazi administrative official who issued behests to thuggish subordinates for the perpetration of atrocities was a direct participant in those atrocities even if he sat in his office hundreds of miles away from them. His edicts were a direct and necessary condition for the occurrence of the carnage over which he presided, and they were thus paradigmatic instances of evil conduct.

Not everyone whose actions contribute to the perpetration of iniquities is so directly implicated, of course. If the degree of involvement associated with some contribution is extremely tenuous, then the contribution might not be wrongful (much less evil). For example, if the factories that produced firearms in Germany during the late 1930s and early 1940s had not been supplied with electricity, the armaments necessary for the outrages of the *Einsatzgruppen* would have become depleted. Some of those outrages might thus have been averted. On the one hand, the managers of the electricity suppliers who continued the flow of electricity to the firearms factories were probably thereby committing wrongs, albeit wrongs that were mitigated by the dearth of palatable alternative courses of action. On the other hand, the lower-level employees of the suppliers (whose menial tasks may have been essential for the sustainment of the flow of electricity) were probably not committing any wrongs by performing their humble roles. Of course, if anyone among them was motivated by sadistic relish at the thought of participating in a large-scale project of evil, then he or she was acting wrongfully. However, very likely most of the low-level employees in an electricity supplier had little or no sense of the causal chains that ran between their endeavours and the massacres carried out by the *Einsatzgruppen*. Moreover, given the lengthiness and tortuousness of those chains, the lower-echelon employees were not at fault for failing to grasp how they themselves were remotely contributing to the horrors in which those chains culminated. Hence, at least in most cases, the low-ranking employees were not culpably heartless or reckless or negligent. Their actions were not wrongful and were certainly not evil.

On more dubious ground ethically were the employees of the firearms manufacturers themselves. Anyone working at a firearms factory in Germany during the late 1930s and early 1940s, even in a low-level position, was contributing more directly to the perpetration of iniquities. Still, although anybody who worked for such an employer during the Nazi period was *ipso facto* acting wrongly, the gravity of the wrongs in many cases was mitigated by the fewness of any palatable alternative courses of action. Furthermore, among the low-level employees at the munitions factories, even those who could have obtained jobs in less unwholesome organizations were in most cases not behaving evilly. Though they were committing wrongs by not availing themselves of the opportunities open to them for alternative employment, the connections between their menial tasks and the *Einsatzgruppen*'s atrocities were for the most part too distant to support the claim that their performance of those tasks was evil. Of course, if some of the low-level employees were motivated by the thought that they would be facilitating the perpetration of the atrocities, then they were indeed behaving evilly. Whether their motivations were sadistic or heartlessly chauvinistic, the connections between their odious outlooks and the infliction of egregious harms were sufficient to render their actions evil. However, the other

low-level employees of the munitions manufacturers, who were not similarly motivated, were acting wrongly but not evilly. Although they should have taken jobs
elsewhere, their not having opted for alternatives was wrong rather than wicked.

Notwithstanding the brevity of this discussion of the minor roles that are played by
certain people in large-scale evils, my remarks have gone some way toward revealing
that the matter of connections between potentially evil outlooks and serious harms
is not entirely distinct from the matter of the potentially evil outlooks themselves. In
particular, when those connections are physically and normatively remote, attributions of evil heartlessness or recklessness to the people involved will often be incorrect.
This point becomes evident when we compare the situation of the low-level function-
aries in the firearms factories with the situation of low-level assistants at the sites of the
Einsatzgruppen's massacres. Except for people who were brutally coerced into helping,
anyone who worked in any capacity in support of those massacres and in physical
proximity to them was guilty of evil conduct. No mentally competent adult in such a
position could fail to be aware of the horrors to which he was contributing (albeit in
a minor role). Hence, unless any such person was acting under the pressure of brutal
coercion, his frame of mind was itself evil: sadistically malicious, heartless, or reckless. Markedly different was the situation of the low-level employees of the munitions
manufacturers. Although those employees were culpable for performing jobs in firms
that were integral to the Nazis' prosecution of large-scale enterprises of evil, the culpability in many cases was negligence rather than heartlessness or extreme recklessness.
To be sure, some of the low-level employees may have been sadistically malicious or
heartlessly chauvinistic. Anyone so motivated was acting evilly by performing menial
tasks in a weapons factory. However, very likely many of the low-level employees
were not so motivated. They had only a limited sense of the monstrosities to which
they were contributing in their small ways, and they were thus largely able to block
out from their minds the fact that they were indeed contributing to the perpetration of
those monstrosities. Accordingly, their outlooks were negligent rather than heartless
or extremely reckless. Their wrongful behaviour—consisting in their fulfilment of
their humble work-related responsibilities—was not evil.

This point about the negligence (rather than heartlessness or recklessness) of people who contribute remotely to wicked undertakings is of considerable importance
in much of the contemporary world. People in many countries play minor roles in
bringing about iniquities elsewhere—through investments, through purchases of
various products, and so forth—but in most cases the operative outlooks are negligent rather than sadistic or heartless or reckless. Hence, in most cases, the small and
distant contributions of people to the occurrence of atrocities in foreign lands are
not evil. Although the people involved should take more care to ascertain the consequences of their actions and should not so readily block out those consequences from
their minds, their remissness does not amount to wickedness.

At any rate, this discussion of tenuous connections between culpable states of mind
and large-scale projects of evil can remain terse. Fascinating and vital though the

topic is in sundry contexts, we do not need to explore it extensively in this book. After all, even when the culpable states of mind are sadistic or heartless, and thus even when the actions and omissions impelled by those states of mind are wicked (despite the remoteness of the connections between the actions or omissions and the ultimate infliction of atrocities), the wickedness is not at a level that would trigger the purgative rationale for the death penalty. That penalty would never be apposite in response to such small contributions to iniquities.

Let us briefly look afresh, for example, at the low-level employees of munitions manufacturers in Nazi Germany. Some of them were acting evilly by performing their menial tasks, if they were carrying out those tasks on the basis of sadistic malice or heartless chauvinism and if they were thus aiming to facilitate the vile endeavours of the *Einsatzgruppen* and other Nazi murderers. However, their evil conduct, unlike the evil conduct of the *Einsatzgruppen*, was not extravagantly heinous. No executions of those minions would be justifiable under the purgative rationale for capital punishment. We should reach a corresponding conclusion about consumers who deliberately buy products from certain countries (such as Iran or China or Burma or Syria) in order to express their approval of the rebarbative regimes that rule those countries. Much the same is true of investors who make a point of purchasing shares in companies that help to prop up such despicable regimes. Acting on the basis of sadistic malice or heartless greed, those consumers and investors are behaving evilly. Moreover, their actions might contravene criminal prohibitions within their own jurisdictions. However, because they are only bit players who participate at a distance in the wide-ranging projects of evil which they gladly support, their repellent conduct is far from extravagantly heinous. *Sans plus*, no execution of any such person could be justified on the ground that his continued existence blights the moral fabric of his community. (Of course, we should draw a different conclusion about an investor who knowingly is the sole or dominant financial backer of some monstrous regime or terrorist gang. Even if such a person does not participate in directing the details of the activities of the loathsome regime or terrorist organization which he funds, the connection between his evilly culpable outlook and the commission of atrocities is sufficiently close and ample to warrant his being held guilty of those atrocities.)

6.2.2.1.4. *Spectatorial pleasure*

In my discussion of sadistic malice in § 6.2.1.1, the matter of voyeuristic or spectatorial wickedness has surfaced. If somebody derives sadistic pleasure from a film about the perpetration of genocide by the Khmer Rouge in Cambodia, and if he knows that the events depicted are real (or are based on reality), then his conduct as a viewer is a low-grade variety of evil. He is deriving ghoulish gratification from the infliction of appalling harms. Even though his connection to the harms is only spectatorial, and even though that connection is itself mediated through film, his relishing of the butchery of hapless Cambodians is at odds with any elementary respect for their humanity and with any elementary concern for them as beings who are capable of experiencing intense pain. Because his grotesque frame of mind is connected through the film's vivid portrayals to other people's genuine suffering of anguish of the direst sort, his sadistic voyeurism is evil. As Luke Russell writes, 'the enjoyment of extremely harmful actions counts as an evil act.... [E]vil acts are wrongful acts that are either extremely harmful, or are connected in certain ways to extreme harms, and...acts of appreciation or enjoyment of extreme harms are so connected' (Russell 2007, 672).

As the quotation from Russell implies, instances of evilly sadistic voyeurism can be focused on dreadful afflictions that have not themselves arisen from wicked conduct. If Margaret experiences sadistic glee while viewing the maimed and mangled bodies of the victims of an earthquake, her spectatorial conduct is wicked even though the deaths and horrible injuries of the victims are not attributable to any acts of evil. Of course, if Margaret is at the scene of the earthquake and is declining to offer any help while she chortles sadistically, her non-assistance—if prompted by her sadism rather than (say) by any physical disabilities on her part—is itself evil. However, even if she is thousands of miles away from the earthquake in a land where she witnesses on television the ghastly results of the disaster, her experiencing of sadistic exuberance in response to those results is evil. Despite her physical distance, and despite the fact that the misery which she relishes is due to a natural catastrophe rather than to any wrongful actions, her unsavoury delight upon beholding that misery is evil.

6.2.2.2. Is severe harm necessary for evil?

As this chapter has contended, evil conduct involves connections between certain types of culpability and extreme harm. What has been stressed so far is that only certain types of culpability are potentially productive of evil. That point has needed emphasis, since it sometimes gets overlooked in theories of evil. Russell, for example, suggests that evil actions are 'culpably wrong actions that have a certain kind of connection to extreme harms, in that they either produce extreme harms, are intended to produce extreme harms, contribute to extreme harms, or are acts of appreciation of extreme harms'.[17] He states: 'In many ways, this is an attractive account of evil.' Yet, given that such a conception would classify numerous merely negligent actions as evil, it is not really attractive. Russell errs in suggesting that culpability of every type can be constitutive of evil conduct. On the contrary, sadistic malice and heartlessness and extreme recklessness are the only kinds of culpability that can be so constitutive. Negligence is never enough, regardless of how much harm an instance of negligent conduct might produce. (Russell does go on to broach a couple of alternative criteria 'according to which evil actions can flow only from certain motives'. However, each of those criteria is highly problematic. Under the first of them, on which Russell does not elaborate at all, 'evil actions necessarily are malicious actions, performed out of a desire to harm others'. A criterion of that sort is untenable, for it generates

---

[17] All the quotations in this paragraph are from Russell 2007, 676.

the conclusion that the wickedly reckless actions discussed in § 6.2.1.3 above—such as Wilbur's volley of shots at the hapless bystanders and the lethally reckless stunts of the daredevil drivers—are not evil. Under the second of Russell's two alternative criteria, 'evil actions necessarily are defiant actions, performed despite the agents' knowledge that they are wrong'.[18] Such an understanding of evil is patently unsatisfactory, for it assesses moral obtuseness favourably. As Russell himself observes, albeit without expressing any disapproval, this latest understanding of evil would oblige us to conclude that 'many terrorist actions are not evil[,] . . . because the terrorists mistakenly believe that what they are doing is morally right'. Anyone endorsing such a conception of evil would think that most of the atrocities by the Nazis and the Khmer Rouge and nearly all massacres by terrorists and most of the lynchings by the Ku Klux Klan should not be characterized as evil. A theory of wickedness that would yield such ridiculous conclusions is not to be taken seriously.)

Claudia Card has stumbled in broadly the same manner as Russell, in her important work on evil. On the opening page of her book on the topic, she proclaims that 'evils are foreseeable intolerable harms produced by culpable wrongdoing' (Card 2002, 3). Like Russell's purportedly attractive account of evil, this formulation entails the classification of numerous negligent actions as wicked. That implication appears to be embraced by Card in her next few sentences: 'On my theory, the nature and severity of the harms, rather than perpetrators' psychological states, distinguish evils from ordinary wrongs. Evils tend to ruin lives, or significant parts of lives. It is not surprising if victims never recover or are never quite able to move on, although sometimes people do recover and move on' (Card 2002, 3–4). Casebooks on tort law abound with judgments that recount how various instances of negligent conduct have ruined the lives of the people who are detrimentally affected by them. Hence, Card's way of distinguishing between evils and ordinary wrongs will place myriad instances of negligent conduct on the former side of that dichotomy. No theory of wickedness that carries such an implication is satisfactory. Card herself may appear to recognize as much in the sentences that immediately follow those which have just been quoted: 'Evildoers, however, are not necessarily malicious. Oftener they are inexcusably reckless, callously indifferent, amazingly unscrupulous' (Card 2002, 4). Given that Card here omits any mention of negligence, she may appear to be confining the class of potentially evil states of mind to sadistic malice, heartlessness, and extreme recklessness. However, quite apart from the fact that an apt restriction of that sort is not reflected in her general statement of the nature of evil actions which I have quoted above, some brief later remarks by her on negligence make clear that she does regard it as a type of culpability that can give rise to evil conduct. While

---

[18] Albert Hofstadter expressed such a view as follows: 'In true moral evil the actor is convinced that the norm he violates is morally right. He is convinced that he is setting himself against what he ought to do, intentionally doing what he ought not to do. Evil cannot exist save in and through this active opposition to what is perceived as good and right.' Hofstadter 1973, 5–6, quoted in Kekes 1990, 86. A more sophisticated but equally misguided version of the view held by Hofstadter is elaborated in Milo 1984, chs 2 and 7.

differentiating among degrees of evil by reference to the viciousness of the kinds of culpability that can underlie wicked conduct, she maintains that 'there are "degrees" of inattentiveness: recklessness is grosser than neglect or carelessness'.[19] Her inclusion of negligence in the class of potentially evil states of mind is further confirmed somewhat later when she writes as follows:

[A]n evil *intention* is a culpable intention to do someone intolerable harm, or to do something with that foreseeable result, even if the intention does not succeed. In an evil *deed*, the intention succeeds. An evil intender may not foresee harm, owing to culpable recklessness, negligence, or even a choice to ignore. But the harm must be foreseeable if one were to attend with reasonable care. Culpability in an evil intention can take many forms, such as (1) the aim to bring about intolerable harm, (2) the willingness to do so in the course of pursuing an otherwise acceptable aim or in adhering to some other value or principle, or (3) the failure to attend to risks or take them seriously. [Card 2002, 20, emphases in original]

Though Card's theory can be modified to exclude all instances of merely negligent conduct from the category of evil actions, it currently includes many such instances in that category and is therefore unacceptable as it stands. Card has not overcome this problem through her recent indication that she wishes to substitute 'inexcusable' for 'culpable' in her central formulation of the nature of evils (Card 2008, 6). Altered in that fashion, the formulation would declare that 'evils are foreseeable intolerable harms produced by inexcusable wrongdoing'. Card is somewhat idiosyncratically taking excuses to be certain mitigating factors. More specifically, a Cardian excuse reduces the blameworthiness of someone who has committed a misdeed, because 'there was some *good reason* for the deed, although not good enough to justify that deed on the whole' (Card 2008, 6, emphasis in original). Given this understanding of excuses—or, indeed, a more common understanding of them as factors that absolve people of responsibility for their wrongful conduct[20]—many instances of negligent conduct are inexcusable. Thus, Card continues to classify countless negligent actions and omissions as evil. Her theory should be rejected *pro tanto*, whatever may be its virtues in a number of other respects.

Let us glance at one further philosopher who commits a similar misstep. Stephen de Wijze, in a thought-provoking article, maintains that an action or project is evil if it 'will gratuitously inflict, or bring about, one or more of "The Great Harms"

---

[19] Card 2002, 14. Card errs in claiming that recklessness is a variety of inattentiveness. Recklessness consists in the *deliberate* and gratuitous hazarding of risks (usually acute risks). Card commits a similar misstep in the next passage which I quote from her. In fairness to her, I should note that the distinction between recklessness and negligence has not always been as widely marked among jurists as it is today. Moreover, a few major contemporary legal philosophers have tentatively played down the distinction; see, for example, Moore and Hurd 2011.

[20] I have argued elsewhere that excuses so understood are strictly legal phenomena. There are no excuses in morality; instead, there are only justifications and mitigations. See Kramer 2004, 249–94; 2005. However, my approach to excuses is quite different from Card's, since many of the mitigating factors to which I advert are considerations that bear on the responsibility of individuals. Card, by contrast, distinguishes such considerations from the mitigating factors on which she focuses.

to sentient beings with the relevant moral standing'. He explains that the 'Great Harms' to which he refers are calamities such as 'great physical suffering, illness, starvation, death, destruction of home or habitat and the misery of continual and unrelenting terror and harassment' (De Wijze 2002, 218, 219, endnote omitted). Since calamities of nearly all these kinds can be inflicted upon people by the negligent conduct of others, and since de Wijze does not specify any *mens rea* component other than gratuitousness, he has joined Russell and Card by attaching himself to the proposition that numerous instances of negligence are to be classified as evil. Like Russell and Card, he unacceptably dilutes the shuddersomeness of the property of evil by holding in effect that a multitude of negligent actions partake of that property.

Philosophers go astray when they obscure the distinctiveness of the modes of culpability that can underlie evil conduct. At this juncture, however, we need to take account of a converse error that has been committed by some philosophers: the error of discounting or underestimating the factor of severe harm as a necessary constituent of wickedness. Of course, as has been contended at length in this chapter, the factor of severe harm can figure as an element of wicked conduct in a number of ways. Not every instance of such conduct involves the actual occurrence of deaths or injuries. Still, unless that factor does play some role—that is, unless it is connected in some relevant manner to a potentially evil mode of culpability—any conduct under consideration is not evil. Certain philosophers have mistakenly denied this point and have submitted that evil actions do not have to involve severe harm at all. To complete my account of evil (before moving on to the topic of defilement), this chapter will examine the arguments that have been propounded by those philosophers. As will be seen, they do not succeed in establishing that any instance of evil conduct can ever be wholly unconnected to the infliction of severe harm.

6.2.2.2.1. *Concomitants of harm*

Garrard has most forcefully and frequently contended that some evil conduct is not connected to grievous harm in any fashion. She has offered one of her principal examples in two slightly different versions. We should look at both of those versions, in order to mull them over in combination. Garrard articulates the first of them as follows: 'A tyrannical state executes by firing-squad a young dissident; and then bills the grieving relatives for the cost of the bullet. Clearly the main disvalue produced in this case is the killing of the young man. But it is the charging for the bullet that is more likely to strike us as evil' (Garrard 1998, 45). A few years later, she slightly modifies and amplifies her scenario. She refers to 'the case of the Iraqis during the occupation of Kuwait [in 1990] who, having shot a young boy, demanded money from the boy's family to pay for the bullet. Here the principal suffering was caused by the killing; but it is the charging for the bullet which strikes most people as evil' (Garrard 2002, 327, endnote omitted). In the first version of the scenario, the slaying of the young man is a heartlessly deliberate execution of a dissident by a ruthless regime. In the second version, by contrast, the circumstances of the killing are unspecified.[21] To confront Garrard's position in its strongest form, let us assume that the fatal shooting is accidental and that it is therefore not evil in itself. Hence, the wickedness of charging the decedent's family for the bullet is not derivative of any other evil. Nonetheless, the example does not illustrate the point which Garrard is seeking to make.

Although the inadvertent shooting of the boy is not itself evil, it is grievously harmful (both for the boy and for his family). Were the charge to the family for the bullet not connected to that grievously harmful event or to some comparable incident, the charge would not be evil. If the bullet had missed or had merely grazed the boy, the billing of the family for the cost of it would still have been wrongful and cavalier but would not have been wicked. In the absence of any link to serious harm, the billing would be haughtily intimidating but would not exemplify the attitude that is characteristic of evil conduct: an attitude (sadistically malicious, heartless, or extremely reckless) of utter disdain for the humanity and elementary well-being of someone else, who is regarded as a mere plaything to be destroyed or otherwise grossly mistreated for one's own sinister purposes. When the charge to the parents for the bullet is made in the aftermath of the slaying of their son, that quintessentially evil attitude is precisely what is being conveyed to them.

Garrard's scenario, as I have construed it, does show that two actions can be wicked in combination even though neither of them would be wicked in isolation. However, it does not show that any action can be evil without being connected to the infliction of grievous harm. What makes the difference between the wickedness of charging for a bullet that has *killed* a boy and the mere wrongfulness of charging for a bullet that has *grazed* a boy is precisely the presence or absence of grievous harm. Garrard is mistaken in thinking that no such harm need be involved in evil conduct.

6.2.2.2.2. *Tortured cats and bullied children*

Garrard adduces a couple of other examples, which can be considered here together. In her original article on evil, she writes as follows: 'Think of someone slowly torturing a cat, or gloatingly bullying a terrified child. In the scale of the world's catastrophes the disvalue produced by these actions is pretty insignificant, and yet we might well want to call these actions evil rather than just wrong' (Garrard 1998, 45). Garrard returns to the first of these examples in her later article: '[C]onsider the person who, with gloating enjoyment, slowly tortures a cat. In the scale of the world's sufferings it barely registers, nonetheless it can plausibly be called evil' (Garrard 2002, 327). The position which Garrard appears to be opposing here is markedly different from the position which I am defending. She appears to be assailing the view that no instance of conduct is ever wicked unless it produces misery and deaths on the scale of the Soviet system of slave-labour camps or the Cambodian genocide or the Maoist Cultural

---

[21] The circumstances of the killing are likewise unspecified in the source of Garrard's example: Glover 1999, 36.

Revolution. As she states: 'We should at least leave open the possibility of there being small-scale actions where the production of disvalue is minuscule, compared to the huge paradigm cases such as the Holocaust or slavery, and yet these actions may be qualitatively such as to merit the judgement that they are evil' (Garrard 1998, 45).

When Garrard's stance is elaborated along these lines, no sensible philosopher would disagree with it. Precisely because no sensible theorist of evil would disagree with such a stance, however, her defence of it is somewhat puzzling. Consider here two points.

First, the account of evil which Garrard is impugning would be truly preposterous. Such an account, in maintaining that only calamities on the scale of the Holocaust or the Cultural Revolution can correctly be classified as evil, would imply that each individual atrocity within the Holocaust or the Cultural Revolution was not evil. After all, each such atrocity produced anguish on a scale that was minuscule in comparison with the extent of the anguish caused by the Holocaust or Cultural Revolution as a whole. Likewise, the several instances of torture and cannibalistic murder committed by Jeffrey Dahmer in Wisconsin in the 1980s and 1990s were productive of misery on a scale that paled in comparison with the degree of the misery caused by the Cambodian or Rwandan genocide as a whole. Consequently, according to the theory of evil which Garrard is contesting, the smashing open of a Jewish baby's head against a concrete wall by a sadistic Nazi concentration camp guard was not evil, and Dahmer's acts of cannibalizing young men after bludgeoning and hacking them to death were not evil. Any analysis of the concept of evil that generates such conclusions is absurd—which is why Garrard's confutation of that analysis is puzzling. Why does Garrard feel any need to combat a doctrine that is so patently outlandish?

Secondly, when marshalling her other examples, Garrard does not in fact take that ridiculous doctrine as her target. Instead, her target is the far more sensible proposition that no instance of conduct is evil unless it involves the actual or envisaged infliction of very serious harm. For example, when she deals with the scenario of the shooting in Iraq—which we have examined above—Garrard does not contrast the Iraqi government's charge for the bullet with a massive catastrophe such as the Holocaust. Rather, she contrasts it with the shooting for which the charge has been imposed. Yet, given that that shooting has caused deleterious consequences on a scale that is vastly surpassed by the scale of a massive catastrophe, her benchmark would make little sense if she were addressing herself to the outlandish view which I have discussed in the last few paragraphs. She must instead be addressing herself to the far more sensible proposition that has just been stated. That is, she must be trying to refute the proposition that every instance of evil conduct involves grievous harm. We should therefore assess her examples of the cat and the bullied child by reference to that proposition.

Torturing a cat, whether slowly or otherwise, is manifestly a way of harming it grievously. Moreover, since the torture is sadistically malicious—it is carried out with 'gloating enjoyment'—it is underlain by an evil-inclining mode of culpability. With a close connection between that mode of culpability and the infliction of severe harm, the torture is a straightforward instance of evil conduct unless the nature of the victim as a non-human animal somehow makes a decisive difference. Initially the subhuman nature of the cat may appear to make such a difference, since this chapter's discussions of evil and this book's earlier discussions of human dignity have highlighted the humanity of the victims of evil actions. However, as has been emphasized at a number of junctures in those discussions, human beings should receive not only respect in their capacity as reflective agents but also solicitude in their status as sentient beings who are capable of undergoing positive experiences and prone to feeling intense pain. That latter status is shared by many non-human animals and certainly by cats. Consequently, although the focus of this book lies on evils perpetrated against human beings—since only such evils can ever warrant the imposition of capital punishment—my account of evil can quite readily extend to wicked actions perpetrated against animals. Someone who sadistically tortures an animal is displaying a wholesale lack of concern for its well-being as a creature that is prone to experiencing agony. He is treating the animal as a plaything that can be subjected to excruciating pain for his own perverse pleasure. In the absence of any mitigating circumstances, somebody who sadistically or heartlessly exploits the capacity of a sentient creature to feel exquisite pain is behaving wickedly.

In sum, then, Garrard's scenario of the torturing of the cat does not go any way toward confirming her thesis that some instances of evil conduct involve no serious harms. On the contrary, her scenario depicts an action that causes very serious harm. Does her example of the gloatingly bullied child fare any better? The answer to that question is negative, though her extremely brief presentation of the example would have to be amplified before we could gauge its precise import. If the bullying does not result in any significant physical injuries, and if it occurs only once or twice, then it is seriously wrong but not evil. Contrariwise, if it results in significant physical injuries, or if it occurs on many occasions, then it is indeed evil. Under such circumstances, however, the bullying plainly involves the infliction of severe harm (physical or psychological). In other words, inasmuch as the mistreatment of the child is correctly classifiable as evil, it is so because it involves the very factor—grievous harm—which Garrard is claiming to be inessential. Far from clinching her case, her example of the bullied child contributes to the disconfirmation of her position.

6.2.2.2.3. Sadistic voyeurism again

Garrard adduces one further scenario which she believes to be supportive of her stance: a scenario of sadistic voyeurism. Given that this chapter has already probed evil conduct of that kind (in § 6.2.2.1.4) and has shown that such conduct connects sadistic malice to the occurrence of severe harm, we do not need to ponder her scenario at any length. However, we should note in passing that Garrard and especially Russell characterize the effects of sadistic voyeurism misleadingly. Garrard refers to 'the sadistic voyeur, who chooses to observe, with intense relish, the sadistic acts of another. Here nothing is added to the sum of suffering by his voyeuristic behaviour; nonetheless we might wish to call it evil' (Garrard 2002, 327, endnote omitted). Russell similarly writes that 'the enjoyment of extremely harmful actions counts as an evil act, even when such enjoyment is not additionally harmful itself' (Russell 2007, 672). The first half of this quoted remark by Russell is of course unexceptionable, but the second half—which presumably builds, in a utilitarian fashion, on Garrard's observation that the sadistic voyeurism adds nothing to the 'sum of suffering'—is misguided.

Suppose that Peter derives sadistic pleasure from viewing photographs of people who have been badly injured or killed. Or perhaps he furtively visits the sites of automobile accidents and other fatal misadventures in order to gain sadistic gratification from beholding the carnage. Whatever may be the details, a key feature of this scenario is that the people whose misery or destruction provides Peter with pleasure are not aware of his ghoulish witnessing of their woes. Consequently, as Garrard suggests, his sadistic spectatorship does not add to the sum of their sufferings. Her suggestion along those lines is misleading, however, because it all too easily lends itself to Russell's utilitarian inference that the victims of the misadventures have not been harmed in any way by Peter's voyeurism. Though their anguish has not been intensified (*ex hypothesi*), they have—unbeknownst to them—been harmed by being subjected to the indignity of furnishing Peter with sadistic amusement. His use of them and their tribulations for his own perverse enjoyment has harmed them by demoting them to the status of playthings. Their posture as moral agents entitled to respect, and as sentient creatures entitled to concern, has been besmirched by his abominable behaviour. Though he has not increased their pain, he has subordinated them grotesquely to his own purposes. Subordinated in that fashion, they have been harmed by the contravention of their dignity.[22]

6.2.2.2.4. *A face-saving reply*

Garrard is not the only philosopher who has argued that some evil actions involve no serious harms. Morton's formulation of his conception of evil acts is patently consistent with the proposition that some such acts are connected only to minor harms: 'A person's act is evil when it results from a strategy or learned procedure which allows that person's deliberations over the choice of actions not to be inhibited by barriers against considering harming or humiliating others that ought to have been in place' (Morton 2004, 57, italics removed). This formulation does not specify that, whenever an evil act is performed, the harm caused or contemplated is extremely serious. Morton leaves wide open the possibility of evil conduct in which a barrier-lowering mentality is connected to harm of quite a trifling sort. He goes on to proclaim as much, when he remarks that his conception of evil 'allows small-scale evil, evil acts that do not involve killing, major suffering, or life-destroying humiliation. For sometimes you shouldn't even consider doing something that harms another person, although the harm is comparatively minor' (Morton 2004, 60).

---

[22] My point about Peter's harming of the victims of the misadventures is applicable whether or not the victims are dead at the time of his voyeurism. Some philosophers have argued that people cannot be harmed posthumously. See, for example, Fabre 2008. Several of my objections to Fabre's view are articulated (and attributed to me) in her essay. For some of my arguments in favour of the proposition that dead people can be harmed, see Kramer 2001, 49–52, 54–5.

If Morton is to vindicate this feature of his account of evil, he will have to supply some persuasive examples of wicked actions that do not involve any very serious
harms. His first example is as follows:

Suppose that I am giving a lecture and a student asks me a question that I don't know the
answer to. One way of saving face is to retort: 'The fact that you ask that question shows how
little you grasp the topic. Does someone have an intelligent question?' This will certainly shut
the student up, and it will also produce dismay and possibly depression. It is something that
should not even occur to me. [Morton 2004, 60–1]

A cruel and self-indulgently deceitful riposte of the kind recounted in this passage is plainly
wrongful. It is palpably an abuse of the power that is wielded by a professor over the students who attend his lectures, and it is at odds with the educational responsibilities that
are incumbent on any academic. However, the concept of evil is stretched outlandishly if
we apply it to the depicted misbehaviour. A spur-of-the-moment retort that disparages a
student in order to spare the lecturer himself from embarrassment is hardly a manifestation
of a thoroughgoing lack of respect for the student's reflective agency and a thoroughgoing
lack of concern for the student's basic well-being. Wrong and self-serving though the retort
is, its petulance is not the grotesque perversity of evil. An appropriate emotional reaction to
the lecturer's behaviour is that of indignation rather than a shuddering sense of horror.

Admittedly, Morton avouches that the lecturer's brusque reply is 'towards the
lower edge of what most people would regard as evil' (Morton 2004, 61). Let us leave
aside any empirical question about the lower reaches of what most people would
regard as evil; such an empirical question, apropos of which Morton does not provide
any evidence, is beside the point here. Let us focus instead on the philosophical and
moral question concerning what is in fact towards the lower edge of evil. On that
question, Morton's position—his claim that the lecturer's rejoinder is evil, albeit at a
low level—is unpersuasive.

On the one hand, there are of course low-grade instances of evil conduct. As has
already been noted, for example, someone who watches a documentary film about
the Holocaust or the Tiananmen Square massacre in order to experience sadistic glee
is engaging in behaviour that is at the lower end of the spectrum of evil. Moreover,
given that the property of wickedness is vague, the range of low-level instances of
wicked conduct will shade into the range of instances of conduct that are neither
determinately wicked nor determinately not wicked; the demarcation between the
former range and the latter is encompassed by higher-order vagueness. As a consequence, we plainly need to be circumspect when judging whether low-grade
instances of wickedness are such instances or not.

On the other hand, due circumspection should scarcely inhibit anyone from recognizing that the lecturer's sharp reply in Morton's scenario is not wicked, even at a
low level. Though the reply is an abuse of power and is thus wrongful, its reasonably
foreseeable impact is only moderately and ephemerally harmful. Consequently, the
heartless frame of mind that impels such a face-saving reply is not akin to the heartless

frame of mind that leads somebody to shoot innocent people at point-blank range or to administer excruciating tortures. Albeit the difference between those frames of mind is a quantitative matter of degree, it is also a qualitative matter of kind. Whereas a person who adopts the latter frame of mind is viewing other people as playthings entirely subordinate to his own nefarious purposes, no such cavalierly god-like disdain for the fundamental interests of others is bespoken by a retort that enables a lecturer to extricate himself from an embarrassing plight.

Indeed, Morton's assertion that the retort 'should not even occur to me' is itself implausibly censorious. Although the lecturer should have firmly repressed the temptation to escape from his predicament by belittling the student, the notion that such an escape should not even have occurred to the lecturer—in other words, the notion that he should not even have felt tempted—is implausibly demanding. Experiencing a temptation to deliver a face-saving reply is not per se wrong (much less evil). A lecturer's indulgence of that temptation is of course wrongful, but, because of the transitoriness and mildness of the harm that is the reasonably foreseeable effect of the indulgence, such conduct falls well short of being evil.

6.2.2.2.5. *An embarrassing secret*

Morton adduces one further example of conduct which he believes to be both evil and only modestly harmful. He asks us to 'consider someone who has been entrusted with an extremely embarrassing secret, and tells it to the world. This too has something in common with much more serious evil-doing: it ignores a barrier against the humiliation of others' (Morton 2004, 61). To judge whether this scenario depicts an instance of evil conduct, we would need to know more about the content of the secret and about the sensibilities of the person whose confidentiality has been betrayed. We would also need to know more about the circumstances surrounding the concealment and the disclosure. However, what can be stated in abstraction from such specifics is that the disclosure is evil only if the reasonably foreseeable effects of its occurrence are severely harmful to the person whose secret has been divulged. If the content of the revealed information is such that the person betrayed will be likely to undergo agonizing humiliation and other seriously untoward effects (such as the loss of a job and the loss of all or most of her friends), and if she herself is a sensitive person who is apt to feel devastated by the betrayal and the other effects, and if there is no solid moral consideration that weighs in favour of the act of disclosure, then that act is evil. The heartlessness or sadism that underlies the disclosure is directly connected to very serious harm; as Morton himself accepts in a passage quoted above, life-ruining humiliation is a very serious type of harm indeed. By contrast, if the content of the revealed information is such that the humiliation caused by the divulgence of it is likely to be transient with no other seriously untoward consequences, and if the person whose confidences have been violated is not especially delicate in her sensibilities, then the breach of her trust is not evil (though of course it is wrong, unless the person with the secret has herself been behaving immorally by keeping certain information concealed). On a spectrum between the envisaged situation where the disclosure is clearly evil and the envisaged situation where it is clearly not evil are many possible intermediate situations whose ethical bearings are less clear-cut. In every case, however, a key factor is the gravity of the harms that are the reasonably foreseeable effects of the revelation of some secret.

To ponder these abstract points at a more concrete level, we should briefly consider the interplay of characters in Charles Dickens's *Bleak House*. In that novel, the loathsome lawyer Tulkinghorn goes to great efforts to apprise himself of a secret long kept by Lady Dedlock, the wife of his chief client. He eventually discovers that, before marrying her husband, she had borne another man's child out of wedlock. Tulkinghorn's motivations for striving to learn Lady Dedlock's secret are not entirely clear. Paramount among them, as far as can be discerned, are a heartlessly fierce determination to protect the perceived interests of his client and a sense of sadistic gratification derivable from his being in a position to wield power over Lady Dedlock.[23] At any rate, in the ethical climate of early Victorian England, his revelation of the information about her past indiscretion will foreseeably harm her severely. It will bring severe and lasting disgrace upon her, and it will very likely ruin her marriage. To be sure, when Lord Dedlock does eventually become aware of his wife's secret, he proves to be magnanimous. However, given that his personality theretofore has been generally obtuse and unappealing, he has furnished no strong grounds for his wife or anyone else to anticipate that a display of magnanimity on his part is a probable upshot of the disclosure of her past behaviour. Even when broaching the possibility of such an upshot in a conversation with Lady Dedlock, Tulkinghorn is dismissive of its likelihood: 'Sir Leicester is devoted to you almost to infatuation. He might not be able to overcome that infatuation, even knowing what we know. I am putting an extreme case, but it might be so. If so, it were better that he knew nothing' (Dickens 1971, 636 [ch 41]). Furthermore, even though Lord Dedlock himself turns out to react in an enlightened fashion to the information about his wife's premarital fling, the reactions of the people in his and Lady Dedlock's social circles would almost certainly have been sanctimoniously stern if they too had learned of that information during Lady Dedlock's lifetime. Consequently, given that a number of grievously damaging effects are liable to ensue from any widely propagated revelation of Lady Dedlock's secret, and given that no genuinely weighty considerations militate in favour of such a revelation, the divulgence of her secret by Tulkinghorn to Lord Dedlock and to the broader world would be an evil course of action. Tulkinghorn is in fact murdered before he can engage in such a course of action, but he would have been behaving wickedly if he had engaged in it.

---

[23] Tulkinghorn's dehumanizing heartlessness is perhaps best conveyed by the following description of his demeanour in a colloquy with Lady Dedlock about her secret: '[H]e methodically discusses his matter of business, as if she were any insensible instrument used in business' (Dickens 1971, 715 [ch 48]).

What is of central importance here is that the wickedness of such a disclosure by Tulkinghorn would be due to the combination of (1) his heartless or sadistic frame of mind and (2) the severity of the damaging consequences that are likely to follow from his publicizing of Lady Dedlock's secret.[24] The latter factor is crucial, just as is the former. Had the events of *Bleak House* taken place in a much more permissive society where the exposure of Lady Dedlock's past would predictably have carried very few detrimental effects, and had Lady Dedlock herself not been a very sensitive person (in contrast with the character portrayed by Dickens), the exposure would not have been evil. It would have been wrong, of course, especially in light of the heartlessness or sadism of Tulkinghorn's outlook. However, when such an outlook is unconnected to any serious harm (whether actual or envisaged), the conduct that it impels is not evil.

In sum, Morton's second example is no more successful than his first in showing that some instances of evil conduct do not involve any serious harm. If the imparting of confidential and highly embarrassing information is evil, it is so partly because of the grievously harmful effects that are expected to flow from it. Of course, like the example of the lecturer's curt retort, the example of the divulged information does tend to draw attention to the actuality or possibility of borderline cases. Along with the property of evil that comprehends it, the property of severe harmfulness is vague. Between the extremes of harmfulness and harmlessness—that is, between the countless situations in which disclosures of embarrassing secrets would be extremely damaging (like the situation depicted in *Bleak House*) and the countless situations in which such disclosures would be largely innocuous—are throngs of intermediate cases. Some of those intermediate cases are borderline situations in which revelations of embarrassing information are neither determinately evil nor determinately not evil, because the harms that can reasonably be expected to follow from those revelations are neither determinately very serious nor determinately not very serious. We should readily recognize as much, while also recognizing that the role of very serious harm as an actual or envisaged consequence of a breach of confidentiality is a necessary condition for the status of the breach as evil.

6.3. Defilement and death

As has been argued, evil conduct is underlain by sadistic malice or heartlessness or extreme recklessness that is connected to severe harm in the absence of any significant extenuating circumstances. However, not every instance of evil conduct should elicit the death penalty. On the contrary, that penalty is appropriate for only a small

---

[24] Even though some of the severely damaging consequences might not ultimately have materialized, the perceived likelihood of them at the time of the disclosure would have been dispositive. Tulkinghorn would have expected them and would have acted in pursuit of them (as is plain from his remark that the premarital escapade by Lady Dedlock should be kept concealed if Lord Dedlock would not disown her after learning of it). Insofar as any of the expected consequences would not ultimately have ensued, the exposure of Lady Dedlock's secret would have stood as a failed attempt.

proportion of such instances. After all, as the preceding chapters have collectively maintained, none of the standardly propounded rationales for capital punishment is successful (either in isolation or in combination). Hence, if such punishment is justifiable at all, its justification is to be found in the purgative rationale.[25] Yet that last-mentioned rationale certainly does not extend to every instance of evil conduct. Rather, it extends only to instances of evil conduct that are so heinous as to render defilingly abominable the continued existence of their perpetrators. Given that most instances of evil conduct are not so heinous, the reach of the purgative rationale—the reach of the only sound justification for the death penalty—is narrow. Accordingly, to understand that rationale and to gain some sense of the scope of its applicability, we need to go beyond an account of evil. We need to mull over the nature of defilement.[26]

6.3.1. Nothing supernatural

Let us begin our exploration of this issue by pondering a quotation from Morton:

We have a visceral revulsion from extremely evil acts. The revulsion is most vivid when the acts involve physical violence, but it extends to other acts produced by similar patterns of motivation, even if they do not have the same emotional immediacy. Evil acts have a quality that in ancient times would have made us fear that the gods might send a plague in reprisal, rather than simply making us despair at the incapacities of mere mortals to manage their lives together. [Morton 2004, 13]

This passage is important partly because it harks back to the story of Achan with which this chapter started its discussion of the purgative rationale. (Morton's remarks are also redolent of many other Biblical narratives—such as 2 Samuel 24, where we are told of the pestilence with which God afflicts Israel after King David has sinned by ordering a census of his people.) In addition, the passage makes clear that the provenance of the purgative rationale is not confined to the Hebrew Scriptures. After all, Morton's reference to the sending of a plague by the gods in reprisal for the mishandling of an especially iniquitous crime immediately calls to mind the opening scene of *Oedipus Rex*, where the land of Thebes suffers because

---

[25] Obviously, I am assuming that the purgative rationale is the sole credible alternative to the standardly propounded rationales. I know of no other alternatives.

[26] The secular philosophical literature on defilement is much less extensive than the secular philosophical literature on evil. Moreover, some of it is not very helpful. For example, the murky discussion of defilement in the first main chapter of Ricoeur 1969 is focused chiefly on the defilement of wrongdoers by their wrongs rather than on the defilement of communities by the continued existence of evildoers. Much more readable and interesting—indeed, often fascinating—is Douglas 1966. However, Douglas's perspective was that of an anthropologist rather than that of a philosopher. Her concern was with suggesting how various beliefs about defilement complicatedly correspond to certain aspects of primitive social structures (and how they serve to reinforce or sometimes modify those aspects). Among the few secular philosophical treatments of defilement, I should make particular mention of two works: the piquantly illuminating but laconic discussion in Nozick 1989; and the astutely probing reflections in Stump 2004.

the murderer of the former king Laius has not yet been apprehended or punished. (Unbeknownst to everyone in Thebes, of course, Oedipus himself is the murderer.) One's alertness to the defilement wrought by the presence of a heinous evildoer can be rooted in the Hellenistic tradition as much as in the Hebraic tradition.

What is common to those traditions, of course, is a belief in the supernatural. Defilement has generally been understood in those traditions as a magical property that arises because of the displeasure of God or a god. According to such an understanding, a devastating plague is the means by which a deity chastises a community for the inadequacy of its response to the vile misdeeds of someone within it who has contravened the deity's will. If the concept of defilement is to play a philosophically and morally respectable role in the purgative rationale for capital punishment, my exposition of that concept will have to move firmly away from these theistic superstitions. As this chapter has already emphasized, its focus will lie on moral principles and their implications rather than on the sulking of deities.

Before we turn to my secular account of defilement, we should note another germane feature of the passage from Morton. Although any philosophically and morally respectable account of defilement has to proceed by reference to moral principles rather than by reference to raw emotions, Morton is quite right to say that acts of extreme turpitude elicit feelings of revulsion in any ordinarily decent people who become aware of those acts. Such visceral reactions, indeed, are reflected in many of the adjectives that routinely get applied to iniquities: 'appalling', 'dreadful', 'shocking', 'repellent', 'disgusting', 'despicable', 'revolting', 'outrageous', 'dismaying', 'rebarbative', 'sickening', 'shuddersome', and so forth. I have used, and will continue to use, such adjectives. However, they should be construed as referring to the extreme gravity of certain actions rather than to the emotional responses which those actions tend to evoke. The ethical bearings of extravagantly wicked modes of conduct are not determined by the reactions which such modes of conduct typically or always arouse. Those bearings are determined by the reaction-independent features of the conduct (including the outlooks with which the conduct is undertaken).[27] In fact, instead of trying to gauge the extravagant wickedness of any actions by ascertaining people's reactions to them, we should proceed in the opposite direction. That is, we can gauge the soundness of the moral sentiments of people by ascertaining whether they experience revulsion when confronted with actions that are extravagantly evil. If someone does not feel outraged and sickened in response to such actions, then his moral outlook is defective *pro tanto*.[28] Powerful emotions of outrage and disgust are appropriate precisely because the perpetrators of extravagantly wicked actions are

---

[27] Of direct pertinence here are my objections to relativism, subjectivism, and response-centred accounts of morality in Kramer 2009a, 30–46, 56–67.

[28] I here disagree with Nussbaum 2004, 163–71. Nussbaum believes that indignation, rather than disgust, is the emotion that should accompany outrage in response to terrible crimes. My remarks in the text, of course, do not in any way exclude the appropriateness of indignation as a reaction to such crimes.

morally responsible agents. Those emotions would not be appropriate if the destruction and suffering inflicted by such actions were inflicted instead by wild animals or
natural forces.

6.3.2. Paradigmatic cases

My account of defilement can unfold most smoothly if we have in mind a couple of
paradigmatic cases of extravagantly evil conduct. These sketches are not put forward
here as accurate summaries of real-life crimes, though the first of them is based fairly
closely on the iniquities perpetrated by Richard Ramirez in California, while the
second of them is based extremely loosely on the evils committed by Josef Fritzl in
Austria. (Heinous though Fritzl's evils are, they are not so heinous as to trigger the
purgative rationale for the death penalty. Hence, the actions recounted in the second
scenario below are not only significantly different from his misdeeds but also considerably worse. They roughly resemble some of the hideous 'medical' experiments
conducted under the direction of another Josef—Josef Mengele at Auschwitz.) The
vast majority of cases of extravagantly evil conduct involve multiple murders that
have been committed in especially vile ways; the first of my scenarios is just such a
case. By contrast, the second scenario is propounded here largely in order to indicate
that some conceivable cases of extravagantly evil conduct do not involve murders.

Two points should be highlighted at the outset. First, although every murder is
wrongful, and although every murder committed in the absence of extenuating circumstances is evil, most murders are not extravagantly evil. As has already been emphasized, the scope of the applicability of the purgative rationale for capital punishment is
cabined indeed. It encompasses very few of the murders that take place in any normal
year in this or that jurisdiction. Hence, the gruesomeness of the crimes recounted
below is not incidental or included gratuitously. Rather, extreme gruesomeness—or
extravagance in other respects, including the sheer numbers of victims who are severely
and deliberately harmed—is what sets apart the instances of evil conduct that trigger
the purgative rationale.

Secondly, the presentation of some paradigmatic cases of extravagantly evil actions is
important not only because it will facilitate my discussion of defilement, but also because
it will underscore the abiding possibility and occasional actuality of such cases. This point
should be emphasized because the properties that are constitutive of extravagantly evil
conduct—extreme gruesomeness and destructiveness, sadistic malice or heartlessness
or grotesque recklessness, and so forth—are all vague. Consequently, on the spectrum
between extravagantly evil behaviour and merely evil behaviour (or merely wrongful
behaviour), there are many borderline modes of wickedness that are neither determinately extravagant nor determinately non-extravagant. Furthermore, the very distinction
between the extravagant and the non-extravagant is itself vague at a higher-order level.
Hence, innumerable possible instances of evil are not determinately extravagant, just as
innumerable possible stretches of time during which some students await the results of

their examinations are not determinately lengthy. Whenever any instances of evil are not determinately extravagant, the purgative rationale for capital punishment does not apply. Borderline instances are all to be resolved against the imposition of the death penalty. However, we should scarcely conclude that no possible instances of conduct are extravagantly evil. Just as innumerable possible stretches of time during which some students await the results of their examinations are determinately lengthy, so too innumerable possible instances of wickedness are determinately extravagant. Many of those instances are not only determinate but also straightforward. To any such straightforward instances the purgative rationale for capital punishment is applicable. Thus, by orienting my discussion toward a couple of clear-cut cases of extravagantly evil conduct, this chapter can accentuate the import of the purgative rationale. My presentation of those cases will help to make clear that that rationale does carry major implications for the world at large. Although any indeterminacy is to be resolved against the sentencing of an offender to death, such sentencing is appropriate and indeed morally obligatory in connection with iniquities that are unmistakably extravagant—iniquities such as those recounted immediately below.

6.3.2.1. Richard's Case

After having taken up the worship of Satan for some years, Richard engages in a string of grisly murders over several months. Breaking into houses at night, he binds his victims and then rapes and tortures and mutilates them before slaughtering them. Some of them he decapitates, whereas others he strangles or shoots. His victims vary in age from infants to elderly women. Richard experiences intense sadistic pleasure as he rapes and tortures and mutilates them, and he derives even greater pleasure when he ultimately murders them. Their screams and terror fill him with exhilaration. He sometimes drinks the blood of his victims, and he usually consumes sundry parts of their bodies (often while they are still alive to witness his cannibalism). He gloatingly tells his victims what he intends to do to them, as he proceeds to make use of them and their bodies for his ghoulish gratification.

Not long after he has committed his thirteenth murder, Richard is identified and apprehended. Fleeing from his captors, he is eventually overpowered and is arrested and placed in prison. While he awaits his trial, he boasts with remorseless glee of his many acts of rape and torture and murder.

6.3.2.2. Joseph's Case

Unlike Richard, Joseph does not perpetrate any outright murders. However, he kidnaps several girls, ranging in age from seven to fourteen. He places each girl in a separate soundproof cell of an underground network of rooms beneath his home. He shackles each girl's torso firmly to fixtures in the wall, and, in order to avert any escapes, he amputates each girl's hands and each girl's legs above the knees. Joseph has some medical training and is therefore able to perform the amputations without killing any of his victims, but he uses no anaesthesia for the process. He is invigoratingly amused by the girls' screams and agony, and he feels a god-like sense of elation as he fundamentally reshapes their bodies. After he has conducted the amputations on each girl, he keeps her chained to the wall in her cell for many months. He feeds each of the girls twice a day, and he intermittently cleans each of them. For hours or even days at a time, however, each of Joseph's captives is left to sit amidst her own urine and excrement. In addition to visiting each girl daily for feeding, Joseph quite frequently visits each of them for sessions of rape and torture. He has abducted his victims precisely because he wishes to subject them to such sessions. He satisfies his overweening concupiscence with the girls, and he tortures them both to gratify his sadistic impulses and to indulge his pseudo-scientific curiosity concerning the reactions of human beings to severe pain. Day after day for many months, the girls undergo these horrible sessions with no glimmer of hope for an end to their bondage. Even while not undergoing rape and torture, they with their mutilated bodies spend their time in the grim loneliness and squalor of their dungeons.

A repairman on a professional visit to Joseph's house notices that something very strange has been occurring in the basement, and he summons the police. After a short investigation, the police uncover Joseph's appalling mistreatment of his captives. Though Joseph has not killed any of them, he has refrained only because they would no longer have served his sadistic and lascivious purposes if they had been dead. In any event, although he has not killed them, he has ruined their bodies and their lives in the most ghastly fashion. Having been mutilated by him and immured by him in their cells for more than a year, the girls emerge from their travails as physically and psychologically shattered remnants of human beings.

6.3.3. Defilement and purgation

The crimes recounted in Richard's Case and Joseph's Case are paradigmatic specimens of extravagantly evil conduct, in that they are straightforwardly classifiable as such specimens by virtually everyone who acknowledges the possibility of the occurrence of extravagantly evil conduct at all.[29] Neither Richard nor Joseph has committed the worst atrocities imaginable—since the sheer numbers of victims could have been augmented—but each of them has perpetrated grotesque iniquities that besmirch the moral standing of the community in which each of them respectively abides. Though there is not any collective responsibility for the original iniquities themselves (in the absence of any facts that would implicate people who were acting as public officials), there is collective responsibility for the continued existence of each of the perpetrators. Because there is collective responsibility of the latter kind,

---

[29] Worth noting here is that the property of paradigmaticity is not equivalent to the property of determinacy (Kramer 2009a, 90–101). The former property is epistemic, whereas the latter is ontological. A paradigmatic instance of extravagantly evil conduct is something that is uncontroversially or straightforwardly classifiable as an instance of such conduct. Evil behaviour that is *determinately* extravagant might or might not be *paradigmatically* so, since its determinacy—unlike its paradigmaticity—does not depend on whether its status as extravagantly wicked is obvious to everybody (or virtually everybody) who is competent to judge that status.

and because the continued existence of Richard or Joseph defiles any community which bears that responsibility, such a community is under a moral obligation to resort to capital punishment.

Why is the continued existence of Richard or Joseph defiling? That is, why does the continued existence of either of them taint the moral posture of the community concerned? On the one hand, if Richard or Joseph were allowed to live without being punished in any significant way, the blemish on the relevant community's moral standing would be manifest. Richard's or Joseph's impunity would be grossly at odds with the equality and human dignity of his victims, and would thus be grossly at odds with any aspiration of a community to embody an upright moral order. Such a state of affairs would also flagrantly clash with other morally worthy objectives (such as deterrence and incapacitation and denunciation) that can legitimately be pursued through the imposition of reasonable punishments. On the other hand, as the preceding chapters of this book have argued, neither retributivistic ideals nor any of the other commonly invoked aims of punishment can justify the use of the death penalty. If Richard and Joseph are each sentenced to imprisonment in supermaximum conditions of solitary confinement for hundreds of years without parole, then the ideals of retributivism and the other commonly invoked aims of punishment will have been fulfilled. In what sense, then, would the continued existence of Richard or Joseph be defiling? If the continued existence of each of them (in conditions of supermaximum detention) does not contravene any of the ideals or aims just mentioned, then what ethical considerations does it contravene?

To discern the answers to these questions, we have to take account of the distinctiveness of the purgative rationale. According to the traditional understanding of that rationale in ancient Israel and Greece, a purgative execution is carried out to rectify the relationship between a community and an external being (God or some god). In that respect, the purgative rationale differs saliently from each of the standardly proffered justifications of capital punishment. Retributivism, for example, concerns the relationships—of human equality and moral accountability—that prevail within a community. Of course, its egalitarian ideal embraces all human beings (and, indeed, any other possible moral agents); but retributivists concentrate on the use of punishments to effectuate that ideal within the boundaries of each jurisdiction, to ensure that the long-term and transitory members of a community are governed by relationships of basic equality and moral responsibility. Similarly, the proponents of the various consequentialist theories of punishment have sought to promote the realization of certain desiderata (deterrence, incapacitation, denunciation) within each jurisdiction. To be sure, those proponents believe that their respective theories recount the proper bases for punishments in all societies governed by liberal-democratic regimes. However, the schedule of the punishments required under each of those theories is jurisdiction-specific. Instead of being based on the relationships between a particular jurisdiction J and anything external, the appropriate levels of the punishments in J under each of the consequentialist theories are determined by the peculiarities of J's circumstances.

The purgative rationale for the death penalty is quite different. On the one hand, as has already been stressed, no philosophically and morally respectable elaboration of that rationale can appeal to any relationship between a community and some deity. On the other hand, such an appeal would be patently superfluous as well as preposterously misconceived. Instead of being focused on the relationship between a community and a wrathful divinity, my secular exposition of the purgative rationale is focused on the relationship—a normative relationship—between each community and the rest of humanity. Central to that focus is the extravagance of the atrocities committed by the people to whom the purgative rationale applies. In other words, central to my focus is the very property that brings those atrocities within the scope of the purgative rationale.

When iniquities are on the scale of those perpetrated by Richard or Joseph, they bespeak not only utter contempt for particular individuals and for the moral order of the community in which the iniquities occur, but also utter contempt for basic human capacities and thus for humankind as a whole. Contempt of the latter sort, whereby helpless and innocent members of humankind are repeatedly subjected to destruction and excruciating pain for the sake of one's own twisted purposes, is what a secular rendering of the purgative rationale should recognize as depravity. Such depravity, embodied by Richard or Joseph, poses an affront to humankind so long as either of them remains alive. That depravity therefore taints the relationship between Richard's community or Joseph's community and the rest of humanity. Removing the taint in each case requires terminating the existence of Richard or Joseph.

6.3.3.1. A first query: humankind as a whole?

Someone might object that the extravagance of the evils committed by Richard or Joseph bespeaks utter contempt not for humankind as a whole but for a portion of humankind. After all, every one of Richard's victims and Joseph's victims is female. Most other serial killers likewise principally target women (especially prostitutes) or homosexual men. Similarly, the Nazis perpetrated their atrocities chiefly against Jews and gypsies and Slavs and homosexuals, and the Khmer Rouge concentrated their ferocity primarily on intellectuals and urban dwellers. Given as much, someone might maintain that the depravity of Richard or Joseph pertains to females rather than to all of humanity, and that the depravity of other heinous evildoers is also typically circumscribed.

Even if this objection were correct, it would not undermine the purgative rationale for capital punishment. An ethical blot on the relationship between Richard's or Joseph's community and all females would in itself be a very grave matter. Still, the posited objection is unsustainable. Though the crimes committed by Richard or Joseph do especially blight the relationship between each man's community and all females, those crimes also blight the relationship between each man's community and the rest of humanity as a whole. What should have kept Richard and Joseph from committing their atrocities are the very features of the victims—most notably the capacity of each of them to experience intense pain and the status of each of them

as an agent with ends of her own—that are characteristic of human beings generally. (Of course, as Chapter 3 has prominently remarked, not every human being
is possessed of the capabilities of a reflective agent. However, those capabilities are
characteristic of human beings in that every normal member of the human species
does possess them.) By going ahead with their monstrous crimes, Richard and Joseph
have demonstrated their wholesale disdain for those features of human beings in a
deeply grotesque fashion. They have thereby demonstrated their wholesale disdain
for human beings generally, even while they have also evinced a special animosity
toward females.

Much the same can be said about the Nazis and about others who have engaged in
depravedly evil behaviour. Although the Nazis' iniquities were indeed crimes against
specific groups (as well as against particular individuals, naturally), they were also
crimes against humanity and were rightly classified as such at Nuremberg. Through
the extravagant savagery and abundance of those iniquities, the Nazis manifested their
unremitting contempt for basic features of people—again, the vulnerability of people
to excruciating pain and the competences of people as reflective agents—that unite the
members of humankind as a species. When the Nazis repeatedly treated their victims'
screams of agony at best as matters of indifference and at worst as stimuli for the infliction of further torment, they showed themselves to be sweepingly disdainful of the very
properties of human beings that should elicit concern and respect. Precisely owing to
the sheer outlandishness of their displays of cruel brutality, those displays were offences
not only against particular individuals and certain religious or ethnic groups but also
against humanity. The scale and outrageousness of those brutal actions made them
crimes against human dignity as well as against particular possessors of that dignity. (Of
course, unlike the crimes committed by Richard and Joseph, the atrocities committed
by the Nazis were undertaken on behalf of the German nation. Hence, whereas neither
Richard's community nor Joseph's community is collectively responsible for Richard's
or Joseph's horrible misdeeds, the German nation was collectively responsible for the
Nazis' iniquities. However, the chief point made in this paragraph is independent of any
ascription of collective responsibility for those iniquities. It is a point that assimilates the
Nazis' atrocities to the odious crimes of Richard and Joseph.)

6.3.3.2. A second query: capital punishment for mere contempt?

As has been contended, the continued existence of Richard or Joseph is defiling
because each of them has demonstrated his thoroughgoing contempt for humankind.
Somebody might object that a display of contempt for humankind is not a sufficient
basis for the imposition of any serious punishment, much less for the imposition of the
death penalty. After all, a person can display contempt for human beings *en masse* by
railing against them in the manner of King Lear. Although such fulminations might
warrant an arrest for a breach of the peace, they would scarcely amount to a capital
offence. Thus, a critic of my arguments might maintain, I have not correctly specified
any basis for subjecting Richard and Joseph (or anyone else) to capital punishment.

An objection along those lines is plainly misconceived. For expository conven-ience, let us concentrate here on Richard. If he is executed, the proper ground for putting him to death is that his numerous vile acts of rape and torture and murder have made his life a moral blight upon the relationship between his community and the rest of humanity. His life has cast such a blight because his crimes in their cumula-tive magnitude and ferocity constitute a repudiation of humankind through mon-strous behaviour rather than merely through intemperate ranting. In other words, my references to Richard's contempt for humankind are not specifying a detachable basis for the execution of Richard—a basis that could somehow be separated from the outrageous actions that embody it. Rather, my references to his contempt are specifying the full significance of those actions. His rapes and murders and acts of torture are obviously wicked crimes against particular individuals, but they are also cumulatively something more. When I attribute to him an attitude of thoroughgo-ing disdain for precious and fundamental features of human beings, I am indicating what the something more is. With that attribution, I am indicating that his crimes are crimes against humanity. Such an attribution hardly implies that an attitude of thoroughgoing disdain in itself—in abstraction from hideous crimes that give effect to it—would be enough to warrant the execution of Richard. His execution is indeed warranted, but only because his contempt for humankind takes the form of profuse and horrendous acts of violence.

6.3.3.3. A third query: whence the community's involvement?

As has been seen, a key to the purgative rationale for capital punishment is that some arrays of offences are so overwhelmingly vile that they cumulatively lead to a tainting of the relationship between the offender's community and the rest of humanity. Yet, as has also been observed, a community is not collectively responsible for the perpe-tration of crimes such as those committed by Richard and Joseph. (In that respect, their crimes differ from the atrocities committed by the Nazis.) Now, given that there is no collective responsibility for the perpetration of those crimes, a critic might query why the *community's* relationship with the rest of humanity can get morally tarnished by them. Why does not any moral blot extend only to the relationship between the *offender* and the rest of humanity? Why, for example, can Richard's murders and rapes and mutilations lead to a tainting of the relationship between his community and the rest of humankind? Why is Richard not the only party whose relationship with the rest of humankind has been sullied by his terrible crimes?

These questions highlight the importance of distinguishing between different stages at which a community bears responsibilities, and also the importance of specifying the contents of those responsibilities quite precisely. At the stage when Richard is com-mitting his initial crimes, the legal-governmental system of his community owes a general responsibility to any members of the public to take all reasonable steps to pro-tect them from invasions of their legal rights by others. Unless the officials of the legal-governmental system have been remiss in some significant way, the success of Richard in carrying out his initial crimes does not amount to a breach of the responsibility just mentioned. An obligation to take all reasonable steps to keep citizens safe from invasions of their legal rights can be fulfilled even though some serious invasions do occur. Reasonable steps do not include the suffocating levels of surveillance and security that are characteristic of a repressive tyranny. (Moreover, even the stifling measures adopted by such a tyranny are not guaranteed to avert all serious crimes. Murders by private individuals occur in China and Iran as well as in liberal democracies.) If Richard is deftly clever and ruthless in evading apprehension, and if the authorities have therefore not been significantly remiss in failing to arrest him after his early iniquities, even the occurrence of his later atrocities can be consistent with the authorities' fulfilment of their public-safety responsibilities. It can also be consistent, accordingly, with the community's fulfilment of its responsibilities to the rest of humanity. When Richard is eventually apprehended, however, the situation has changed. Although the community has not become collectively responsible for his heinous crimes, and although (*ex hypothesi*) the community's legal-governmental system has not breached its public-safety obligations, the community through that system has now become collectively responsible for the subsequent handling of Richard's case. His fate, including the very continuation of his existence, is now in the community's hands. Thus, although his crimes initially tarnish only *his* relationship with the rest of humankind—and his more specific relationships with his own community and with the individual victims of his outrages—the relationship between his *community* and the rest of humankind is now at stake.

Richard's community is morally obligated to preserve his life and basic well-being during the full time requisite for a fair trial and for any credible appeals, which might extend over quite a long period. Throughout that period, the community's legal-governmental officials are not morally entitled (or legally entitled, in any liberal democracy) to put Richard to death. Throughout that period, the relationship between his community and the rest of humanity is untarnished by the preservation of his life. When a fair trial and all the non-frivolous appeals have ended with the authoritative ascertainment of his guilt, however, his community through its legal-governmental system is morally obligated to terminate his life. Thereafter, the continuation of his life—beyond the time required for a legally prescribed execution—is something that defiles the relationship between his community and the whole of humanity. His continued existence thenceforward is an affront to humankind.

The community's relationship with the rest of humanity is now at stake because the community through its legal-governmental system plays a decisive role in continuing or discontinuing Richard's life. It plays a decisive role in determining whether resources are to be devoted to prolonging or terminating his existence. Note that the devotion of resources to the prolongation of his existence will be especially heavy if Richard is subjected to highly restrictive confinement as an alternative to being executed. As was remarked in Chapter 4, supermaximum imprisonment is very expensive. Hence, if Richard is sentenced to such imprisonment as an alternative to the death penalty—because it is perceived as the only mode of confinement for him that will preserve the safety of other prisoners, or because it is perceived as the only humanely available alternative to the death penalty that is suitably harsh—his community will be expending a particularly large quantity of resources on the continuation of his existence. In so doing, it will be expending a particularly large quantity of resources on the persistence of a state of affairs that sullies its relationship with the rest of humanity. Hence, the imposition of a severe sanction that falls short of the death penalty is not a means whereby a community can remove the blight that lies on its relationship with the rest of humankind. On the contrary, the infliction of such a sanction is an especially costly measure for keeping in existence the cause of that blight. (My point in this paragraph does not depend on any claims about the source of the funding that will be devoted to the preservation of Richard's life. Even in the very unlikely event that Richard is wealthy with a large savings account that can be seized for the purpose of defraying the costs of his imprisonment, the legal-governmental system that confines him is determining that those funds are to be used for keeping him alive rather than for terminating his life or for other purposes. Hence, even if Richard's assets are sufficient to cover the expenses of his detention, his community through its legal-governmental system is directly implicated in the continuation of his existence. His community makes the key decisions concerning the disposition of those assets. Consequently, the preservation of his life defiles not only his own relationship with humankind but also that of his community. Additionally worth noting here is that the discussion in this paragraph does not presuppose that a practice of executing vile offenders is less costly per person than a practice of subjecting such offenders to lifelong imprisonment. In a legal-governmental system with an apparatus of capital appeals as elaborate as that in the United States, the former practice can be more expensive per person than the latter. However, the greater expenditures by a community under the former practice are for the purpose of terminating the lives of vile offenders, whereas the expenditures by a community under the latter practice are oriented toward the sustainment of those lives.)

We can now see why banishment or ostracism is not a suitable alternative to capital punishment for offenders who have committed extravagantly heinous crimes. Under some traditional renderings of the purgative rationale for capital punishment, admittedly, banishment is on a par with the death penalty as an apposite punitive response to extravagantly wicked conduct. In the opening scene of *Oedipus Rex*, for example, we are explicitly told by Creon that those sanctions are equally fitting as means of overcoming the defilement of a community that has ensued from the presence of a horrible murderer. Under my own secular rendering of the purgative rationale, however, banishment cannot ever aptly serve as a substitute for the death penalty. Banishment can result in a vast physical distance between a defilingly evil offender and his community, but it does not result in any comparable normative distance. After all, the whole process of exiling such an offender will have allocated a considerable quantity of resources to the prolongation of his life. It is an officially chosen route for continuing rather than terminating his existence. Accordingly, it is an officially chosen route for perpetuating an affront to humanity. When a defilingly evil offender is exiled rather than executed, the blight on the relationship between his community and the rest of humanity persists. (Of course, if such an offender is banished to a place where he will predictably die quickly, the point made in this paragraph is not applicable. Banishment in such circumstances is itself a mode of execution, and any resources expended on it are thus devoted to ending the life of the offender. Though a sanction of that type will probably be in contravention of the purgative rationale's prohibition on cruelty in methods of execution, it will not be at odds with the rationale's insistence on putting noxious offenders to death.)

6.3.3.4. A fourth query: why death?

My response to the foregoing query will undoubtedly induce some readers to broach yet another objection. Granting that terrible evils such as those committed by Richard or Joseph are cumulatively crimes against the whole of humanity, and granting that the relationship between humankind and Richard's or Joseph's community can become tainted by the aftermath of those crimes, somebody might nonetheless query why the death penalty is the uniquely appropriate punitive response to either man's misconduct. Why is the execution of Richard the only means of preventing or expunging his defilement of his community's moral standing? Suppose that the legal-governmental system in his community were to sentence Richard to multiple terms of lifelong imprisonment-without-parole in austere conditions of solitary confinement. As has already been noted, such a way of dealing with his iniquities would satisfy the ideals and concerns of retributivists, and—on highly plausible empirical assumptions—it would also contribute to the realization of the objectives of deterrence-oriented, incapacitative, and denunciatory accounts of punishment. While accepting that the purgative rationale has correctly adverted to the humankind-hating aspect of Richard's crimes as a dimension of them that exceeds the reach of retributivism or any of the other accounts of punishment just mentioned, somebody can still wonder why that aspect of his dastardly crimes cannot be satisfactorily handled by a sanction less severe than the death penalty. Suppose that the grim austerity of the conditions of Richard's imprisonment is explicitly imposed by the court in order to repudiate his contempt for humanity (rather than to further any other punitive objectives). Would not that intensification of the unpleasantness of his confinement be sufficient to avert or remove any stain on his community's relationship with humankind as a whole? After all, an intensifying measure of that sort would constitute his community's forceful rejection of his own repudiation of human dignity. Given that that measure would constitute a palpable disavowal of his hatred of humanity, why would it not be enough to prevent the defilement of his community? If it is enough, moreover, then the Minimal Invasion Principle requires that it be employed in lieu of the death penalty. As a milder sanction that is nevertheless satisfactory for the purpose of purgation, the intensification of the bleakness of Richard's imprisonment is to be favoured over capital punishment on the basis of fundamental liberal-democratic principles of political morality. Or so some readers may be disposed to contend.

To grasp how this latest query is to be rebutted, we should begin by noting that the purgative rationale's claims about the tarnishing of the relationship between an offender's community and the rest of humankind are not socio-psychological or anthropological propositions concerning what is likely to be demanded. Though popular sentiment has remained supportive of capital punishment in many of the countries where such punishment has been abolished, the purgative rationale does not rely on any suggestion that a community containing a loathsomely evil offender will be confronted with demands from overseas for his execution. There is no suggestion here, in other words, that the people or governments of other countries will be clamouring for Richard or Joseph to be put to death in order to remove the ethical stain that is constituted by either man's continuing presence. Any thesis to that effect would be empirically dubious and would in any event be irrelevant.

My claims about a blight on the relationship between Richard's or Joseph's community and the rest of humankind are straightforwardly ethical rather than socio-psychological. Whether or not the citizens and governments of other nations, if suitably well informed, would favour the execution of Richard or Joseph—that is, whether or not they would be inclined to press for the fulfilment of the obligation incumbent on Richard's or Joseph's community to carry out such an execution—the infliction of that sanction is essential for the removal of the aforementioned blight, which exists independently of what people think about it or about the proper way of dealing with it. For stylistic convenience here, let us concentrate again on Richard. Through the depravity of his monstrous crimes, he has manifested his hatred of humankind as well as of particular human beings. Although his grievous wrongs against his community and against his particular victims can be handled satisfactorily through lifelong imprisonment-without-parole in conditions of solitary confinement, his besmirching of the relationship between his community and humanity cannot similarly be rectified through the intensification of the drabness of his confinement or through any other punitive measure short of the death penalty. By adopting any such measure in lieu of an execution, his community would be allocating resources to the prolongation of his life. That point is crucial not only for a well-founded ascription of responsibility to the community (as has been argued), but also for a sound explanation of the impropriety of any punitive approach that would eschew the use of the death penalty against Richard. With the sheer extravagance of his array of iniquities, he has established that his life is antithetical to the dignity of humankind. He has set himself firmly against such dignity rather than in support of it, as he has committed atrocities which in their overweeningness are determinative of the ethical character of his whole life. Those atrocities vest his life with its horrible significance, for they ethically dominate the sundry other things that he has done. Having dedicated himself to the murderous destruction and perverse exploitation of features of people that are fundamentally characteristic of them as human beings, he has pitted his life against the nature of humanity generally. His life therefore stands as an affront to the dignity of humankind and as a blot on the relationship between humankind and his community, especially if his community is assigning large quantities of resources to the sustainment of his existence.

In short, because Richard has made his life a fierce repudiation of humanity through his monstrous exploits, his community will have placed itself in an ethically untenable dilemma if its legal-governmental system declines to sentence him to death. Either the humanity-repudiating dimension of his crimes will go entirely unpunished, or else it will be punished within an overall package of sanctions whereby the community apportions significant resources to the continuation of his life. In either case, his community will have failed to remove the taint that sullies its relationship with the rest of humanity. It will have reached an authoritative decision to keep Richard in existence and thus to preserve a life that constitutes a grotesque rebuff to humankind.

Given the character of the life that Richard has constructed for himself, his community is morally obligated to execute him. No one is ethically empowered to waive that obligation, for it is owed to the past, present, and future members of humanity at large. Although Richard has outrageously wronged some particular individuals, the ground for executing him is the outrageous wrong against humankind that is immanent in the evils which he has committed against the particular individuals. Because of the savagery and abundance of those evils, his life has become a horrific renunciation of humankind; accordingly, the continuation of his life is irreconcilable with his community's upholding of the dignity of humanity.

Of course, the obligation to impose capital punishment on Richard is susceptible to being overtopped in normative importance by countervailing ethical considerations. For example, my next chapter will discuss some procedural or administrative inequities that can militate against the use of capital punishment in certain contexts. Other countervailing ethical factors, too, can weigh heavily against the imposition of the death penalty in various circumstances. However, even when such factors do exceed in importance the moral obligation of a community to execute a defilingly evil offender, that latter obligation abides as such. Any failure to fulfil it is a persistent wrong against humankind.

Thus, unlike the commonly advanced rationales for the institution of capital punishment, the purgative rationale complies with the Minimal Invasion Principle. It calls for the application of the death penalty when and only when the termination of an offender's life is the sole means of rectifying the sullied relationship between the offender's community and humankind as a whole. In any such situation, sanctions that are less severe will not suffice to achieve the purgative purpose that is incumbent on the community.

6.3.3.5. A fifth query: a role for repentance?

As has been contended, a key to the purgative rationale for capital punishment is that the scale and depravity of an offender's hideous crimes can invest his entire life with a humanity-hating significance. His other doings, be they commendable or deplorable or neutral, are ethically overwhelmed by those hideous crimes. Some readers may therefore wonder whether the purgative rationale leaves any room for life-changing repentance—namely, repentance that might render inappropriate the application of the death penalty to an offender for whom such a penalty would otherwise be appropriate. If an offender is guilty of a string of grotesquely brutal crimes, can the defilingness of his life be overcome through genuine and lasting contrition on his part?

The topic of repentance is very complex, and any full-scale treatment of it lies well beyond the scope of this book.[30] However, several observations here are germane. First, even if it were unproblematically true that a defilingly evil criminal can in principle become genuinely repentant and thereby cease to be defilingly evil, this point would be fully consistent with my effort to justify the use of capital punishment in certain cases. After all, most of the criminals who fall under the purgative rationale for such punishment do not evince attitudes that could credibly be characterized as penitent. On the contrary, most such criminals are gloatingly boastful and defiant in their public and private pronouncements about their iniquities. Hence, even if there were no other difficulties surrounding the proposition that a defilingly evil offender can reinvest his life with some positive worth by becoming durably contrite and by giving effect to his contrition through his behaviour, the practical importance of the purgative justification of the death penalty would be only slightly diminished. Nearly all of the executions required under that justification in abstraction from any considerations of repentance would still be required after such considerations are fully taken into account. In most cases, there is no repentance to be taken into account; in most cases, defilingly evil offenders exhibit no traces of remorse.

Secondly, the very notion of repentance when applied to anyone responsible for numerous acts of appalling turpitude is in fact deeply problematic. This second observation is not a psychological claim about the unlikelihood that anyone responsible for such acts will ever undergo durable feelings of contrition.[31] Nor am I yet broaching the epistemic limitations that make so formidable the task of ascertaining whether any expressions of such feelings are sincere or not. Instead, this second observation is a grave moral doubt. Repentance consists not only in feelings of profound remorse and humility, but also in conduct that gives effect to those feelings by atoning adequately for the wicked misdeeds that have occasioned them. As Antony Duff writes: '[U]ndertaking a penance, giving this outward and materially burdensome expression to the painfully burdensome recognition of one's own wrongdoing, is a way of taking the matter seriously; it part[ly] *constitutes* the repentant sinner's earnest repentance' (Duff 2003, 299, emphasis in original). In regard to monstrously evil crimes, however, there might well be nothing—short of unflinchingly abject submission to capital punishment—that would amount to a satisfactory form of atonement. This point is especially clear with reference to political despots who have sent millions of innocent people to

---

[30] For a brief but insightfully suggestive discussion of repentance, see Stump 2004, 49–52. I do not entirely agree with the conclusions which Stump tentatively reaches, but she asks the right questions.

[31] I of course agree with that psychological claim, but it is not the point which I am currently making.

their deaths. Apart from abasedly voluntary submission to the death penalty, nothing on the part of Hitler or Goebbels or Stalin or Pol Pot could have come close to atoning for the frenzied ruination of millions of innocent lives. In that respect, the monstrousness of each of those men was beyond repentance. Even in connection with atrocities on a smaller scale, moreover, the sheer feasibility of repentance (as a moral matter) is exceedingly dubious. In the extremely unlikely event that Richard or Joseph comes to feel profoundly and lastingly contrite, the attainment of full repentance by either of them will require his giving effect to his remorse through some mode of conduct that will constitute his atonement for his vile crimes. Yet in each case the crimes are so overweeningly horrific that no mode of conduct other than the abject undergoing of an execution could satisfactorily atone for them. The very features of the crimes that bring them within the purgative rationale for capital punishment—their extravagant vileness and profuseness—also place them collectively beyond repentance. Only the voluntary undergoing of an execution would adequately give effect to genuine penitence on the part of Richard or Joseph. Anything less would make a mockery of the devastation that each man has so depravedly wrought, and a mockery of the contempt for humankind which the wreaking of the devastation has manifested.

Thirdly, given the depravity of the crimes that trigger the purgative rationale for capital punishment, the epistemic difficulties pertaining to the occurrence of genuine repentance are huge. One problem, of course, resides in the impediments to a court's differentiating between utterances of contrition that are sincerely felt and utterances of apparent contrition that are craftily articulated. In the rare cases when defilingly evil offenders give voice to contrite-sounding utterances at all, the obstacles to ascertaining their veracity are considerable—notwithstanding that the courts rely on expert psychologists for assistance. Nearly as important, however, is the problem of self-deception. Even if we leave aside the moral impossibility of an offender's adequately atoning for his grotesque atrocities while remaining alive, any putative feelings of remorse experienced by such an offender are apt to be products of his own wishful thinking induced by the pressures on him to show contrition. For example, the ostensible penitence displayed by Albert Speer in the aftermath of the downfall of the Third Reich was probably in large part a mixture of mendacity and self-deception (Fest 2001). Someone with mental processes that lead to his perpetration of atrocities is hardly likely to be an astute judge of his own subsequent reflections on what he has done. Coming from such a person, then, even sincere utterances of remorse are not really trustworthy.

Fourthly, despite the preceding three observations, the purgative rationale for capital punishment does leave a bit of room for the efficacy of repentance. In particular, there can be some room in a case where the extravagantly evil conduct of someone has occurred on only a single occasion rather than on multiple occasions over an extended period. On the one hand, a massacre on a single occasion can be sufficiently grave (in its motivations and scale) to invest with negative worth the life of anyone who has perpetrated it. Its immensity makes it definitive of the tenor—the profoundly humanity-hating tenor—of the perpetrator's whole life. When someone has carried out such an atrocity, the sustainment of his life will sully the relationship between his community and humankind as a whole. On the other hand, if the person in question has not previously or thereafter committed any iniquities, he might be able to redeem himself through genuine and perdurable repentance.

Consider, for example, the situation of Timothy McVeigh. Although he had engaged in some low-level criminality before he murdered 168 people by blowing up a federal office building in Oklahoma in 1995, and although he had for quite some time held to a dangerously paranoid view of the federal government in the United States, he had not theretofore done anything really evil. Now, McVeigh in fact remained stonily unrepentant throughout his trial and the subsequent period leading up to his execution. Let us counterfactually suppose, however, that he had become profoundly remorseful in the aftermath of his terrible crime. Having learned of all the deaths (including the deaths of many children) that he had brought about, McVeigh might have finally recognized the poisonousness of the outlook to which he had long adhered. He might have shed his paranoid fantasies about the government and his anti-Semitism and his other unsavoury beliefs, and he might have resolved firmly to do his utmost to disabuse other people of the vile misconceptions to which he had succumbed. He might have indicated that he was fully ready to accept the death penalty as a just sanction for his iniquity, but that he was also prepared to dedicate a lifelong term of imprisonment to warning others against the fascist ideology that had beguiled him. If the criminal-justice authorities could have satisfied themselves concerning the genuineness and lastingness of his repentance, they would have been well advised—in these circumstances, which are markedly different from the actual circumstances of his behaviour—to commute his death sentence to a term of lifelong incarceration. Horrendous though his act of mass murder was, he could have reinvested his life with positive value through genuine repentance. Because his perpetration of an appalling atrocity was confined to one occasion, genuine repentance on his part could have separated that atrocity from the rest of his life sufficiently to render the purgative rationale for capital punishment inapplicable.

6.3.3.6. A sixth query: difficult backgrounds and extenuation

Does the purgative rationale leave any room for taking into account the dire backgrounds of some defilingly evil offenders, for purposes of extenuation? On the one hand, many such offenders come from normal families in which they were not subjected to any special hardships as youngsters. Hence, even if the answer to the question just broached were robustly affirmative, the purgative rationale would still call for the imposition of the death penalty in quite a few cases. On the other hand, some defilingly evil offenders (such as Charles Manson) have indeed come from troubled backgrounds. Consequently, this question about extenuation and the aetiology of monstrousness does have to be addressed. Though this book does not aim to specify the ambit of the purgative rationale in fine detail, a general delineation of that ambit has to include a treatment of this topic.[32]

Like the matter of repentance, the matter of the extenuative effects of offenders' backgrounds is a large issue that can only be touched upon here. Its ramifications extend well beyond the purgative rationale for capital punishment, but my present (very brief) discussion will ponder only the bearing of this issue on the justifiability of executing the monstrous offenders whose crimes are of the sort which the purgative rationale covers. When the sentence for such an offender is pronounced, should it be lightened if the offender has indeed grown up in the travails of terrible circumstances? In other words, should the purgative rationale be deemed inapplicable to a vile criminal if his perpetration of ghastly crimes can plausibly be attributed in part to his having emerged from such travails?

6.3.3.6.1 *General inflexibility*

Although there are some exceptions to the inflexibility of the purgative rationale on this point, the answer to each question above is generally negative. Whatever may be the extenuative effects of an offender's dire background in a less serious case, the extenuative effects in cases that trigger the purgative rationale for the death penalty are typically nil. In any case of the latter kind, the crimes that have been committed are depravedly brutal and devastating. The mentality that leads anyone to perpetrate such crimes is monstrous. Albeit a cruel and abusive upbringing undoubtedly makes the development of such a mentality more likely than does a kind and supportive upbringing, the increased likelihood amounts to a (fairly weak) tendency rather than an irresistible impetus. Heinous offenders have played major roles in forming their own characters, even though they have of course done so within the constraints and pressures of their environments.[33] For some such offenders, those constraints and pressures have been hellish. Any community is under a general moral obligation to take all reasonable steps to avert or eliminate such deplorable conditions, not only because of their criminogenicity but also because of their intrinsic wrongness. (Accordingly, opponents of capital punishment are quite mistaken insofar as they believe that the imposition of such punishment 'sends the message that society bears no responsibility for the wrongdoer's situation and hence no obligation to improve it' [Kahan 1999, 44].) Still, most of the people who grow up in harrowing conditions do not become iniquitous murderers and torturers, and most of the people who do become iniquitous murderers and torturers have not hailed from egregiously bad backgrounds. At lower levels of criminality, where transgressions can sometimes be

---

[32] Among the discussions of this topic in debates over the death penalty and other sanctions (though not over the purgative rationale specifically, of course) are Bedau 2002, 8; Buss 1997; Dolinko 1992, 1648–9, 1654–6; Hampton 1992, 1698–9; Haney 1995; Markel 2009, 1193–4; Moore 1995, 636–7, 649; Murphy 1973, 231–43; Nussbaum 2004, 167–8; Primorac 1982, 147–8; Reiman 1985, 131–3; Reiman 1998, 125–8; Steiker 2005, 766–8; Stolz 1983, 168–9; Sunstein and Vermeule 2005b, 852–4; Van den Haag 1985a, 167–9; Weiler 1978, 316–18.

[33] I advance these remarks from the perspective of a compatibilist.

intelligible though wrongful responses to desperate circumstances, facts about the dismayingly bad backgrounds of some offenders should in certain cases be treated as mitigating considerations. By contrast, at the level of extravagant turpitude that would warrant the imposition of the death penalty under the purgative rationale, there is usually no comparable room for leniency. However arduous the conditions of an offender's upbringing may have been, his perpetration of grotesque murders and tortures is an affront to humanity. As the offender performs rebarbative crimes with glee or indifference while his victims scream in agony, the horror of his atrocities is not lessened by any wrongs that may have been committed against him in the past. His wholesale contempt for the features of human beings that militate so powerfully against his wicked actions is monstrous, even if he has formed his depraved outlook partly in reaction to ordeals which he himself has undergone in his youth. In its inflexibility on this point, the purgative rationale for capital punishment concurs with the retributivism of Michael Moore, who complains as follows about the conde-scension and moral torpor involved in excessive indulgence toward criminals:

We invent for the wrongdoers a set of excusing conditions that we would not tolerate for a moment in ourselves. When [virtuous people] transgress, [they] know how ill it lies to 'excuse' themselves by pointing to their own childhood or past, their lack of parental love, their need for esteem, and other causes. Virtuous people do not use the childish 'something made me do it' because they know that that denies their essential freedom in bringing about some harm. They know that they did it, chose to do it, caused though that choice surely was by factors themselves unchosen. Yet we cannot stand to apply to criminals the same standard of responsibility that we apply to ourselves because we cannot stand to acknowledge that there is such a thing as evil in the world—and, worst of all, that it is not 'inhuman' but a part of creatures not so different from ourselves. Lack of anger at criminals, if it does not represent simple indifference to the sufferings of others, may represent our self-deception about the potential for evil in humanity. [Moore 1995, 649, citation omitted]

Interestingly, Sarah Buss, who favours an expansive view of the circumstances under which criminals should be absolved of blame for their wrongdoing, largely agrees with Moore and with the purgative rationale in her remarks on the worst offenders:

Most [serial killers] are men who derive intense sexual pleasure from doing things to/with human bodies that the rest of us find revolting. If anyone is sick, then these men are. Yet does their illness necessarily exempt them from blame? Most juries have thought otherwise. And it seems to me that, from a moral point of view, they are correct. After all, there is no good reason to think that most of these men were incapable of restraining themselves when they committed their crimes. It seems, rather, that they simply did not *want* to restrain themselves... [W]hat is truly abnormal about these people is the content of their desires, not the degree to which they were capable of exercising self-control when they committed their crimes.[34]

---

[34] Buss 1997, 369 n 53, emphasis in original. For a similar view of psychopaths, see Morton 2004, 74–6. For a slightly more indulgent (though largely non-committal) view, see Milo 1984, 60–3, 77.

Buss's remarks raise an issue—the issue of mental illness—to which we shall return shortly. For the moment, the key point is that defilingly evil offenders are reflective agents rather than automatons. Having formed their profoundly evil characters within the limits of their genes and their environments, they are rightly held fully responsible for their heinous crimes against humanity.

6.3.3.6.2. Some exceptions

Despite the general inflexibility of the purgative rationale, there are some exceptions to the proposition that offenders who commit monstrously evil crimes are to be held responsible by being subjected to the death penalty. Among the main considerations that support the inflexibility of the purgative rationale is the role of each offender in forming his own character within the confines of genetic and environmental factors. In some cases that are not utterly fanciful, however, offenders have not played any roles in forming their own monstrous characters. They are therefore not to be held fully responsible for the wicked crimes which they perpetrate. They have to be imprisoned in furtherance of public safety, of course, but they should not be executed.

Suppose for example that a law-abiding man with a normal temperament is involved in an automobile accident through no serious fault of his own. In the accident he suffers a severe concussion, and he lapses into a coma. When he emerges from the coma, his whole personality has changed dismayingly. He is now violently brutal and sadistic, whereas he was previously of a pacific disposition. Before long, he commits a number of savage rapes and murders, each of which involves cruel torture. Had he carried out those horrific crimes on the basis of inclinations developed through the course of his life, the death penalty would have been warranted under the purgative rationale. However, given that he has not in fact participated in the formation of his newly vile character, the death penalty is inappropriate for him. He cannot rightly be held responsible for the monstrous personality that has taken hold of him, even though the choices which he makes in the grip of that personality are indeed his choices. Thus, although he has become a sadistic thug and has committed terrible crimes accordingly, the purgative rationale for the death penalty is not applicable to him.

Other credible scenarios can illustrate this same point. For example, suppose that—instead of having been injured in an automobile accident—the man discussed in the preceding paragraph has innocently drunk a beverage into which somebody has slipped a personality-altering drug. As a result of ingesting the drug, the man lapses into a coma. When he emerges from the coma, he is a monstrous psychopath. If he goes on to commit some appalling crimes, the purgative rationale for capital punishment will not be applicable to him. As has been stated in the preceding paragraph, he cannot rightly be held responsible for a profoundly evil outlook that has become his through no fault of his own. Having found that outlook foisted upon him, he should not be subjected to the death penalty for the horrendous crimes which he perpetrates while in its sway.

Exceptions to the general inflexibility of the purgative rationale are very rare, but they are credibly possible. When someone has become a heinous psychopath because of changes in his brain induced entirely by some event(s) over which he has not been able to exercise any control, he cannot rightly be executed for the atrocities which he commits. He of course should be imprisoned for life on the basis of incapacitative considerations, but the focus on moral responsibility which the purgative rationale shares with retributivism is not pertinent in application to him. His crimes fall outside the ambit of the purgative rationale. Given the exceptional circumstances, the aetiology of his monstrousness is dispositive.

6.3.3.7. A seventh query: mental maladies and shortcomings

As has been suggested by the quotation from Buss, the problem of mental illness raises a few of the same issues of moral responsibility that are raised by the problem of offenders' backgrounds. A key point for the purgative rationale is that a monstrously psychopathic state of mind does not amount to an insane outlook in any sense that precludes moral responsibility. Undoubtedly, violent psychopathy is a serious mental aberration. However, although psychopaths generally lack empathy and feel no moral inhibitions, they are (reflectively though not affectively) aware of the dichotomy between right and wrong, and they are fully aware of the pain and terror which they inflict upon their victims. They have to be aware of the pain and terror in order to derive pleasure therefrom; they do not preposterously think that their victims are inanimate objects. Nor are such offenders automatons. As Buss rightly indicates, violent psychopaths choose to act upon their grotesque and strongly felt desires even though they are capable of restraining themselves (if only on prudential grounds). They are morally responsible for the atrocities which they perpetrate. As the psychologist Roy Baumeister affirms: '[Psychopaths] are not mentally ill in the usual sense. They function reasonably well in society, they are well in touch with reality, and their actions are freely chosen rather than being driven by compulsions or irresistible urges' (Baumeister 1997, 137).

6.3.3.7.1. Mistakes about harmfulness versus mistakes about morality

Of considerable importance for any discussion of this matter is a distinction between fundamental mistakes about the harmfulness of one's own conduct (or the conduct of one's associates) and fundamental mistakes about other non-normative features of the world or about moral principles.[35] If Herbert is so mentally deranged as to believe sincerely that the heads of other people are inanimate baubles that can be smashed or shot without the arousal of pain in anyone, and if many of his other beliefs about the effects of his own actions are similarly crazy, then he is devoid of moral responsibility

---

[35] This distinction is overlooked in Dolinko 1986, 589–90; and Nussbaum 2004, 165. For some remarks on a related though less nuanced distinction, see Milo 1984, 9–10, 31–3; Moore 1997, 676.

by virtue of insanity. If he shoots someone in the head or smashes someone's skull open with a hammer, then he should be detained indefinitely in a top-security facility for the violently insane but should not otherwise be punished. Even if he has wrought such havoc against several victims, his conduct does not fall within the purgative rationale for capital punishment. His outlook is insanely deranged rather than evil. He is extremely dangerous but not culpable—or, if he is culpable, his malice is that of a minor vandal rather than that of a murderer. When he causes the carnage that he does, he is not acting on the basis of any serious misapprehensions of moral principles. Instead, he is acting on the basis of some lunatically mistaken beliefs about the harmfulness of his own conduct.

By contrast, a murderous psychopath is finely attuned to the extreme harmfulness of his actions. As has been stated, he amply recognizes the pain and fear which his brutal crimes induce. He acts not on the basis of mistaken beliefs about the injuriousness of his misdeeds, but instead on the basis of gross misapprehensions of moral principles. He is reflectively aware of the contents of various moral principles, but affectively he takes them to be inapplicable to himself. He consequently rapes and tortures and murders people without compunctions, while he knows fully well the misery that he is causing. Like Antonio in Shakespeare's *The Tempest*, he feels not the deity of conscience in his bosom. The failings in his outlook are egregious errors of moral judgement, rather than a crazy blindness to the destructive impact of his actions on other people. He is not insane; he is defilingly evil. (Likewise defilingly evil rather than insane is a vicious bigot who tortures and murders various Jewish individuals because he believes that Jews are conspiring to take over the world. He acts on the basis of appalling errors of moral judgement and on the basis of preposterous mistakes about certain non-normative facts, but he is under no illusions about the injuriousness of his onslaughts.)

6.3.3.7.2. Mental retardation

Of course, the tidy dichotomy between the insanity of Herbert and the evil of a ruthless psychopath will be tested in reality by sundry intermediate cases. In those intermediate cases, errors about morality and errors about harmfulness can intertwine in complicated combinations. Especially problematic are some of the appalling crimes committed by malefactors who are mentally retarded (Blecker 2003, 296–7). On the one hand, many of the cases involving such malefactors are clear-cut, for sheer unintelligence is consistent with full responsibility for wickedness. A mentally retarded person who commits crimes akin to those of Richard or Joseph—with the sadism or heartlessness of Richard or Joseph—is rightly liable to be sentenced to death for crimes against humanity. On the other hand, some credibly possible cases involving mentally retarded offenders are less straightforward.

Suppose for example that a mentally retarded mother becomes convinced that her five children are possessed by demonic spirits and that the only way to keep them from going to Hell is to decapitate each of them. (This scenario is a variant of the actual case of Andrea Yates in Texas, who was mentally ill rather than retarded and who drowned her children instead of decapitating them.) When the mother does indeed decapitate her children, she has done so both on the basis of an outlandish error about the overall harmfulness of her actions and on the basis of an appalling error of moral judgement. Still, given that she would not have mistreated her children in any fashion if she had not fallen prey to her error about the overall harmfulness of decapitating them, and given that she has acted out of a desire (albeit a hideously warped desire) to secure the well-being of her children, her conduct falls outside the sway of the purgative rationale for capital punishment. She should be incarcerated for the rest of her life but should not be executed.

Suppose, however, that the scenario in the preceding paragraph were to be modified so that the mother has decapitated her five children not with the aim of sparing them from Hell but with the aim of sparing herself therefrom. She has heartlessly committed atrocities against them for her own selfish purposes.[36] Unless there are some substantial extenuating factors (such as her having been subjected repeatedly to vehement warnings and expostulations from a clergyman, as Andrea Yates was), her conduct falls within the ambit of the purgative rationale for capital punishment. Although she is of subnormal intelligence, and although she has proceeded under the influence of a staggering misconception about the presence of demonic spirits, she has not been under any illusions concerning the direly injurious impact of her beheadings on her children. She has acted solely in furtherance of her own perceived interests and not in furtherance of their interests. Her mental retardation is no bar to her full responsibility for her repellently evil conduct.

6.3.3.7.3. Mental illness

This chapter has already indicated that, if atrocities are committed by someone with a mental aberration that consists in egregious misapprehensions of moral principles, the atrocities are straightforwardly covered by the purgative rationale for capital punishment. No such aberration precludes full responsibility under that rationale. Some other serious mental maladies are different, however. They produce not only egregious misapprehensions of moral principles, but also major failings in a person's recognition of the harmfulness of his own behaviour. If failings of the latter sort are central to a mentally ill person's performance of actions that would ordinarily amount to extravagantly evil iniquities, then typically the person should be detained indefinitely in a top-security institution for the violently insane. Typically, that is, the person should be held to lie beyond the reach of the purgative rationale for capital punishment.

---

[36] Worth remembering here is that heartlessness need not involve a complete absence of qualms. See § 6.2.1.2.2 above.

We have seen that mentally retarded people who commit terrible crimes on the basis of preposterous errors in their perception of the injuriousness of their own behaviour should be imprisoned rather than executed. A partly parallel conclusion follows for people afflicted with serious mental illnesses who commit such crimes on the basis of such errors; those people should be detained in mental institutions rather than executed. This partial similarity between the mentally retarded and the mentally ill has been signalled by my scenario of the mother who decapitates her children, for—as was stated—that scenario is a variant of an actual situation involving a mentally ill woman in Texas.

Some mental illnesses are so debilitating, of course, that they completely disengage their sufferers from reality. As Michael Davis remarks: 'Some of the insane are so deranged that trying to communicate with them is like trying to communicate with the wind' (Davis 1996, 157). If anybody in the grip of such lunacy has somehow harmed others badly, he or she cannot rightly be held criminally responsible at all. However, even a serious mental illness that does not completely undo a person's grip on reality can result in his or her making fundamental mistakes about the damagingness of his or her own conduct. If the person is acting squarely under the influence of such mistakes when he or she commits outrageous misdeeds, then he or she should be treated as dangerously insane rather than as defilingly evil.

6.3.3.7.4. Insanity after conviction

Let us suppose that, after the conviction and sentencing but before the implementation of the sentence, Richard or Joseph becomes thoroughly insane. He altogether loses his engagement with reality and becomes an inarticulate madman (or a raving madman) with no sense of connection to his past life or indeed to anything else beyond his delusions. Suppose, for example, that he sits throughout the day with his hand tucked into his shirt across his chest under the firm conviction that he is Napoleon. His state of insanity goes well beyond the major errors of cognition that have plagued the mother in my scenario of the decapitated children. In accordance with the common expression, Richard or Joseph has 'lost his mind.' In such circumstances, the execution of Richard or Joseph should not go ahead. Under the purgative rationale, someone is properly liable to undergo the death penalty if and only if a fair trial can establish that the continuation of his existence defiles the relationship between his community and humankind. In the circumstances envisaged here, where Richard or Joseph has become thoroughly insane, he has permanently or temporarily ceased to exist as the person who carried out extravagantly evil atrocities. Thus, the implementation of his death sentence should permanently or temporarily be set aside.[37] What justifies the imposition of the death penalty under the purgative rationale is also what limits the scope of the rationale's applicability. When an offender properly sentenced

---

[37] Could the officials in a system of criminal justice legitimately seek to deprive monstrous offenders of their sanity, as an alternative to executing them? The reasons for a negative answer to this question are largely similar to the reasons for the illegitimacy of any punitive practice of torturing or mutilating monstrous prisoners. I expound those reasons at length in my forthcoming book on torture.

to death has completely lost his mind during the interval between the time of sentencing and the scheduled time of his execution, the justificatory basis for proceeding with the execution has permanently or temporarily vanished—just as it would have permanently vanished if the offender had died during that interval. In the absence of that justificatory basis, the purgative rationale is inapplicable. Consequently, until the offender recovers his sanity (if he ever does), he should not be executed but should instead be detained indefinitely in a top-security institution for the deranged.

6.3.3.8. An eighth query: failed attempts afresh

As this chapter has argued (in § 6.2.2.1.1), sadistic or heartless attempts to produce dreadfully harmful consequences can be evil whether or not the consequences ultimately ensue. Should we reach a similar conclusion about extravagantly evil conduct? If somebody repeatedly tries to bring about horrible massacres or other iniquities, and if his efforts repeatedly come to naught, do those efforts cumulatively fall within the sway of the purgative rationale? Suppose for example that a terrorist leader repeatedly sends out his underlings to blow up airplanes and trains and hotels. Because of the vigilance of the passengers and crew on the airplanes and trains, and because of the effectiveness of the security personnel at the hotels, each of the terrorist leader's plots is foiled. Apart from the underlings themselves, nobody is injured (much less killed) by any of the endeavours of the terrorist gang. If the terrorist leader is eventually apprehended and placed on trial, should he be subjected to the death penalty? He has repeatedly done his utmost to bring about mayhem and carnage among innocent people on a catastrophically large scale. His failure to produce such dire results has not been due to any want of determination and fanatical sedulity on his part. Through his persistent striving to engage in mass murder, he has exhibited his contempt for the features of human beings that should have dissuaded him from forming and pursuing his odious plots. Through the sheer extravagance of the multiple atrocities which he has sought to mastermind, he has manifested his profound contempt for humanity. Should he, then, be sentenced to death under the purgative rationale?

Now, as was stated in my earlier discussion of this matter, the present chapter is not the place for exploring at length the problem of moral luck or the more specific problem of criminal attempts. There is, in any event, no need for us to delve into either of those problems in any depth. As should be evident from my reply to the query about the prospect of executing people who have merely expressed sentiments of deep contempt for humankind (in § 6.3.3.2), the answer to each question in the preceding paragraph is negative. Although the conduct of the terrorist leader has been unmistakably evil, and although his accomplishment of his deadly aims would certainly have warranted the imposition of the death penalty under the purgative rationale, the thwarting of those aims is enough to bring his case outside the reach of that rationale. He should be imprisoned for life—perhaps in supermaximum conditions—but he should not be executed.

As has been emphasized in § 6.3.3.2, forceful displays of contempt for humanity are not themselves monstrously evil unless the displays have consisted in extravagantly malign actions that visit appalling harm upon other people. Railing repeatedly against humanity in the manner of Jacques in Shakespeare's *As You Like It* is not a monstrously evil mode of conduct; indeed, it is not per se evil at all. Although endeavouring repeatedly to perpetrate massacres in the manner of the terrorist leader depicted above is certainly an evil mode of conduct, it does not make his life defilingly evil unless some or all of the massacres have occurred. It exhibits contempt for humankind, but—unless some of the massacres occur—the contempt is not embodied in actions that visit appalling harm upon other people. Because such harm has not materialized, the relationship between the terrorist leader's community and the rest of humanity will not be vitiated by his being kept alive. Only when a humankind-hating attitude has been given effect through the infliction of carnage is it an element of some crimes against humanity. Unsuccessful attempts to commit those crimes exemplify such an attitude but do not produce any grievous harm. Their exemplification of that attitude is therefore not of the sort that is encompassed by the purgative rationale. Unless an offender's hatred of humankind has issued in evil actions that actually produce grievous harm on an extravagant scale, the purgative rationale is not triggered. As has been stressed in § 6.3.3.2, an attitude of hostility toward humankind that falls within the ambit of the purgative rationale is not separable from the appallingly harmful atrocities that embody it; it is the underlying tenor or significance of those atrocities. If an offender with his evil actions has not in fact managed to inflict any harm, there is no swath of ruination in which his contempt for humanity is immanent. Although an attitude of hostility toward humankind can of course exist in such circumstances—that is, although an attitude of that type can exist independently of the infliction of hideous harm—it does not then make the offender's life *defilingly* evil. Only when that attitude is immanent in dreadfully destructive conduct that embodies and effectuates it, can it lead to the defilement of the relationship between an offender's community and the rest of humankind.

Thus, although the terrorist leader with his bootless plots has behaved evilly to the point of manifesting contempt for humankind, he has not tainted the whole relationship between his community and the rest of humanity. Despicable though his outlook is, it has not taken effect in horrible consequences that would embody it and would thereby materially impugn the dignity—the basis for self-respect—of every member of humankind. Because no such consequences have ensued, the life of the terrorist leader is evil without being defilingly evil. Though he has striven to produce carnage on an odiously extravagant scale, his intentions and efforts have not brought about any actual carnage that would constitute a standing affront to humanity. For him, then, lifelong imprisonment rather than death is the morally requisite sanction.

6.3.3.9. A ninth query: jurisdictional complexities

My reference to the terrorist leader's community helps to highlight some of the jurisdictional complexities that surround the implementation of the purgative rationale for capital punishment. This chapter has repeatedly referred to the relationship between an offender's community and the rest of humankind because in a typical case the atrocities covered by the purgative rationale are committed within the jurisdiction of the community to which the perpetrator belongs as a citizen or resident. However, plainly, quite a few cases will depart from that typical pattern. Such departures are especially likely in a country (such as the United States) that is itself composed of multiple jurisdictions with separate sets of laws; but they can happen anywhere.

Outrages perpetrated by Middle Eastern terrorists are often marked by jurisdictional complexities, as they are frequently initiated far from the terrorists' own communities, and as their harmful effects are sometimes inflicted far from the locations in which the outrages have been initiated. Consider, for example, the complexities arising from the bombing of Pan Am Flight 103, which exploded over Lockerbie (Scotland) in 1988. Even in connection with crimes that do not partake of the labyrinthine international tangles of the Lockerbie bombing, moreover, the jurisdictional complications can be daunting. For example, the serial killer Ted Bundy committed his murders in at least six American states.

Because of these potential gnarls, my references to the communities of offenders should be understood along the following lines. In each particular case, any community with jurisdiction over the perpetration of some iniquities is morally obligated to take all reasonable steps (through its legal-governmental system) to ensure that anyone responsible for those iniquities is brought to justice. Such a community may be where some or all of the iniquities have been initiated; or where the ghastly effects of some or all of the iniquities have been felt; or where some person responsible for those iniquities normally resides; or where the aforementioned person holds his citizenship; or where that person has fled; or where the victims of the iniquities held their citizenship or normally resided. In an exceptionally complicated case, all of the roles just listed are filled by different communities. In a straightforward case, a single community fills each of those roles. At any rate, a community that does indeed have at least one of these connections (or some other special connection) to the offences or the offender is under a moral obligation to strive to bring the offender to justice.

If someone responsible for extravagantly evil crimes is within the territory of a community, then the reasonable steps to be taken are as they have been sketched in § 6.3.3.3. That is, the community through its criminal-justice system is morally obligated to undertake all reasonable endeavours to apprehend the offender and to subject him to a fair trial. He must also be provided with opportunities to lodge any non-frivolous appeals. If he is convicted of the heinous crimes that have been imputed to him, and if his appeals are unsuccessful, then the appropriate sanction for him is the death penalty. A community will be in dereliction of its moral obligations if its criminal-justice system does not impose the death penalty in such circumstances.

If there is some other community C2 with an even stronger claim to jurisdiction over the crimes (perhaps because they were all committed there), then the community C1 whose legal-governmental officials have apprehended the offender may well be under a moral duty to extradite him to C2. Whether such a moral duty is incumbent on C1 will depend principally on the fairness and efficiency of the criminal-justice system in C2, and also on the fairness and efficiency of the criminal-justice system in C1. It likewise depends to some degree on the substance of the prevailing transnational laws that govern competing jurisdictional claims. Most important for the purposes of this chapter, the existence or inexistence of a moral duty-to-extradite depends on whether any practice of capital punishment with a purgative orientation is operative in C2 for especially outrageous crimes. If somebody is credibly charged with such crimes, and if capital punishment with a purgative orientation has been eliminated (or never adopted) in C2, the absence of such punishment is a moral consideration that militates against acceding to C2's request for extradition.[38] That consideration might be exceeded in importance by countervailing moral factors, but it obtains as an obligatory moral reason for declining to comply with C2's request. After all, if the guilt of the accused person is established by a fair trial, then—given the extravagant evil of his crimes—the purgative rationale requires that he be sentenced to death. A community without the institution of capital punishment is unable to abide by the purgative rationale's requirement. It is unable to remove the moral blight on its relationship with the rest of humankind, and also the moral blight on the relationship between C1 and the rest of humankind. The prospect of the persistence of that blight is something that weighs heavily against an affirmative response to the request for extradition. (Of course, if C1 itself has eliminated or never adopted the institution of capital punishment with a purgative orientation, the absence of such punishment in C2 does not militate in favour of placing the accused person on trial in C1 instead. Neither C1 nor C2 will be able to remove the taint on its relationship with the rest of humanity. If some other community C3 also has jurisdiction over the crimes in question, and if the death penalty with a purgative orientation is employed in C3 for terrible offences, then *ceteris paribus* C3 is the community in which the suspect should be tried.)

Let us now assume that C1 declines to extradite the suspect to C2; the reason for the negative response is that the authorities in C1 want to offer refuge and protection to the suspect. (Suppose, for example, that Argentina is C1, Israel is C2, and the suspect is Adolf Eichmann.) C1 is patently in breach of its moral obligations, but the trickier question is whether C2 likewise remains distinctively tarnished by the continued existence of the suspect. What should be remembered here is that a community's association with a vile offender places the community under a moral obligation to take all reasonable steps to ensure that the offender is brought to justice. Thus, although C2 is under a moral obligation to exhort C1 to extradite the suspect, and although C2 is likewise morally obligated to place pressure on C1 through various economic and diplomatic measures, it is not morally obligated to go to war with C1 over the matter. If C2 has undertaken within its power all reasonable economic and diplomatic measures in order to induce C1 to

---

[38] I am assuming here that the alternative to the use of capital punishment with a purgative orientation is no capital punishment at all, since the use of the death penalty with any other orientation would be morally illegitimate.

deliver the suspect for trial, then—even if the measures have proved to be futile—C2 has fulfilled the moral obligations that are incumbent upon it by dint of its association with the suspect. The members of C2 are tarnished by the continued existence of the suspect, but not any more so than the members of communities which have no special association with him or with his crimes.

Still, although C2 is not morally obligated to engage in acts of war against C1 for the purpose of gaining possession of the suspect, some forcible actions that normally would be morally impermissible are morally permissible in the circumstances. For example, when Israel abducted Eichmann from Argentina in 1960, its capture of him was morally permissible and indeed commendable. Israel was not morally duty-bound to seize Eichmann from Argentinian territory, but in the circumstances it was morally at liberty to do so. It deserved plaudits for doing so, since it thereby brought to justice someone who was the very incarnation of the defilingness of extreme evil. Abductions of people from the territory of other countries are not ordinarily permissible, of course, but the capture of Eichmann from the territory of Argentina was admirable. Such a feat was a deft way of overcoming the Argentinians' obstruction of justice and their perpetuation of the blight cast upon humankind by Eichmann's continued existence.

If C2 does succeed in bringing under its control a suspect accused of monstrously evil offences, it will then be morally obligated to proceed in the manner outlined four paragraphs ago. That is, it will be obligated to provide a fair trial and ample time for any non-frivolous appeals. If the guilt of the suspect has been established at the end of the process, then C2 will be morally obligated to carry out the death penalty.

In sum, a defilingly evil offender's community is any community that bears some special association with the offender or with his atrocities. The relationship between each such community and the rest of humanity is particularly tainted by the continuation of his life. If no such community is prepared to bring him to justice—or if no such community is morally entitled to execute him, because each such community is governed by an illiberal regime—then any liberal-democratic country in the rest of the world is morally entitled to assert extra-territorial jurisdiction over his crimes. After all, the extravagance of his iniquities has demeaned every member of humankind. Still, although the assertion of extra-territorial jurisdiction is morally permissible in a situation of that type, it is a last resort. Highly susceptible to abuse, the exercise of such jurisdiction is to be undertaken charily (not least because a trial administered by a community that has no special connections to the offender or his offences is unlikely to be fair in the absence of extensive cooperation from the communities that do have such connections). In some circumstances, however, the importance of removing the moral taint produced by a defilingly evil offender is sufficient to outweigh the importance of the reasons for circumspection.

6.3.3.10. A tenth query: vagueness and aggravating factors

Some readers may be worried by the fact that my exposition of the purgative rationale for capital punishment has had to rely on vague concepts such as those of extravagance and grievous harm. As has been remarked at several junctures in this chapter, any accurate account of evil or defilement does indeed have to invoke vague concepts. Because evil and defilement are themselves vague properties, no theory of either of them can do without such concepts. As a consequence, any system of criminal justice that operates in accordance with the purgative rationale will be faced with the abiding possibility and likelihood of borderline cases that neither fall determinately within that rationale nor fall determinately outside it.

Of course, in the respect just mentioned, the administration of the purgative rationale for capital punishment is not fundamentally different from the other workings of a criminal-justice system. Every crime is defined with vague concepts, as is every defence. Whenever judges and other legal-governmental officials implement the terms of various laws, the possibility of indeterminate borderline cases is ineliminable. Anyone who hopes to overcome vagueness altogether in the operations of a legal system is pursuing a chimera (Kramer 2007, 36–37). Hence, the sheer fact that vague concepts figure in the purgative justification of capital punishment is not distinctively problematic at all.

6.3.3.10.1. *The concerns of the opponents of the purgative rationale*

However, for two reasons, someone might feel unease about the vagueness of the concepts with which the purgative justification is constructed. First, the stakes are especially high when the applicability or inapplicability of the purgative rationale is at issue. By reference to that rationale, judges and juries are to differentiate between defilingly evil offenders (for whom the death penalty is appropriate and obligatory) and other evil offenders (for whom such a penalty is inappropriate). Though vagueness is undoubtedly a characteristic of every standard for decision-making in any legal-governmental system, the decisions concerning the applicability or inapplicability of the purgative rationale are literally matters of life and death. Given that so much hinges on those decisions, some readers might feel particularly troubled by the prospect of indeterminacy in any cases that are to be resolved under the purgative criterion.

Secondly, such readers might feel further troubled by the extent of the vagueness of the chief concepts in the purgative rationale. While allowing that all or virtually all legal concepts are vague, they might nonetheless maintain that the range of the borderline cases associated with each of the chief concepts in the purgative rationale is disquietingly ample. In comparison with most other legal concepts—so such readers might claim—the concepts of extravagance and grievousness (and other concepts that are integral to the purgative rationale) are very vague indeed. A complaint along those lines would suggest that the indeterminacy surrounding the implementation of the purgative rationale is troublingly more abundant than the indeterminacy surrounding the implementation of most other legal standards.

Now, every proponent of the purgative rationale for the death penalty should accept that the first of these concerns is well-founded. It is indeed true that the stakes are peculiarly high when legal-governmental officials and juries are deciding whether the purgative rationale is applicable to particular offenders or not. Much more dubious is the second of the concerns just recounted. Though the concepts central to the purgative rationale are doubtless vaguer than some of the technical concepts in various regulatory statutes, they are not much vaguer than many of the familiar concepts in criminal law and in other areas of law. For example, they are not vaguer than the concept of reasonableness, which figures so saliently in many statutes and in much of the common law. Nevertheless, even if the concern about the degree of the vagueness of the principal concepts in the purgative rationale is misplaced, the concern about the high stakes is sufficient in itself to warrant great caution.

6.3.3.10.2. *Dealing with vagueness*

Proponents of the purgative rationale can and should respond in two ways to the need for caution. First, as has already been emphasized, the outcome in any indeterminate case should be against the applicability of that rationale. Although an offender's crimes in such a case do not fall determinately outside the scope of the purgative justification for the death penalty, they do not fall determinately within that scope, either. Hence, there is no basis for the imposition of the death penalty in such a case. Moreover, given that the burden of proof is always arrayed against supporters of capital punishment, any significant uncertainty concerning the determinacy of a particular offender's case is enough to undermine the justifiability of the imposition of such punishment on that offender. Only clear-cut cases of monstrously evil conduct—such as those of Richard and Joseph—can justifiably trigger the infliction of the death penalty.

Secondly, the admittedly vague standard of the purgative rationale can be cashed out with less vague standards through statutory or adjudicative specifications of the aggravating features of crimes that cumulatively render justifiable the imposition of the death penalty. Indeed, statutory specifications of such features are a longstanding aspect of the practice of capital punishment in the United States (McCord 1998, 115–22; Note 2001, 1604 n 38, 1607–10; Nussbaum 2004, 164, 168). However, although most of the features singled out by statutes in various American states are relevant to inquiries about the applicability or inapplicability of the purgative rationale for capital punishment, some others are of doubtful pertinence. On the one hand, the statutory provisions are generally appropriate insofar as they direct the judge or jurors in any particular case to ask whether there are multiple victims, and whether torture or rape has been involved, and whether the body of any victim has been mutilated either before or after death, and whether the defendant has previously been convicted of very serious crimes, and whether any victim has been stabbed or shot numerous times, and so forth. On the other hand, far less helpful are statutory provisions that direct the judge or jurors in any particular case to ask whether the victim was a stranger to the perpetrator, and whether the murder has been committed in order to avoid arrest, and whether the murder has been committed during an armed robbery. Each of those factors in certain circumstances can be of some relevance to inquiries about the applicability of the purgative rationale, but none of them per se bears directly or typically on such inquiries.

Unhelpful for a markedly different reason are statutory provisions which direct the judge or jurors in any particular case to ask whether the crimes under examination are especially heinous, cruel, and depraved (or outrageously and wantonly vile and inhuman, or indicative of an utter disregard for human life). Such provisions single out considerations that are obviously relevant to inquiries about the applicability of the purgative rationale, but the shortcoming of the provisions is that they virtually restate the purgative criterion instead of explicating it. After all, the point of statutorily specifying various types of aggravators is to cash out the vague concepts of the purgative rationale through recourse to criteria that are less vague. That point will go unfulfilled if the specifications of the aggravating factors invoke the very concepts—the vague concepts of the purgative rationale—which they are supposed to be expounding. If the problem addressed through statutory specifications is that the purgative rationale for capital punishment as a direct guide to judges and juries will generate too much uncertainty and too many inconsistent decisions, that problem will not be alleviated by specifications that are too close to the purgative rationale itself. (Of course, notwithstanding what has just been said, judges and juries should certainly be guided by the purgative rationale. They need to be aware that that rationale is what they are seeking to implement when they are asked to focus on the presence or absence of aggravating factors. However, the guidance provided by the rationale itself is a general orientation rather than a more concrete set of instructions.)

Exactly how the specifications of aggravating features should be formulated is a matter of detail that will not be tackled here, for it is partly dependent on empirical findings by psychologists concerning the ways in which human decision-makers tend to respond to different patterns of wording. Likewise not to be tackled here is the matter of determining how many aggravating factors must be present and how they are to be cumulatively weighed. Abstract reflections on that latter issue are of limited value, as Robert Blecker suggests: 'It's not the number of aggravators[,] because that allows a jury in fact to avoid its responsibility by deluding itself into believing it is engaging in a weighing process whose outcome is predetermined by the legislative list. It's not the numbers; it's the quality' (Symposium 2003, 174 [remarks by Robert Blecker]). Blecker regrettably overstates his point, for the numbers do matter. However, he is right to suggest that *in abstracto* there is no talismanic formula for cumulatively weighing the aggravating and mitigating features of any murderous offender's crimes. Specifications of such features can guide the decisions of judges and juries more concretely than can the purgative rationale for capital punishment itself, but they do not transform the process of decision-making into a mechanical endeavour of adding and subtracting. Though the specifications must include general instructions concerning the ways in which the aggravating characteristics of ghastly crimes are to be considered in combination, the instructions reduce vagueness without eliminating it. They certainly cannot eliminate the need for careful attention to the specificities of each case. A jury or a judge will have to pay such attention in order to answer the underlying question whether the crimes of any particular offender amount to a clear-cut instance of extravagantly evil conduct.

6.3.3.11. An eleventh query: permissibility as well as obligatoriness?

Let us ponder one further query. This chapter has argued that the use of capital punishment against defilingly evil offenders is morally obligatory. The death penalty for any such offender is morally obligatory because it is the only means—and is thus the least invasive means—by which his community can remove the blight which he has cast upon its relationship with the rest of humankind. Readers who accept that conclusion might nonetheless wonder whether the imposition of the death penalty is also morally permissible. Let us keep in mind, after all, that this book is attempting to show that capital punishment can be strongly justified in some circumstances. To show as much, this chapter has to establish two points:

1. The imposition of capital punishment is morally obligatory in certain actual or credibly possible cases.

2. In some of the cases in which the imposition of capital punishment is morally obligatory, it is also morally permissible.

As has been stated above, this chapter has argued at length in support of 1. Some readers may query whether 2 is also sustainable. Given that this book's aim of strongly justifying the application of the death penalty in suitable situations will go unfulfilled unless 2 is sustainable, this final query—though straightforwardly resolvable—is of considerable importance.

6.3.3.11.1. *When permissibility is missing*

We should begin our examination of this matter by noting something that has already been readily acknowledged in this chapter. In some of the contexts to which the purgative rationale for capital punishment is applicable, going ahead with executions in conformity to that rationale is not morally permissible. In any context of that sort, some countervailing moral duties require the officials of a legal-governmental system to refrain from conducting any executions. As has already been remarked, and as will be explored squarely in my next chapter, some notable factors that can give rise to such countervailing moral duties are irregularities in the implementation of the death penalty. Those procedural irregularities can be sufficiently invidious to render any executions morally impermissible. In that event, the procedural dimension of the institution of capital punishment in some community is in conflict with its substantive dimension. On substantive grounds expounded by the purgative rationale, the officials in a liberal-democratic system of governance are morally obligated to put defilingly evil offenders to death after those offenders have been duly tried for their iniquitous crimes; yet, on procedural grounds that will be probed in my next chapter, those officials are sometimes morally obligated to refrain from carrying out any executions.

In a situation of this sort, where the officials face a genuine moral conflict, the administering of an execution is not strongly justified. It is only morally obligatory rather than both morally obligatory and morally permissible. However, although the administering of an execution in such a situation is not morally permissible and is thus not strongly justified, it might well be justified in the weaker sense of amounting to the morally best course of action available. Whether it will be justified in that weaker sense is dependent on the relative importance or strength of the conflicting obligations. If a community's moral duty to remove the blight produced by the continuation of the life of some monstrous offender is weightier than the community's moral duty to forgo any executions amidst conditions of procedural irregularities, then the application of the death penalty to the offender is morally justified in the weaker sense delineated above. It is morally the best course of action in the circumstances, notwithstanding its impermissibility and its consequent engendering of remedial duties. Contrariwise, if the community's moral obligation to execute some monstrous offender is less weighty than its moral obligation to eschew executions as a result of procedural irregularities, then the application of the death penalty to the offender is not morally justified at all. Which of these upshots will obtain in a context marked by the moral impermissibility of executions is a matter that obviously hinges on the specificities of each such context.

6.3.3.11.2. *When executions are permissible*

If no executions were ever morally justified in the strong sense, then this book's fundamental aim could not be fully realized. As my next chapter maintains, however, there are no solid grounds for thinking that the institution of capital punishment will inevitably be so badly flawed as to undermine the moral legitimacy of each instance of such punishment. Though the import of procedural irregularities is hardly to be discounted, their occurrence at damagingly high levels is contingent rather than ineluctable. Procedural aberrations, when properly contained, do not warrant any sweeping pessimism about the potential legitimacy of executions. What we should briefly ponder here is whether there are any other grounds for such pessimism. Are there any inherent substantive features of capital punishment that render it morally impermissible, even when it is required under the terms of the purgative rationale?

The answer to this question is negative, not least because the very property of capital punishment that makes it morally obligatory under the purgative rationale is something that also makes it morally permissible. Whereas capital punishment is not the least invasive means for attaining any of the desiderata commended by most of the commonly propounded rationales for such punishment, it is the least invasive means (indeed, the only means) for attaining the objective commended by the purgative rationale. Thus, whereas the use of capital punishment on the basis of the commonly propounded justifications does not satisfy the Minimal Invasion Principle, the use of such punishment on the basis of the purgative justification does indeed satisfy that principle.

Because the death penalty is the only sanction that can cleanse the moral blight with which a defilingly evil offender has afflicted the relationship between his community and the rest of humanity, the application of that penalty to such an offender is morally obligatory. For exactly the same reason, however, the application of that penalty is morally legitimate. Since no sanction that is less severe will remove the aforementioned blight, the use of the death penalty for that purpose is consistent with the Minimal Invasion Principle and is thus consistent with the fundamental principles of liberal democracy. Purgative executions, unlike executions conducted in pursuit of other objectives, do not run athwart those principles.

Moreover, because the death penalty is the only sanction for which the purgative rationale ever calls, any punishment harsher than an execution through the most humane available method is not countenanced by the purgative rationale. No greater degree of harshness would contribute to the realization of that rationale's aim, and therefore no greater degree of harshness is ever authorized thereunder. Consequently, unlike the deterrence-oriented justification of capital punishment and some of the other frequently advanced justifications, the purgative justification places a principled and credible ceiling on the severity of the sanctions which it prescribes. In contrast with those other justifications, then, the purgative rationale is not deprived of its moral force by an inability to set such a ceiling. In contrast with those other justifications, it never calls for torture or mutilation or any barbarous methods of putting people to death. Hence, the executions which it requires are not delegitimized by being attributable to a punitive principle that would call for such horrors.

Nor is the purgative rationale a punitive principle that disregards the value of moral responsibility. Whereas the various consequentialist justifications of punishment are deprived of their legitimacy by their failure to insist that only people who are morally responsible for crimes can properly be subjected to sanctions, the purgative rationale does indeed insist on responsibility as a necessary condition for the legitimacy of any infliction of the death penalty. Only a person who is morally responsible for appalling crimes will ever fall within the compass of the purgative rationale. Under that rationale, such a person is to be executed precisely because he is responsible for horrific crimes—and precisely because the continuation of his existence is therefore defiling. Like retributivism, then, the purgative rationale is a doctrine that ascribes a central place to the ideal of moral responsibility in its punitive prescriptions. Far from contravening the value of responsibility, the executions required by the purgative rationale are morally permissible partly because they uphold that value.

Still, despite all the foregoing grounds for concluding that capital punishment undertaken on the basis of the purgative rationale is morally permissible, some readers may feel that such punishment is impermissible because it violates the right to life of each executed offender. That line of argument is often voiced in public debates over the legitimacy of the death penalty—as is remarked in Cahill 2010, 13—but its flimsiness has been clear-sightedly recognized by the leading philosophical opponent of capital punishment, Hugo Adam Bedau (1990, 484; 1993, 162–5; 1999, 43–4). As Bedau is well aware, most of the great philosophers in the early modern period who affirmed the existence of a fundamental right to life were in favour of capital punishment. They believed that the right to life is inalienable, but they also believed that it can be forfeited through extremely grave misconduct. Just as somebody who launches a serious and unprovoked attack against other people will have forfeited his right to life if the slaying of him is necessary to ward off the attack, so too somebody who has committed terrible crimes will have forfeited his right to life if the execution of him is necessary to deal adequately with the effects of those crimes. Of course, as Bedau rightly points out, any supporter of capital punishment who invokes the notion of forfeiture in this manner will then have to show that the imposition of such punishment on vile offenders is indeed necessary to deal adequately with the effects of their atrocious crimes. Bedau correctly submits that that burden of proof cannot be discharged by the proponents of any deterrence-oriented, retributivistic, or incapacitative rationale for the death penalty. However, like virtually everyone else in the contemporary debates over capital punishment, he does not address the purgative rationale at all. As this chapter has endeavoured to establish, the purgative justification—within its scope—succeeds where the other attempted justifications of capital punishment have failed. Hence, proponents of the purgative rationale can soundly argue that executions of monstrous offenders are morally permissible because each of those offenders through his hideous crimes has forfeited his right to life.

Some critics of capital punishment have adopted a further tack that is closely related to the invocation of a right to life. They have declared that the infliction of such punishment is inconsistent with the dignity of human beings. However, as has already been contended in some of my earlier chapters, such an allegation runs together the property of human dignity with the property of moral worth. On the one hand, even the most terrible offender remains a human being and is thus possessed of human dignity. Consequently, there are clear limits on what a system of criminal justice can legitimately do to such an offender. Torture and mutilation are always morally impermissible, as is the use of any method of capital punishment that is gratuitously painful. No punitive exploitation of an offender's capacity to experience agonizing pain is ever permissible; any such exploitation would be at odds with the moral integrity of the community on whose behalf it is carried out. On the other hand, the moral worth of the life of a demonically evil offender is negative. Having perpetrated atrocities that cumulatively constitute a repudiation of humankind, such an offender blights his community through his continued existence. So long as he is put to death through the gentlest method available, his execution will reflect his moral worth and will not clash at all with his human dignity. The application of the death penalty to him will have held him responsible for defiling his community so heinously, and will thus have treated him as someone endowed with reflective agency. In so doing, it will not have exploited his capacity to feel intense pain, nor will it have mutilated him before or after his death. On all counts, then, the execution of a grotesquely evil offender on the basis of the purgative rationale is consistent with his human dignity. In that respect as well as in every other respect that has been pondered here, the institution of capital punishment on such a basis can be morally permissible. Given that it is also morally obligatory, such an institution can be morally justified in the strongest sense.

6.4. Conclusion: why only liberal democracies?

This chapter will conclude by tersely addressing a topic that has surfaced fleetingly at several previous junctures in this book. Why is the moral force of the purgative rationale for capital punishment operative only in liberal democracies? Why is the application of such punishment to a defilingly evil offender not justifiable in every country with which the offender or his odious criminality is specially connected, regardless of the political complexion of the regime that reigns therein? After all, the atrocities committed by a defilingly wicked criminal are such as to constitute an affront to the whole of humankind. Why, then, does the justifiability of putting such a criminal to death depend on the moral worthiness of the system of governance within which he is punished?

6.4.1. An ancillary reason: procedural fairness

One secondary but still important reason for the limitedness of the reach of the purgative rationale is that the likelihood of a scrupulously fair trial in any given case—with, for example, a stringent burden of proof placed on the prosecution rather than on the defendant—is markedly higher under a liberal-democratic system of governance than under a repressive autocracy. Until someone accused of outrageous crimes has undergone a fair trial with ample opportunities for non-frivolous appeals, he cannot legitimately be executed on the basis of the purgative rationale and therefore cannot legitimately be executed, period. (My remarks here pertain to all circumstances that arise during any normal operations of a system of criminal justice. In an overwhelmingly dire emergency, caused by a full-scale invasion of a country or by multiple terrorist attacks with nuclear weapons or by a dreadful natural cataclysm such as the impact of a sizeable asteroid, the normal procedures and precautions within a criminal-justice system can legitimately be streamlined.) Thus, since many of the procedural safeguards that are routinely present in any liberal democracy will usually be missing from the trials held under the auspices of a tyrannical regime, those trials are not sufficiently fair to ground the legitimacy of purgative executions. Any despotic regime is like a liberal-democratic regime in that it is under a moral obligation to conduct fair trials and also under a moral obligation to execute monstrous offenders whose guilt has been duly ascertained through such trials and any subsequent appeals. However, because a despotic regime typically declines to fulfil the first of those obligations, it excludes itself from being in a position to fulfil the second of those obligations. It excludes itself from being in a position to carry out any morally justified executions, even if it explicitly invokes the purgative rationale in support of its practice of capital punishment.

Two caveats should be entered here. First, this initial approach to explaining the limitedness of the reach of the purgative rationale is merely of ancillary importance because it applies only contingently to any particular case. Indeed, the contingency of the applicability of this initial explanation has been overtly signalled by my use of qualifiers such as 'typically' and 'usually'. Although a repressive autocracy will typically invert liberal-democratic values by proceeding against a criminal defendant with a strong presumption of guilt rather than with a presumption of innocence, and although such an autocracy will likewise typically eschew various other liberal-democratic safeguards that are crucial for the fairness of a trial, there is always the possibility of an exceptional case (from time to time) in which a defendant accused of atrocious crimes is tried with adequate fairness. Hence, if the procedural concerns recounted above were the only grounds for the confinedness of the range of contexts in which the purgative rationale is operative, that rationale would countenance some of the actual or credibly possible executions conducted by odious tyrannies. Accordingly, if this book is to substantiate its claims about the inoperativeness of the purgative rationale in societies that are governed by tyrannical regimes, it will have to go beyond the aforementioned procedural considerations. Important though those considerations are, they do not in themselves support the proposition that every execution undertaken on the basis of the purgative rationale by a despotically illiberal government is morally illegitimate.

Secondly, although this brief discussion has emphasized that the trials of criminals under repressive systems of governance tend to be unfair, it has not thereby suggested that those trials generally arrive at inaccurate verdicts more often than the fair trials that are conducted under liberal-democratic systems of governance. Fairness is not equivalent to epistemic reliability, though the two can converge. What is unfair about a typical trial under an authoritarian regime is that the protections against a false positive—that is, the protections against an inaccurate verdict of guilt—are quite meagre. At the same time, however, that very feature of the trial reduces the probability of a false negative (an inaccurate verdict of innocence). By substantially lowering the likelihood that innocent people will be convicted of crimes, liberal-democratic procedural precautions substantially increase the likelihood that guilty people will be acquitted. Those precautions favour false negatives over false positives. *In abstracto*, then, we cannot say whether the verdicts reached in a system of criminal justice that includes the liberal-democratic safeguards are more frequently accurate or less frequently accurate than the verdicts reached in a system that eschews such safeguards. Everything will hinge on the specifics of the respective systems.

Now, under any credible account of the principles of liberal democracy, the possible epistemic drawbacks of the sundry procedural precautions in the trials of criminals are a price worth paying. By any liberal-democratic reckoning, false positives are considerably worse morally than false negatives. That order of priorities is reflective of broader values within the principles of liberal democracy, just as the inverse order of priorities is reflective of broader values within authoritarianism. Whereas the proponents of authoritarianism believe that the interests of a legal-governmental system take moral precedence over the interests of individual citizens whenever the former are in conflict with the latter, the proponents of liberal democracy recognize that the order of moral precedence is actually the reverse in a wide array of contexts. One such context is the trial of anyone who has been charged with some serious crime(s). Even if the interests of a legal-governmental system and the safety of the public would be furthered by requiring some particular criminal defendant to overcome a presumption of guilt when he is placed on trial, the officials who run the system are morally obligated to adhere instead to a presumption of innocence. They are likewise morally obligated to abide by a number of other procedural safeguards that together endow any trial with fairness. Instead of consisting solely in epistemic reliability—which might or might not be enhanced overall by the procedural protections—such fairness consists also and principally in the respect shown to a defendant (even a vile defendant) as someone possessed of human dignity. That respect is shown when a trial is structured with precautions which treat false positives as far worse than false negatives.

Of course, there is room for the proponents of liberal-democratic principles to disagree reasonably about the extent to which the occurrence of false positives is morally worse than the occurrence of false negatives. There is, consequently, room for reasonable disagreement about the stringency of the safeguards that should be in place for trials of criminal defendants. After all, the occurrence of false negatives is hardly an inconsequential matter, as dangerous miscreants are set free. Similarly, there is room for variations among liberal democracies in the specific sets of safeguards which they adopt. Such variations do indeed obtain among the systems of criminal justice in liberal-democratic countries (Kramer 2007, 184–5).

Nonetheless, what is common to those systems is that their procedures for trials of criminal defendants uphold the basic priorities of liberal democracy by tilting palpably in the direction of individual rights vis-à-vis the state. That is, the procedures tilt palpably in the direction of guarding against the subjection of innocent people to punishments. The precautions that effect such a tilt, whatever their specific substance, are essential for the fairness of a trial. Since the purgative rationale is applicable only to defendants who have been tried fairly, it is applicable only when the procedures of a trial have been conducted in accordance with liberal-democratic values. Because the procedures of the trials in jurisdictions ruled by autocratic regimes are very seldom conducted in accordance with such values, the reach of the purgative rationale is generally confined to liberal-democratic countries.

6.4.2. The chief reason: purgation in a moral community

As has been observed, the considerations of procedural fairness outlined above are not in themselves sufficient to account fully for the limitedness of the purgative rationale's sphere of application. To see why executions conducted on the basis of that rationale by tyrannical regimes are never morally legitimate, we need to probe more deeply into the rationale's orientation. In so doing, we can also discern more clearly why purgative executions are legitimate only when they ensue from fair trials. My discussion in the preceding subsection has taken for granted that the legitimacy of such executions is dependent on a regime's compliance with the requirements of procedural fairness. This final subsection will help to explain that dependence.

The key point here has been stated laconically in Chapter 1, and can now be fleshed out with reference to my elaboration of the purgative rationale in the current chapter. As has been argued, the continued existence of an extravagantly wicked offender would defile his community because the offender through his grotesque crimes has repudiated humankind. His continued existence would therefore sully the relationship between his community and the rest of humanity. By executing such an offender after his guilt has been confirmed through a fair trial along with any relevant appeals, a community saves its moral probity from the blight that would have been cast upon it by the continuation of the offender's life. Such is the purgative rationale for capital punishment. Now, if that rationale is properly to be given effect by the legal-governmental institutions of a community, those institutions must themselves be promotive of the community's moral probity. They must themselves enhance and consolidate the character of the community as a moral grouping. Liberal-democratic institutions perform just such a role, as they give expression to the political inclinations of the people in a community while respecting the fundamental rights of everyone. They promote the moral flourishing of any society over which they govern, by enabling the achievement of salutary collective projects that would not otherwise be feasible, and by upholding the general moral values of democratic self-determination and equality and individual freedom and moral responsibility. Such institutions can rightly profess to further the good moral standing of a community by ensuring that those democratic and liberal values are richly instantiated therein. They consequently possess the moral authority to invoke the purgative rationale against any defilingly evil offenders. Because a liberal-democratic system of governance through its own workings will have bolstered the moral health of a society, it can legitimately and pertinently implement a rationale for capital punishment that is focused precisely on that moral health.

Quite different is the position of a repressively autocratic system of governance. Instead of contributing valuably to the moral uprightness of the community over which it reigns, such a system of governance tarnishes the community's moral character by acting squarely athwart the liberal and democratic values which it should be championing. It crushes any democratic aspirations that people harbour, and it stifles many of the freedoms (or combinations of freedoms) that are enjoyed by individuals in liberal-democratic countries. It likewise makes a mockery of the value of equality by sustaining so great a gulf between its own posture of dominating ascendance and the lowliness of the downtrodden people who suffer under its sway. Its despotic workings detract hugely from the moral hygiene of the society in its thrall. Hence, the officials who run such a system of governance are not in any position of moral authority to invoke and apply the purgative rationale for capital punishment. They cannot aptly claim to be caretakers of the moral probity of the community over which they rule; quite the contrary. Accordingly, any endeavours by them to execute defilingly evil criminals are morally illegitimate—even in the unlikely event that those criminals have received fair trials, and even in the unlikely event that the officials have acted with the specific intention of rectifying the moral relationship between their own community and the rest of humanity. Although the defilingly evil criminals should indeed be put to death on the basis of the purgative rationale, the officials in a heavy-handedly authoritarian regime have disqualified themselves from carrying out any of the requisite executions legitimately. Because their own regime sullies the moral standing of their community and of humankind, any purgative executions conducted by them will be instances of hypocrisy rather than measures that genuinely reaffirm the character of their community as a moral grouping. The situation will be akin to that denounced by King Lear:

> Thou rascal beadle, hold thy bloody hand!
> Why dost thou lash that whore? Strip thy own back;
> Thou hotly lusts to use her in that kind
> For which thou whip'st her. The usurer hangs the cozener.
> Through tattered clothes small vices do appear;
> Robes and furred gowns hide all.[39]

Because purgative executions are not morally legitimate unless they serve to redeem the moral character of a society, and because they cannot fulfil such a purpose in a society governed by an iniquitous regime, the purgative rationale does not authorize such a regime to put anyone to death.

The last couple of paragraphs have drawn a stark dichotomy between liberal-democratic regimes and tyrannical regimes. Whereas the former regimes are possessed of the moral authority to invoke and apply the purgative rationale legitimately, the latter are not. Now, plainly, the realities of political life are not as tidily bifurcated as the last two paragraphs might together imply. Every liberal-democratic system of governance is imperfect to a greater or a lesser degree, and some despotic regimes are less thuggishly repressive than others. There is no talismanic point of transition from the moral benignity of liberal democracies to the moral bankruptcy of autocratic systems of governance. Across the gamut of actual or possible intermediate specimens, the diverse systems of governance that are endowed with the moral authority of liberal democracies will have gradually shaded into the diverse systems of governance that are devoid of such authority. Any system of governance that is not determinately endowed with the authority of a liberal democracy—because it is determinately devoid of such authority, or because it is neither determinately devoid nor determinately possessed thereof—cannot legitimately conduct any executions on the basis of the purgative rationale for capital punishment.

---

[39] *King Lear*, IV.vi.161–7. For some reflections on the fact that various otherwise legitimate and pertinent strictures are illegitimate when they are articulated hypocritically, see Cohen 2006.

Of course, legal-governmental institutions can be determinately possessed of liberal-democratic moral authority even though they fall well short of perfect benignity in some of their workings. So long as a system of governance is predominantly and sincerely devoted to the fulfilment of liberal-democratic requirements and ideals, its imperfections do not bar it from legitimately invoking and applying the purgative rationale. Its applications of that rationale to defilingly wicked offenders do not amount to instances of hypocrisy, and are therefore supportive rather than destructive of the moral order which the purgative rationale upholds.

We can now see why the purgative rationale for capital punishment is legitimately invocable only when a defilingly evil offender has received a fair trial (with an abundance of opportunities for non-frivolous appeals). A system of governance is not predominantly and sincerely devoted to the fulfilment of liberal-democratic requirements and ideals unless its mechanisms of criminal justice satisfy the demands of procedural fairness to a high level. Unless the trials of criminal defendants within a jurisdiction are generally fair, the institutions of criminal justice there will not be morally positioned to draw legitimately upon the purgative rationale for capital punishment. Those institutions, in such circumstances, do not belong to a flourishingly liberal-democratic system of governance. Furthermore, unless the trial of an egregiously evil offender has itself been conducted in compliance with the constraints of procedural fairness to a high degree, any sentencing of that offender to death on the basis of the purgative rationale will be an instance of hypocrisy that undermines the rationale's moral aspiration. An unfair trial would make a mockery of the very values of liberal democracy on which the purgative justification rests. Hence, no purgative execution is morally legitimate if the offender upon whom it is administered has not been tried fairly.

In the final chapter of this book, we shall look further at considerations of procedural fairness. This penultimate chapter has endeavoured to show that purgative executions are in principle both morally obligatory and morally legitimate in certain circumstances, and that the legitimacy of any such executions will depend partly on the fairness of the procedures by which they have been imposed. Some opponents of capital punishment have submitted that certain features of the administration of such punishment render it intrinsically unfair. In so arguing, they in effect maintain that capital punishment is never morally legitimate in practice. We should now turn to examine their lines of reasoning.

7

The Death Penalty in Operation

In principle, the use of capital punishment against defilingly evil offenders is morally permissible. In this final chapter, we shall consider whether the use of such punishment against such offenders is ever morally permissible in practice. Is the administration of the death penalty inevitably so defective as to rule out the legitimacy of every application of that penalty? Do the procedural aspects of the institution of capital punishment ineluctably taint the substantive aspects of that institution?

Some caveats and disclaimers should be entered at the outset. First, as should be evident from the closing portions of Chapter 6 and from some other parts of this book, the matters broached by this chapter are live issues only in the context of a system of governance that is generally liberal-democratic. Under a system of governance that is repressively illiberal—such as the present regime in China, where far more people are executed each year than in the rest of the world combined—the institution of capital punishment is morally illegitimate across the board (for reasons expounded at the end of the preceding chapter). Under a repressive system of governance, then, worries about the administration of the death penalty are superfluous. Even if all such worries could be allayed, any application of that penalty by the mechanisms of criminal-law enforcement in a thuggish regime would be morally impermissible. Hence, throughout the present chapter, my discussion is addressed to liberal democracies and their imperfections. Tyrannical regimes are excluded from consideration altogether. Having no authority whatsoever to execute anyone, those latter regimes are not in a position to be deprived of such authority by the administrative concerns recounted in this chapter.

Secondly, as Chapter 1 has readily acknowledged, many of the worries about the administration of capital punishment are heavily empirical in their general tenor. Though this chapter will make a few references to some of the relevant empirical literature, it does not itself make any contribution to the gathering of data. It is philosophical rather than social-scientific in its orientation—as is the rest of this book, of course. Now, philosophical reflection can greatly help to clarify what is at stake in some of the empirical controversies over the administration of capital punishment, but obviously it cannot directly resolve any points of contention that are genuinely empirical. However, this chapter is not aiming to resolve such points of contention. It is not aiming to provide and assess data on the administration of capital punishment in any part of the United States or in the other few liberal democracies (most notably Japan) where such punishment is still practised. Instead, as has been stated above, my aim is to determine whether the shortcomings in every credibly possible set of procedures for the imposition of the death penalty are inevitably destructive of the moral permissibility of any such imposition. Can there credibly be a system of criminal-law enforcement in which those procedures are robust enough to sustain the moral legitimacy of executions? For the purpose of grappling with that question, philosophical ruminations—along with some reformative proposals and some plausible abstract empirical hypotheses—are singularly appropriate.

Thirdly, this chapter is presupposing the soundness of the purgative rationale for capital punishment, and is not seeking to amplify or bolster the arguments which Chapter 6 has propounded in favour of that rationale. On the one hand, the problems broached in this chapter are especially worthy of attention because the purgative rationale is sound. If there were no substantive basis for the institution of capital punishment, then allegations of procedural shortcomings would be of secondary importance. To be sure, those allegations if correct would be specifying some additional reasons for eschewing or abandoning the death penalty, and they might in any event be of great tactical value for opponents of that penalty who are unable to persuade other people of the substantive case against the use of such a sanction. However, if there were no satisfactory substantive basis for putting any prisoners to death, the primary reason for eschewing or abandoning the institution of capital punishment would be the very absence of such a basis. Thus, the fact that there is a solid substantive foundation for putting certain prisoners to death—in other words, the fact that the purgative justification of capital punishment is sound—will have heightened the noteworthiness of the allegations of procedural inequities. As this chapter endeavours to rebut or defuse those allegations, it takes for granted that the substantive grounds for the imposition of capital sentences are indeed solid. On the other hand, while taking as given that the purgative rationale for the death penalty is correct, this chapter does not itself set out to strengthen that rationale any further. Instead of adding to the arguments in favour of the purgative justification of capital punishment, this chapter will highlight the practical import of that justification by casting doubt upon claims that the use of capital punishment can never be morally legitimate in practice. Because those claims are about the practical significance of the purgative rationale rather than about the rationale itself, my ripostes to them are likewise about that practical significance. The purgative justification itself, as opposed to its practical importance, is not at stake in this chapter.

Fourthly, although I shall be arguing that institutions of capital punishment can credibly be legitimate in their operations, this chapter is not trying to vindicate those institutions as they currently exist in various jurisdictions of the United

States or elsewhere. As has already been remarked, my discussions will not marshal any data concerning the practice of capital punishment in its contemporary forms. What is more, the arguments herein are consistent with the proposition that the procedural safeguards in every contemporary system of capital punishment are insufficient for the moral legitimacy of any such system. Though the truth of that proposition is rather unlikely, it is not ruled out by anything that will be maintained in this chapter. What will be contended here is that any grave procedural inadequacies in a regime of capital punishment are not insuperable, and that the moral legitimacy of such a regime in its practical workings is therefore credibly possible. Whether that possibility has been realized through the procedural precautions in any of the current systems of capital punishment is not a matter on which this book takes a position. Instead, I warn against some fallacies and oversimplifications that can too readily lead people to dismiss the moral propriety of a practice of putting heinous offenders to death.

7.1. Mistakes and irrevocability

Every supporter of the purgative rationale for capital punishment should be troubled by the prospect of executions of innocent people. After all, one of the chief vices for which this book has criticized the deterrence-oriented and denunciatory accounts of capital punishment is the tendency of those accounts to call for executions of innocent people in certain situations where the people in question are known by legal-governmental officials to be innocent. Of course, the *countenancing* of executions of innocents is the peculiarly grave sin of those consequentialist approaches to the death penalty. However, that sin is so grave precisely because such executions are themselves terrible events. Furthermore, the terribleness of those events is only lessened—and is certainly not eliminated—in situations where the innocence of the executed prisoners is unknown to any legal-governmental officials. Putting to death an innocent person through the mechanisms of a system of criminal-law enforcement is dismayingly wrong even if all the officials involved in ordering and implementing the execution have not had any reasonable grounds for doubting that the person is guilty of atrocious crimes. Some wrongs are serious wrongs despite the faultlessness of the outlooks of the people who are responsible for them.

Now, any institution operated by human beings can never entirely eliminate the possibility of errors in its operations. Because the workings of a system of criminal justice impinge so heavily on the lives of people who become caught up in those workings, the officials who run such a system in any liberal democracy will take great pains to avoid mistakes; however, there can never be any absolute guarantee that their efforts will succeed in each particular case. Hence, every supporter of the purgative rationale for capital punishment should acknowledge that the possibility of an execution of an innocent person can never be excluded completely—even if such a possibility is happily never realized within some system of criminal justice. As has already been stated, the inextirpability of that possibility is of course troubling. What should be pondered here is whether the abidingness of that possibility is sufficient to delegitimize every practice of capital punishment, however scrupulously and carefully conducted the practice may be.

7.1.1. A preliminary point: clarifying an ambiguity

Before this chapter addresses the foregoing question directly, we should note an ambiguity in the concept of innocence (Dolinko 1986, 585 n 211; Nathanson 2001, 126–7; Radin 1980, 1156–7; Steiker and Steiker 2005, 597–600). Let us examine that concept with reference to an array of crimes for which somebody might be charged and tried. The crimes cumulatively are extravagantly evil. Now, the concept of innocence can be construed narrowly to cover everyone who is not at all culpably involved in any of the crimes under consideration, or it can be construed more expansively to cover everyone who has not been culpably involved in those crimes at any level that would warrant the imposition of the death penalty under the purgative rationale. When the concept of innocence is construed in the more expansive fashion, it extends not only to people who are innocent in the narrower sense but also to anyone whose culpable involvement in the specified crimes has fallen short of being monstrously evil.

Suppose, for example, that Victor and Hugo are two burglars who together enter the home of a large family one evening in order to steal what they can. Victor is unarmed, and he inaccurately believes that Hugo is also unarmed. Hugo is in fact carrying a gun, and he proceeds to slaughter the members of the family mercilessly while Victor is in another part of the house. Hugo escapes before the police arrive, whereas Victor is apprehended as he separately tries to flee. If Victor is subsequently charged not only with burglary but also with all the murders, and if he is sentenced to death on the basis of the purgative rationale, then a serious mistake will have been made. Victor is not innocent in the narrow sense, but he is innocent in the more expansive sense. He has not committed any crimes that would warrant the imposition of the death penalty under the purgative rationale. If he is executed, then an innocent man—in the more expansive sense of 'innocent'—will have been put to death.

In any liberal democracy's system of criminal-law enforcement where capital punishment is practised, an execution of a person who is innocent in the narrower sense will be extremely unlikely in any particular case but will be an especially serious wrong whenever it does occur. Executions of people who are innocent in the broader sense will be somewhat more common, but the wrongness of many of those executions will be somewhat less serious than the wrongness of any executions of people who are innocent in the narrower sense. For instance, in connection with the punishment levied for the murders committed by Hugo, the wrongness of executing

Victor is slightly less serious than the wrongness of executing somebody who has not in fact played any part in the burglary by Hugo and Victor.

There is not really any need for my discussion of mistaken executions to distinguish between innocence in the narrower sense and innocence in the broader sense. Putting to death a person who qualifies as innocent in either sense is a serious wrong, and the extreme rarity of executions of people who are innocent in the narrower sense is offset by the peculiar gravity of those executions. Any supporter of the purgative rationale for capital punishment should feel uneasy about the possibility of executions of people who are innocent in either sense. Still, because mistaken executions are particularly problematic when they are carried out against people who are innocent in the narrower sense, my discussion usually can best be construed as focusing on just such people. All the same, every major point in this section is applicable likewise (*mutatis mutandis*) to executions of people who are innocent only in the more expansive sense.

7.1.2. Intentional killings of innocents?

If we are to think clearly about the problem of mistaken executions, we need to avoid an oversimplification that has beguiled some of the theorists who have addressed that problem. The oversimplification consists in the claim that mistaken executions amount to intentional killings of innocent people. Such a claim, left unembellished as an accusation, broaches the problem of mistaken executions in a highly emotive fashion that elides some important distinctions. It impedes any rigorous analysis of the matter.

7.1.2.1. A specious argument

Richard Lempert has propounded a peculiarly dubious version of the assertion about the intentional killing of innocents. In an ill-advised Appendix to a very important article on capital punishment, he first goes astray by suggesting that the execution of an innocent person is morally tantamount to murder. He declares that retributivists justify the death penalty for murderers 'by reference to the awesomeness of the crime—that is, to the evil of intentionally taking an innocent life,' and he contends that 'if the system which imposes the ultimate punishment cannot proceed without inevitably replicating the momentous harm—the slaying of the innocent—that justifies such punishment, the basis for the system is undermined'. He reiterates that 'if a state punishes capitally it will inevitably commit the terrible act [of murdering an innocent person] necessary, in the retributivist scheme, to justify the killing of man' (Lempert 1981, 1225, 1226). To this moral equation between executions of innocent people and murders, the obvious response is that the malicious intentionality which underlies the crime of murder is missing from a mistaken execution (Sorell 1987, 47). Lempert anticipates such a retort, and he avouches that 'it may be sound at the level of individual sentencing. A jury sentencing a man to death may not, if it has found the facts competently and in good faith, be held morally accountable for the wrong of condemning an innocent person.'[1] However, he believes that supporters of the institution of capital punishment are morally in a much shakier position than are the members of a jury who sentence an innocent person to death after a scrupulously fair trial:

[T]he moralist who advocates a system of capital punishment is not in the same position as the juror who mistakenly condemns. Unless the moralist is ignorant of the history of capital punishment and of the fallibility of human beings, he knows that if the death penalty exists such mistakes are inevitable. If he intends to have a system of capital punishment, he intends to take innocent lives whether or not he wants to. Intentions are not defined by desires.

...If the retributivist's principles do not allow the intentional taking of the innocent life as a means to greater justice—and for most moral retributivists they do not—they will not justify a system that makes such takings inevitable. [Lempert 1981, 1226]

Slightly later in his Appendix, Lempert pushes his position to its extreme when he writes that in a system of capital punishment 'we do not want to kill the innocent, but everyone we kill we kill intentionally and...we intend a system designed (albeit in small measure) to take innocent life' (Lempert 1981, 1227). Quite remarkable is the notion that a system of capital punishment in a liberal democracy has been 'designed...to take innocent life'. Furthermore, even the somewhat milder allegation in the long excerpt above has ridden roughshod over the distinction between intended consequences and foreseen consequences.

David Dolinko, who himself opposes capital punishment on substantive grounds, has replied forcefully to Lempert (Dolinko 1986, 591–4; 1992 1633 n 35). As Dolinko points out, the confidently foreseeable but undesired consequences of a course of action are usually not intended consequences. He offers a few examples, which I slightly modify here (Dolinko 1986, 593). If some Islamist terrorists seize a couple of American hostages in Iraq and declare truculently that both hostages will be decapitated unless all American troops are withdrawn forthwith, and if the American President decides to keep his country's military forces in Iraq, the subsequent deaths of the hostages are not intended consequences of his course of action. The claim that the President has intended the beheadings is grossly distortive rather than illuminating. Similarly, although the people who run a company that manufactures automobiles are aware that the use of their vehicles on the roads each year will result in some deaths of innocent drivers and passengers and pedestrians, those deaths are not intended consequences of the company's processes of production. To say that the people who run the company have intended the deaths of the innocent victims of automobile accidents is to mischaracterize grotesquely the nature of their outlooks and conduct. Similarly, if a Minister of Education knows (on the basis of extensive empirical studies) that the introduction of more effective and rigorous pedagogical methods into his country's schools will result in small increases in the annual levels of suicides among schoolchildren, and if he nonetheless goes ahead with the new methods in order to improve the

---

[1] Lempert 1981, 1226. As will be remarked presently, Lempert has here significantly misstated the issue which he is addressing.

educational achievements of his country's students, any additional suicides that occur are not intended consequences of his course of action.

To be sure, there are some contexts in which the confidently foreseeable but undesired results of people's actions are correctly classifiable as intended consequences thereof. Consider, for example, a scenario that has been familiar to philosophers for decades (Foot 1978, 21–2). As some spelunkers are starting to leave a cave through its narrow mouth—the only means of exit—the fattest member of their party becomes immovably stuck. His corpulent body fills the mouth of the cave and thus prevents everyone else from exiting. Flood waters begin to rise dangerously inside the cave; if the spelunkers do not leave its confines within a few hours, they will all be drowned. They have some explosives with them, which are not sufficiently powerful to breach a separate opening in the cave but which are sufficiently powerful to dislodge the fat man from the cave's mouth by blowing him to pieces. If the spelunkers resort to using the explosives in order to remove the fat man from the orifice, they can hardly claim with any credibility that they did not intend to kill him. Although they would be delighted if he were miraculously to survive while being thrust out of the way by the explosives, they know that he will in fact be killed, and they opt for killing him as the lesser of two evils. With huge reluctance they choose to kill him in order to save themselves, and they therefore intend to kill him. As Philippa Foot remarked, we would rightly scoff if the trapped explorers 'were to argue that the death of the fat man might be taken as a merely foreseen consequence of the act of blowing him up'. As she contended, the following line of reasoning from the explorers would be risible: ' "We didn't want to kill him...only to blow him into small pieces" or even "...only to blast him out of the cave" ' (Foot 1978, 21–2).

In Foot's scenario of the subterranean adventurers, intention and desire do come apart in the manner suggested by Lempert. However, the actions of those adventurers are plainly distinguishable from the actions of people who support and design a system of capital punishment. The latter actions are much closer in character to those of the people in Dolinko's second and third examples: namely, the executives who run an automobile manufacturer and the Minister of Education who adopts some improved methods of instruction. Like the people in those two examples—and unlike the explorers in Foot's scenario—the supporters and designers of a system of capital punishment do not resort to killing any innocent human being (even with great reluctance) in pursuit of their own aims. Instead, they resign themselves to the fact that the undesired byproducts of their system of capital punishment will probably include small numbers of deaths of innocent defendants. Like the deaths of innocents in all three of Dolinko's examples, and unlike the death of the fat man in Foot's scenario, the executions of innocents that might take place in a system of capital punishment are directly due to determinative decisions reached by people other than those on whom we are focusing.[2] Hence, these sundry thought-experiments together militate

---

[2] Of course, the jurors who condemn an innocent defendant to death might themselves be among the supporters and designers of the system of capital punishment within which they reach their judgment.

strongly against Lempert's view that the supporters of a system of capital punishment in a liberal democracy intend to slay some innocent defendants.

Lempert might be tempted to retreat without fully surrendering. That is, he might maintain that the supporters of a system of capital punishment exhibit recklessness when they advocate an institution that will very likely lead to the deaths of some innocent people. He might cite in his support a different scenario offered by Foot, who referred to a 'case of wicked merchants selling, for cooking, oil they knew to be poisonous and thereby killing a number of innocent people' (Foot 1978, 22). Such a retort, however, would be highly assailable in at least two respects.

First, Lempert would face a difficulty parallel to the one that has just been recounted. In other words, he would be committing himself to the proposition that the manufacturer of automobiles and the Minister of Education in Dolinko's examples are reckless with regard to the lives of motorists and schoolchildren respectively. After all, the endeavours in which the manufacturer and the Minister engage are not relevantly distinguishable from the endeavours undertaken by supporters of capital punishment. Quite untenable, however, is the notion that the managers of a company which produces well-functioning automobiles—with engines designed not to enable the vehicles to reach perilously high speeds—are displaying recklessness with regard to the lives of innocent motorists and pedestrians who might be killed by the careless driving of the users of the automobiles. Likewise untenable is the notion that a Minister of Education who introduces new pedagogical methods after careful deliberation on their merits and drawbacks is behaving recklessly in relation to the lives of schoolchildren. Equally untenable, then, is the notion that people act recklessly when they support a system of capital punishment that is endowed with numerous safeguards against the conviction of innocents. The advocates of such a system are scarcely displaying a reckless disregard for the lives of innocent defendants, even though they know that no institution designed and run by human beings is absolutely guaranteed against the making of mistakes.

A second problem that will obstruct any attempt by Lempert to attribute recklessness to proponents of capital punishment is related to the first problem. When the hazarding of risks (usually acute risks) is reckless, it is not only deliberate but also gratuitous. One of the chief reasons for holding that the activities of the automotive managers and of the Minister of Education are not reckless is that their respective decisions and conduct are grounded on very solid considerations. The automotive managers oversee the production of an extremely useful product, while the Minister of Education strives to improve the modes of pedagogy in his country's schools. Their decisions and conduct are far from gratuitous.

Lempert will undoubtedly seek to differentiate capital punishment from the manufacture of automobiles and the improvement of education, on the ground that there are no solid considerations that support the imposition of such punishment. He

---

However, they will decide the verdict and sentence *qua* jurors rather than *qua* supporters and designers. No comparable division of roles is present in Foot's scenario of the spelunkers.

correctly believes that no such considerations are adduced by deterrence-oriented and retributivistic justifications of the death penalty, but he does not examine any other rationales for that penalty. In particular, like everyone else in the contemporary debates heretofore, he has not scrutinized the purgative rationale at all. As Chapter 6 has maintained, purgative considerations do suffice to render the death penalty morally obligatory in appropriate contexts. Purgative reasons for action are strong reasons; when people support the institution of capital punishment on the basis of such reasons while also urging the adoption of proper safeguards that minimize the likelihood of mistaken executions, they are not hazarding any risks gratuitously. They are not acting recklessly. Thus, unless Lempert can rebut the purgative rationale for capital punishment, he cannot succeed in relevantly distinguishing such punishment from the manufacture of automobiles and the tightening of educational standards. He has not met this challenge and indeed has not yet attempted to meet it.

7.1.2.2. Intentional or not?

Let us return to the judges and juries who mistakenly sentence innocent defendants to death. In connection with such people, Lempert oddly misstates the question which he is addressing and which is currently under examination here. In a concessionary statement that has already been quoted, he suggests that the relevant question is whether judges and juries who mistakenly sentence defendants to death are morally accountable for the commission of wrongs. In addition to framing the question inappositely, Lempert provides an incorrect (negative) answer. To the question about moral accountability for the commission of wrongs, the correct answer is affirmative. Whenever a judge or jury has mistakenly sentenced someone to death, a serious wrong has been committed—even if the deliberations undertaken by the judge or jury have been scrupulously careful and thoughtful. Although the gravity of the wrong is mitigated by the faultlessness of the deliberations and by the institutional responsibilities of the judge or jury, a wrong has indeed occurred. For that wrong, the deciding judge or jury is morally accountable. We shall return to this point later.

For the moment, the relevant question is not about moral accountability but about intentionality. When that latter question is asked about the legislators and citizens who support a system of capital punishment, the answer—as has been argued—is negative. Those legislators and citizens do not intend to kill innocent people. How should the question about intentionality be answered when it is asked in relation to the judges and juries who actually sentence innocent defendants to death, and in relation to the prison officials who implement the sentences? Do the judges and juries and prison officials intend to execute innocent defendants? We should assume, of course, that they are acting in good faith with meticulous circumspection. Do they nonetheless intend to kill innocents?

This question cannot be answered until we disambiguate it. When the question is construed in one way, an affirmative answer to it would warrant the conclusion that the judges and juries are behaving wickedly (rather than merely wrongly) by sentencing innocents to death. When the question is construed in another way, an affirmative answer to it does not warrant any such conclusion. Now, as will be seen, when the question is construed in the former of these two ways, the only sustainable answer to it is negative. When the question is construed in the latter of these two ways, by contrast, the correct answer to it is affirmative; but that affirmative answer does not carry the strongly condemnatory force which the opponents of capital punishment seek to convey when they allege that the long-term practice of such punishment will result in intentional executions of innocents. However the notion of intentionally killing innocent people might be understood, nobody can correctly invoke that notion in support of the proposition that judges and juries are behaving wickedly when in good faith they mistakenly sentence people to death.

7.1.2.2.1. The de dicto/de re distinction

What is needed here is a distinction between understanding a statement *de dicto* and understanding a statement *de re*. Exactly how this distinction should be formulated at a general level is a matter of controversy among logicians and philosophers of language (McKay and Nelson 2010; Richard 1990, 128–33), but the distinction can easily be illustrated through some examples. Let us ponder a slightly modified version of an example from a classic paper on the topic (Quine 1956). 'Ernest is seeking to kill a lion' can be interpreted either *de dicto* or *de re*. We interpret the statement *de re* if we construe it to mean that there is some particular lion which Ernest is seeking specifically to kill. Such an interpretation will be natural, for instance, if a lion has escaped from a circus and if Ernest has been hired to protect members of the public by shooting the beast. Alternatively, we can interpret the statement *de dicto* by construing it to mean that Ernest is seeking to kill any lion among an array of such creatures. That interpretation will be natural, for instance, if Ernest is participating in an African safari. Construed *de re*, the statement is to be analysed as 'There is some x, such that x is a lion and Ernest is seeking to kill x.' Construed *de dicto*, the statement is to be analysed as 'Ernest is seeking to bring it about that there is some x, such that x is a lion and Ernest has killed x.'

Let us briefly mull over one further example: 'Ben intends to marry the tallest woman in Topeka.' Construed *de re*, the statement is to be analysed as 'There is some x, such that x is the tallest woman in Topeka and Ben is intending to marry x.' So interpreted, the statement posits a relationship between Ben's intention and a particular woman. The positing of that relationship does not imply that Ben knows that the particular person whom he intends to marry is the tallest woman in Topeka. When the statement is interpreted *de re*, it can be true even if Ben has not the slightest inkling that his fiancée is taller than every other Topekan woman. Construed *de dicto*, by contrast, the statement is to be analysed as 'Ben intends to bring it about that there is some x, such that x is the tallest woman in Topeka and Ben has married x.' When the statement is interpreted *de dicto*, it implies that Ben's fulfilment of his intention will involve his knowing that his bride is the tallest woman in Topeka.

7.1.2.2.2. *The distinction applied*

We are now in a position to assess the allegation that a judge intentionally orders the killing of an innocent defendant when she mistakenly convicts such a defendant and sentences him to death. Such an allegation, plainly, can be interpreted either *de dicto* or *de re*. Construed in the latter fashion, the allegation is correct but is not a harsh condemnation. Construed in the former fashion, the allegation is a harsh condemnation but is not correct. (I am assuming, as I have been assuming, that every judge or other decision-maker involved in capital sentencing within any liberal democracy has acted in good faith with reasonable care. In the final subsection of my discussion of mistaken executions, I shall relax that assumption.)

Suppose that Morgan is innocent and that he has nonetheless been convicted of some repellently heinous crimes for which he is to be sentenced after a scrupulously fair trial. Suppose that he is sentenced to death, and that the sentence is eventually implemented after his appeals have failed to overturn the conviction. When Morgan's guiltlessness later becomes apparent, the judge or the executioner is accused of having intentionally killed an innocent person. Is the accusation correct? If it is interpreted *de re*, it is correct.[3] So construed, it maintains that (1) the judge or executioner has intentionally killed the particular person Morgan and (2) the particular person in question has turned out to be innocent of the crimes for which he was put to death. Each conjunct of the conjunction in this *de re* accusation is true, and thus the accusation as a whole is true. It is to be analysed as 'There is some *x*, such that *x* has been intentionally put to death by the judge or executioner and *x* has subsequently turned out to be innocent.' When the accusation is understood in this fashion, it does not in any way imply that the judge or executioner was aware of Morgan's innocence at the time of the sentencing and the execution. It allows that the execution of Morgan is similar to an incident of 'friendly fire' in the military, where soldiers—acting in good faith with reasonable care—intentionally kill an ostensible enemy who later turns out to be one of their own troops. The soldiers have intentionally killed their comrade, but only because they have mistakenly believed that he is a foe rather than a comrade. Similarly, the judge and executioner have intentionally killed Morgan, but only because they have mistakenly believed that he is guilty of the appalling crimes for which he has been tried. Consequently, although the allegation about the intentional killing of an innocent defendant is correct when it is construed *de re*, it is not harshly condemnatory. It does not suggest that the mistakes committed by the judge and executioner are evil; their mistakes are morally wrong and dismaying but are far from wicked.

---

[3] Thus, the following remark by Louis Pojman is simplistic, notwithstanding that the position which he rejects is even more facile: '[Opponents are] incorrect in saying that mistaken judicial execution is morally the same or worse than murder, for a deliberate intention to kill the innocent occurs in a murder, whereas no such intention occurs in wrongful capital punishment' (Pojman 1998, 54).

Alternatively, the allegation can be construed *de dicto*. So interpreted, the allegation is to be analysed as 'The judge and executioner have intended to bring it about that there is some x, such that x is a person innocent of any crimes and x has been put to death by the judge and executioner.' Construed in this fashion with reference specifically to Morgan's case, the accusation implies that the judge and executioner have been aware of the innocence of Morgan when they respectively sentence and execute him. Such an accusation is strongly condemnatory. If it were true, the actions of the judge and executioner would be evil rather than merely wrong. However, on the assumptions that have been operative throughout this discussion, the allegation understood *de dicto* is false. Both the judge and the executioner at the time of the sentencing and the execution have firmly believed that Morgan is guilty of the loathsome crimes for which he has been convicted after fair legal proceedings. Accordingly, their putting him to death has not been undertaken in the knowledge that he is innocent. Hence, although their putting him to death is a serious wrong that has given rise to remedial obligations, it does not partake of the wickedness that would be correctly ascribable to it if the allegation above were correct when construed *de dicto*.

Supporters of the death penalty should be on their guard whenever their opponents assert that, even if everybody involved in the workings of a criminal-justice system is acting in good faith, the use of such a penalty over a long period will very likely result in a few intentional killings of innocents. As has been observed, such a charge is correct only if it is interpreted *de re* rather than *de dicto*. Nonetheless, the opponents of capital punishment who voice such an indictment are probably hoping to capitalize on the severely condemnatory force which the indictment carries if it is interpreted *de dicto*. The point here is not that the people who resort to such an accusation are typically indulging in chicanery. Rather, the point is that—especially in debates outside scholarly circles—some of those people are insufficiently attuned to fine philosophical distinctions and are therefore conflating the two ways in which the accusation can be construed. If they simply want to highlight the similarities between mistaken executions and incidents of 'friendly fire' in the military, then their assertions are substantively unexceptionable though perhaps misleading. In most contexts, however, their assertions appear to be advanced as harsh denunciations that specify an evil-making property (rather than merely a wrongness-intensifying property) of the mistaken executions. Their pronouncements appear to be aimed at eliciting shudders that go beyond consternation. So aimed, the pronouncements are misconceived.

7.1.3. Sweeping too broadly

In respect of many of the objections to capital punishment that focus on the possibility of mistakes, one major reason for querying their damagingness is that they sweep too broadly. If the objections were correct in telling against the subjection of murderous thugs to the death penalty, they would also tell against the subjection of such thugs to any other severe punishments. To say as much, of course, is not to deny the differences between the death penalty and the other harsh sanctions. As has been readily accepted throughout this book, capital punishment is a more severe imposition than any other punitive measure that is employed within liberal democracies. Nevertheless, if some of the worries about mistaken executions were sufficient to delegitimize every use of capital punishment, they would also delegitimize the use of any alternative sanctions. Given that those worries do not suffice to undermine the moral tenability of all the alternative sanctions, we can quite safely infer *modus tollens* that they likewise do not expose any fatal flaws in the morality of capital punishment.[4]

7.1.3.1. Lempert's reasoning afresh

As has been remarked by some of the scholars who have trenchantly criticized Lempert's argument about the supporters and designers of systems of capital punishment (Alexander 1983, 234–36; Dolinko 1986, 592), the soundness of his argument would morally doom not only capital punishment but also every other onerous sanction. After all, if executions of innocents will occasionally occur in virtually any large-scale institution of capital punishment, so too will lengthy terms of imprisonment occasionally be imposed on innocents in virtually any criminal-justice system that uses imprisonment as a punitive technique. Thus, if executions of innocents are intended by the supporters and designers of every system of capital punishment—as Lempert maintains—then so too the imprisoning of innocents for lengthy terms will have been intended by the supporters and designers of every criminal-justice system. As far as Lempert's argument is concerned, there are no grounds for distinguishing between mistaken executions and mistakenly imposed terms of imprisonment. Whilst the former are confidently foreseeable though undesired and rare consequences that ensue from the functioning of virtually any large-scale institution of capital punishment, the latter are confidently foreseeable though undesired and rare consequences that ensue from the functioning of virtually any criminal-justice system. Lempert believes that, because the occurrence of some erroneously imposed executions is a confidently foreseeable consequence of virtually every large-scale regime of capital punishment, the supporters and designers of any such regime intend to have innocent people put to death. Thus, he has committed himself to a parallel claim about the supporters and designers of any criminal-justice system; they intend to have innocent people sentenced to lengthy terms of imprisonment. He further suggests that the intendedness of the executions of innocents is sufficient to preclude the moral legitimacy of any institution of capital punishment. (He actually maintains that the intendedness is sufficient to render that institution incompatible with retributivism's prohibition on any deliberate slaying of innocent people. However, given that such a prohibition is a correct principle of morality—*pace* any consequentialists who might think otherwise—Lempert's position can safely be formulated as a thesis about the moral legitimacy of the aforementioned institution.) Lempert has therefore committed himself to the cognate view

---

[4] A *modus tollens* inference is of the following form. From the premises 'If P, then Q' and 'It is not the case that Q,' we can validly infer 'It is not the case that P.'

that the intendedness of the imprisoning of innocents is sufficient to preclude the moral legitimacy of every system of criminal justice.

Nothing in the preceding paragraph has elided the differences between the death penalty and other punishments. Although death is the most severe sanction imposed in any liberal democracy, the disparity between it and any lengthy term of imprisonment is not enough to block the generalization of Lempert's argument to every such lengthy term. If the intentional execution of an innocent defendant is morally wrong—as it plainly is—then the intentional subjection of someone to a protracted term of incarceration for some crime(s) which he has not committed is likewise morally wrong. Moreover, although the former wrong is graver than the latter, the gap between them is too small to salvage the moral legitimacy of a system of criminal-law enforcement that has been designed partly in order to condemn innocent people to long terms of imprisonment. Were Lempert correct in his reasoning about the legitimacy of the institution of capital punishment, he would be correct in extending that reasoning to call into question the legitimacy of every credible regime of criminal-law enforcement.

As has already been argued, Lempert's reasoning about the institution of capital punishment is in fact unsustainable. It is unsustainable principally because of its untenable ascriptions of intentions to the supporters and designers of systems of capital punishment, as we have seen. However, as will be contended later, a further reason for rejecting it is that it overestimates the morally vitiating effects of dubious intentions. Even if intentions of the sort which Lempert recounts were correctly imputable to some of the people who favour each system of capital punishment, we could not validly infer that every such system is morally illegitimate in all of its workings. Some such systems might still be morally legitimate overall as institutions. We shall return to this point.

7.1.3.2. Intentionality at the level of decision-making, once again

Like Lempert's attributions of intentions to the supporters and designers of institutions of capital punishment, any allegations about judges' and executioners' intentional killings of innocents are generalizable to other onerous punitive impositions. If judges and other criminal-justice officials are acting intentionally in capital cases, they are likewise acting intentionally in cases where they hand down and implement sentences of lifelong imprisonment (or other lengthy terms of incarceration). If the allegations about intentional killings of innocents in cases of mistaken executions were correct when construed *de dicto*, then—as has been remarked—those executions would be wicked rather than just seriously wrong. Similarly, if allegations about the intentional imprisoning of innocent people for life (or for other lengthy terms) in cases of mistaken incarceration were correct when construed *de dicto*, the punishments imposed in those cases would be wicked rather than just seriously wrong. Although the death penalty is a more severe sanction than any lengthy term of incarceration, someone who knowingly condemns other people to long periods in prison for crimes which they have not committed is behaving evilly.[5] The evil in any particular case would be nearly as great as the evil committed by someone who knowingly condemns an innocent person to death. Thus, since cases of mistaken incarceration are virtually inevitable in any large-scale system of criminal justice, the allegations about the intentional imprisoning of innocents would be hugely damaging to the moral status of every such system if those allegations were correct when construed *de dicto*.

In fact, of course, such allegations are generally unsupportable when they are interpreted *de dicto*. We have seen as much in connection with the accusations of intentional killings of innocents in cases of mistaken executions, and a parallel point applies here. In a liberal democracy, the imprisoning of innocent people will never (or hardly ever) be undertaken in the knowledge of their innocence. Accordingly, allegations about the intentional imprisoning of innocents are true in a liberal democracy only when they are construed *de re*. So construed, of course, the allegations are far less scathing than when they are understood *de dicto*.

At any rate, the key point here is that the accusations about intentional killings of innocents in cases of mistaken executions do not single out a problem that (in its general contours) is unique to capital punishment. If the problem highlighted by those accusations were sufficiently damaging to imperil the moral legitimacy of every system of capital punishment—as is typically assumed by the people who articulate the accusations—a cognate problem would imperil the moral legitimacy of every system of criminal justice that employs onerous sanctions such as lengthy terms of imprisonment. Now, quite outlandish is the notion that the system of criminal justice in every liberal democracy is bereft of moral legitimacy. Insofar as we would be led to such a notion if we were to credit the accusations of intentional killings just mentioned,[6] we have good grounds for distrusting those accusations as they are typically understood. For reasons partly indicated in the preceding paragraph and partly indicated later, the distrust turns out to be well-founded indeed.

7.1.3.3. Steiker and Steiker on the distinctive harms of mistaken executions

In a highly illuminating article about the recent tendency of opponents of capital punishment to focus their efforts on the occurrence of mistaken convictions, Carol Steiker and Jordan Steiker briefly mention 'two distinctive harms that flow from executing the innocent' (Steiker and Steiker 2005, 588). To be sure, the dialectical

---

[5] Here and elsewhere in this book, I leave aside any truly exceptional circumstances in which a lengthy term of imprisonment is imposed on some innocent person for his own safety and with his eager collusion. Though such circumstances are extremely rare, they can conceivably arise even in a flourishing liberal democracy. For example, somebody who defects from an organized-crime syndicate and testifies against some of his erstwhile comrades might well be safer within the confines of a maximum-security penitentiary than in the outside world, for quite an extended period.

[6] We would be led to such a notion not as a matter of logical entailment but as a matter of substantive morality. Though there are morally pregnant differences between capital punishment and lengthy terms of imprisonment, the morally pregnant similarities between them are such that the queries about mistaken executions will be applicable as well (*mutatis mutandis*) to mistakenly imposed terms of imprisonment.

situation of their remark is different from that of Lempert's comments. At this stage in their article, they are arguing specifically against the view that the occurrence of mistaken executions is comparable to the occurrence of accidental deaths during major public-works projects such as the erection of highways and bridges. When they refer to two harms as distinctive, they mean that those harms are not characteristic of the accidental deaths that have been compared by some theorists to mistaken applications of the death penalty; Steiker and Steiker are not seeking to maintain that the harms in question are never associated with any mistakenly imposed sanctions other than executions. Still, given that they do not indicate that the specified harms are indeed associated with other sanctions, we should take note of that point here.

Steiker and Steiker first point out that, unlike the victims of accidents during public-works projects, 'those who are innocent and sentenced to death suffer the additional devastation of being blamed for a terrible crime; their names, families, and entire lives are forever tainted by such ignominy, quite apart from the death of their bodies' (Steiker and Steiker 2005, 588). Worth mentioning briefly here is a matter that will receive further attention presently. Because the erroneousness of a mistaken execution can be discovered posthumously, not everyone who undergoes such an execution will be tainted forever by ignominy. In any particular case, such an upshot is contingent rather than inevitable. At any rate, the chief point to be noticed at the moment is that the stigmatizing effects of conviction and punishment will attach to people who are mistakenly found guilty of heinous crimes, regardless of whether the penalty for such crimes in a particular jurisdiction is death or instead some other onerous sanction. Perhaps the stigma will be slightly greater if the death penalty is imposed, but the unwarranted infamy in each case derives principally if not entirely from the fact that someone has been convicted and severely punished for seemingly having perpetrated some appalling crimes. The special severity of the death penalty will make little if any difference to the level of the infamy that accrues. Even if a defendant is sentenced to lifelong imprisonment rather than to death for the terrible crimes that have been imputed to him, the level of the notoriety will be very high. Moreover, unless he is incarcerated in isolation from other convicts, he is likely to be the target of lethal attacks by them.

Steiker and Steiker next train their attention on the legitimacy-impairing effects of mistaken executions. They declare that 'when such errors are discovered, as some but by no means all of them eventually will be, they deeply undermine the legitimacy of the entire criminal justice system' (Steiker and Steiker 2005, 588). As the Steikers refer to the discovery of errors, they are clearly concentrating on the *perceived* legitimacy of a criminal-justice system. However, their point can readily be extended to the *actual* legitimacy of any such system and can thereby encompass mistakes that remain undiscovered as well as those that are eventually brought to light. Now, admittedly, both with respect to perceived legitimacy and with respect to actual legitimacy, the corrosiveness of mistaken executions is somewhat greater than the corrosiveness of mistakenly imposed terms of imprisonment. Nevertheless, the difference is a fairly small matter of degree. If an innocent person is convicted of ghastly crimes and condemned to a lifelong term of incarceration, and if the error is unearthed much later—perhaps after his death in prison—both the perceived legitimacy and the actual legitimacy of the prevailing criminal-justice system will have been damaged quite badly. Mistaken inflictions of any severe punishments detract significantly from the legitimacy of the criminal-justice institutions in which the inflictions have occurred. Such legitimacy-attenuating effects are especially pronounced in capital cases, but are hardly unique thereto.

As has been indicated, my remarks here are not disagreeing with anything asserted by Steiker and Steiker. Whereas I am contending that the detrimental results of mistaken executions ensue also (albeit usually somewhat less damningly) from mistaken impositions of other severe penalties, the Steikers are concerned to distinguish mistaken executions from the fatalities that occur in public-works projects. My conclusions are entirely consistent with their apt conclusion that there is 'ample reason to weigh erroneous executions quite differently from unavoidable deaths in the [public-works] context'.[7] Nevertheless, because the Steikers' reference to 'two distinctive harms that flow from executing the innocent' is susceptible to misunderstanding, my remarks here have warned against anyone's inferring that those harms follow only from mistaken executions and not additionally from mistaken applications of other heavy sanctions. If any readers were to seize upon the general possibility of those harms as a basis for rejecting the institution of capital punishment, they would be sweeping too broadly. Save in the highly unlikely event that the mistakes within some particular jurisdiction are more common in the administration of capital punishment than in the administration of other severe penalties, someone who seeks to avoid the stigmatizing and legitimacy-impairing ramifications of erroneous executions by opposing the institution of capital punishment will have committed himself to opposing as well the imposition of any other heavy sanctions. If he does not relish the latter commitment, he should rethink the former. (Again, the commitments to which I refer here are moral rather than logical. Given that the stigmatizing and legitimacy-impairing effects of mistaken confinements of people for long terms in prison will fall little short of the corresponding effects of mistaken executions, someone who regards the prospect of the latter effects as intolerably outweighing any benefits of the institution of capital punishment should adopt a similar stance with respect to other sanctions down to a fairly low level of punitive severity. Although the stigmatizing and legitimacy-enfeebling consequences of mistaken applications of the other sanctions are somewhat smaller than the homologous consequences of mistaken

---

[7] Steiker and Steiker 2005, 588. Somewhat oddly, the Steikers do not mention another reason: whereas the fatalities in public-works projects are accidental, the deaths of innocent people who undergo executions are intentional. Of course, as has been observed at some length in this chapter, we need to be very careful about the sense in which those deaths are intentional. Nonetheless, the fact that they are intentional in some sense is a feature that *pro tanto* renders them worse than the fatal mishaps in public-works projects.

executions—and although there are some moral differences between the benefits of the institution of capital punishment and the benefits of the employment of the other sanctions—such disparities are too small to enable anyone plausibly to invoke the stigmatizing and legitimacy-enfeebling consequences as grounds for opposing the death penalty while not also opposing the use of other onerous punishments.)

7.1.4. Irrevocability?

When opponents of capital punishment endeavour to specify why mistaken executions are qualitatively worse than mistakes in the administration of other harsh penalties, they frequently submit that executions are uniquely irrevocable. If such a contention on their part is to be sustainable, it will have to draw upon a pertinent criterion (or a pertinent set of criteria) that will distinguish capital punishment from other sanctions. Let us explore some of the criteria that have been broached.

7.1.4.1. Compensability

Sometimes the complaints about the irrevocability of capital punishment are centred on our supposed inability to compensate innocent people for executions to which they have mistakenly been subjected. In that respect, the opponents of capital punishment contend, death is markedly different from any other sanction. Although someone wrongly imprisoned cannot receive back the years during which he has been immured, he can be compensated to some degree for the loss of those years. By contrast, someone wrongly executed is not only unable to receive back the life that has been taken from him, but is also beyond any possibility of compensation. So argue many of the opponents of capital punishment—including some of the most sophisticated opponents thereof—who seek to explain why errors in the administration of such punishment are uniquely terrible.

Hugo Adam Bedau, for example, writes that '[d]eath makes compensation for error impossible, whereas it is always possible to compensate (at least in part) any wrongly convicted life term prisoner,' and that '[d]eath...makes compensation impossible, whereas it is possible to compensate a prisoner in some way for wrongful confinement even if it is not possible to give back any of the liberty that was taken away' (Bedau 1990, 490; 1993, 176). Dolinko has likewise maintained that '[w]e can at least partially remedy, repair, or eliminate the consequences to a person of imprisonment, but not those of execution,' and that 'infliction of the death penalty automatically makes it impossible to do anything to rectify a mistake' (Dolinko 1986, 576 n 187, 586 n 216). Dan Markel has put forward some similar pronouncements:

By precluding executions, at least there is a chance for error to be recognized, apologized for, and, in some cases, recompensed appropriately.... The anxiety about punishing or executing the wrong person means that the state must leave itself avenues in which it can undertake its own reparations and apologies to persons it has mistakenly punished. The hubris and final-ity associated with an execution forecloses the state's opportunity to take those steps toward rectifying the injustice it has caused.[8]

In sounding this theme, these opponents of the death penalty are joined by one of its most prominent advocates, Ernest van den Haag: '[A] prison sentence may be remitted once the prisoner is found innocent; and he can be compensated for the time served (although compensation ordinarily cannot repair the harm). Thus, though (nearly) all penalties are irreversible, the death penalty, unlike others, is irrevocable as well' (Van den Haag 1968, 280). Another supporter of capital punishment, Igor Primorac, has also declared that mistaken executions are uniquely non-compensable: '[T]hose [mistakes made by judges and jurors] with most disastrous repercussions—those which result in innocent men being executed—can never be rectified. In all other cases of mistaken sentencing we can revoke the punishment, either completely or in part, or at least extend compensation' (Primorac 1982, 144).

For the moment, let us leave aside the innocent people who are sentenced to long terms in prison. We shall return to them in the next subsection. Here our focus lies on the proposition that any innocent person who undergoes an execution can never be compensated for the wrong that has been done to him or her. Are Bedau and Dolinko and these other writers correct when they endorse that proposition? As has been recognized by some other theorists who have pondered these matters (Davis 1996, 97–103; Gale 1985, 1024–5), the answer to this question is negative. Although an innocent person who is mistakenly subjected to capital punishment cannot be compensated for the error during his lifetime, some compensation and other modes of rectification can occur after his death by way of his estate or surviving relatives. Just as the victim of a tort can be compensated posthumously through payments of damages to his estate—regardless of whether he has died from the tort itself or from something else during the litigation that arises from it—so too the victim of an erroneous execution can be compensated posthumously. A court can order that payments be made to his estate for distribution to his heirs, and an appropriate official from the judicial or executive branch of government can furnish an authoritative expression of apology and consternation.

To be sure, any such compensation and apology will hardly undo all the effects of the execution. Those measures will not magically bring the deceased person back to life. Still, compensation as a remedy in countless situations quite apart from capital punishment is inadequate to undo the effects of sundry wrongs. One such situation, of course, is the plight of an innocent person who has been erroneously convicted and imprisoned. If such a person is incarcerated for a lengthy period before the mistake is finally discovered (if it ever is), the many years squandered in prison are lost to him forever. Numerous other probable ramifications of his confinement—the falling away of his family and friends, the dissolution of his sense of purpose in life and his sense of self-reliance, the disruption and termination of his career, the coarsening of

---

[8] Markel 2005, 468, 478. See also Markel 2009, 1203.

his personality, and so forth—are likewise insusceptible to being undone fully if at all. Hence, although posthumous compensation and apologies are manifestly imperfect as means of remedying the wrong suffered by a person who has been erroneously subjected to capital punishment, the fact that they are imperfect does not make them qualitatively different from remedies for wrongs in myriad other contexts.

Worth remarking here is that this subsection's point about the posthumous compensability of mistaken executions has been recognized—albeit fleetingly and inconspicuously—by some opponents of capital punishment who are disposed to characterize executions as irrevocable. For example, Jeremy Waldron writes as follows: 'If a person turns out to have been innocent of some offense for which he was punished with a penalty other than death, there is something we as a society can do to make up for the suffering, loss of liberty, or inconvenience we have imposed on him. If he has been executed there is nothing we can do for him (though we may be able to compensate his estate or his dependents)' (Waldron 1992, 39). Markel, from whose work I have quoted above, also laconically adverts to the possibility of posthumous compensation: 'When the guillotine drops,...the state cannot demonstrate its own sense of remorse to the offender, even if it could make some amends to the surviving family.' To his credit, Markel again tersely acknowledges the possibility of posthumous compensation when he is discussing the imprisonment of innocent people: '[L]ost time [spent in prison] cannot itself be restored, but that does not preclude civil plaintiffs from obtaining a remedy in tort for harms endured on account of false imprisonment, nor does it mean that a victim of false imprisonment, or her allies *and survivors*, would not appreciate the expression of apology and recompense from the state.'[9]

Though these avowals of the possibility of posthumous remedies for mistaken executions are very brief, they correctly indicate that claims about the unique irrevocability of the death penalty are not tenable insofar as those claims are focused on the putative uncompensability of such executions. Detractors of capital punishment will have to resort to some other way of cashing out the notion of irrevocability.

7.1.4.2. Remedies during one's lifetime

Presumably aware that compensation for any erroneous wielding of the death penalty can be paid posthumously—and that other rectificatory measures, inadequate though they are, can likewise be undertaken posthumously—opponents of that penalty have often trained their attention on the fact that compensation or other remedies for a mistaken execution will never be provided *during the lifetime of the executed person*. Unlike any claim that a mistaken execution cannot be remedied at all, this claim that a mistaken execution of a person P cannot be remedied during P's lifetime is correct in itself. Furthermore, this way of explicating the property of irrevocability trades on an ethically significant distinction. Compensation or any other remedy provided during the lifetime of a wronged person is more meaningful than compensation or any other remedy

---

[9] Markel 2005, 463, 468–9 n 258, emphasis added. See also Markel 2009, 1198.

provided posthumously. However, the key question here is whether such an understanding of the property of irrevocability can serve to differentiate between the subjection of
an innocent person to capital punishment and the subjection of an innocent person to
lifelong imprisonment-without-parole.

Many of the theorists who write on this matter seem to assume that any innocent
person subjected to lifelong imprisonment is immortal. On the one hand, obviously, if
those theorists were asked directly whether people mistakenly incarcerated are immortal, they would answer in the negative. On the other hand, in a host of pronouncements
by an array of writers, an assumption of immortality appears to be operative.

Some of the statements quoted in the preceding subsection are among those pronouncements, including the first of the statements by Bedau. Two further declara-
tions by Bedau, which resemble each other closely, likewise presuppose that wrongly
imprisoned people are immortal. He asserts that '[d]eath is interminable, whereas it
is *always* possible to terminate by revocation a life prison sentence,' and that '[d]eath
is interminable, whereas it is *always* possible to revoke or interrupt a life sentence'
(Bedau 1990, 490, emphasis added; 1993, 175–6, emphasis added). Larry Laudan
adopts much the same position when he writes as follows: 'If someone is erroneously
sent to prison for life, there is *always* the prospect that the conviction, if false, can be
undone by pardon or retrial, if suitably exculpatory evidence emerges' (Laudan 2006,
58, emphasis added). Ernest van den Haag chimes in with a similar remark: 'Death
alone is irrevocable. A life sentence can *always* be revoked; the law can be changed;
appeals may be successful; a pardon may be granted. Not least, there is *always* the hope
of escape' (Van den Haag and Conrad 1983, 257, emphases added). With the instances
of 'always' in the foregoing statements, these philosophers implicitly ascribe immortality to people who are wrongly incarcerated.

A somewhat more subtle version of this misstep is to be found in a very insightful
essay on the irrevocability of capital punishment, by Michael Davis. Davis submits
that 'the death penalty makes compensation during one's lifetime impossible while
imprisonment does not' (Davis 1996, 98). Davis here commits a stumble which he
perceptively criticizes elsewhere in his essay. That is, he here relies on a comparison between (1) the culmination of a process of administering a death sentence and
(2) any stages of imprisonment that are antecedent to the culmination of a lifelong
sentence. As he himself recognizes slightly later: '[I]f we are to consider whether the
sentence of death, once executed, is irrevocable in a way imprisonment is not, we
must be careful to compare the outcome of the death penalty with the outcome of
imprisonment.'[10] When we do compare the outcome of a process of implementing
a death sentence and the outcome of a process of implementing a lifelong sentence,
we find that the consummation of each of those processes is a defendant's death. If
each sanction is carried out fully before any mistake is discovered, then the person

---

[10] Davis 1996, 104. This point is likewise well made in Barkow 2009, 1174. See also my discussions in
§§ 3.3.1.2 and 3.3.1.3 of Chapter 3.

who has been subjected to the sanction cannot be compensated during his lifetime. In that respect, lifelong imprisonment-without-parole is no different from capital punishment—notwithstanding this paragraph's first quotation from Davis.

Dolinko too has erred by pursuing an inapposite comparison. He writes as follows:

> It is of course possible that in a particular case a person wrongly sent to prison will have died before the error is discovered, so that he cannot be released or compensated. This is a kind of 'irrevocability' to which *any* human action is liable. But what is unique about capital punishment is its *inherent* irrevocability: infliction of the death penalty automatically makes it impossible to do anything to rectify a mistake...And much of the force of the mistake argument derives from the belief that finite, fallible creatures ought not to 'play God' by imposing a penalty guaranteed to be irrevocable rather than one which might, like any human action, be made 'irrevocable' by adventitious supervening events. [Dolinko 1986, 586 n 216, emphases in original]

Let us here overlook the fact that Dolinko in this passage is referring to compensation or rectification *tout court* instead of referring more narrowly to compensation or rectification that is undertaken during the lifetime of the person affected. Even if that misstep is put aside, his comparison between capital punishment and imprisonment is tendentious. He poses a contrast between a completed process of administering a death sentence and an uncompleted process of administering a sentence of lifelong imprisonment-without-parole. If we compare like with like by juxtaposing the completion of the former process and the completion of the latter, we find that the culmination of each of them is the death of the convicted person. Thus, each of those sanctions when fully imposed is guaranteed to be irrevocable, and each of them when fully imposed is possessed of inherent irrevocability. What Dolinko says about capital punishment in the passage above is fully applicable as well to lifelong imprisonment-without-parole. Whenever a sentence of lifelong imprisonment-without-parole is consummated, there is no prospect of undertaking compensation or any other remedy during the lifetime of the person on whom that sanction has been inflicted.

Yet another incisive theorist goes astray when Markel writes that 'the state cannot be said to *intentionally* foreclose the opportunity to make amends to a wrongly convicted person when...the defendant dies in prison before her name can be cleared...But the problem with capital punishment, is that it is unusual among punishments because executions take an *affirmative* step to prevent the possible recognition of wrongful convictions in the future' (Markel 2009, 1202–3, emphases in original). Though the closing statement in this quotation is worded quite puzzlingly, it appears to be asserting that the execution of an innocent prisoner will prevent any future recognition of the erroneousness of her conviction. Assertions of that sort have been oppugned in § 7.1.4.1 above. Still, Markel more likely means to say that the erroneousness of the conviction cannot be recognized during the prisoner's lifetime, once the prisoner has been executed. So construed, his contention is correct but is also true *mutatis mutandis* of lifelong imprisonment-without-parole. Exactly what Markel means to convey through his italicization of 'affirmative' is not clear, but the steps undertaken by the officials in a system of criminal-law enforcement to confine a prisoner for life without parole are affirmative by any reasonable reckoning. If we compare the intended culmination of their steps with the intended culmination of the steps undertaken by law-enforcement officials against a prisoner who is to be executed, we find that the upshot is the same. Like an execution, lifelong imprisonment-without-parole ends in death.

Insofar as the first statement in the quotation from Markel is applied to an innocent person P who has been sentenced to lifelong imprisonment-without-parole, it is true only when interpreted *de dicto*. If the statement is instead interpreted *de re*, it incorrectly suggests that the intended completion of a term of lifelong incarceration does not eliminate opportunities for the making of amends directly to the person who has been incarcerated. On the contrary, when P is sentenced to lifelong imprisonment-without-parole, what is intended is that she should be incarcerated until she is dead—at which point no further communications with her will be possible, of course. Hence, the first statement in the quotation from Markel is tenable only as a *de dicto* assertion. As such an assertion, the statement in effect denies that P was known to be innocent during the period when she was condemned in good faith to spend the rest of her life behind bars. As such an assertion, however, the statement can readily be extended to cover innocent defendants who are sentenced in good faith to be executed. Their innocence, too, has not been known during the time when their punishment has been administered. Thus, like the closing portion of the quotation from Markel, the opening portion adverts to a feature that is shared by capital punishment and lifelong imprisonment-without-parole. Markel has not succeeded in isolating any feature that is unique to the death penalty.

In short, although the hallmark of the irrevocability of a punishment imposed on a person P is the fact that the punishment can never be remedied during P's lifetime, a focus on that hallmark does not enable us to differentiate between capital punishment and a term of lifelong imprisonment-without-parole. Whenever either of those sanctions is fully implemented, it is irrevocable in the specified sense. If the detractors of capital punishment wish to single out some aspect of it that sets it apart from all other sanctions as uniquely problematic, they will have to look elsewhere.

What those detractors have presumably had in mind, when training their attention on the fact that no remedies for an erroneous execution can ever be undertaken during the lifetime of the person who has been executed, is that the process of administering a death sentence is typically shorter in its duration than is the process of implementing a sentence of lifelong imprisonment-without-parole (Davis 1996, 107–8). On the one hand, because a system of capital punishment cannot be morally legitimate unless ample opportunities for appeals are provided to people who have been sentenced to death,[11] the process of implementing a capital sentence in a morally legitimate manner will frequently extend over a long period (as does indeed happen, sometimes to an extravagant extent, in the United States at present[12]). On the other hand, notwithstanding the lengthiness of the interval between the sentencing and the execution in many a capital case, that interval is typically briefer than the period spent in prison by someone who serves out a term of lifelong incarceration. Accordingly, the span of time during which the innocence of a sentenced defendant can be uncovered prior to his death is typically shorter in a case where he is executed than in a case where he has been sent to prison for life. *Ceteris paribus*, then, the occasions on which the defendant's innocence might be exposed during his lifetime are typically fewer in a case of the former sort than in a case of the latter sort.

This difference between capital punishment and lifelong imprisonment-without-parole—a difference that resides in what typically obtains rather than in what always obtains—is probably the very thing toward which the opponents of capital punishment are gesturing when they write as if imprisoned defendants are immortal. Contrary to what is so often contended, the divergence between those sanctions does not lie in the irrevocability of the one versus the revocability of the other. If irrevocability is cashed out as irremediability during the lifetime of a punished defendant, then each of those sanctions is irrevocable when it is fully put into effect. Instead, the divergence between them lies in the rapidity with which each of them typically gets put into effect fully. That divergence is a genuine difference, but it is obviously a matter of degree rather than a qualitative matter of kind. Within our assessments of the moral status of capital punishment, that divergence should enter as one factor to be weighed against others. Let us now turn to an outline of such an assessment—at a high level of abstraction—in order to ponder briefly how the moral status of the death penalty is affected by the ineliminable possibility of mistakes in the application of that penalty.

7.1.5. Capital punishment in the shadow of mistakes

Although claims about the unique irrevocability of capital punishment and about the intentionality of executions of innocents have turned out to be unsustainable in the forms in which they are usually propounded, this chapter has come up with some attenuated versions of those claims that are defensible. Mistaken executions are indeed worse than mistaken impositions of the other sanctions that are employed in liberal democracies, even though the distinctive badness of such executions has frequently been mischaracterized

---

[11] For some indications why an ample structure of appeals is so important—despite the costly cumbersomeness of such a structure and its proneness to abuse—see, for example, Grann 2009; Lithwick 2009; Nathanson 2001, 124–6; Rowan 2004, 392–9; Schwartz 2010; Tabak 2003.

[12] Another peculiarity of the administration of capital punishment in the United States, not directly relevant here, is that some states condemn substantial numbers of convicts to death while executing hardly any of them. For an insightful exploration of this matter, see Steiker and Steiker 2006.

and exaggerated. What is the moral upshot of the abiding possibility that some innocent people will be put to death within any system of capital punishment?

As has been stated, an execution of an innocent person is a serious wrong even if the trial and appeals that lead up to the execution have been admirably fair. The wrong inflicted is especially grave if the defendant is innocent in the narrower and more demanding sense that was specified in § 7.1.1 above, but it is serious in any event. However, the persistent possibility of some executions of innocents does not delegitimize a system of capital punishment unless such executions actually occur at a level of frequency that removes the moral basis for the system to invoke and apply the purgative justification of the death penalty. Of course, the level of frequency that would produce such an effect is not something that can be specified *in abstracto*. Among the considerations that bear on the matter, apart from the sheer incidence of the erroneous executions, are the extent and nature of a system's safeguards against the conviction and execution of innocent people (including, for example, the quality of the legal representation available to indigent defendants upon whom the death penalty might be imposed); the extent, if any, to which the decisions reached within the system have been inflected by bigotry or malice or any other dubious attitudes; the robustness of the virtues of the overall legal-governmental apparatus within which the system of capital punishment is operative; and the amplitude of the remedies that are undertaken when any mistakes are brought to light. How these considerations and other factors are to be appraised in combination in any particular case is heavily dependent on the specificities of the case. It is not inconceivable that the wrongs and other drawbacks of institutions of capital punishment will always in practice outweigh the estimable features of those institutions and will thus vitiate the moral status thereof. Such institutions might always lack the moral wherewithal to carry out executions legitimately for the purpose of purgation. However, an upshot of that kind is hardly preordained. If a regime of capital punishment oriented toward the purgative rationale for such punishment is designed with extensive procedural safeguards in a flourishing liberal democracy, its moral illegitimacy as a regime is unlikely. (Of course, notwithstanding that the regime as a whole is legitimate, any mistaken executions within it are serious wrongs.)

Because of the gravity of the wrong inflicted by any mistaken execution, the safeguards for ensuring the fairness of trials and appeals should be especially stringent in capital cases. Unless those safeguards are sufficiently solid, the officials who run a system of capital punishment will not be able to invoke and apply the purgative rationale without hypocrisy—and, as Chapter 6 has observed, such hypocrisy will delegitimize the system. The general aim of the procedural precautions in any institution of capital punishment has been summarized aptly and simply by Stephen Nathanson (who himself opposes the death penalty):

[I]f the death penalty is to be justified, we must have good reason to believe that our system is on the whole quite reliable and that very few innocent people will ever be executed. We must do our utmost to provide stringent safeguards that will make such executions highly unlikely—even if this means bearing extra legal costs, putting up with long delays, and sometimes seeing death sentences overturned for what appear to be merely 'legal technicalities.' Moreover, we must be confident that these safeguards will work. [Nathanson 2001, 123]

7.1.5.1. Confidence rather than certainty

Though the passage above from Nathanson is extremely sketchy, it is important in two contrasting respects. First, by indicating that we must have good reason to believe in the reliability of our criminal-justice system's trials and appeals and that we must have grounds for confidence in the efficacy of the procedural protections with which those trials and appeals are structured, Nathanson wisely avoids going too far. As he recognizes, confidence and good reason for belief—rather than certainty—are the epistemic desiderata for which we should be striving. Some opponents of capital punishment insist that nothing less than certainty will suffice for the moral legitimacy of any application of such punishment. In other words, no such application is legitimate unless any reasonable assessment of the evidence against a defendant warrants a conclusion that there is no probability whatsoever of a mistake in the proceedings by which he has been convicted. As Thom Brooks, among others, has proclaimed: '[W]e must have certainty of a person's guilt before imposing death. The problem is that we can never have absolute certainty through the judicial process' (Brooks 2004, 194). Brooks is correct in claiming that a requirement of absolute certainty can never be fulfilled through any judicial process. What is more, such a requirement cannot be fulfilled through any process of empirical investigation or moral deliberation at all. Hence, an insistence on certainty in the administration of capital punishment is a substantive stance against the use of such punishment, even though that stance is dressed up as a concern over procedural shortcomings. It presupposes that the pursuit of the ethical desideratum of purgation is rendered illegitimate by any non-zero probability of the innocence of a person who is scheduled for execution. Yet, given that there always is a non-zero probability of the innocence of anyone scheduled for execution, the presupposition just stated is tantamount to the view that the desideratum of purgation cannot ever be attained permissibly. Such a view is patently a substantive doctrine, which stands in need of a substantive defence. Reiterated assertions that 'we are unable to have certainty of a person's guilt for a capital offense' and that 'there can be no certainty regarding a person's guilt' and that 'we will never be able to know with absolute certainty a defendant's guilt' do not go any distance toward vindicating that substantive doctrine.[13] Any substantive vindication would have to explain why the administering of capital punishment is to be held up to a superhumanly stringent epistemic standard—a standard which is bound to be unfulfilled and which is not applied to any other governmental or military endeavours. Repeated invocations of that standard and of its unsatisfiability do not contribute to the provision of an explanation.

---

[13] The quotations are from Brooks 2004, 188, 192, 193. Among the various other writings that insist on certainty in the administration of capital punishment are Rowan 2004, 406–7; and Symposium 2003, 140–2 (remarks of Jeffrey Kirchmeier).

Let us briefly examine an attempt to explain why that cripplingly unfulfillable standard should be applied to the administration of capital punishment and not to any other governmental or military activities. Michael Rowan submits that singling out the administration of capital punishment in this manner is appropriate because 'the stakes are extraordinarily high in capital punishment, higher perhaps than with any other consequence of government action' (Rowan 2004, 390). It is indeed true that the stakes are higher in the imposition of the death penalty than in the imposition of any other sanction that is employed by a liberal democracy's system of criminal justice. This book has readily accepted and indeed emphasized as much. However, the imposition of sanctions within a criminal-justice system is hardly the sole function of the full array of legal-governmental institutions in any country, and Rowan is quite wrong to suggest that the stakes in the administration of capital punishment are higher than those in the performance of every other function of government. In many military undertakings, the lives at stake are far more numerous than the lives terminated each year in a liberal-democratic regime of capital punishment. In some actions of policing—especially involving the rescue of hostages—the lives at stake outnumber the life terminated in any particular application of the death penalty. Still, despite the extraordinarily high stakes, no requirement of absolute certainty is germane. Indeed, truly ludicrous is the notion that the aforementioned undertakings and actions should not go ahead unless the soldiers or policemen who perform them are absolutely certain that no innocent people will be killed (or that any innocent people who are killed will be greatly outnumbered by the innocent people who are saved). That notion is ludicrous because the standard of absolute certainty is manifestly unsatisfiable; no military engagements or policing endeavours could ever proceed if they had to meet such a standard. Anyone who insists on certainty for the legitimacy of those engagements and endeavours is taking a substantive stand unremittingly against the use of the military and the police, under the guise of expressing procedural concerns over the possibility of mistakes. Rowan is doing much the same by adverting to the high stakes in a regime of capital punishment as a reason for applying a requirement of absolute certainty to every such regime. He is taking a substantive stand unremittingly against the use of capital punishment. To sustain his position, he will have to marshal arguments to show that the good of purgation is never sufficient to legitimize the incurring of small risks of mistakes in the administration of executions. He has not yet begun that task of substantive argumentation.

Before we move on, we should note—for the sake of clarity—the two main levels at which one's confidence or certitude about the workings of a system of capital punishment is operative. That is, we should distinguish between an epistemic attitude toward a particular execution and an epistemic attitude toward the overall institutional apparatus within which the death penalty is administered. If Mary feels absolutely certain in her beliefs about the guiltiness of the particular defendants who are executed within such a system, then she is not fully rational unless she also feels absolutely certain that the system as a whole has not put to death any innocent person.

By contrast, if Mary feels very confident but not absolutely certain in her beliefs about the guiltiness of the particular defendants who are executed, and if the number of people subjected to capital punishment in her community over a long period of time is considerable, then she is not fully rational if she very confidently believes that the institution which imposes such punishment has never put any innocent person to death. On the contrary, she should be confident—though not absolutely certain, of course—that at least one mistake has been made at some point, whether or not it has ever come to light. (The degree of confidence which she should rationally attach to that latter belief will depend on the degrees of confidence with which she holds her beliefs about the guiltiness of the individual defendants who have been executed.) In other words, unlike absolute certainty, confidence about the absence of any mistake at the level of every individual execution does not rationally carry over into confidence about the absence of any mistakes at the level of a large-scale institution of capital punishment. Instead, what is rationally consistent with confidence at the level of every individual execution is confidence that the incidence of mistakes in the overall institution is extremely low. Strong and well-founded confidence of the latter sort, rather than the chimera of certainty, is the epistemic state which a morally defensible system of capital punishment must strive to sustain. (Note, as a short digression, that the remarks in this paragraph make clear that a certain philosophical conundrum known as the 'paradox of the preface' is not really a paradox at all.[14] Suppose that an author of a scholarly book has carefully checked each assertion in the book and that he nonetheless includes a sentence in the volume's preface along the following lines: 'The errors to be found in this book are solely my own responsibility.' According to the standard exposition of the paradox of the preface, the author's belief about the presence of errors in his volume is rationally inconsistent with his beliefs about the correctness of the individual assertions in the volume. Nevertheless, if the author has indeed checked each of his assertions carefully, then all the beliefs in question are admirably reasonable. His inability to harbour those beliefs in combination without rational inconsistency is thus paradoxical, or so the standard exposition maintains. In fact, any appearance of paradoxicalness arises from a failure to keep in view the differing degrees of robustness with which someone can hold beliefs. If the author is audacious enough to feel absolutely certain when he ponders the veracity of each assertion in his book, then—unless he is arrantly irrational—he will not include any sentence in the preface which declares or presupposes that there is a non-zero probability of the presence of errors in the volume. If he is rational, his absolute certainty at the level of each belief about the correctness of each individual assertion will have carried over into absolute certainty at the level of his belief about the unfailing accuracy of the volume as a whole. If the author more sensibly feels very confident but not certain about the veracity of each assertion in his book, he can without any rational

---

[14] For the seminal (and pleasingly pithy) exposition of the so-called paradox of the preface, see Makinson 1965. For a terse account, see Sainsbury 1988, 148.

inconsistency include a sentence in the preface which declares or presupposes that there are a few errors in the volume. Such a sentence expresses a belief that is itself held with confidence rather than with certainty, if the author is rational. Given that each of his beliefs about the veracity of each of his individual assertions is held with confidence rather than with certainty, and given that the book contains a large number of assertions, he can rationally believe with confidence—short of certainty—that the book as a whole contains a few errors. When he includes a statement to that effect in his preface, he is not being irrational at all. Because his reasonable beliefs in combination are rationally consistent when each of them is held with confidence rather than with certitude, the ostensible paradox of the preface is not genuinely a paradox.)

7.1.5.2. Exasperation as the price of legitimacy

A second respect in which the passage from Nathanson deserves attention is that it straightforwardly acknowledges that the procedural safeguards which secure the moral legitimacy of a system of capital punishment are sometimes quite exasperating in practice. Some criminal-defence lawyers who stand implacably opposed to the death penalty are inclined to exploit those safeguards—through the lodging of far-fetched appeals, for example—in order to stymie the workings of a system in which that penalty is imposed. Though some such misuses of procedural protections can be averted through suitable reforms, any scheme of protections that is sufficiently ample to confer moral legitimacy upon a regime of capital punishment will leave quite a bit of latitude for questionable manoeuvres. The removal of all such latitude would involve the removal of most of the procedural precautions themselves. For example, given how vexingly difficult it can be to distinguish between frivolous appeals and unusual but serious appeals, any strong efforts to crack down on the former are likely to stifle many of the latter as well. Thus, in any institution of capital punishment that sustains its moral legitimacy by guarding against mistakes with careful diligence, some irksome loopholes and delays will be present. Nathanson is right to highlight that point and to suggest that the proponents of capital punishment have to put up with exasperation as the price of legitimacy.

   Well beyond the scope of this book are the details of the procedural precautions that would be stringent enough in any particular jurisdiction for the legitimacy of a regime of capital punishment. Many of the relevant issues have been thoughtfully plumbed by the Massachusetts Governor's Council on Capital Punishment, which began its deliberations in September 2003 and which presented its final report in May 2004.[15] Though the Council of course did not consider the purgative rationale for the death penalty (or any other rationale, for that matter), nearly all of its recommendations are consistent with that rationale.

---

[15] See Massachusetts Governor's Council on Capital Punishment 2004. For a well-informed discussion by a leading member of the Council, see Hoffmann 2005.

Let us glance here at one important issue. DNA testing is crucial in every case where evidence is available that would enable such testing to go ahead. DNA analyses are best known as an exculpatory technique, of course, and some discussions of the matter—such as that in Brooks 2004, 192–4—proceed as if the only role for those analyses were exonerative. Obviously, however, DNA testing can also play a powerfully inculpatory role. In fact, some opponents of capital punishment worry that the guilt-confirming potency of DNA analyses will greatly strengthen the institution of such punishment: 'DNA has and will surely continue to indicate guilt in many cases, both at trial and during the post-conviction process....[T]he long-term impact of DNA actually might be to legitimate capital punishment.'[16] Because DNA testing when conducted properly is far more reliable than virtually any alternative type of evidence, it can play a key procedural function—whether incriminating or exonerative—in the cases where genetic material is available for subjection to such testing. When genetic material is indeed available, DNA testing (at public expense) should be mandatory in any advanced criminal-justice system.

Nevertheless, despite the salutariness of the development of DNA analyses, two caveats should be entered prominently here. First, even when DNA testing is carried out impeccably, it does not warrant the attachment of absolute certainty to any conclusions which it supports (Steiker and Steiker 2002, 423). Its probative power vastly exceeds that of virtually any other kind of evidence, but it establishes extremely high probabilities rather than certainties. Of course, if the results of the DNA testing in a given case are inculpatory and are consistent with the other evidence that has been adduced, then the extremely high probabilities attached to those results are easily sufficient to justify the conviction of the defendant. If the crimes for which the defendant is convicted are so heinous as to fall within the ambit of the purgative rationale for the death penalty, then the imposition of that penalty on the defendant will be both morally obligatory and morally legitimate. When an execution has been conducted on such a basis, it is admirably fair (even if, *mirabile dictu*, it ultimately turns out to have been mistaken and thus illegitimate). When I emphasize here that DNA testing does not generate certainty, I am hardly thereby seeking to suggest that the results of such testing are inadequate for convicting and executing offenders who have perpetrated extravagantly wicked crimes. My purpose is in fact the opposite. By insisting that even a probative technique as redoubtable as DNA testing will have led to high probabilities rather than to certainties, this chapter is again maintaining that absolute certainty is a chimera and that the fairness of any conviction and execution does not require such certainty. Very high probabilities are all that we can attain, and they are enough.

Secondly, everything said so far about DNA analyses is premised on the assumption that those analyses are carried out capably. Patently, however, there is never

---

[16] Rowan 2004, 403, 402. For some broadly similar expressions of anxiety, see Liebman 2002, 547–8 n 73, 549; Steiker and Steiker 2002, 418, 421; Steiker and Steiker 2005, 621–2; Wefing 2001.

any guarantee that the testing of genetic material in this or that particular case has been conducted adeptly. Disconcerting reports about the testing in Harris County of Texas have surfaced from time to time, for example (Markel 2005, 450). To be sure, incompetent DNA testing can err in the direction of false negatives as well as in the direction of false positives. Even more important, there are very solid grounds for thinking that such testing is generally carried out with great proficiency in the United States at present (Giannelli 2007, 208–11), and there are plainly no grounds for thinking that incompetence is widespread or inevitable. Nevertheless, the ineliminable possibility of the mishandling of DNA analyses in any particular case should engender some wariness. Marvellously reliable though such analyses are when they are conducted properly, their being conducted properly is not something that can be taken for granted. For the sake of endowing trials and appeals with fairness, the courts in every advanced system of criminal justice are morally obligated to draw upon DNA analyses in any cases where testable material is available; but the testing must itself be monitored to guard against incompetence and malfeasance.

7.2. Arbitrariness

The spectre of erroneous convictions and executions is not the only aspect of the administration of capital punishment that has worried many opponents of such punishment. Another complaint that has quite frequently been voiced is that there are no principled bases that would enable courts to differentiate non-arbitrarily between very serious crimes for which the death penalty should be imposed and very serious crimes for which that penalty should not be wielded. Such a complaint differs from the concerns about the possibility of erroneous executions, for those latter concerns are consistent with the thesis that capital crimes and non-capital crimes can be distinguished in a principled manner. Moreover, whereas the allegations of mistakes are focused on particular cases in isolation, the allegations of arbitrariness are inherently comparative. As Dolinko rightly characterizes the charge of arbitrariness: 'It is a *systemic* argument— a claim that in general no principled distinction separates murderers who are executed and those who are not—rather than a claim that *in particular cases* such a principled distinction might be lacking' (Dolinko 1986, 577, emphases in original).

Of course, as Dolinko goes on to observe, an accusation of arbitrariness can intelligibly be voiced with reference to a particular case in isolation. However, the arbitrariness highlighted by such an accusation does not consist in a dearth of respectable standards for discriminating between capital crimes and non-capital crimes. Rather, it consists in the misapplication of some such standards that bear on the case at hand. Hence, an accusation of 'arbitrariness' along those lines is an objection claiming that a mistake has been made. By contrast, the complaints about arbitrariness under examination here are contending that there are no respectable standards of the sort just mentioned. Such standards are never misapplied, but only because they do not exist—or so the writers who articulate these complaints have maintained.

Bedau is among the philosophers who have criticized the administration of capital punishment in this fashion. He declares that 'the actual study of why particular persons have been sentenced to death and executed does not show any careful winnowing of the worst from the bad. It shows that those executed were…the losers in an arbitrary lottery that could just as well have spared them' (Bedau 1993, 190). Lempert in a broadly similar vein refers to 'an inevitably capricious system of capital punishment,' as he bitingly asserts that 'the person who applauds the execution of the murderer is applauding what is literally unprincipled state action' (Lempert 1981, 1182). Austin Sarat likewise proclaims that capital punishment cannot ever be 'administered in a manner that is compatible with our legal system's fundamental commitments to fair and equal treatment' (Sarat 2001, 251). Charles Black, whose book on the topic is subtitled *The Inevitability of Caprice and Mistake*, insisted that 'the official choices—by prosecutors, judges, juries, and governors—that divide those who are to die from those who are to live are on the whole not made, and cannot be made, under standards that are consistently meaningful and clear' (Black 1981, 29). Carol Steiker joins this chorus as she asseverates that 'the fact that defendants from otherwise similar counties in the same [American] state face radically different prospects of receiving capital punishment calls into question not only the procedures by which those deserving of capital punishment are chosen but also the reliability of the underlying judgment that any particular defendant so chosen deserves the death penalty' (Steiker 2005, 768). Jeffrey Kirchmeier similarly worries that 'even if you come up with a smaller group [of the worst murderers] than we have now, you will still have arbitrariness within the system. Even if you make the categories smaller, you will still end up, within that category, having discretion and arbitrariness.' Contending that 'problems of arbitrary discretion will still be there within the system,' he poses what he takes to be a rhetorical question: 'Obviously, all homicides are horrible, so how do you say that some are especially heinous, cruel or depraved and some are not?' (Symposium 2003, 136, 137 [remarks of Jeffrey Kirchmeier].)

Though each of these statements has derived from rumination upon the practice of capital punishment in the United States, each of them goes beyond declaring that the actual implementation of such punishment in various American jurisdictions has been capricious. Each of them submits that the capriciousness is inevitable in any system for the administration of the death penalty. These complaints are about the absence of any meaningful standards rather than about misapplications of such standards. They are thus to be distinguished from the following line of criticism of executions in the United States that has been pressed by Jack Greenberg among others: 'Since at least 1967, the death penalty has been inflicted only rarely, erratically, and often upon the least odious killers, while many of the most heinous criminals have escaped execution' (Greenberg 1986, 1670). Greenberg is here presupposing the existence of meaningfully ascertainable differences between the most heinous criminals and the least odious killers, and he is criticizing the administration of the death penalty in the United States for failing to track those differences. He might think that the failures are insurmountable in principle, but he does not say so in the statement just quoted or at any other point in his article. He is lamenting the systematic misapplication of meaningful standards, rather than the absence of any such standards. That same lament is expressed when he writes that Americans 'have a system of capital punishment that results in infrequent, random, and erratic executions, one that is structured to inflict death neither on those who have committed the worst offenses nor on defendants of the worst character' (Greenberg 1986, 1675). Although such a statement affirms that capriciousness pervades the administration of capital punishment in the United States, it does not go further by maintaining that capriciousness is unavoidable in principle whenever such punishment is administered.

Still, although Greenberg's complaint about systematic misapplications of potentially proper standards is different from the complaints about the inevitability of standardlessness, the differences between them sometimes become blurred. (For example, the quotation from Bedau in the penultimate paragraph above could be construed in either way.) Fittingly enough, then, some of my rejoinders will throw doubt upon Greenberg's indictment as well as upon the bolder claims about arbitrariness that have been advanced by many other opponents of the death penalty.

7.2.1. A markedly inadequate response

Throughout his writings on capital punishment, Ernest van den Haag was inclined to dismiss the concerns of philosophers and jurists who bemoan the arbitrariness of the distinctions that are drawn among defendants convicted of heinous crimes. He believed that considerations of comparative justice can be separated sharply from considerations of non-comparative justice, and he concentrated squarely on the latter. As a result, he tended to deal distortively with the complaints about arbitrariness as if they were focused on individual cases in isolation.

Consider, for example, the following remark from one of his essays: '[E]ven when capriciousness is thought reducible, one wonders whether releasing or retrying one guilty defendant, because another equally guilty defendant was not punished as much, would help reduce capriciousness. It does not seem a logical remedy' (Van den Haag 1985b, 961 n 25). Van den Haag was here presuming that the sentence imposed on the executed defendant is non-capricious whereas the sentence imposed on the defendant who has been spared from execution is capricious. He indicated that he was pondering a scenario in which 'a guilty person, or group of persons, may get away with no punishment, or with a light punishment, while others receive the punishment they deserve' (Van den Haag 1985b, 961). However, as has already been emphasized, the allegations of arbitrariness under examination here are not focused on individual cases in isolation. The gist of those allegations is that no available standards enable us to differentiate in a principled fashion among defendants who have committed murders. With reference to that class of defendants, no principled criteria separate the people who should be executed from those who should not be. So, at any rate, the aforementioned allegations insist. Hence, contrary to what van den Haag apparently thought, the property of capriciousness as understood in those allegations is systemic rather than something that can be ascribed to any defendant's case on its own. In van den Haag's scenario, accordingly, both the sentence imposed on the executed defendant and the sentence imposed on the defendant who escapes execution are capricious in the relevant sense. Because not all convicts who have committed murders should be subjected to the death penalty, and because there are no respectable standards for selecting some of those convicts and not the others—or so we are told—any process of differentiating among them that does take place is arbitrary in respect of those who are selected for execution as well as in respect of those who are not. Thus, given the liberal-democratic premise that (within certain limits) the imposition of excessively severe sanctions is worse than the imposition of unduly lenient sanctions, and given that we cannot know which murderers ought to be spared from the death penalty while others should be subjected to it, the levelling down of every murderer's punishment to something short of the death penalty would be a plausible response to the accusations of arbitrariness. To be sure, any such response would itself be deeply problematic, as we shall soon behold. However, the difficulties besetting it were not correctly identified by van den Haag.

Even more misguided is van den Haag's insistence—repeated on many occasions—that shortcomings in the distribution of capital sentences do not have any bearing on the moral legitimacy of the use of the death penalty. Van den Haag persistently contended that considerations of comparative justice in the imposition of capital punishment are always trumped by considerations of non-comparative justice. Let us look at a few of his numerous expressions of this view.

Near the outset of an essay published in 1986, van den Haag wrote as follows: 'If capital punishment is moral, no distribution would make it immoral. Improper distribution cannot affect the quality of what is distributed, be it punishments or rewards. Discriminatory or capricious distribution thus could not justify abolition of the death penalty' (Van den Haag 1986, 1662–3). Construed generously, the first two statements in this passage are correct. It is indeed true that the moral status of the death penalty as a general type of sanction is not affected by the maladministration of that penalty in any particular jurisdiction. Insofar as the first two statements in this passage are about the death penalty as a general type and are not about tokens of that type, they are correct. However, so construed, those statements are consistent with the proposition that the use of the death penalty is morally illegitimate in any jurisdiction where it is seriously maladministered. In the closing portion of the passage, van den Haag denied that very proposition. He maintained that the woeful maladministration of the death penalty would never undermine the legitimacy of particular applications of that sanction to nefarious criminals. Such a contention is arrantly unsustainable, for—as has been argued in Chapter 6—the moral legitimacy of any application of capital punishment depends not only on the fairness of the legal proceedings which have eventuated in that application, but also on the broader fairness of the system of criminal justice wherein those proceedings have taken place. Unless the particular proceedings and the overall system are reasonably fair, the imposition of a death sentence is an instance of gross hypocrisy and is thus condemnable (even if the person on whom the sentence has been imposed is a defilingly wicked perpetrator of atrocities).

Admittedly, van den Haag was not addressing the purgative rationale for capital punishment at all, and he therefore cannot appropriately be censured for having failed to take into account the conditions that are necessary for the justifiability of any executions conducted on the basis of that rationale. However, the point here about hypocrisy is also pertinent from the perspective of retributivists with their insistence that punishments are wielded in order to give effect to the values of human equality and moral accountability. If the imposition of a sanction as severe as the death penalty is the culmination of a haphazard legal proceeding, it scarcely serves as a means of upholding those values. Likewise, if a legal-governmental system is generally marked by capriciousness in its operations through which it subjects people to criminal penalties, then—even if a particular proceeding has been fair—the system as a whole cannot without hypocrisy impose a severe sanction such as the death penalty in furtherance of the values of retributivism. In other words, retributivism is a doctrine that is amply attuned to the importance of comparative justice in securing the legitimacy of punitive institutions and the legitimacy of particular punitive measures. Given that van den Haag affiliated himself to a large degree with retributivism and invoked key retributivistic concepts such as that of desert, he too should have recognized that the legitimacy of any punitive imposition hinges partly on considerations of comparative justice.

Among the myriad of passages in which van den Haag discounted the importance of comparative justice is the following:

Some lawyers have insisted that the death penalty is distributed among those guilty of murder as though by a lottery and that the worst may escape it. They exaggerate, but suppose one grants the point. How do those among the guilty selected for execution by lottery become less deserving of punishment because others escaped it? What is wrong is that these others escaped, not that those among the guilty who were selected by the lottery did not. [Van den Haag 1985b, 963–4, footnote omitted]

This passage combines some of the errors that have already surfaced in van den Haag's pronouncements. For one thing, van den Haag here again took for granted that the murderers who get selected for execution by lottery are deserving of their fate. However, one of the chief claims of the philosophers and jurists who perceive widespread arbitrariness in the administration of capital punishment is that we have no grounds for presuming that the death penalty is appropriate for the murderers who are selected to undergo it. Those philosophers and jurists, like the vast majority of other people who discuss these matters, believe that not all murderers should be put to death for their crimes. Capital sentences are appropriate only for some murderers rather than for all. Given as much, and given that the processes through which some murderers get singled out for execution are arbitrary (as the aforementioned philosophers and jurists believe), van den Haag's blithe assumption about the deservedness of each execution is glib at best. Van den Haag may have idiosyncratically believed that everyone convicted of murder is deserving of capital punishment,[17] but, if so, it is hard to understand how he could have taken himself to be coming to grips with the line of reasoning which he purported to be contesting. After all, that line of reasoning begins from the very widely endorsed premise that not everybody convicted of murder is properly subject to the death penalty.

Moreover, even if that premise were to be left aside *arguendo*, van den Haag's riposte to the allegations of arbitrariness would be otiose. Suppose that capital punishment is an appropriate sanction for everyone correctly convicted of murder, when his or her case is considered in isolation. Even so, we cannot validly infer that capital punishment is an appropriate sanction for *any*one (much less for everyone) when his or her case is considered in combination with other murderers' cases. *Pace* van den Haag, the pursuit of non-comparative justice can be delegitimized by considerations of comparative equity. If a system of criminal-law enforcement singles out murderers for execution on the basis of a lottery or some other aleatory procedure—or on the basis of hair colour or skin colour or surname or any other morally irrelevant factor—the system lacks the moral wherewithal to put anyone to death legitimately. Justified executions are conducted in order to uphold the basic moral values that are grossly transgressed by extravagantly heinous crimes, yet a system of criminal-law enforcement with capricious or invidious procedures for selecting people to undergo executions will itself thereby be flouting those values. Operating high-handedly in contravention of the ideals of liberal democracy, such a system will lack the moral authority to invoke and apply the purgative rationale for the death penalty legitimately.

Indeed, as Dolinko pertinently remarks (Dolinko 1986, 573), van den Haag's disregard of the importance of comparative justice leads to some repellent conclusions. Let us compare the following two systems of criminal-law enforcement. In System 1, everybody convicted of murder is imprisoned for life. In System 2, every non-Hispanic person convicted of murder is imprisoned for life while every Hispanic person convicted of murder is executed, even though the murders committed by Hispanics are generally no more wicked than those committed by non-Hispanics. Under van den Haag's apparent assumption that everyone convicted of murder is deserving of capital punishment, System 1 does not inflict on any murderer the sanction which he or she deserves. System 1, then, is an institution in which 'we would give up justice for the sake of equality. We would reverse the proper order of priorities' (Van den Haag 1985b, 964). By contrast, System 2 levies on each Hispanic murderer the punishment which he or she deserves, even while it treats non-Hispanic murderers with unjust leniency. Hence, given van den Haag's belief that considerations of non-comparative justice always trump those of

---

[17] Van den Haag was opposed to mandatory capital punishment for the crime of murder, but only because it 'risks jury cancellations'. Van den Haag 1985b, 959 n 14.

comparative justice—that is, given his belief that '[m]orally, [non-comparative] justice must always be preferred to equality' (Van den Haag 1978, 55)—System 2 is unequivocally to be preferred to System 1. If the regime of criminal-law enforcement in some society evolves from operating in the manner of System 1 to operating in the manner of System 2, it will have improved by van den Haag's reckoning. As Dolinko tellingly snorts: 'A theory according to which society *improves* by shifting from imprisoning all murderers to executing only [Hispanic murderers] is a theory hard to take seriously' (Dolinko 1986, 573).

7.2.2. Another unsatisfactory response

Although Dolinko's article on the issues pertaining to the administration of capital punishment is among the most astute and sophisticated writings in the whole literature on the topic, one of his rejoinders to the complaints about arbitrariness is doubtful in the light of my first retort to van den Haag. Dolinko contends that the accuracy of those complaints would undermine the legitimacy not only of capital punishment but also of any other severe sanctions. Replying specifically to Charles Black's animadversions on the practice of capital punishment in the United States, Dolinko submits that 'what Black has given us is not an argument against *capital* punishment, but an argument against imposing *any* serious form of punishment on convicted criminals'. Dolinko declares: 'I cannot see...how it could be rational to respond to Black's picture of the criminal justice system by abolishing the death penalty but continuing to administer other punishments' (Dolinko 1986, 575).

To see why these remarks by Dolinko are unpersuasive, we should recall that the queries raised by Black and others about the arbitrariness of the administration of capital punishment are focused on the standards for differentiating among murderers. According to these critics, the touchstones for separating the worst murderers from other murderers are hopelessly problematic and nebulous. Because those touchstones are so dubious, we cannot have any reasonable confidence that the murderers singled out for execution are undergoing a type of punishment that is appropriate for their crimes. We cannot believe with any reasonable confidence that each of the executed murderers has been subjected to a sanction that is no more severe than what he has deserved. Such is the conclusion for which these opponents of capital punishment have argued.

Dolinko's worry seems to be based on the following line of thought. If some other sanction such as lifelong imprisonment is substituted for the death penalty as the most severe punishment to be imposed in a given jurisdiction, then we will still need to differentiate between the worst murderers (who will be subjected to that punishment) and the remaining murderers (who will each be subjected to a less severe punishment). However, the shift from the death penalty to lifelong imprisonment as the harshest sanction within the jurisdiction will not in itself do anything to alleviate the capriciousness of the procedures by which some murderers are classified as the worst.[18] Hence, whereas the death penalty has heretofore been imposed on selected murderers in an arbitrary fashion, lifelong imprisonment will now be imposed on selected murderers in an arbitrary fashion. Since lifelong imprisonment is itself a very severe sanction, we should be nearly as troubled by arbitrariness in the administration of it as we are by arbitrariness in the administration of capital punishment. If imprisonment for thirty years were to replace lifelong imprisonment as the heaviest sanction to be levied in the jurisdiction, the problem of administrative arbitrariness would in turn afflict it—and so forth. Professor Black and any like-minded theorists thus appear to be committed to the implausible conclusion that no heavy sanctions can ever legitimately be employed in any system of criminal-law enforcement.

If the line of thought recounted in the preceding paragraph is indeed what underlies Dolinko's claims about the generalizability of Black's arguments, then those claims are unfounded. One of the chief worries of the theorists who perceive rampant arbitrariness in the administration of capital punishment is that some or all of the murderers selected for execution are being punished more severely than is warranted. No cognate worry will be applicable if everyone convicted of murder is subjected to a punishment that is no more severe than the lightest sanction that is appropriate for anyone who has perpetrated such a serious crime. Suppose for example that a term of thirty years in prison is just such a sanction, and that it is imposed on everybody correctly convicted of murder. In that event, nobody is being punished more severely than is warranted. To be sure, such an arrangement will subject some murderers—the worst murderers—to a level of punishment that is less severe than the appropriate level for their terrible crimes. However, because (*ex hypothesi*) there is no principled way of differentiating between the worst murderers and the remaining murderers, and because within certain limits the imposition of excessively severe penalties on offenders is worse than the imposition of unduly lenient penalties, the imprisonment of every murderer for thirty years is the optimal upshot that can be attained within the constraints envisaged by Black and like-minded theorists. It is certainly a better upshot—by the reckoning of those theorists as well as by any ordinary reckoning—than the elimination of all heavy sanctions.

In the preceding paragraph, I have referred to everyone *correctly* convicted of murder. Dolinko's rejoinder to Black would withstand scrutiny if the complaints by Black and like-minded theorists were about arbitrary convictions rather than about arbitrary sentencing. If those theorists were contending that the standards for determining guilt or innocence in murder trials are themselves hopelessly problematic and amorphous, then Dolinko would be correct in holding that such theorists are committed to gainsaying the legitimacy of any onerous punishments for people who have been convicted of murder. In fairness to Dolinko, it should be noted

---

[18] Like me, Dolinko does not think that such procedures are in fact damagingly capricious. He assumes *arguendo* that they are, however, in order to draw out what he takes to be a dismaying implication of Black's arguments.

that Black himself did sometimes suggest that the standards operative in murder trials are arbitrary in their application. For example, as Dolinko remarks, Black tried to show that some American courts manipulate the notion of premeditation in first-degree murder trials to convict defendants who would very likely have been acquitted of first-degree murder in other American courts (Black 1981, 57–8). Nevertheless, Black directed his strictures predominantly against practices of sentencing. Like the other theorists whose worries about arbitrariness in the administration of capital punishment have been quoted in this chapter, he was primarily concerned to reveal that such arbitrariness suffuses the processes for differentiating between murderers who should be sentenced to death and murderers who should be sentenced to prison. When the complaints about capriciousness in capital sentencing are so focused, they are not vulnerable to Dolinko's critique. Their natural conclusion is not that perpetrators of the crime of murder should never be punished with any onerous sanctions, but instead that every such perpetrator should be punished with a sanction that is no more severe than what is appropriate for the least odious token of that crime-type.

7.2.3. Distortive exaggeration

Although the allegations of arbitrariness in the administration of capital punishment do not fall prey to the rejoinders that have been examined so far, they are distortively exaggerated. Neither in practice in the United States nor in principle under the purgative rationale for the death penalty is the task of singling out the worst criminals a matter of caprice.

7.2.3.1. Processes of differentiation in practice

Because the workings of systems of capital punishment in practice are ascertainable only through empirical studies, and because this book is philosophical rather than social-scientific, my observations in this subsection will be very terse. Nonetheless, because the discussion in § 7.2.3.2 below (in keeping with Chapter 6) will maintain that the categorization of offenders as defilingly evil under the purgative rationale is far from arbitrary, some brief remarks on actual practices of sentencing in the United States are pertinent here. Even though those practices will have to be altered markedly if capital punishment in the United States is placed on a solid footing by being based henceforth on the purgative rationale, there are of course some affinities between the current practices and purgative practices. Most notably, the focusing of judges' or jurors' attention on aggravating and mitigating factors will continue to play a key role, as will appellate reviews of comparative sentencing. Hence, if the current practices were marred by rampant capriciousness, we would have some grounds for pessimism about the implementation of the purgative rationale. Conversely, if inconsistencies in capital sentencing are much lower than they are sometimes alleged to be, we have reasonable grounds for optimism.

7.2.3.1.1. Studies cited by Dolinko

Dolinko adverts to two empirical studies from the mid-1980s.[19] The authors of the first of those studies, Samuel Gross and Robert Mauro, are primarily concerned to show that the race of the victim in a capital murder trial affects the likelihood that a death sentence will be imposed. (In the next main section of this chapter, we shall probe the influence of invidious biases in the administration of capital punishment.) However, in addition to trying to establish that decisions about sentencing are inflected to some degree by considerations of race, Gross and Mauro highlight the bearing of three other matters on such decisions: the fact that a murder has been perpetrated in the course of the perpetration of another felony; the fact that a murder has been perpetrated against a stranger; and the fact that more than one person has been murdered.[20] Each of those three matters very strongly increases the likelihood that a death sentence will be imposed. For example, whereas only 0.8 per cent of the single-victim homicides in Illinois from 1976 to 1980 led to death sentences, 15.3 per cent of the multiple-victim homicides during that same period eventuated in such sentences. Given that each of these three determinants is at present a statutorily specified aggravating factor in many American jurisdictions, and given that the status of someone's crimes as extravagantly evil will almost always hinge partly on the third of these determinants and will sometimes hinge partly on the other two, the powerful influence of these considerations on patterns of capital sentencing is reassuring. Far from indicating that the processes for differentiating between the worst murderers and other murderers are sweepingly arbitrary, the study by Gross and Mauro suggests that most of the judges and jurors who participate in such processes are training their attention on germane factors. That upshot of the Gross/Mauro study would presumably become even more evident if sundry other aggravating factors—such as the previous major crimes of offenders, and the occurrence of torture or mutilation or especially gruesome methods of slaughter—were also to be taken into account.[21]

In the other study cited by Dolinko, Arnold Barnett has found that capital sentencing in Georgia during the mid-1970s was heavily influenced by the following three factors: the persuasive potency of the evidence pointing toward the conclusion that the defendant in a given case had deliberately slain some other person(s); the status of the victim as a stranger to the defendant; and the heinousness of the murder(s). Barnett elucidates the third of those factors by offering some examples of particularly odious crimes: 'Among vile slayings are those with multiple victims, those preceded

---

[19] Dolinko 1986, 575 n 182. The studies to which he refers are Barnett 1985 and Gross and Mauro 1984.

[20] Gross and Mauro 1984, 56–75. Two other matters—the fact that the victim of a murder is female, and the fact that a gun has been used—unsurprisingly turn out to bear more weakly on the likelihood of a capital sentence in any given case.

[21] 'Case-by-case reviews [from the 1960s] suggested that when a killing involved multiple victims, sexual torture, or a bizarre weapon, a consensus for death [between the presiding judge and the jury] was especially likely.' Barnett 1985, 1332.

by psychological torture or sexual abuse, and those involving bizarre weapons or mutilated bodies' (Barnett 1985, 1341). Another consideration that played a significant role in the capital sentencing, in combination with the three foregoing factors, was a defendant's prior record of criminality.

Although the first of Barnett's factors is more evidentiary than substantive, its role is manifestly indispensable for any effort to implement satisfactorily the purgative justification of capital punishment. As has been emphasized already in this chapter, the evidentiary and other procedural standards in capital trials must be stringent to guard against mistakes as far as is reasonably possible. Of course, the standards are not to be so demanding as to stymie all capital prosecutions in a chimerical quest for certainty. Nonetheless, their stringency should reflect the special severity of the sanction to which such prosecutions may lead. Consequently, quite reassuring is the fact that decisions on capital sentencing are powerfully influenced by the cogency of the incriminating evidence.

Also reassuring is each of the other factors highlighted by Barnett, especially the third. Although the absence of any previous acquaintance between a victim and the person who has slain her is not necessarily connected with the iniquity of the crime, there is a contingent link. (For example, the lack of familiarity between the parties will have lowered the likelihood that the crime is due to a grievance-fueled hatred of a particular person and will have increased the likelihood that it is due instead to a hatred of people generally.) Much more obviously of relevance to the purgative rationale for capital punishment is the third of Barnett's determinants. The heinousness of an offender's crimes is precisely that on which a judge or jury should be concentrating when deciding whether those crimes have rendered the offender's life defilingly evil. Thus, the influence of that factor on the sentencing in capital cases is exactly what a proponent of the purgative rationale would hope to discover. Also a ground for optimism is that such sentencing is swayed to some degree by the previous major crimes of offenders. When gauging whether the life of a malefactor is defilingly evil as a result of the latest vile crimes for which he has been convicted, a judge or jury should be attentive to the question whether the malefactor has committed any comparably vile crimes in the past.

Before we move on, we should note two additional points relating to Barnett's survey of the data from Georgia. First, although his survey also finds that the race of the victim in any capital case affected the probability of the imposition of a death sentence, his analysis of the cases on that very point is moderately encouraging—because the detected effect is quite small and is almost entirely confined to mid-level cases that would clearly not fall under the scope of the purgative rationale. (We shall return to this matter later in the chapter.) Secondly, Barnett's findings are especially interesting because they have been gathered from the initial trials without taking account of any subsequent appeals and reversals (Barnett 1985, 1338 n 38). Since one key role of a system of appeals is to smooth out anomalies, the high levels of consistency in the patterns of sentencing studied by Barnett are particularly noteworthy.

7.2.3.1.2. McCord on aggravating factors

Like Dolinko, David McCord is an opponent of the death penalty. Nevertheless, again like Dolinko, McCord is largely unconvinced by the theorists who allege that arbitrariness inevitably and wide-rangingly afflicts the administration of that penalty. McCord draws partly on the large array of cases from Georgia that have also been analysed by Barnett, and partly on his own survey of twenty-five capital cases in Georgia from the mid-1980s and early 1990s.[22] Having examined those arrays of cases, McCord—who refers to the most heinous instances of criminality as 'highest condemnation cases'—concludes that 'jurors are actually able to easily recognize and respond consistently to highest condemnation cases. In such cases, virtually any juror who is not [excludable from serving on a capital jury because of his or her categorical opposition to the death penalty] will vote for a death sentence even if, in the abstract, the person prefers the [life-long imprisonment-without-parole] alternative' (McCord 1998, 19). Directly addressing the sundry accusations of capriciousness that have been hurled against the administering of the death penalty in the United States, McCord writes as follows:

> The consistency of sentencers in choosing death in highest condemnation cases has been obscured by the oft-repeated claim of abolitionist zealots that the system of capital punishment in the United States operates so 'freakishly' as to render receipt of a death sentence as unpredictable as being struck by lightning. The evidence is clear, however, that if any freakishness inheres in the system, it manifests itself at the lower culpability ranges, not at the higher ones: sentencers clearly recognize and unambiguously respond to the highest condemnation cases with death sentences. [McCord 1998, 22, footnotes omitted]

McCord's findings tally strikingly with those of Barnett. Whatever might be the inconsistencies of sentencing in the mid-level capital cases, there is a remarkably high degree of consistency in the most egregious cases. Indeed, as McCord points out, a death sentence was imposed in every one of the thirty-four most iniquitous capital cases in Georgia during the mid-1970s. For any advocate of the purgative justification of capital punishment, the extraordinary measure of consistency in the treatment of such cases is welcome indeed. Only such cases fall within the reach of that justification. Hence, like the other empirical writings that have been adduced here, McCord's observations suggest that judges and juries are amply capable of coming to grips with the sorts of questions that will confront them when they are called upon to prescribe sentences in fulfilment of the purgative justification.

7.2.3.2. Differentiation in principle

Having glanced at some empirical studies which discern a very high level of consistency among the sentences handed down in cases that involve crimes of sufficient

---

[22] McCord's own survey is presented in McCord 1997, 582–90. The materials on the cases from Georgia in the 1970s, studied by both Barnett and McCord, are magisterially presented in Baldus, Pulaski, and Woodworth 1983; and Baldus, Woodworth, and Pulaski 1990.

turpitude to trigger the purgative rationale for the death penalty, we should now turn briefly to the issues of principle that pertain to the application of that rationale. On the one hand, as Chapter 6 has readily acknowledged, the chief concepts in the purgative rationale are vague. Consequently, some actual cases and countless potential cases will neither fall determinately within the scope of the rationale nor fall determinately outside that scope. On the other hand, as has also been emphasized in Chapter 6, many actual cases and countless possible cases fall squarely within that scope or squarely beyond it. The indeterminacy of some cases should scarcely blind us to the determinacy of others. Moreover, the decisions on sentencing in all the indeterminate cases are to go against the applicability of the purgative rationale. Unless a person's crimes lie determinately within the sway of the purgative justification, they do not provide any sufficient basis for the wielding of the death penalty.

Cases involving capital crimes of mid-level seriousness—the very cases in regard to which the complaints about capriciousness and invidious discrimination are empirically of some pertinence—do not fall determinately within the ambit of the purgative rationale. Nearly all of them lie determinately outside that ambit, and the few remaining mid-level cases are indeterminate. Properly drafted instructions on sentencing in a system of capital punishment that is oriented toward the purgative rationale will firmly exclude all those cases from the imposition of such punishment. In so doing, the instructions will have to refer directly to the purgative rationale itself and also to germane specifications of aggravating circumstances.

Direct references to the purgative rationale itself are essential for underscoring how appalling any crimes must be if they are to trigger the death penalty. Unless someone's conduct is so extravagantly rebarbative that it bespeaks a repudiation of humankind by evincing complete disdain for some characteristic features of human beings—namely, their capacities as reflective agents, their abilities to undergo pleasurable experiences, and their susceptibility to intense pain—the conduct is not such that the continued existence of the person who has performed it will defile his or her community. It is therefore not the sort of conduct that would warrant the execution of that person on the basis of purgative considerations.

As the preceding chapter has suggested, references to specifications of aggravating circumstances are essential for providing concrete indications of the features of crimes that activate the purgative rationale. As Chapter 6 has likewise made clear, any specifications which suitably flesh out that rationale will coincide only partly with those that are variously contained at present in the statutes of American death-penalty jurisdictions. Within a system of capital punishment oriented toward the desideratum of purgation, any enumeration of aggravating circumstances is to be centred on gauging whether offenders' crimes are so horrific as to render morally untenable the continuation of their lives. Many of the current formulations of aggravating circumstances would facilitate efforts by judges and jurors to determine whether offenders' lives are defiling, but not all of those formulations would do so. Some of them, as they currently stand, are either irrelevant or too broad. They would thus tend to elicit the imposition of the death penalty in cases that do not lie within the compass of the purgative rationale.

For example, one of the circumstances that are statutorily classified as aggravating in most death-penalty jurisdictions in the United States is the fact that a murder has occurred during the commission of some other felony. Such a classification is too expansive. In a system of criminal justice that carries out executions for the purpose of purgation, the role of any co-occurrent felony has to be defined more narrowly. The decisive matter is whether the co-occurrent felony itself bespeaks the same humanity-contemning attitude that underlies the gruesome murder(s) which the felony accompanies. Some felonies, such as rape and aggravated assault, do usually betoken such an attitude and therefore do contribute to a repudiation of humankind. Some other felonies, however, such as burglary and grand larceny and narcotics sales and robbery, do not in themselves bespeak a comparably depraved outlook. Accordingly, the sheer fact that a murder has been perpetrated in the course of one or more of those lesser felonies is not something that militates in favour of subjecting the murderer to a purgative execution.

Of course, a lesser felony such as a burglary can be carried out in a depravedly brutal fashion—in which case a purgative execution might well be an appropriate punitive response (especially if the perpetrator has been responsible for similarly brutal actions in the past). However, the triggering of the purgative rationale in such a situation is due entirely to the occurrence of the grotesque violence. If that violence when perpetrated in the course of a burglary is at a level sufficient to activate the purgative rationale, it would also have been sufficient if no burglary had been involved. Conversely, if the brutality in the absence of a burglary is not sufficient to activate that rationale, it would not have been sufficient even had it been perpetrated in the course of a burglary. Thus, for the purpose of applying the purgative justification of the death penalty, the commission of a lesser felony is not to be categorized as an aggravating circumstance. (Naturally, the commission of such a felony can quite properly be counted as an aggravating circumstance for some other purposes. For example, it should obviously be taken fully into account when the length of a term of imprisonment is set for an offender whose combined crimes warrant his being incarcerated rather than executed.)

In sum, the implementation of the purgative rationale for capital punishment will necessitate a number of adjustments in any of the current sets of procedures for administering such punishment. Consistency in sentencing is vital for any such implementation, but the consistency must derive from attentiveness to the features of offenders' doings that make their lives defilingly evil. When decisions on sentencing are indeed reached by reference to the presence or absence of such features, the resultant consistency will reflect the determinacy of the purgative rationale in application to most cases that involve very serious crimes. Most such cases reside either determinately within the reach of that rationale or determinately outside it. For instance, Richard's Case and Joseph's Case from Chapter 6 are both straightforwardly within the purview of that rationale. Furthermore, as has already been stated, there is a determinately correct upshot for any case that does *not* fall straightforwardly within that purview; in any such circumstances, the death penalty is not to be imposed.

Thus, the allegations of rampant and inevitable arbitrariness in the administration of capital punishment are not only empirically dubious but also theoretically unmotivated. Especially if the statutory classifications of circumstances as aggravative are modified to fit more tightly with the purgative rationale for the death penalty, there is no reason to think that judges and juries will generally be unable to mark the distinctions which the implementation of that rationale will require them to mark. In other words, there is no reason to think that they will generally be unable to differentiate between conduct that is extravagantly heinous and conduct that is not.

7.2.4. Residual arbitrariness

Of course, to maintain that the worries about capriciousness in the administration of capital punishment are greatly overblown is not to maintain that those worries are utterly unfounded in every particular. In any institution operated by human beings rather than by infallible deities, some inconsistencies and aberrations will arise. Though appellate reviews of comparative sentencing can help to minimize the occurrence of such anomalies, those reviews are themselves conducted by human beings and are thus not apt to avert or remove every incongruity.

Moreover, the distinction between crimes that are determinately humanity-repudiating and crimes that are neither determinately humanity-repudiating nor determinately not humanity-repudiating is itself vague (owing to higher-order vagueness, which encompasses the division between the determinate and the indeterminate). Consequently, there will in some possible cases not be any determinately correct answers to questions about the justifiability of wielding the death penalty—even though there is in place a rule of closure which deals with all first-order vagueness by prescribing that the death penalty is inappropriate in any case that involves crimes which are not determinately humanity-repudiating. Any attempt to deal with the higher-order vagueness through the adoption of some further rule(s) of closure would be caught in an infinite regress. Hence, there is an ineliminable possibility of some cases in regard to which neither the purgative rationale itself nor any specifications of aggravating circumstances can prescribe determinately whether the death penalty is appropriate or not. In that respect, there is an ineliminable possibility of some arbitrariness within any system of capital punishment that is founded on the purgative rationale. No matter how effective and extensive the consistency-promoting safeguards within such a system may be, they cannot entirely close off the possibility just mentioned.

What should we conclude? Does the ineliminable possibility of some modicum of arbitrariness in every regime of capital punishment undermine the moral legitimacy of each such regime? A conclusion along those lines would be as misguided as any corresponding conclusion that might be focused on our inability to come up with absolute guarantees against the erroneousness of the outcomes in particular cases. (That latter inability has been discussed in § 7.1.5.1 above.) Just as infallibility and absolute certainty are chimerical objectives, so too is the removal of all indeterminacy. This chapter has already argued that, if the officials who run a system of capital punishment have taken an abundance of reasonable steps to guard against mistaken executions, their non-attainment of infallibility and absolute certainty does not per se preclude the legitimacy of their overall endeavours (though, of course, any mistaken execution is itself a serious wrong). Likewise, so long as those officials have taken an abundance of reasonable steps to promote the principled consistency of the sentencing in their system, their having fallen short of perfection in that respect does not per se preclude the legitimacy of their overall operations.

Some opponents of capital punishment contend that any dram of arbitrariness in the administration of such punishment is enough to delegitimize all the executions that are carried out. My riposte to such an objection resembles my earlier riposte to the claim that nothing short of infallibility and absolute certainty is sufficient to vindicate the overall workings of a regime of capital punishment. That is, when opponents suggest that even the smallest residuum of arbitrariness in any system of capital punishment is morally crippling for the system as a whole, they are taking a substantive position that has been dressed up as a procedural query. This point is made trenchantly by Dolinko:

[T]his attempt to revivify the *procedural* arbitrariness argument actually derives such force as it possesses from a concealed *substantive* claim that [capital punishment] is immoral no matter what procedures are used to impose it...[A]ny punishment system devised and operated by human beings is bound to have some amount of 'standardless discretion'; it is humanly impossible to define crimes and assign penalties by rules anticipating all the unique variations in circumstances that might possibly arise in particular cases. Hence the demand that the death penalty be administered by a completely discretionless, perfectly rational procedure is in reality a demand that it not be inflicted at all by human beings; and *that* demand must rest on an argument that the nature of death makes its deliberate infliction as a punishment morally improper—i.e., on what I have called a substantive argument. [Dolinko 1986, 577, 578–9, emphases in original]

In any substantive argument of the sort to which Dolinko refers, a detractor of capital punishment would have to explain why the purgative objective realized by a properly oriented system of such punishment is of no moral importance or virtually no moral importance. After all, the argument would be maintaining that even the modicum of arbitrariness in institutions of capital punishment which contain arrays of consistency-promoting safeguards is enough to delegitimize the pursuit of purgation through executions. Such a position would presuppose that the salutariness of purgation counts for nothing or for hardly anything—since the moral drawbacks of the residuum of arbitrariness in the aforementioned institutions are slight. (Whereas an execution of an innocent person is always a serious wrong, executions of offenders whose heinous crimes fall within the residuum of arbitrariness in a well-designed system of capital punishment are only minor wrongs.) Suffice it here to say that no opponent of the death penalty has yet taken on the task of arguing that the moral good of purgation is of no account or virtually no account. Thus, any claims about the systematically delegitimizing force of the residuum of arbitrariness in a well-designed regime of capital punishment remain wholly unsubstantiated.

7.3. Invidious discrimination

Let us ponder one further objection that has often been pressed against the administration of capital punishment in the United States. Numerous studies have suggested that decisions about the levying of capital sentences are inflected by considerations of race.[23] More specifically, the race of the victim of any murder is a factor that affects the likelihood of the imposition of a death sentence for the murder. The conclusion drawn by many opponents of the death penalty is that the judges and juries who engage in capital sentencing are inclined to value the lives of white people more highly than those of black people. Now, insofar as any invidious discrimination of this sort is really operative in a system of capital punishment, it seriously tarnishes that system. If such discrimination is extensive, it can even undo the whole system's moral legitimacy. It is problematic not only because invidious discrimination on the basis of race is repugnant in every situation, but also because the stakes in any context of capital sentencing are so high.

Patently, the complaints about racism in capital sentencing cannot satisfactorily be countered through the ostrich-like retorts of van den Haag. Most of his pronouncements in which he discounted the importance of comparative justice—some of which have been quoted in § 7.2.1 above—were made in response to various worries about racial discrimination as well as in response to worries about capriciousness. Those pronouncements with their devaluation of comparative justice are no more persuasive in reply to the former worries than in reply to the latter (Dolinko 1986, 579–80). If racism plays a wide-ranging role in the processes of selecting among offenders for the death penalty in some jurisdiction, then the moral soundness of the system which administers that penalty may well be vitiated. In that event, the system cannot legitimately conduct any executions on the basis of the purgative rationale; after all, such executions would be administered in furtherance of moral values which *ex hypothesi* the system as a whole is flouting. Executions conducted in such circumstances are morally impermissible manifestations of hypocrisy, even if each person executed has committed appalling crimes that render his life defilingly evil. Thus, given that the aim of this chapter is to explore whether the institution of capital punishment can be morally legitimate despite shortcomings in its administration, van den Haag's head-in-the-sand approach to the issue is singularly unhelpful.

[23] For overviews of quite a few studies through the early 1980s, see Barnett 1985, 1330–4, 1358–60; Gross and Mauro 1984, 38–49. For some more recent studies, see Baldus, Woodworth, and Pulaski 1990; and Baldus, Woodworth, Zuckerman, Weiner, and Broffitt 1998.

7.3.1. Extrinsicality

Whereas the possibility of mistaken executions and some modicum of arbitrariness in the administration of capital punishment cannot ever be completely overcome, the influence of racism in capital sentencing is entirely extrinsic. Though racial prejudices might affect the selection of defendants for the death penalty in any particular jurisdiction, the role of such noxious prejudices is far from inevitable. Especially if appellate reviews of comparative sentencing are duly attentive to the factor of race, the sway of those prejudices in the selection of defendants can be averted or eliminated. As Dolinko aptly contends:

> [E]ven if we accept both the statistical evidence and the inference of discrimination drawn from it, the discrimination argument requires a further step. We must agree that racial discrimination in capital punishment cannot be eradicated. Otherwise, the appropriate response to the demonstration that such bias exists would be 'eliminate the discrimination,' not 'abolish capital punishment.' Where is the proof that we cannot administer the death penalty in a racially neutral fashion? Abolitionists commonly rely on assertions that prejudice in capital punishment is 'so deeply rooted that little can be done in practice to eradicate it'—a counsel of despair not on its face unassailable. [Dolinko 1986, 581–2, footnote omitted, quoting Bedau 1982, 186.]

Even if the rooting out of racial prejudices from any society is not a realistically attainable goal—save, perhaps, over several generations—the use of procedural safeguards (such as appellate reviews) to keep those prejudices from biasing any decisions about capital sentencing is eminently realistic. Moreover, we should recall that the only countries relevantly under consideration here are those which are governed by liberal-democratic regimes. Only in such countries can the death penalty be legitimately administered on the basis of the purgative rationale. Given as much, and given that the adherence of liberal-democratic regimes to the values of equality and freedom is highly conducive to the diminution of bigotry, the aim of progressively reducing and marginalizing bigotry in countries that can legitimately practice capital punishment is itself not wildly unrealistic. Of course, any claim to that effect should be coupled with an unflinching awareness of the centuries-long presence of racism and anti-Semitism and other ugly hatreds in the lands that are now liberal democracies. However, all or nearly all of those lands became liberal democracies only recently. For instance, some American states—disfigured first by slavery and later by institutionalized racial dominance and disenfranchisement—did not become liberal democracies until the past few decades. During the brief period since each existing liberal democracy gained its character as such, there has generally been significant progress (albeit not without setbacks) toward the elimination of bigotry.[24] Though racial and religious prejudices might never disappear completely in any liberal democracy, there are ample grounds for thinking that such prejudices can realistically be reduced to the point where they

---

[24] One of the setbacks in recent years has been a surge in anti-Semitism among many Muslim citizens of some European liberal democracies.

would not inflect decisions on life-or-death matters such as the imposition of capital punishment.

To be sure, most of the opponents of capital punishment who worry about racism in the selection of defendants for such punishment do not allege that the problem lies in gross bigotry. Rather, the problem is usually said to derive from much subtler and largely subconscious prejudices that lead many jurors unreflectively to attach greater value to the lives of white victims of murders than to the lives of black victims (Baldus, Woodworth, Zuckerman, Weiner, and Broffitt 1998, 1723; Barnett 1985, 1356–7 n 59). Still, insofar as any anomalies in the dispensation of death sentences are indeed due to such insidious prejudices, those anomalies should be avoidable through proper procedural precautions. Appellate reviews of comparative sentencing are obviously of importance, but so too are monitory instructions from judges in the phases of the original trials during which the sentences are decided. After all, many of the people who harbour subconscious prejudices would be dismayed by them if they were brought to light. Hence, there are grounds for optimism about the efficacy of instructions from judges which would refer to any germane social-scientific studies and which would caution jurors to be alert to the possibility of the influence of sub-liminal prejudices. In combination with other procedural safeguards, such instructions can go a long way toward overcoming any race-based aberrations that do exist in capital sentencing.

Thus, although the legitimacy of the use of the death penalty in any particular jurisdiction can of course be destroyed by the wide-ranging sway of racial prejudices in patterns of sentencing, the legitimacy of the death penalty as a general punishment-type will remain wholly unimpaired. The legitimacy of that general type of punishment remains wholly unimpaired because the influence of racial discrimination on capital sentencing is meaningfully avoidable both in principle and (gradually if not immediately) in practice.

7.3.2. A couple of complexities and the key rejoinder

Although there is little doubt that the administration of the death penalty in certain American states is skewed to some degree by considerations of race, the situation is more complicated and equivocal than might initially be thought. For one thing, the problem of the devaluation of black victims is partly due to efforts to rein in any invidiously overzealous prosecution of black defendants (Dolinko 1986, 581). Because the vast majority of murders in the United States are intraracial, a significant increase in the dispensation of capital sentences for murderers of black people would almost certainly involve a significant increase in the number of such sentences for black defendants. Conversely, endeavours to hold down the latter number are partly responsible for the apparent slighting of the lives of black victims.

A related point that should be noted here is that the racial discrimination detected in some systems of capital punishment in the United States during recent decades has been centred mostly on black victims of murders—the undervaluing of their lives—rather than on black defendants (Abramson 2004, 138). Although an array of studies have seemed to reveal that black murderers are sentenced to death disproportionately, the appearance of invidious discrimination usually dissipates when the data are analysed to take account of the heinousness of the murders and the number and seriousness of the murderers' past offences. (By contrast, the appearance of *victim-centred* discrimination across mid-level cases of murder generally does persist even when other factors are taken into account.) Admittedly, there are exceptions to this general point. For instance, the authors of a major study undertaken in Philadelphia in the 1990s submit that their findings 'clearly support an inference that the race of the defendant is a substantial influence in the Philadelphia charging and sentencing system, particularly in jury penalty trials' (Baldus, Woodworth, Zuckerman, Weiner, and Broffitt 1998, 1714). Since the authors of the Philadelphia study have controlled for many of the variables that have to be taken into account to ensure that their findings of invidious discrimination against black defendants are reliable, their conclusions are dismaying even though their sample sizes are small. Nevertheless, Patrick Lenta and Douglas Farland are correct when they state that in general the 'evidence that black capital defendants are discriminated against relative to white capital defendants is scantier [than the evidence of discrimination pertaining to black victims of murders in comparison with white victims]' (Lenta and Farland 2008, 275).

In any event, the Philadelphia study is consistent with the central observation that should be made here about the evidence of discrimination against black victims of murders and against black capital defendants. Like the evidence of arbitrariness in the administration of capital punishment, the evidence of racial discrimination indicates that the suspect patterns of decision-making arise predominantly in cases of mid-level seriousness—cases that are definitely excluded from the scope of the purgative rationale. As the authors of the Philadelphia study affirm: 'The Philadelphia results are consistent with the results of earlier studies that tested the "liberation hypothesis." This theory posits that race and other arbitrary factors are likely to have the most profound effect in midrange cases in which the decision maker is "liberated" from the "grip of fact" that virtually compels a particular result when the case is very clear cut' (Baldus, Woodworth, Zuckerman, Weiner, and Broffitt 1998, 1716). This result concurs with the findings of an earlier survey by some of the same authors, in which they declare that 'race-of-victim and race-of-defendant effects are not uniform across the cases, but appear primarily in cases in the midaggravation range'. They conclude that 'when the crime involved was either extremely aggravated or comparatively free from aggravating circumstances, the choice between a life and a death sentence was relatively clear; and, regardless of racial factors, Georgia prosecutors and juries responded accordingly' (Baldus, Woodworth, and Pulaski 1990, 145). Indeed, quite uncontroversial is the proposition that the race-based skewing in processes of capital sentencing is concentrated in the mid-level range of cases. For example, Ronald Tabak, an outspoken opponent of the death penalty, has written as follows: 'The Baldus studies and others show the great disparities based on the race of the victim in middle range cases. The middle range problem could be eliminated by adopting pro-death penalty Ninth Circuit Judge Alex Kozinski's idea of narrowing death eligibility to include only the most heinous murders' (Tabak 1999). Richard Dieter, another fierce critic of capital punishment, has similarly acknowledged that the influence of race on decisions about capital sentencing is not significant in the very cases that are covered by the purgative rationale for the death penalty:

> Race does not affect all cases equally. Notorious serial killers like Ted Bundy or John Wayne Gacy, both white, are nearly certain to receive the death penalty regardless of their race. In the most highly aggravated cases, the fact that the defendant is black is less of a factor pushing a case toward a death sentence. The same can be said for cases of very low severity: race is less likely to be a factor in cases where there is little inflammatory evidence. But in the 'mid-range' of severity (or aggravation), race plays a very significant role. When cases were ranked from 1 to 8 in increasing severity, cases in categories 1 (least severe) and 8 (most severe) showed little or no discrimination against black defendants. But in the middle categories 3 through 7, the disproportionate treatment of black defendants, as compared to all other defendants, was quite pronounced. [Dieter 1998]

In short, like the problem of arbitrariness, the problem of racial discrimination in the administration of the death penalty is largely absent from the cases to which the purgative rationale is applicable. In this respect, the limitedness of the reach of that rationale is a major advantage.

7.3.3. No severe punishments? A first look

Complaints about racial discrimination in the administration of the death penalty are usually focused on the processes whereby some murderers are selected for that penalty while other murderers in the same jurisdiction are selected for lesser sanctions. When the complaints are so focused, there is no danger of their leading to the conclusion that murder cannot legitimately be punished with any severe sanction. Instead, as might be inferred from the discussion in § 7.2.2 above, they will lead at worst to some less disconcerting conclusions. Let us first assume that the discrimination pertains to the race of each perpetrator of murder. In that event, the following conclusion may well ensue. If and only if the racial discrimination in the aforementioned processes of selection cannot be surmounted or greatly reduced (despite all my arguments hitherto), each black murderer should be subjected to a sanction that is no more severe than the gentlest sanction imposed upon any white murderer. Such a conclusion will commend itself only if the non-comparative injustices wrought by the levelling down of the sanctions for black murderers are more than offset in moral importance by the termination of the invidiously unfavourable treatment of black defendants. Note that this prescription for levelling down does not entail the abolition or suspension of the death penalty for white defendants, among whom a relevant selection can still be undertaken without any taint of racism.[25]

Let us now assume that the discrimination pertains to the race of each victim of murder, and let us assume *arguendo* that the discrimination cannot be overcome or greatly reduced. In that event, the following conclusion may well ensue. Everyone convicted of murder should be subjected to a sanction that is no more severe than the punishment that is appropriate for the least evil instance of the crime. Such a conclusion is a morally superior alternative to another proposition that might be embraced on the basis of the complaints about discrimination against black victims of murders: namely, the proposition that each murderer of a black person should be subjected to a sanction that is no less severe than the harshest sanction imposed upon any murderer of a white person. The implementation of that latter proposition would result in the punishing of many murderers of black people more severely than would be appropriate for their crimes. It would consequently violate a principle of liberal democracy invoked in § 7.2.2—the principle that (within certain limits) the imposition of excessively severe sanctions is morally worse than the imposition of unduly lenient sanctions. It would also dismayingly increase the number of black defendants who are subjected to the death penalty. Hence, the best conclusion to be drawn from the complaints about discrimination against black victims of murders in the administration of capital punishment is the conclusion stated at the outset of this paragraph. (Of course, in line with what has been said in the preceding paragraph, the levelling down of the punishments for all murderers is morally superior to the continuation of the prejudice-marred status quo only if the non-comparative injustices wrought by the levelling down are more than offset in moral importance by the termination of the invidiously unfavourable treatment of black people who have been slain.)

7.3.4. No severe punishments? A second look

Though the philosophers and jurists who raise concerns about racial prejudice in the administration of capital punishment have usually trained their attention on the sentencing stages of trials at which some people convicted of murder are distinguished from other such people by being singled out for execution, the concerns occasionally pertain to earlier stages of the processes in systems of criminal-law enforcement. Michael Cholbi, for example, has contended that a 'good deal of the justifiable suspicion harbored by African-Americans and other racial minorities toward the criminal justice system has little to do with events in the courtroom. Rather, they are acutely aware of the extra-judicial discrimination that takes place before a defendant even enters a courtroom.' He elaborates: 'Examples of such discrimination include prosecutors who, aware of jurors' prejudices, more frequently opt to prosecute African-Americans for murder, and police officers who more aggressively pursue

---

[25]   This point is missed in Hurka 2001, 27.

and prosecute crime in African-American neighborhoods.' He maintains that the safeguards introduced during recent decades to avert racial discrimination in the sentencing of capital defendants have exacerbated the discrimination that occurs at the earlier stages of legal proceedings: '[A]s many predicted, the reforms instituted after Furman (sentencing guidelines that limit judge and jury discretion in imposing death; bifurcated trials with distinct guilt and penalty phases; automatic appeals of death sentences; and state reviews to determine if a given sentence aligns with those in similar previous cases, etc.) shifted racial discrimination to these earlier stages of the judicial process' (Cholbi 2006, 257–8).

7.3.4.1. An opening reply to Cholbi

In response to these claims by Cholbi, three observations are pertinent. First, when he alleges that the procedures leading up to trials and convictions of black suspects are suffused with racism, his allegations are somewhat in tension with the main drift of the recent studies on racism in the administration of capital punishment. Although a few of those studies have produced some evidence of defendant-centred discrimination that persists even when the authors have controlled for the relative heinousness of the defendants' murders and the seriousness of the defendants' past crimes, the emphasis in recent decades has been principally on victim-centred discrimination. Cholbi is aware of the findings of such discrimination, and he later discusses and endorses them (Cholbi 2006, 267–9). However, given that a large majority of the instances of the most serious crime-types in the United States are intraracial, his claims here about defendant-centred discrimination—with his apparent view that criminality should be pursued less aggressively in African-American neighbourhoods—are not easily squared with the notion that black victims of crimes are receiving inadequate protection by the police. If the policing of serious crimes in black communities is to be scaled down in accordance with Cholbi's apparent wishes, the protection extended to black victims of such crimes will be curtailed commensurately.

7.3.4.2. A further reply to Cholbi

Secondly, if Cholbi were correct about the pervasiveness and intractability of racial discrimination on the part of the police and other law-enforcement officials in the United States, the conclusion to be drawn with reference to black defendants there would go well beyond the moratorium on capital punishment for which Cholbi calls. Rather, as Dolinko suggests in reply to a somewhat different line of argument (Dolinko 1986, 582–3), the conclusion to be drawn with reference to black defendants in the United States is that they cannot properly be subjected to any severe sanctions. After all, Cholbi is in effect maintaining that arrests and convictions of black defendants are unreliable indicators of the defendants' guilt. If such a contention were correct across a wide range of cases, then the imposition of any severe sanctions on black defendants within American courts would be morally illegitimate.

Although the death penalty is of course a more severe sanction than a long term in prison, the latter punishment—or any other heavy sanction, such as a medium-length term in prison—would also be morally illegitimate if it were inflicted on a defendant whose arrest and conviction are probably attributable to racism. Thus, if Cholbi really believes that racism in American policing and criminal proceedings is very widespread and tenacious,[26] he ought to be calling for a moratorium on the use of any onerous punishments against black defendants.

7.3.4.3. A final reply to Cholbi

Thirdly, Cholbi's denunciation of the treatment of black people by the systems of criminal-law enforcement in the United States is entirely consistent with the retention of capital punishment for white defendants whose crimes are extravagantly evil. Cholbi anticipates a reply of this sort to some of his other arguments, and he seeks to parry it. He asserts that, if a moratorium on capital punishment were to cover black defendants but not white defendants, it would 'introduce[e] a new injustice, this time to whites'. He explains: 'If whites could expect to be executed for murder whereas African-Americans could not, then whites would face a greater cost for murdering than would African-Americans.... We would simply have turned the switch of injustice in the other direction' (Cholbi 2006, 270).

7.3.4.3.1. Fair discrimination

Cholbi's anticipatory response should be met with two rejoinders. In the first place, if his complaints about ubiquitous racism against blacks in American policing and legal proceedings were correct, the retention of capital punishment for white offenders in combination with the discontinuation of such punishment (and of any other severe sanctions) for black offenders would not be unjust toward the whites. Under such an arrangement, the worst of the white offenders would be subjected to capital punishment not because they are white but because they have been reliably convicted of horrific crimes. Their situation would be very different from that of black defendants in the contemporary United States as portrayed by Cholbi. Black defendants, according to him, have not been reliably convicted of anything. When any black defendants are subjected to the death penalty—in the United States as depicted by Cholbi—there is a high likelihood that the defendants are undergoing such treatment because of their skin colour and that they have not genuinely committed any serious crimes. Consequently, the retention of capital punishment or any onerous sanctions for black convicts is morally unsustainable. Decidedly different is the retention of such punishment for the vilest of white offenders. As has just been remarked, those white offenders would be executed because of the appalling crimes

---

[26] As should be evident, I myself do not subscribe to such a belief. Nevertheless, only an extraordinarily naïve person would think that racism is altogether absent from policing and from criminal proceedings in the United States (and indeed in other liberal democracies—to say nothing of the numerous non-Western countries in which racist and ethnic/tribal hatreds are rampant).

of which they have been reliably convicted. There is virtually no likelihood that the actions of law-enforcement officials in arresting and convicting those offenders have been prompted by their skin colour, and there is only a minute likelihood that the offenders have not actually perpetrated the iniquities for which they have been tried and convicted. Hence, there are no grounds of fairness for objecting to their executions.

Supporters of Cholbi will probably think that I am missing his point, which is about comparative justice rather than about the non-comparative desideratum of purgation. They might be happy to allow that the worst of the white offenders have committed repulsive crimes which fall within the scope of the purgative rationale, and they might therefore concede that the execution of each such vile offender is worthy of approbation when it is assessed in isolation. However, when we take account of the fact that black culprits who have perpetrated equally appalling crimes are not being subjected to the death penalty or indeed to any onerous sanctions, we can recognize that the treatment of the white culprits is inequitable. Or so the supporters of Cholbi will insist. Indeed, they will contend that the inequitability extends to white citizens generally. In the remarks quoted just above, Cholbi is implicitly appealing to a principle which he has formulated earlier in his article:

Principle of Equal Status: Individuals do not enjoy equal legal status relative to a given crime if (a) the law or legal practices provide different individuals with different expectations about the likely costs of committing that crime, and (b) the differences in expectations are best explained by a factor other than differences in individuals' desert. [Cholbi 2006, 263]

In the scenario that I am envisaging, where white people convicted of appalling crimes are liable to undergo the death penalty while black people convicted of such crimes are subject only to much lighter penalties, the expected costs of committing heinous crimes will generally be higher for white citizens than for black citizens. Accordingly, the supporters of Cholbi will be apt to think that the state of affairs depicted in my scenario is in contravention of the Principle of Equal Status. They will thus conclude that Cholbi is correct in asserting that capital punishment can never legitimately be suspended only for blacks and not also for whites.

Though my next subsection will impugn the Principle of Equal Status, that principle can be left uncontested for the moment—because the situation depicted in my scenario is fully consistent with it. After all, the reason why the expected costs of committing vile crimes are higher for white citizens than for black citizens in my scenario is tied to the factor of responsibility for the perpetration of crimes. Specifically in connection with the imposition of the death penalty, the decisive factor is responsibility for the perpetration of extravagantly evil crimes. (Of course, Cholbi's Principle of Equal Status refers to desert rather than to responsibility. However, because this book's rationale for the death penalty is purgative rather than retributivistic, and because the property of responsibility is highlighted both by the purgative rationale and by retributivism, my discussion here will substitute 'responsibility' for 'desert' in Cholbi's principle.) In the contemporary United States as portrayed by Cholbi, the responsibility of black individuals for the commission of crimes is not reliably ascertainable. Because of the poisonous sway of racism throughout the operations of American criminal-law enforcement, the conviction of a black person for some crime(s) does not reliably indicate that he is responsible for the crime(s). By contrast, the responsibility of white individuals for the commission of crimes is reliably ascertainable. In any typical circumstances, the conviction of a white person for some crime(s) does reliably indicate that he is responsible for the crime(s). Consequently, white defendants can and should be punished straightforwardly in accordance with their criminal responsibility. Except by sheer happenstance, contrariwise, black defendants cannot be punished by an American court straightforwardly in accordance with their criminal responsibility—since, *ex hypothesi*, any such court lacks the means to determine reliably whether black people are responsible for particular crimes. Thus, although the expected costs of perpetrating atrocities are much higher for white citizens than for black citizens in my scenario, the Principle of Equal Status countenances the disparity. That disparity arises from the divergence between the *reliability* of the courts' attributions of criminal responsibility to white citizens and the *unreliability* of the courts' attributions of criminal responsibility to black citizens.

Supporters of Cholbi might query whether the purgative rationale for the death penalty is compatible with the retention of that sanction for white defendants in systems of criminal justice which are so plagued by racism that they cannot legitimately execute any black defendants. Given what has been said in Chapter 6 about the hypocrisy and consequent illegitimacy of any execution conducted on the basis of the purgative rationale by an illiberal regime, the retention of capital punishment for white defendants in my scenario may itself seem clearly illegitimate. How can racist systems of criminal justice ever invoke the purgative rationale without hypocrisy? If they cannot, then Cholbi is correct in holding that any moratorium on capital punishment should apply to white defendants and black defendants alike.

Such an attempt to vindicate Cholbi would be unsuccessful, since the suspension of capital punishment and other onerous punishments for black defendants in my scenario will counteract the delegitimizing effects of racism and will thereby enable the proper use of the death penalty—on the basis of the purgative rationale, of course—against white defendants. Suppose that the US Supreme Court were to agree with Cholbi's dismal picture of the treatment of blacks by policemen and prosecutors and many judges in the United States. Suppose that, in response to the perceived problem of racism, the Court were to place a moratorium on the use of capital punishment and lengthy prison terms against black defendants. Such a move would not eradicate the problem of racism, but it would eliminate the most pernicious effects of that problem within the systems of criminal justice over which the Court presides. It would thereby shore up the moral standing of those systems to the point where the purgative rationale for the death penalty could legitimately be invoked within them against whites who are convicted of grotesquely heinous crimes. Of course the Supreme Court might take the view that, because some jurisdictions in the United States have been so heavily implicated in invidious practices against black defendants, the courts in those jurisdictions now lack the moral wherewithal to invoke the purgative rationale against anyone (white or black) without hypocrisy. Any such courts should indeed be placed under a transracial moratorium on capital punishment. Other state and federal courts, however, could legitimately continue to sentence to death any white defendants whose odious crimes give rise to a pressing need for purgation. Thus, Cholbi errs when he submits that his account of the systems of legal governance in the United States should lead to a blanket moratorium on capital punishment. Were that account correct, it would warrant only a partial moratorium at most.

7.3.4.3.2. A dubious principle

Worth remarking here is that Cholbi's Principle of Equal Status is untenable as it stands. We can see as much by noting that, in any jurisdiction, malefactors who are cannily deceitful and ruthlessly resistant will typically be less likely to undergo sanctions than will malefactors who are less adept at dissimulation and less willing to resort to extreme violence in order to remove witnesses or evade capture. *Ceteris paribus*, then, the expected costs of committing crimes will be lower for the crafty and pitiless malefactors. Under the operations of any credible legal system, such villains will tend to fare better in eluding apprehension and sanctions. Moreover, their advantage in that respect is hardly due to their being less deserving of punishment or less viciously responsible for misdeeds than the criminals who are not comparably endowed with clever furtiveness and ruthlessness. Quite the contrary. Hence, 'the differences in expectations [namely, the lower costs of criminality that face the cunning and relentless wrongdoers] are best explained by a factor other than differences in individuals' desert'.

In short, Cholbi's Principle of Equal Status is contravened by every possible legal system—including every possible legal system that is impeccably free of invidious discrimination—in relation to every type of crime. Any legal-governmental system's operations will be such that the likelihood of apprehension is lower for miscreants who are especially canny and unscrupulous. For such miscreants, *ceteris paribus*, the expected costs of committing various crimes will be lower than for other people. In that very regard, the operations of every legal system fail to comply with the requirement laid down by Cholbi's principle. Quite outlandish, however, is the notion that in every such system the legal status occupied by the shrewdly devious and violent criminals is unequal to that occupied by people who are less capable of outwitting and outshooting the law-enforcement authorities. Likewise preposterous is the notion that the latter people are wronged by the sheer fact that the cleverly devious and ruthless villains are more likely to escape legal punishment. In the absence of invidious discrimination or negligence on the part of the law-enforcing authorities, the fact that those villains are more likely to escape punishment does not constitute a wrong against anybody. Ergo, given that the greater likelihood of their escaping punishment nonetheless amounts to a vio-lation of Cholbi's Principle of Equal Status by every operative legal system, and given that any violation of a genuine moral requirement constitutes a wrong, we can soundly infer that Cholbi's principle does not set forth any genuine moral requirement.

7.3.4.4. A brief summation

As should be evident, I do not favour the implementation of the conclusions which I have drawn from Cholbi's account of policing and legal proceedings in the United States. That is, I do not favour a moratorium on capital punishment and other severe sanctions for black defendants.[27] If Cholbi's dire account were accurate, then the draw-backs of such a moratorium in regard to non-comparative justice might be exceeded in moral importance by the virtues of such a measure in regard to comparative justice.[28] However, because Cholbi's remarks on the influence of racism in policing and legal proceedings are significantly overstated (at least in connection with the appalling crimes that are covered by the purgative rationale for the death penalty), the matter of assessing the relative importance of the drawbacks and benefits associated with a partial morato-rium does not arise.

At any rate, the chief point in my discussion of Cholbi has been to make clear that his line of argument—even if otherwise successful—does not warrant the conclu-sion that a transracial moratorium on capital punishment should be introduced in the United States. At the very most, his argument would support the conclusion that a moratorium on such punishment and on other severe penalties should be imposed for cases involving black defendants. His own principles do not support any more sweep-ing conclusion. Even if he could vindicate his dismal picture of policing and legal proceedings in the United States, and even if he could show that the non-comparative drawbacks of suspending capital punishment and other onerous sanctions for black defendants would be surpassed in moral importance by the gains in comparative jus-tice, he would not thereby have established that the use of the death penalty on the basis of the purgative rationale is morally illegitimate in the United States across the board. Such a penalty would remain legitimate (and obligatory) in cases involving white defendants who have perpetrated terrible iniquities.

7.3.5. Substance dressed up afresh as procedure

Despite what has been said about the negligible influence of racial biases on the sentencing in the sorts of cases that fall within the ambit of the purgative rationale

---

[27] I in fact favour a moratorium on capital punishment for defendants of all races, though my reasons are different from those adduced by Cholbi. A comprehensive moratorium should last in each jurisdic-tion of the United States until the system of capital punishment in each jurisdiction has been firmly reoriented toward the purgative rationale for such punishment.

[28] On some of the complexities surrounding this issue, see Lenta and Farland 2008, 287–9. (The ante-penultimate and penultimate paragraphs of the discussion by Lenta and Farland contain an error that does not detract from the main points which they are making.)

for the death penalty, there are obviously no guarantees that the decisions in those cases will never be inflected by such biases. Safeguards such as appellate reviews of comparative sentencing are designed to counter any effects of biases, but there are of course no guarantees that the safeguards will themselves always fulfil their assigned purpose. Racial prejudices might occasionally creep in, and they might sometimes (however rarely) go uncorrected. Do these possibilities vitiate the moral standing of every institution of capital punishment, because the life-or-death stakes of the decisions within any such institution are so momentous? Would the occasional actualization of these possibilities—through the intrusion of racial considerations into some processes of capital sentencing—undo the overarching moral legitimacy of any institution within which the tainted processes of sentencing have taken place?

Plainly, any judgments that have been skewed by racial prejudices are morally illegitimate, even if the sentences handed down would have been correct in themselves. For example, if a black defendant who has committed atrocious crimes is sentenced to death, and if the judge and jury who determine his sentence would have opted for a lighter punishment if he had been white, then the execution of him is morally illegitimate notwithstanding that his crimes have made his life defilingly evil. However, the questions posed in the preceding paragraph are not about the moral legitimacy of particular executions, but are instead about the moral standing of institutions. Is the overall moral legitimacy of an institution of capital punishment stymied by the sheer possibility and occasional actuality of the influence of racism in some aspects of the institution's workings?

An answer to this question will depend on the frequency of the actual emergence of that baleful influence. If a significant proportion of the sentences in a system of capital punishment are swayed by racial biases, then the system is discredited to the point where the purgative rationale for executions cannot be invoked without hypocrisy. Every execution administered by a system so tarnished, including every execution that is itself wholly unprompted by any racial discrimination, is then deprived of moral legitimacy by the role of such discrimination in the overall operations of the system. By contrast, if racism and other invidious biases seldom or never impinge on decisions about capital sentencing (after such decisions have been refined, if necessary, through appellate reviews), then the institution of the death penalty within a given jurisdiction can retain its legitimacy indefinitely. In such an institution, any executions which are otherwise appropriate and which are not themselves prompted by any invidious prejudices will be morally legitimate. Such executions are not deprived of their moral legitimacy by the few occasions on which the handling of certain other capital cases is skewed by racism. Gravely wrong though any such skewing is, its confinedness prevents it from delegitimizing the whole system of capital sentencing in which it occurs.

Some opponents of capital punishment might of course take a contrary view. They might maintain that, because the stakes are so high in capital cases, any element of racial discrimination in some such cases is enough to invalidate morally the whole institution of the death penalty. Having recourse to such a position, the opponents of capital punishment will have forsaken their putative focus on issues of procedure and will instead have adopted a firm substantive stand against the use of such punishment. As Dolinko pointedly observes, their position 'requires more than an appeal to an assertedly firm, widely-shared societal condemnation of racism; it requires that we grapple with just those intractable problems about the unique moral status of capital punishment that procedural arguments are supposed to avoid' (Dolinko 1986, 584). After all, nobody could argue credibly that the whole institution of policing or of military defence is rendered morally illegitimate by the fact—if it is a fact—that a small number of the decisions reached in each of those institutions are prompted by racist sentiments. Of course, if any legal-governmental operations were *pervaded* by racial discrimination, those operations as a whole would indeed be morally illegitimate. However, when the sway of racial biases is highly cabined within some large-scale institution, the overall workings of the institution are not stripped of legitimacy by the handful of contexts in which those ugly biases do influence people's judgements. If opponents of the death penalty wish to maintain that on this very point the institution of capital punishment is different from the institution of policing or of military defence, then they will need to supply substantive arguments to back up their claims. They will need to explain why a system of capital punishment oriented toward the desideratum of purgation is uniquely susceptible to a loss of legitimacy. They cannot vindicate their position by simply adverting to the life-or-death stakes of the decisions to be reached in such a system; many of the decisions to be reached in the institutions of policing and military defence are likewise life-or-death matters. Instead, the detractors of capital punishment will have to explain why the desideratum of purgation is of such little importance that the pursuit of it can so easily be rendered illegitimate. As Dolinko suggests, any argument to that effect will have to deal with the substantive moral status of capital punishment—the very moral matter from which some detractors of capital punishment have hoped to prescind through their concentration on procedural issues.

7.4. A few words in conclusion

As this chapter has stated near its outset, its arguments are to some degree inconclusive. Left open here is the possibility that the imposition of capital punishment in the United States or in any other liberal-democratic jurisdiction is morally impermissible. When the chief objections to the administration of capital punishment are developed in connection with any particular jurisdiction, they are partly empirical. Though this chapter has touched upon some of the empirical studies that have been conducted in various American jurisdictions, it has done so principally in a cautionary spirit. That is, it has warned against any easy acceptance of the inferences that are drawn from those studies by people who are strongly opposed to the death penalty. The relevant matters are much less straightforward than they might at first appear.

Having warned as much, I have naturally had to be somewhat tentative in drawing my own inferences from the empirical surveys.

Still, even though this chapter has not sought to affirm robustly that the conditions in any particular jurisdiction (in the United States or elsewhere) are suitable for the retention or introduction of the death penalty, it has supplied some grounds for optimism. Most notably, my discussions have maintained that it is realistically possible to reduce any problems in the administration of the death penalty to levels at which those problems do not undermine the legitimacy of the whole system of capital punishment in which they surface. In maintaining that point, I have presupposed that the purgative rationale for the death penalty prescribes an objective that is of great moral importance. Hence, this chapter's reflections on the administration of capital punishment depend partly on Chapter 6's exposition of the purgative rationale. If (and only if) that rationale is correct—as I obviously take it to be—my discussions of procedural issues here have gone a long way toward confirming that the institution of capital punishment can be morally legitimate under conditions that are realistically attainable in liberal-democratic societies. Under circumstances that are far from fanciful, in other words, the use of the death penalty as a means of purgation is strongly justified.

Nonetheless, because there is not at present any jurisdiction in which the sole basis for the imposition of the death penalty is the purgative rationale, a corollary of this book's arguments is that a moratorium should be placed on every existing scheme of capital punishment. Only when the practice of such punishment in a liberal-democratic society is reoriented toward the objective of purgation (and toward no other objective), can the moratorium there rightly be lifted. Such a reorientation will involve the tightening of procedural safeguards and the scaling down of the range of cases in which the death penalty is imposed. It will also, of course, involve some major substantive adjustments in the underpinnings—the theoretically elaborated underpinnings and the practically articulated underpinnings—of the practice of capital punishment. When such a practice is so reordered, however, its pursuit of purgation will be on a solid moral grounding which the institution of capital punishment has heretofore lacked.

References

Abernethy, Jonathan. 1996. 'The Methodology of Death: Reexamining the Deterrence Rationale.' 27 *Columbia Human Rights Law Review* 379–424.

Abramson, Jeffrey. 2004. 'Death-is-Different Jurisprudence and the Role of the Capital Jury.' 2 *Ohio State Journal of Criminal Law* 117–64.

Alexander, Larry. 1983. 'Retributivism and the Inadvertent Punishment of the Innocent.' 2 *Law and Philosophy* 233–46.

Allen, Ronald and Shavell, Amy. 2005. 'Further Reflections on the Guillotine.' 95 *Journal of Criminal Law & Criminology* 625–36.

Andenaes, Johannes. 1974. *Punishment and Deterrence*. Ann Arbor, MI: University of Michigan Press.

Arendt, Hannah. 1963. *Eichmann in Jerusalem: A Report on the Banality of Evil*. Harmondsworth: Penguin Books.

Austin, John. 1885. *Lectures on Jurisprudence*. Fifth Edition. Volume I. Edited by Robert Campbell. London: John Murray.

Austin, John. 1995. *The Province of Jurisprudence Determined*. Edited by Wilfrid Rumble. Cambridge: Cambridge University Press. Originally published in 1832.

Baldus, David, Pulaski, Charles, and Woodworth, George. 1983. 'Comparative Review of Death Sentences: An Empirical Study of the Georgia Experience.' 74 *Journal of Criminal Law & Criminology* 661–753.

Baldus, David, Woodworth, George, and Pulaski, Charles. 1990. *Equal Justice and the Death Penalty*. Boston, MA: Northeastern University Press.

Baldus, David, Woodworth, George, Zuckerman, David, Weiner, Neil Alan, and Broffitt, Barbara. 1998. 'Racial Discrimination and the Death Penalty in the Post-*Furman* Era: An Empirical and Legal Overview, with Recent Findings from Philadelphia.' 83 *Cornell Law Review* 1638–770.

Barkow, Rachel. 2009. 'The Court of Life and Death: The Two Tracks of Constitutional Sentencing Law and the Case for Uniformity.' 107 *Michigan Law Review* 1145–205.

Barnett, Arnold. 1985. 'Some Distribution Patterns for the Georgia Death Sentence.' 18 *University of California-Davis Law Review* 1327–74.

Baumeister, Roy. 1997. *Evil: Inside Human Cruelty and Violence*. New York: W.H. Freeman and Company.

Beccaria, Cesare. 1995. *On Crimes and Punishments*. In *On Crimes and Punishments and Other Writings*. Edited by Richard Bellamy. Translated by Richard Davies, Virginia Cox, and Richard Bellamy. Cambridge: Cambridge University Press. Originally published in Italian in 1764.

Bedau, Hugo Adam. 1978. 'Retribution and the Theory of Punishment.' 75 *Journal of Philosophy* 601–20.

Bedau, Hugo Adam. 1982. *The Death Penalty in America*. Third Edition. Oxford: Oxford University Press.

Bedau, Hugo Adam. 1985. 'Thinking of the Death Penalty as a Cruel and Unusual Punishment.' 18 *University of California-Davis Law Review* 873–925.

Bedau, Hugo Adam. 1990. 'Imprisonment vs. Death: Does Avoiding Schwarzschild's Paradox Lead to Sheleff's Dilemma?' 54 *Albany Law Review* 481–95.

Bedau, Hugo Adam. 1993. 'Capital Punishment.' In Tom Regan (ed), *Matters of Life and Death*. Third Edition. New York: McGraw-Hill, pp 160–94.

Bedau, Hugo Adam. 1999. 'Abolishing the Death Penalty Even for the Worst Murderers.' In Austin Sarat (ed), *The Killing State*. New York: Oxford University Press, pp 40–59.

Bedau, Hugo Adam. 2002. 'The Minimal Invasion Argument against the Death Penalty.' 21 (# 2) *Criminal Justice Ethics* 3–8.

Benn, Stanley. 1985. 'Wickedness.' 95 *Ethics* 795–810.

Bennett, Jonathan. 1981. 'Morality and Consequences.' In Sterling McMurrin (ed), *The Tanner Lectures on Human Values: 1981*. Cambridge: Cambridge University Press.

Bennett, Jonathan. 1995. *The Act Itself*. Oxford: Oxford University Press.

Bentham, Jeremy. 1962. *Principles of Penal Law*. In *The Works of Jeremy Bentham*, Volume I, 365–580. Edited by John Bowring. New York: Russell & Russell. Originally published in 1838.

Berman, Mitchell. 2010. 'Two Kinds of Retributivism.' *University of Texas School of Law Public Law and Legal Theory Research Paper Series*. Paper # 171, 1–32.

Berns, Walter. 1979. *For Capital Punishment*. New York: Basic Books.

Binder, Guyora. 2002. 'Punishment Theory: Moral or Political?' 5 *Buffalo Criminal Law Review* 321–71.

Binder, Guyora and Smith, Nicholas. 2000. 'Framed: Utilitarianism and Punishment of the Innocent.' 32 *Rutgers Law Journal* 115–224.

Black, Charles. 1981. *Capital Punishment: The Inevitability of Caprice and Mistake*. Second Edition. New York: W.W. Norton.

Blecker, Robert. 2003. 'The Death Penalty: Where are We Now?' 19 *New York Law School Journal of Human Rights* 295–304.

'Book Review.' 1983. 81 *Michigan Law Review* 1210–14. Reviewing Hugo Adam Bedau (ed), *The Death Penalty in America*.

Bowers, William and Pierce, Glenn. 1980. 'Deterrence or Brutalization: What is the Effect of Executions?' 26 *Crime & Delinquency* 453–84.

Bradley, Gerard. 1999. 'Retribution and the Secondary Aims of Punishment.' 44 *American Journal of Jurisprudence* 105–23.

Braithwaite, John and Pettit, Philip. 1990. *Not Just Deserts: A Republican Theory of Criminal Justice*. Oxford: Oxford University Press.

Brooks, Thom. 2004. 'Retributivist Arguments against Capital Punishment.' 35 *Journal of Social Philosophy* 188–97.

Burgh, Richard. 1982. 'Do the Guilty Deserve Punishment?' 79 *Journal of Philosophy* 193–210.

Buss, Sarah. 1997. 'Justified Wrongdoing.' 31 *Noûs* 337–69.

Cahill, Michael. 2010. 'Punishment Pluralism.' *Brooklyn Law School Legal Studies Research Papers: Accepted Papers Series*. Paper # 215, 1–23.

Card, Claudia. 2002. *The Atrocity Paradigm: A Theory of Evil*. New York, NY: Oxford University Press.

Card, Claudia. 2008. 'Ticking Bombs and Interrogations.' 2 *Criminal Law and Philosophy* 1–15.

Cholbi, Michael. 2006. 'Race, Capital Punishment, and the Cost of Murder.' 127 *Philosophical Studies* 255–82.

Cohen, GA. 2006. 'Who Can, and Who Can't, Condemn the Terrorists?' 81 *Royal Institute of Philosophy Supplements* 113–36.

Cohen-Cole, Ethan, Durlauf, Steven, Fagan, Jeffrey, and Nagin, Daniel. 2009. 'Model Uncertainty and the Deterrent Effect of Capital Punishment.' 11 *American Law and Economic Review* 335–69.

Conway, David. 1974. 'Capital Punishment and Deterrence: Some Considerations in Dialogue Form.' 3 *Philosophy and Public Affairs* 431–43.

Davis, Lawrence. 1972. 'They Deserve to Suffer.' 32 *Analysis* 136–40.

Davis, Michael. 1983. 'How to Make the Punishment Fit the Crime.' 93 *Ethics* 726–52.

Davis, Michael. 1986. 'Harm and Retribution.' 15 *Philosophy and Public Affairs* 236–66.

Davis, Michael. 1991. 'Criminal Desert, Harm, and Fairness.' 25 *Israel Law Review* 524–48.

Davis, Michael. 1996. *Justice in the Shadow of Death*. Lanham, MD: Rowman & Littlefield.

Davis, Michael. 2002. 'A Sound Retributive Argument for the Death Penalty.' 21 (# 2) *Criminal Justice Ethics* 22–6.

De Wijze, Stephen. 2002. 'Defining Evil: Insights from the Problem of "Dirty Hands".' 85 *The Monist* 210–38.

De Wijze, Stephen. 2009. 'Recalibrating Steiner on Evil.' In Stephen de Wijze, Matthew H Kramer, and Ian Carter (eds), *Hillel Steiner and the Anatomy of Justice*. New York: Routledge, pp 214–32.

Dickens, Charles. 1971. *Bleak House*. Harmondsworth: Penguin Books. Originally published in 1853.

Dieter, Richard. 1998. 'The Death Penalty in Black and White: Who Lives, Who Dies, Who Decides.' URL = <http://www.deathpenaltyinfo.org/death-penalty-black-and-white-who-lives-who-dies-who-decides> (visited in November 2010).

Dolinko, David. 1986. 'Foreword: How to Criticize the Death Penalty.' 77 *Journal of Criminal Law & Criminology* 546–601.

Dolinko, David. 1991. 'Some Thoughts about Retributivism.' 101 *Ethics* 537–59.

Dolinko, David. 1992. 'Three Mistakes of Retributivism.' 39 *UCLA Law Review* 1623–57.

Dolinko, David. 1994. 'Mismeasuring "Unfair Advantage": A Response to Michael Davis.' 13 *Law and Philosophy* 493–524.

Donnelly, Samuel. 1978. 'A Theory of Justice, Judicial Methodology, and the Constitutionality of Capital Punishment: Rawls, Dworkin, and a Theory of Criminal Responsibility.' 29 *Syracuse Law Review* 1109–74.

Donohue, John and Wolfers, Justin. 2005. 'Uses and Abuses of Empirical Evidence in the Death Penalty Debate.' 58 *Stanford Law Review* 791–845.

Donohue, John and Wolfers, Justin. 2006. 'The Death Penalty: No Evidence for Deterrence.' 3 (#5) *The Economists' Voice*, Article 3. URL = <http://www.bepress.com/ev/vol3/iss5/art3> (visited in November 2009).

Douglas, Mary. 1966. *Purity and Danger*. London: Routledge & Kegan Paul.

Dressler, Joshua. 1990. 'Hating Criminals: How Can Something that Feels so Good be Wrong?' 88 *Michigan Law Review* 1448–73.

Duff, RA. 1990. 'Auctions, Lotteries, and the Punishment of Attempts.' 9 *Law and Philosophy* 1–37.

Duff, RA. 2000. *Punishment, Communication, and Community*. Oxford: Oxford University Press.

Duff, RA. 2003. 'Penance, Punishment, and the Limits of Community.' 5 *Punishment and Society* 295–312.

Durkheim, Emile. 1933. *The Division of Labor in Society*. Translated by George Simpson. New York: Macmillan. Originally published in French in 1893.

Dworkin, Ronald. 1986. *Law's Empire*. London: Fontana Press.

Edmundson, William. 2002. 'Afterword: Proportionality and the Difference Death Makes.' 21 (# 2) *Criminal Justice Ethics* 40–3.

Ehrlich, Isaac. 1975a. 'The Deterrent Effect of Capital Punishment: A Question of Life and Death.' 65 *American Economic Review* 397–417.

Ehrlich, Isaac. 1975b. 'Deterrence: Evidence and Inference.' 85 *Yale Law Journal* 209–27.

Ehrlich, Isaac. 1977a. 'The Deterrent Effect of Capital Punishment: Reply.' 67 *American Economic Review* 452–8.

Ehrlich, Isaac. 1977b. 'Capital Punishment and Deterrence: Some Further Thoughts and Additional Evidence.' 85 *Journal of Political Economy* 741–88.

Fabre, Cécile. 2008. 'Posthumous Rights.' In Matthew H Kramer, Claire Grant, Ben Colburn, and Antony Hatzistavrou (eds), *The Legacy of H.L.A. Hart*. Oxford: Oxford University Press, pp 225–38.

Feinberg, Joel. 1970. *Doing and Deserving*. Princeton, NJ: Princeton University Press.

Ferrier, Robert. 2004. '"An Atypical and Significant Hardship":The Supermax Confinement of Death Row Prisoners Based Purely on Status—A Plea for Procedural Due Process.' 46 *Arizona Law Review* 291–315.

Fest, Joachim. 2001. *Speer: The Final Verdict*. Translated by Ewald Osers and Alexandra Dring. New York: Harcourt. Originally published in German in 1999.

Finkelstein, Claire. 2002. 'Death and Retribution.' 21 (#2) *Criminal Justice Ethics* 12–21.

Finnis, John. 1972. 'The Restoration of Retribution.' 32 *Analysis* 131–5.

Finnis, John. 1980. *Natural Law and Natural Rights*. Oxford: Oxford University Press.

Finnis, John. 1999. 'Retribution: Punishment's Formative Aim.' 44 *American Journal of Jurisprudence* 91–103.

Fish, Morris. 2008. 'An Eye for an Eye: Proportionality as a Moral Principle of Punishment.' 28 *Oxford Journal of Legal Studies* 57–71.

Fletcher, George. 1999. 'The Place of Victims in the Theory of Retribution.' 3 *Buffalo Criminal Law Review* 51–63.

Foot, Philippa. 1978. *Virtues and Vices*. Berkeley, CA: University of California Press.

French, Peter and Wettstein, Howard (eds). 2006. *Shared Intentions and Collective Responsibility*. Oxford: Blackwell Publishing.

Gaita, Raimond. 1991. *Good and Evil: An Absolute Conception*. London: Macmillan.

Gale, Mary Ellen. 1985. 'Retribution, Punishment, and Death.' 18 *University of California-Davis Law Review* 973–1035.

Gardner, Romaine. 1978. 'Capital Punishment: The Philosophers and the Court.' 29 *Syracuse Law Review* 1175–216.

Garrard, Eve. 1998. 'The Nature of Evil.' 1 *Philosophical Explorations* 43–60.

Garrard, Eve. 2002. 'Evil as an Explanatory Concept.' 85 *The Monist* 320–36.

Gawande, Atul. 2009. 'Hellhole.' *The New Yorker*, 30 March. URL = <http://www.newyorker.com/reporting/2009/03/30/090330fa_fact_gawande> (visited in January 2011).

Gerstein, Robert. 1974. 'Capital Punishment—"Cruel and Unusual"?: A Retributivist Response.' 85 *Ethics* 75–9.

Gey, Steven. 1992. 'Justice Scalia's Death Penalty.' 20 *Florida State University Law Review* 67–132.

Giannelli, Paul. 2007. 'Wrongful Convictions and Forensic Science: The Need to Regulate Crime Labs.' 86 *North Carolina Law Review* 163–235.

Glover, Jonathan. 1999. *Humanity: A Moral History of the Twentieth Century*. London: Jonathan Cape.

Goldberg, Steven. 1974. 'On Capital Punishment.' 85 *Ethics* 67–74.

Goodin, Robert. 1995. *Utilitarianism as a Public Philosophy*. Cambridge: Cambridge University Press.

Grann, David. 2009. 'Trial by Fire: Did Texas Execute an Innocent Man?' *The New Yorker*, 7 September. URL = <http://www.newyorker.com/reporting/2009/09/07/090907fa_fact_grann> (visited in October 2010).

Greenberg, Jack. 1986. 'Against the American System of Capital Punishment.' 99 *Harvard Law Review* 1670–80.

Gross, Samuel and Mauro, Robert. 1984. 'Patterns of Death: An Analysis of Racial Disparities in Capital Sentencing and Homicide Victimization.' 37 *Stanford Law Review* 27–153.

Hampton, Jean. 1991. 'A New Theory of Retribution.' In Raymond Frey and Christopher Morris (eds), *Liability and Responsibility*. Cambridge: Cambridge University Press, pp 377–414.

Hampton, Jean. 1992. 'Correcting Harms versus Righting Wrongs: The Goal of Retribution.' 39 *UCLA Law Review* 1659–702.

Hampton, Jean. 1998. 'Punishment, Feminism, and Political Identity: A Case Study in the Expressive Meaning of the Law.' 11 *Canadian Journal of Law & Jurisprudence* 23–45.

Haney, Craig. 1995. 'The Social Context of Capital Murder: Social Histories and the Logic of Mitigation.' 35 *Santa Clara Law Review* 547–609.

Hart, HLA. 1968. *Punishment and Responsibility*. Oxford: Oxford University Press.

Hoffmann, Joseph. 2005. 'Protecting the Innocent: The Massachusetts Governor's Council Report.' 95 *Journal of Criminal Law and Criminology* 561–86.

Hofstadter, Albert. 1973. *Reflections on Evil*. Lawrence, KS: University of Kansas Press.

Hood, Roger. 2009. 'Abolition of the Death Penalty: China in World Perspective.' 1 *City University of Hong Kong Law Review* 1–21.

Hudson, WD. 1983. *Modern Moral Philosophy*. Second Edition. Basingstoke: Macmillan Press.

Hurka, Thomas. 1982. 'Rights and Capital Punishment.' 21 *Dialogue* 647–60.

Hurka, Thomas. 2001. 'The Common Structure of Virtue and Desert.' 112 *Ethics* 6–31.

Jones, Hardy and Potter, Nelson. 1981. 'Deterrence, Retribution, Denunciation and the Death Penalty.' 49 *University of Missouri-Kansas City Law Review* 158–69.

Kahan, Dan. 1996. 'What do Alternative Sanctions Mean?' 63 *University of Chicago Law Review* 591–653.

Kahan, Dan. 1999. 'The Secret Ambition of Deterrence.' 113 *Harvard Law Review* 414–500.

Kant, Immanuel. 1964. *Groundwork of the Metaphysic of Morals*. Translated by HJ Paton. New York: Harper & Row. Originally published in German in 1785.

Kant, Immanuel. 1970. *The Metaphysics of Morals*. In *Kant's Political Writings*. Edited by Hans Reiss. Translated by HB Nisbet. Cambridge: Cambridge University Press, pp 131–75. Originally published in German in 1797.

Kaplow, Louis and Shavell, Steven. 2002. *Fairness versus Welfare*. Cambridge, MA: Harvard University Press.

Kekes, John. 1990. *Facing Evil*. Princeton, NJ: Princeton University Press.

Kekes, John. 2005. *The Roots of Evil*. Ithaca, NY: Cornell University Press.

Kennedy, Duncan. 1981. 'Cost-Benefit Analysis of Entitlement Problems: A Critique.' 33 *Stanford Law Review* 387–445.

Kennedy, Joseph. 2000. 'Monstrous Offenders and the Search for Solidarity through Modern Punishment.' 51 *Hastings Law Journal* 829–908.

Kramer, Matthew. 1998. 'Rights without Trimmings.' In Matthew H Kramer, NE Simmonds, and Hillel Steiner, *A Debate over Rights*. Oxford: Oxford University Press, pp 7–111.

Kramer, Matthew. 1999a. *In Defense of Legal Positivism*. Oxford: Oxford University Press.

Kramer, Matthew. 1999b. *In the Realm of Legal and Moral Philosophy*. London: Macmillan Press.

Kramer, Matthew. 2001. 'Getting Rights Right.' In Matthew H Kramer (ed), *Rights, Wrongs, and Responsibilities*. Basingstoke: Palgrave Macmillan, pp 28–95.

Kramer, Matthew. 2003. *The Quality of Freedom*. Oxford: Oxford University Press.

Kramer, Matthew. 2004. *Where Law and Morality Meet*. Oxford: Oxford University Press.

Kramer, Matthew. 2005. 'Moral Rights and the Limits of the "Ought"-Implies-"Can" Principle: Why Impeccable Precautions are No Excuse.' 48 *Inquiry* 307–55.

Kramer, Matthew. 2007. *Objectivity and the Rule of Law*. Cambridge: Cambridge University Press.

Kramer, Matthew. 2009a. *Moral Realism as a Moral Doctrine*. Oxford: Wiley-Blackwell.

Kramer, Matthew. 2009b. 'Consistency is Hardly Ever Enough: Reflections on Hillel Steiner's Methodology.' In Stephen de Wijze, Matthew H Kramer, and Ian Carter (eds), *Hillel Steiner and the Anatomy of Justice*. New York: Routledge, pp 201–13.

Kurki, Leena and Morris, Norval. 2001. 'The Purposes, Practices, and Problems of Supermax Prisons.' 28 *Crime and Justice* 385–424.

Kutz, Christopher. 2000. *Complicity: Ethics and Law for a Collective Age*. Cambridge: Cambridge University Press.

Laudan, Larry. 2006. *Truth, Error, and Criminal Law*. Cambridge: Cambridge University Press.

Lempert, Richard. 1981. 'Desert and Deterrence: An Assessment of the Moral Bases of the Case for Capital Punishment.' 79 *Michigan Law Review* 1177–231.

Lenta, Patrick and Farland, Douglas. 2008. 'Desert, Justice, and Capital Punishment.' 2 *Criminal Law and Philosophy* 273–90.

Liebman, James. 2002. 'The New Death Penalty Debate: What's DNA Got to do with It?' 33 *Columbia Human Rights Law Review* 527–54.

Lithwick, Dahlia. 2009. 'Innocent until Executed.' *Newsweek*, 3 September. URL = <http://www.newsweek.com/2009/09/02/innocent-until-executed.html> (visited in October 2010).

Logan, Wayne. 2002. 'Casting New Light on an Old Subject: Death Penalty Abolitionism for a New Millennium.' 100 *Michigan Law Review* 1336–79.

Lyons, David. 2008. 'The Legal Entrenchment of Illegality.' In Matthew Kramer, Claire Grant, Ben Colburn, and Antony Hatzistavrou (eds), *The Legacy of H.L.A. Hart: Legal, Political, and Moral Philosophy*. Oxford: Oxford University Press, pp 29–43.

Lyons, William. 1974. 'Deterrent Theory and Punishment of the Innocent.' 84 *Ethics* 346–8.

Mabbott, JD. 1939. 'Punishment.' 48 *Mind* 152–67.

MacInnis, Kim. 2002. 'Police Shootings.' In Gregg Lee Carter (ed), *Guns in American Society: An Encyclopedia of History, Politics, Culture, and the Law*. Santa Barbara, CA: ABC-CLIO, pp 471–4.

Makinson, DC. 1965. 'The Paradox of the Preface.' 25 *Analysis* 205–7.

Markel, Dan. 2005. 'State, Be Not Proud: A Retributivist Defense of the Commutation of Death Row and the Abolition of the Death Penalty.' 40 *Harvard Civil Rights-Civil Liberties Law Review* 407–80.

Markel, Dan. 2009. 'Executing Retributivism: *Panetti* and the Future of the Eighth Amendment.' 103 *Northwestern University Law Review* 1163–222.

Markel, Dan and Flanders, Chad. 2010. 'Bentham on Stilts: The Bare Relevance of Subjectivity to Retributive Justice.' 98 *California Law Review* 907–88.

Marquis, Joshua. 2005. 'The Myth of Innocence.' 95 *Journal of Criminal Law & Criminology* 501–21.

Marshall, Lawrence. 2004. 'The Innocence Revolution and the Death Penalty.' 1 *Ohio State Journal of Criminal Law* 573–84.

Massachusetts Governor's Council on Capital Punishment. 2004. 'Final Report.' URL = <http://www.lawlib.state.ma.us/docs/5-3-04Governorsreportcapitalpunishment.pdf> (visited in October 2010).

Massaro, Toni. 1991. 'Shame, Culture, and American Criminal Law.' 89 *Michigan Law Review* 1880–944.

Matravers, Matt (ed). 1999. *Punishment and Political Theory*. Oxford: Hart Publishing.

McCord, David. 1997. 'Judging the Effectiveness of the Supreme Court's Death Penalty Jurisprudence According to the Court's Own Goals: Mild Success or Major Disaster?' 24 *Florida State University Law Review* 545–603.

McCord, David. 1998. 'Imagining a Retributivist Alternative to Capital Punishment.' 50 *Florida Law Review* 1–143.

McGinn, Colin. 1997. *Ethics, Evil, and Fiction*. Oxford: Oxford University Press.

McKay, Thomas and Nelson, Michael. 2010. 'Propositional Attitude Reports: Supplement on the De Re/De Dicto Distinction.' In Edward Zalta (ed), *The Stanford Encyclopedia of Philosophy* (Winter 2010 Edition). URL = <http://plato.stanford.edu/archives/win2010/entries/prop-attitude-reports> (visited in October 2010).

Menninger, Karl. 1968. *The Crime of Punishment*. Harmondsworth: Penguin Books.

Midgley, Mary. 1984. *Wickedness*. London: Routledge & Kegan Paul.

Milo, Ronald. 1984. *Immorality*. Princeton, NJ: Princeton University Press.

Mitias, Michael. 1983. 'Is Retributivism Inconsistent without *Lex Talionis*?' 60 *Rivista Internazionale di Filosofia del Diritto* 211–30.

Moore, Michael. 1984. *Law and Psychiatry: Rethinking the Relationship*. Cambridge: Cambridge University Press.

Moore, Michael. 1995. 'The Moral Worth of Retribution.' In Joel Feinberg and Hyman Gross (eds), *Philosophy of Law*. Fifth Edition. Belmont, CA: Wadsworth Publishing, pp 632–54.

Moore, Michael. 1997. *Placing Blame*. Oxford: Oxford University Press.

Moore, Michael. 1999. 'Victims and Retribution: A Reply to Professor Fletcher.' 3 *Buffalo Criminal Law Review* 65–89.

Moore, Michael. 2007. 'Patrolling the Borders of Consequentialist Justifications: The Scope of Agent-Relative Restrictions.' 27 *Law and Philosophy* 35–96.

Moore, Michael and Hurd, Heidi. 2011. 'The Culpability of Negligence.' In Rowan Cruft, Matthew H Kramer, and Mark Reiff (eds), *Crime, Punishment, and Responsibility*. Oxford: Oxford University Press, pp 311–48.

Morris, Herbert. 1968. 'Persons and Punishment.' 52 *Monist* 475–501.

Mortenson, Julian Davis. 2003. 'Earning the Right to be Retributive: Execution Methods, Culpability Theory, and the Cruel and Unusual Punishment Clause.' 88 *Iowa Law Review* 1099–163.

Morton, Adam. 2004. *On Evil*. New York, NY: Routledge.

Murphy, Jeffrie. 1971. 'Three Mistakes about Retributivism.' 31 *Analysis* 166–9.

Murphy, Jeffrie. 1973. 'Marxism and Retribution.' 2 *Philosophy and Public Affairs* 217–43.

Murphy, Jeffrie. 1979. *Retribution, Justice, and Therapy*. Dordrecht: D. Reidel Publishing.

Murphy, Jeffrie. 1991. 'Retributive Hatred: An Essay on Criminal Liability and the Emotions.' In Raymond Frey and Christopher Morris (eds), *Liability and Responsibility*. Cambridge: Cambridge University Press, pp 351–76.

Murphy, Jeffrie. 1994. 'The State's Interest in Retribution.' 5 *Journal of Contemporary Legal Issues* 283–98.

Nagel, Thomas. 1979. 'Moral Luck.' In *Mortal Questions*. Cambridge: Cambridge University Press, pp 24–38.

Nathanson, Stephen. 1985. 'Does it Matter if the Death Penalty is Arbitrarily Administered?' 14 *Philosophy and Public Affairs* 149–64.

Nathanson, Stephen. 2001. *An Eye for an Eye?* Second Edition. Lanham, MD: Rowman & Littlefield.

Nelkin, Dana. 2008. 'Moral Luck.' In Edward Zalta (ed), *Stanford Encyclopedia of Philosophy (Fall 2008 Edition)*. URL = <http://plato.stanford.edu/archives/fall2008/entries/moral-luck> (visited in April 2010).

Note. 2001. 'The Rhetoric of Difference and the Legitimacy of Capital Punishment.' 114 *Harvard Law Review* 1599–622.

Nozick, Robert. 1974. *Anarchy, State, and Utopia*. New York: Basic Books.

Nozick, Robert. 1981. *Philosophical Explanations*. Cambridge, MA: Harvard University Press.

Nozick, Robert. 1989. 'The Holocaust.' In *The Examined Life*. New York: Simon & Schuster, pp 236–42.

Nussbaum, Martha. 2004. *Hiding from Humanity*. Princeton, NJ: Princeton University Press.

Oldenquist, Andrew. 2004. 'Retribution and the Death Penalty.' 29 *University of Dayton Law Review* 335–43.

Pearl, Leon. 1982. 'A Case against the Kantian Retributivist Theory of Punishment: A Response to Professor Pugsley.' 11 *Hofstra Law Review* 273–306.

Pettit, Philip. 2007. 'Responsibility Incorporated.' 117 *Ethics* 171–201.

Pojman, Louis. 1998. 'For Capital Punishment.' In Louis Pojman and Jeffrey Reiman, *The Death Penalty: For and Against*. Lanham, MD: Rowman & Littlefield, pp 1–66.

Posner, Richard. 1981. *The Economics of Justice*. Cambridge, MA: Harvard University Press.

Primorac, Igor. 1982. 'On Capital Punishment.' 17 *Israel Law Review* 133–50.

Primoratz, Igor. 1989a. *Justifying Legal Punishment*. Atlantic Highlands, NJ: Humanities Press International.

Primoratz, Igor. 1989b. 'Punishment as Language.' 64 *Philosophy* 187–205.

Pugsley, Robert. 1981. 'A Retributivist Argument against Capital Punishment.' 9 *Hofstra Law Review* 1501–23.

Quine, WVO. 1956. 'Quantifiers and Propositional Attitudes.' 53 *Journal of Philosophy* 177–87.

Quinton, Anthony. 1954. 'On Punishment.' 14 *Analysis* 133–42.

Radin, Margaret Jane. 1980. 'Cruel Punishment and Respect for Persons: Super Due Process for Death.' 53 *Southern California Law Review* 1143–85.

Rawls, John. 1955. 'Two Concepts of Rules.' 64 *Philosophical Review* 3–32.

Rawls, John. 1971. *A Theory of Justice*. Cambridge, MA: Harvard University Press.

Reiff, Mark. 2005. *Punishment, Compensation, and Law: A Theory of Enforceability*. Cambridge: Cambridge University Press.

Reiman, Jeffrey. 1985. 'Justice, Civilization, and the Death Penalty: Answering van den Haag.' 14 *Philosophy and Public Affairs* 115–48.

Reiman, Jeffrey. 1998. 'Why the Death Penalty Should be Abolished in America.' In Louis Pojman and Jeffrey Reiman, *The Death Penalty: For and Against*. Lanham, MD: Rowman & Littlefield, pp 67–132.

Richard, Mark. 1990. *Propositional Attitudes*. Cambridge: Cambridge University Press.

Ricoeur, Paul. 1969. *The Symbolism of Evil*. Translated by Emerson Buchanan. Boston, MA: Beacon Press.

Ridge, Michael. 2004. 'If the Price is Right: Unfair Advantage, Auctions, and Proportionality.' 3 *APA Newsletter on Philosophy and Law* 81–6.

Rowan, Michael. 2004. 'Minding Our Skepticism: A Conservative Approach to Capital Punishment.' 31 *Florida State University Law Review* 377–408.

Rubin, Edward. 2003. 'Just Say No to Retribution.' 7 *Buffalo Criminal Law Review* 17–83.

Russell, Luke. 2007. 'Is Evil Action Qualitatively Distinct from Ordinary Wrongdoing?' 85 *Australasian Journal of Philosophy* 659–77.

Sainsbury, R.M. 1988. *Paradoxes*. Cambridge: Cambridge University Press.

Sarat, Austin. 2001. *When the State Kills: Capital Punishment and the American Condition*. Princeton, NJ: Princeton University Press.

Scheid, Don. 1990. 'Davis and the Unfair-Advantage Theory of Punishment: A Critique.' 18 *Philosophical Topics* 143–70.

Scheid, Don. 1995. 'Davis, Unfair Advantage Theory, and Criminal Desert.' 14 *Law and Philosophy* 375–409.

Schwartz, John. 2010. 'In Texas, Death Penalty on Trial.' *International Herald Tribune*, 16–17 October, page 2.

Schwarzschild, Henry. 1990. 'The Death Penalty as a Controversy over Social Values.' 54 *Albany Law Review* 497–500.

Schwarzschild, Maimon. 2002. 'Retribution, Deterrence, and the Death Penalty: A Response to Hugo Bedau.' 21 (#2) *Criminal Justice Ethics* 9–11.

Shafer-Landau, Russ. 1996. 'The Failure of Retributivism.' 82 *Philosophical Studies* 289–316.

Shafer-Landau, Russ. 2000. 'Retributivism and Desert.' 81 *Pacific Philosophical Quarterly* 189–214.

Shepherd, Joanna. 2005. 'Deterrence versus Brutalization: Capital Punishment's Differing Impacts among States.' 104 *Michigan Law Review* 203–55.

Sher, George. 1987. *Desert*. Princeton, NJ: Princeton University Press.

Shiffrin, Seana. 2002. 'Caution about Character Ideals and Capital Punishment: A Reply to Sorell.' 21 (#2) *Criminal Justice Ethics* 35–9.

Sigler, Mary. 2003. 'Contradiction, Coherence, and Guided Discretion in the Supreme Court's Capital Sentencing Jurisprudence.' 40 *American Criminal Law Review* 1151–94.

Sorell, Tom. 1987. *Moral Theory and Capital Punishment*. Oxford: Blackwell.

Sorell, Tom. 2002. 'Two Ideals and the Death Penalty.' 21 (#2) *Criminal Justice Ethics* 27–35.

Statman, Daniel (ed). 1993. *Moral Luck*. Albany, NY: State University of New York Press.

Staub, Ervin. 1989. *The Roots of Evil*. Cambridge: Cambridge University Press.

Steiker, Carol. 2005. 'No, Capital Punishment is not Morally Required: Deterrence, Deontology, and the Death Penalty.' 58 *Stanford Law Review* 751–89.

Steiker, Carol and Steiker, Jordan. 2002. 'Should Abolitionists Support Legislative "Reform" of the Death Penalty?' 63 *Ohio State Law Journal* 417–32.

Steiker, Carol and Steiker, Jordan. 2005. 'The Seduction of Innocence: The Attraction and Limitations of the Focus on Innocence in Capital Punishment Law and Advocacy.' 95 *Journal of Criminal Law & Criminology* 587–624.

Steiker, Carol and Steiker, Jordan. 2006. 'A Tale of Two Nations: Implementation of the Death Penalty in "Executing" versus "Symbolic" States in the United States.' 84 *Texas Law Review* 1869–927.

Steiner, Hillel. 1983. 'How Free: Computing Personal Liberty.' In A Phillips-Griffiths (ed), *Of Liberty*. Cambridge: Cambridge University Press, pp 73–89.

Steiner, Hillel. 2002. 'Calibrating Evil.' 35 *The Monist* 183–93.

Steiner, Hillel. 2009. 'Responses.' In Stephen de Wijze, Matthew H Kramer, and Ian Carter (eds), *Hillel Steiner and the Anatomy of Justice*. New York: Routledge, pp 235–58.

Stephen, James Fitzjames. 1863. *A General View of the Criminal Law of England*. London: Macmillan.

Stephen, James Fitzjames. 1993. *Liberty, Equality, Fraternity*. Edited by Stuart Warner. Indianapolis, IN: Liberty Fund. Originally published in 1873.

Stolz, Barbara Ann. 1983. 'Congress and Capital Punishment: An Exercise in Symbolic Politics.' 5 *Law & Policy Quarterly* 157–80.

Stump, Eleonore. 2004. 'Personal Relations and Moral Residue.' 17 (# 2/3) *History of the Human Sciences* 33–56.

Sunstein, Cass and Vermeule, Adrian. 2005a. 'Is Capital Punishment Morally Required? Acts, Omissions, and Life-Life Tradeoffs.' 58 *Stanford Law Review* 703–50.

Sunstein, Cass and Vermeule, Adrian. 2005b. 'Deterring Murder: A Reply.' 58 *Stanford Law Review* 847–57.

Symposium. 2003. 'Rethinking the Death Penalty: Can We Define Who Deserves Death?' 24 *Pace Law Review* 107–86 (contributions by Martin Leahy, Robert Blecker, William Erlbaum, Jeffrey Fagan, Norman Greene, Jeffrey Kirchmeier, and David von Drehle).

Tabak, Ronald. 1999. 'Racial Discrimination in Implementing the Death Penalty.' URL = <http://www.abanet.org/irr/hr/summer99/tabak.html> (visited in November 2010).

Tabak, Ronald. 2003. 'The Egregiously Unfair Implementation of Capital Punishment in the United States: "Super Due Process" or Super Lack of Due Process?' 147 *Proceedings of the American Philosophical Society* 13–23.

Tasioulas, John. 2004. 'Mercy.' 103 *Proceedings of the Aristotelian Society* 101–32.

Tasioulas, John. 2006. 'Punishment and Repentance.' 81 *Philosophy* 279–322.

Van den Haag, Ernest. 1968. 'On Deterrence and the Death Penalty.' 78 *Ethics* 280–8.

Van den Haag, Ernest. 1978. 'In Defense of the Death Penalty: A Legal-Practical-Moral Analysis.' 14 *Criminal Law Bulletin* 51–68.

Van den Haag, Ernest. 1985a. 'Refuting Reiman and Nathanson.' 14 *Philosophy and Public Affairs* 165–76.

Van den Haag, Ernest. 1985b. 'The Death Penalty Once More.' 18 *University of California-Davis Law Review* 957–72.

Van den Haag, Ernest. 1986. 'The Ultimate Punishment: A Defense.' 99 *Harvard Law Review* 1662–9.

Van den Haag, Ernest. 1990. 'Why Capital Punishment?' 54 *Albany Law Review* 501–14.

Van den Haag, Ernest and Conrad, John. 1983. *The Death Penalty: A Debate*. London: Plenum Press.

Von Hirsch, Andrew. 1978. 'Proportionality and Desert: A Reply to Bedau.' 75 *Journal of Philosophy* 622–4.

Von Hirsch, Andrew. 1990. 'Proportionality in the Philosophy of Punishment: From "Why Punish?" to "How Much?"' 1 *Criminal Law Forum* 259–90.

Von Hirsch, Andrew. 1994. *Censure and Sanctions*. Oxford: Oxford University Press.

Waldron, Jeremy. 1992. 'Lex Talionis.' 34 *Arizona Law Review* 25–51.

Ward, David. 1999. 'Supermaximum Facilities.' In Peter Carlson and Judith Simon Garrett (eds), *Prison and Jail Administration*. Gaithersburg, MD: Aspen Publishers, pp 252–9.

Wefing, John. 2001. 'Wishful Thinking by Ronald J Tabak: Why DNA Evidence Will Not Lead to the Abolition of the Death Penalty.' 33 *Connecticut Law Review* 861–98.

Weiler, Joseph. 1978. 'Why do we Punish? The Case for Retributive Justice.' 12 *University of British Columbia Law Review* 295–319.

Whitman, James. 2003. 'A Plea against Retributivism.' 7 *Buffalo Criminal Law Review* 85–107.

Williams, Bernard. 1981. 'Moral Luck.' In *Moral Luck*. Cambridge: Cambridge University Press, pp 20–39.

Wilson, James Q and Herrnstein, Richard. 1985. *Crime and Human Nature*. New York: Simon & Schuster.

Index